Rewriting Chaucer

REWRITING CHAUCER

Culture, Authority, and the Idea of the Authentic Text, 1400–1602

Edited by

Thomas A. Prendergast
and Barbara Kline

Ohio State University Press
Columbus

Copyright © 1999 by The Ohio State University.
All rights reserved.

Library of Congress Cataloging-in-Publication Data

Rewriting Chaucer : culture, authority and the idea of the authentic text,
1400–1602 / edited by Thomas A. Prendergast and Barbara Kline.
    p.   cm.
Includes bibliographical references (p.   ) and index.
ISBN 0-8142-0811-8 (cloth : alk. paper). — ISBN 0-8142-5011-4
(pbk. : alk. paper)
    1. Chaucer, Geoffrey, d. 1400—Criticism, Textual. 2. Transmission of
texts—History—16th century. 3. Manuscripts, Medieval—England—
Editing. 4. Manuscripts, English (Middle)—Editing. 5. Transmission of
texts—History—To 1500.   I. Prendergast, Thomas A. (Thomas
Augustine)   II. Kline, Barbara.
PR1939.R48   1999
821'.1—dc21   99-19861
                                                                CIP

Text design by Deborah McClain.
Cover design by Gary Gore.
Typeset in Galliard by Graphic Composition, Inc.
Printed by Braun-Brumfield, Inc.

The paper used in this publication meets the minimum requirements
of the American National Standard for Information Sciences—Permanence of Paper
for Printed Library Materials. ANSI Z39.48–1992.

9 8 7 6 5 4 3 2 1

CONTENTS

III
AUTHORITY AND THE PRINTED WORD

Acknowledgments

---◆---

Our special thanks go to Michael Salda and Barbara Hanrahan, who helped this collection become a reality. Thanks are due also to Mary Elizabeth Braun, who provided timely advice, and to our institutions, the College of Wooster and Florida International University, for providing support for this project. Finally, we would like to thank Terry Prendergast and Rob Kline for their material and emotional support.

Introduction:
Writing, Authenticity, and the
Fabrication of the Chaucerian Text

Thomas A. Prendergast

It might be said that the purpose of a good editor is (to paraphrase one of our contributors) to articulate clear boundaries between an "original" authorial text and later "unauthorized" versions of this text. Certainly this has been the position of traditional editors, for example, Paul Maas, Fredson Bowers, and M. L. West. As Seth Lerer and Joseph Dane point out, despite the interrogation of the traditional strictures of editing by social textual critics such as Jerome McGann, the "debates framed by the Bédierists and Lachmannians of nearly a century ago still find themselves played out in the prefaces and articles of professional editors."[1] Even a title like *Rewriting Chaucer* suggests that we remain as strongly invested in the "original" version of Chaucer's texts as we do in palimpsestic "corruptions." Indeed, when Barbara Kline and I first discussed the possibility of putting together this volume, it seemed clear to us that in order to theorize what has been rewritten and why, we needed to distinguish the original source from its reshaped and revised version. The question then became How can we avoid participating in a naive historicism that assumes an ability to recover the "authentic" text without moving to the opposite extreme of finding ourselves unable to say anything at all about the construction of the text? This collection suggests that we need to conceptualize some sort of boundary—no matter how tenuous—between the "original," "authentic" Chaucer and later interpretations of his work, a distinction that enables us to examine the cultural and aesthetic implications of the late medieval and early modern reception of the Chaucerian canon.

Chaucer's manuscripts render the task of conceptualizing such a boundary particularly challenging. As Seth Lerer points out in *Chaucer and His Readers*, our concept of the "authentic" Chaucerian text is fragmentary; we have no holographs of Chaucer's works, only fifteenth-century versions, versions which are already interpretations of his works.[2] Is it, then, possible to "arrive at a unified single version, that can be identified as 'the original?'"[3] Recent critics and scholars of Chaucer have suggested that a certain dose of humility might be in order here, especially when dealing with the unfinished *Canterbury Tales*. Ralph Hanna and Derek Pearsall pinpoint modern critical editions of the *Tales* that privilege the Ellesmere manuscript's readings and tale order. Ellesmere may be particularly attractive by modern editorial standards, but as Hanna and Pearsall point out, it is itself the product of late medieval editorial work that "stands near the end of a variety of experiments at ordering the poem."[4] Perhaps neither Hanna nor Pearsall would go as far as David Greetham, who interrogates the very notion of textual descent, offering instead "a hypertextual model of free-floating links [as] a better simulacrum of medieval textuality than the fixed critical text of the codex ever was."[5] Yet all three share two fundamental beliefs that might enable our explorations of the "unauthorized" Chaucer. First, they agree that the manuscript alternatives often demand that we treat the author's work as a series of texts rather than as a single text. Second, they share the notion that what a text "is" has been conditioned by Romantic assumptions about the genius of the author and the unity of his corpus. These two beliefs may initially seem to disable any exploration of textual rewritings whatsoever, but, as Tim Machan has argued, the conflation of medieval and modern notions of authority is precisely what "obliterates" the "author function of vernacular literature."[6] If Chaucer's complaint to Adam Scriveyn suggests the poet's own interest in maintaining the authority of his text, Machan holds, Chaucer "maintains, through a variety of rhetorical postures, that what he writes is largely determined by the character of the work he is rewriting."[7] Far from indicating an anxiety of influence, these postures exemplify an "anxiety of *originality*."[8] It was in fact Chaucer's unwillingness to lay claim to his own authority that, according to Machan, paradoxically enabled poetic "originality." Such a fluid concept of authority, along with Chaucer's own claims that his rewritings depend heavily on his sources, suggests that Chaucerian texts resist any global attempts to determine how and why they were rewritten. In this book we offer a variety of approaches that encompass the paleographical concerns of Hanna and Pearsall, the New Historical approach of Lee Patterson, and some of the bibliographical methods of Greetham and McGann. We hold that this variety demonstrates both how early redactions of Chaucer shaped this enabling figure into a fifteenth- and sixteenth-century cultural poetics and how the contrasting representations of Chaucer's works reveal the cultural and aesthetic perspectives behind the formation and interpretation of the Chaucerian canon.

In *Negotiating the Past*, Lee Patterson has adumbrated the very different ways that scholars have gone about interpreting Chaucer in the last hundred fifty years. His thesis—that the political struggles which engulfed nineteenth-century England conditioned the modern "recovery" of Chaucer—has offered critics a powerful paradigm by which to historicize our responses to Chaucer. But it is worth noting that neither the liberal humanism that informed the New Critics' "recovery" of Chaucer nor the conservatism that enabled the Exegetics' resistance to a modern "humanistic recovery" has its roots solely in the nineteenth century.[9] Patterson shapes his own historical boundary here by choosing to begin with the great nineteenth-century revival of interest in the Middle Ages.[10] It is part of our thesis that we need to explore the boundaries of Chaucerian interpretation even before that great editorial watershed—Thomas Tyrwhitt's 1775 edition of the *Canterbury Tales*. Tyrwhitt's edition may mark the first full-scale modern editorial intervention in Chaucer studies, but it is part of a hermeneutical and editorial tradition that stretches back to 1400 and, some would argue, even before. The essays that follow theorize distinctions between fifteenth- and sixteenth-century interpretations of Chaucer and the original text, and also articulate how these distinctions ground our own interpretations of Chaucer's works. The conflicted issue of origins, then, is the subtext of this collection. Each essay attempts to recuperate an understanding of the Chaucerian text by locating that understanding in the raw material of the Chaucerian canon—the manuscripts and early editions.

The first part of the collection deals explicitly with the notion of origins and how this notion at once illuminates and problematizes the recovery of Chaucerian texts. John Bowers's essay focuses on the incompleteness of the *Canterbury Tales*, suggesting how politics shaped and mutated early versions of them. The fragmentary nature of the *Cook's Tale* or Chaucer's failure to assign tales to seven of the pilgrims seems to result not so much from carelessness as from self-censorship in a politically controversial age. Yet far from lying unnoticed or untended—as Chaucer might have intended—these incompletions tended to invite later writers to shape additions that answered their own political concerns. Hence, Bowers says, unfinished tales are given closure while complete tales are put into the mouths of formerly mute pilgrims such as the Plowman. These more "complete" versions of the *Tales* satisfied the aesthetic desire for closure and also both authorized and were shaped by politico-literary concerns, such as the desire to claim Chaucer as a champion of Wycliffism.

If, as Bowers argues, it is important at once to establish origins and problematize the possibility of doing so, Míceál Vaughan questions the authenticity of the accepted conclusion of the *Canterbury Tales*. In his essay on the *Parson's Tale* and the *Retractions*, Vaughan argues that close analysis of manuscript rubrics associated with these works reveals that they may have circulated originally as an independent Chaucerian treatise on penitence and the seven deadly sins. Early in the manuscript tradition, however, this treatise on penance was appropriated as a conclusion to the otherwise unfinished *Tales*. Scribes seeking closure to the *Canterbury Tales* had to invent rubrics that both sustained the *Parson's Tale* as part of the larger Canterbury project and separated the end of the treatise (the so-called *Retractions*) from the rest of the tale because of the incompatibility of the Parson's voice with Chaucer's. Later critics have tended to rely on the closure that these "authorizing" rubrics afford even as they acknowledged that the polyvocal aspects of these works problematize that closure. Vaughan suggests that we might investigate the possibility that, far from preserving an "authentic" ending to the *Tales*, the Ellesmere manuscript actually enshrines scribal efforts to provide a fitting conclusion to a work that may have ended with the *Parson's Prologue*.

Where the essays in the first section focus on how fourteenth- and fifteenth-century receptions of Chaucerian texts led to sweeping revisions of the idea of Chaucer, those in the second section focus on localized rewritings of Chaucer. Paul Strohm has pointed out that isolated moments of literary reception are crucial to our understanding of how early audiences read Chaucer. These individual acts of reinterpretation examine totalizing views of the Middle Ages by disclosing how specific historical, geographical, and aesthetic contexts remain crucial to any recovery of Chaucer or the cultures that rewrote him.[11] What is especially interesting about recovering these historical interpretations (as Patterson suggests in his discussion of a fifteenth-century interpretation of Chaucer) is the "amount of interpretation that is required to recover the act of interpretation itself."[12] Discrete revisions of Chaucer require us to rethink how we impose our idea of Chaucer on an audience that is temporally and geographically "other."

Nowhere, as Mary Godfrey demonstrates, is this critical bias more evident than in contemporary treatments of the *Prioress's Tale*. Where current readings of the tale focus on its structural and metaphorical function within the *Canterbury Tales*, many fifteenth-century readers encountered the work in anthologies that presented the tale as one among many other devotional works, like Lydgate's *Legend of Dan Jose*. Not only was the tale in some sense rewritten by this larger devotional context, but its anti-Semitism and violence (which so disturb modern readers) were elided. For readers and editors who preferred to focus on the tale's participation in Marian devotional conventions, those characteristics were beside the point.

Barbara Kline examines how a particular fifteenth-century audience rewrote a Chaucerian text to fit the needs of its ecclesiastical community. As might be expected in this cultural context, the canons responsible for the production of Harley 7333 tended to censor some material antithetical to the Church in their version of the *Canterbury Tales*. What is unexpected is the tendency to reproduce representations of alchemy in the *Canon's Yeoman's Tale*. Considering that the tale's protagonist is a canon, we might expect to find references to a practice often thought to be devilish expunged, not preserved. Kline suggests that the retention of such heterodox material indicates an abiding interest in more arcane kinds of knowledge, to which the residents of Leicester Abbey seemed historically predisposed. At the same time the revisions show that the canons may have been more secular than expected as readers. They seem to have had an understanding of textuality as particularly plastic, responding to the needs of a particular audience rather than having an inherent universal authority.

Edgar Laird addresses himself to the question of how arcane—even suspect—knowledge was propagated under Chaucer's name as he explores the late medieval reception of the *Treatise on the Astrolabe*. More copies of this work survive than any of Chaucer's except the *Canterbury Tales* themselves. This early and ongoing interest in the work perpetuates Chaucer's evident interest in astrology, despite his own denial (in the *Astrolabe*) of "feith" in what he calls "rytes of payens." Curiously enough, though Chaucer's name commanded a fair amount of authority in what we might call the humanistic community of the fifteenth century, it seems to have made little difference to the scientific community, whose members altered and rewrote his work as they might the work of any "lewed compilator."

This cultural tendency for local reading communities to reshape Chaucer's texts in their own image is illuminated by the creation of a "Scottish" Chaucer in Bodleian MS Arch. Selden B. 24. The manuscript is primarily known for its unique conclusion to the *Parliament of Fowls*, which Julia Boffey and A. S. G. Edwards call a "somewhat flamboyant act of linguistic appropriation." But, as Boffey and Edwards point out, what is perhaps more surprising is the extent to which the manuscript is not "Scotticized" for a Caledonian audience. The poems that are spuriously ascribed to Chaucer in the manuscript seem not to be Scottish appropriations, but derive from texts copied by the London scribe John Shirley. Further, the first Selden scribe seems to have limited the extent of his translation of Middle English works into Scots in order to preserve what he saw as "the English flavor. . . . Of an anthology of writings by England's major poet."

If the first Selden scribe can be characterized as wishing to preserve the English flavor of Chaucer, David Parkinson and Carolyn Ives demonstrate that in later anthologies, such as the Bannatyne manuscript, Chaucer was implicated in a specifically Scottish politics of misogyny. Parkinson and Ives argue that Queen Mary's controversial reign, along with the embattled Protestant ascendancy, which in some sense defined the Scotland of the

1560s and 1570s, led to a distinctively Scottish discourse "in reproof and despite of women," which was grounded in the authority of a transformed, Scottified Chaucer. This misogyny had as much to do with prevailing attitudes about politics and religion as it did with well-worn ideas about gender, for even those upstanding Protestant men who sat on the burgh council often had "catholic wives" whose households were seen as "incubators of catholicism." It is not surprising, then, that in a country ruled by a widow and in which women were often seen as favoring the "romish religion," literate men would construct and perpetuate an antifeminist Chaucer who would give voice to their own suspicions about the intentions and capabilities of women.

Beverly Kennedy also interrogates the myth of Chaucer's unremitting misogyny in her essay on the rewritings of the *Wife of Bath's Prologue.* Kennedy argues that the scribe of an early and influential manuscript (Cambridge Dd.4.24) was responsible for adding passages to the *Prologue* that blackened the Wife's character. Most of these passages were picked up by the Ellesmere scribe (other scribes do not replicate them) and made their way into the manuscript tradition. These misogynistic passages, having the authoritative backing of Ellesmere, have been enshrined in modern editions of the *Canterbury Tales,* where they continue to color the way that we read not only the Wife, but Chaucer's general attitude toward women.

The essays in the third section focus on changes in interpretations of Chaucer wrought by the printing press. As Seth Lerer has pointed out, "The importation of the printing press . . . helped transform Chaucer from a remembered presence guiding literary making to a dead *auctor* valued for his exemplarity."[13] What goes along with this exemplarity is an idea of poetic authority that seems to privilege more insistently modern ideas of the authentic text. To some, the ensuing valorization of originality (and later "genius"), which has persisted well into the twentieth century, was enabled by the advent of printing, particularly as printing helped guarantee the perpetuation of the text as an unchangeable object rather than as a mutable subject of aurality.[14] But if, as David Quint has argued, Renaissance critics foreshadowed modern ideas of authorial originality and uniqueness, it was only because "the Renaissance literary text was seeking to reexamine—and represent—the source of its fictions' authority." In other words, the idea of originality comes as a response to the loss of earlier notions of "a nonhistorical transcendent truth which had been advanced for the text by traditional modes of allegorical reading and writing."[15] As the early modern period subjected previous models of literary production to "scientific" study, previous claims of a nonhistorical and divine source were increasingly called into question. In terms of Chaucer's texts, the advent of the printing press, and the concern with notions of the authentic source, led both to an increase in works attributed to Chaucer and to increasing anxiety about the authenticity of such works. As a result, an intense interest in "authentic" manuscripts developed that presumably led editors like William Thynne and Thomas Speght back to the "original" text. Simultaneously, the growing idea of the author as the shaper of an original text led to greater focus on the biography of the poet—as writers attempted to locate the historical origins of the producer of these texts.

Robert Costomiris broaches the problem of how early editors achieved enough consistency among their editorial practices to lay claim to authenticity. Costomiris focuses on the most influential editor of Chaucer in the Renaissance, William Thynne, demonstrating that though Thynne's editorial choices in his two editions *seem* to be haphazard, they in fact suggest that Thynne believed he was returning the *Canterbury Tales* to something approximating its original state. For example, Thynne rejected the *Tale of Gamelyn*, which seemed inconsistent in tone and structure with the other tales in Chaucer's work. But if Thynne was striving for a kind of *editio princeps* in his first edition, then why did he accept such obviously problematic texts as *The Plowman's Tale* in his second? The answer may lie in misattribution of the second edition. Although Thynne's name appears in the preface, he was probably not involved in editing the 1542 edition and should not be held accountable for its inability to live up to the more responsible editing of its predecessor.

Even if Thynne is not responsible for the misattribution of *The Plowman's Tale,* he must be identified as the editor who made one of the more notorious and problematic additions to the Chaucerian canon. Thomas Prendergast examines how Thomas Usk's *Testament of Love,* which appeared in Thynne's 1532 edition, affected and continues to affect Chaucer's literary and biographical reputation. Prendergast illuminates how the misattribution of the *Testament of Love* to Chaucer shaped early lives of Chaucer, at once supplying a demand for authentic biographical facts about the poet and enabling editorial control over "Father Chaucer" by exposing him as a somewhat less than competent political player who needed regal help to escape political trouble. Though Usk's authorship of the work was acknowledged by critics in the nineteenth century, this misattribution continues to shape ideas about Chaucer—no longer telling the critical community who Chaucer is, but who he was not.

Stephanie Trigg examines this crisis of textual authority in her essay on Chaucer's early editors. She argues that Thynne, Stow, and Speght fashioned an authoritative discourse that enabled them to "sell" an "authentic" Chaucerian textuality. These editors emphasized the true (patrilineal) lines of textual transmission by pointing out, for instance, how they needed to purify the text that had been "dirtied" by the commercial hands of the printers. They attempted to legitimate their own recovery of the authentic text by claiming an inspired transmission, but it is clear that, just as the printers differed from them, so too did they differ from Chaucer. Their affinity with him was problematized by their emerging status as "professional" editors. They epitomize the history of Chaucer criticism, in which the attempt to suppress differences between the poet and his editors and critics problematizes the extent to which those editors and critics can acknowledge differences between themselves—even as these differences of gender, nationality, and race become more apparent.

In some ways the conflicts and differences among those who receive Chaucer's texts determine who Chaucer is perceived to be. If Steven Justice is right when he argues that Chaucer's texts demonstrate the poet's "consciousness that the author cannot control the social reach of his text, and that there are potential though unimagined audiences who might make words spoken in innocence something guilty," then Chaucer can be said to be truly prophetic.[16] For though these essays do not always demonstrate "guilt," they do show how many late medieval and early modern redactors of Chaucer's works altered his words to such an extent that Chaucer's consciousness was in part replaced by their own. At the same time these redactors often depended on the fact that the words were authentically Chaucerian, and we still pursue this authenticity today—even as we continue to shape Chaucer into something approximating our own image. It is fitting and perhaps inevitable that the pursuit of authenticity has itself become an object of study. By examining the historical assumptions governing the recovery of the Chaucerian corpus we can begin to examine our own pursuit of the authentic Chaucer.

Notes

1. Seth Lerer and Joseph Dane, "What Is a Text?" *Huntington Library Quarterly* 58 (1996): 1.

2. Seth Lerer, *Chaucer and His Readers* (Princeton: Princeton University Press, 1993), 8.

3. Ralph Hanna III, *Pursuing History: Middle English Manuscripts and Their Texts* (Stanford: Stanford University Press, 1996), 174.

4. Ibid., 181. See also Derek Pearsall, "Editing Medieval Texts: Some Developments and Some Problems," in *Textual Criticism and Literary Interpretation*, ed. Tim Machan (Chicago: University of Chicago Press, 1985), 94. In his introduction Martin Stevens asserts that the notion of "authorship" should include the editorial work that produced manuscripts like Ellesmere (*The Ellesmere Chaucer: Essays in Interpretation*, ed. Martin Stevens and Daniel Woodward [San Marino, Calif.: Huntington Library, 1995], 22).

5. David Greetham, "Phylum-Tree-Rhizome," *Huntington Library Quarterly* 58 (1996): 123. See Pearsall's concerns about "every man his own editor" (*Editing Medieval Texts*, 105) and Hanna's suggestions about what to do if "one cannot openly determine the anteriority of one reading over another" (*Pursuing History*, 192). Both positions indicate an investment in what Greetham calls "the genealogical descent of witnesses" ("Phylum," 99).

6. Tim William Machan, *Textual Criticism and Middle English Texts* (Charlottesville: University of Virginia Press, 1994), 135.

7. Ibid., 116.

8. Ibid.

9. Lee Patterson, *Negotiating the Past* (Madison: University of Wisconsin Press, 1987), 3–39.

10. Ibid., 41.

11. Paul Strohm, "Chaucer's Fifteenth-Century Audience and the Narrowing of the Chaucer Tradition," *Studies in the Age of Chaucer* 4 (1982): 24.

12. Patterson, 116.

13. Lerer, *Chaucer and His Readers*, 19.

14. See for instance, Elizabeth L. Eisenstein, *The Printing Revolution in Early Modern Europe* (Cambridge: Cambridge University Press, 1983); John Guillory, *Poetic Authority: Spenser, Milton, and Literary History* (New York: Columbia University Press, 1983); Walter Ong, *Orality and Literacy: The Technologizing of the Word* (London: Methuen, 1982); and David Quint, *Origin and Originality in Renaissance Literature: Versions of the Source* (New Haven: Yale University Press, 1983).

15. Quint, *Origin and Originality*, x.

16. Steven Justice, *Writing and Rebellion* (Berkeley: University of California Press, 1994), 224.

I

Origins and Authority

Chaucer's *Canterbury Tales* — Politically Corrected

John M. Bowers

M ost literary studies examine what an author wrote. This essay examines what Geoffrey Chaucer did not write.

Though Chaucer left his *Canterbury Tales* in a state far from finished, modern critics have almost unanimously embraced the idea of the work as "unfinished but complete."[1] The assumption of completion has been necessary to enable any discussion of the organic unity of the work and the fulfillment of an authorial design. Yet the fact remains that the work, as it survives, falls drastically short of the 120 tales projected in the *General Prologue* (*CT,* I.790–95).[2] Although Chaucer may ambitiously have intended to surpass the hundred tales of Boccaccio's *Decameron,* he completed only twenty-four tales, including the *Cook's Tale* as a fragment perhaps intended for cancellation, and three other narratives unfinished because of interruptions from other pilgrims: the *Monk's Tale,* Chaucer the pilgrim's *Tale of Sir Thopas,* and quite possibly the *Squire's Tale.*[3] Of the thirty pilgrims introduced in the *General Prologue,* seven are never given any tales at all, fragmentary or otherwise—the Plowman, the Knight's Yeoman, and the Five Guildsmen.

Since Chaucer introduced the Canon's Yeoman as a tale-teller not numbered among the original company of pilgrims gathered at the Tabard Inn, it seems clear that constraints of time and the grim exigencies of mortality cannot fully explain the poet's failure to assign tales to seven of the original pilgrims, the truncation of the *Cook's Tale,* or, for that matter, the failure of the pilgrims to reach their destination at the shrine of St. Thomas in Canterbury. The insertion of the *Canon's Yeoman's Tale* renders the absences of these other sections, promised but not delivered, matters of willful neglect, making them subject to interpretation as issues of authorial intention. The disruption caused by the unexpected entry of a new tale-teller casts Chaucer's decision to omit others into sharp relief. It renders them silent, allows them to slip into partial invisibility, and thereby makes them available for later appropriation or continued neglect.

These omissions become legible as the author's responses to a variety of political energies within the immediate social and textual environment in which he worked—London in the 1390s. Chaucer is rightly praised as a social satirist, and nothing could more clearly underscore his responsiveness to the contemporary scene than his readiness to emend his work in progress. More than any of his earlier writings, the *Tales* stayed keenly alert to the most controversial issues in the immediate civic environment at the moment of their composition *and* at later moments of revision, rearrangement, and recomposition. During the decade from 1389 to 1399 when Chaucer worked on the *Tales,* I believe that he engaged in various acts of self-censorship or, more precisely, partial self-censorship. He canceled portions of his text but allowed materials such as the Man of Law's Endlink to remain available in his working papers. He suspended work on some pieces, for example the *Cook's Tale,* but allowed these fragments to survive as challenges to future speculation. And he abandoned as tale-tellers certain pilgrims introduced in the *General Prologue* but did not replace them, instead sending them forth into the future as agents provocateurs for later literary responses.

The activities of Chaucer's earliest scribes and imitators constitute an important archive for gauging these literary responses.[4] They provide a running commentary on the political challenges to which the text was subjected when it began to circulate, assume a public life, and become "worldly" during the first decades after the author's death. What Gabrielle Spiegel calls "the social logic of the text" had been left rigorously undetermined by Chaucer amid the fragments transmitted to his literary executors and the first generations of copyists. The *Canterbury Tales* emerges as a supreme example of a textual assembly given a whole host of semantic inflections within local circumstances of human relations, shifting systems of material production, and networks of cultural power deployed and redeployed over the next century: "All texts occupy determinate social spaces, both as products of the social world of authors and as textual agents at work in that world, with which they entertain often complex and contestatory relations. In that sense, texts both mirror *and* generate social realities, are constituted by *and* constitute the social and discursive formations which they may sustain, resist, contest, or seek to transform, depending on the case at hand."[5] The reactions of the early fifteenth-century scribes and continuators, whether they sustained Chaucer's omissions or mended these gaps with supplementary materials, can be explored as attempts at rendering a more "politically correct" version of the *Canterbury Tales.*

In addition to the author's own changes of intention, the fifteenth-century compilers who undertook to arrange and copy the unconnected fragments of the *Tales* provide a variety of interpretations in their reactions to Chaucer's omissions. This panoply of reader responses affords the earliest evidence of what Fredric Jameson has classified as texts "always-already-read."[6] The Knight's Yeoman and the Five Guildsmen were allowed to remain voiceless and to slip further into obscurity. The Plowman, however, received two apocryphal tales over the course of the next century. The *Cook's Tale,* whose abrupt cutoff so seriously mars the movement from Fragment I to Fragment II, was variously supplemented with conclusions. In twenty-five manuscripts it was replaced by the astonishingly un-Chaucerian *Tale of Gamelyn;* the scribe of the Bodley 686 manuscript staged an even more daring intervention by adding a violently moralistic conclusion in which the unruly apprentice, Perkyn Revelour, is executed.

According to these critical readings, Chaucer's own principles of exclusion were responsive to the immediate field of competing social energies during the period when he worked on the *Tales.* The act of writing means the process of grounding a poem in the world, and each of Chaucer's new writings, whether it took the form of revising, copying, or anticipating posthumous publication, meant grounding the poem in a new world, one in which the political landscape would be constantly shifting. Never static, a social text is enmeshed in the changes and alterations of the society in which it lives and moves and has its being. Topics that seemed open to barbed satire around 1390 became too sensitive to pursue as the decade wore on and the political scene grew increasingly unstable. Hostility toward the Wycliffites increased during the crisis of 1395, when the *Twelve Conclusions of the Lollards* were posted on the door of Parliament and the king himself was summoned back from Ireland because of the alarm over armed sedition.[7] The civic power of the craft guilds aroused growing suspicions of their loyalty to the Crown, and relations between London and Richard II became so strained that he retaliated by removing three of the most important offices of government from Westminster to York.[8] Although the monarch was placated by the magnificent 1392 pageants offering a concord with the city, Jean Froissart may have more accurately gauged the sentiments of the citizenry when reporting that Londoners figured among the keenest supporters of Henry Bolingbroke's coup in 1399.[9]

Ideological pressures further contributed to shaping the principles of inclusion and augmentation guiding Chaucer's first editors. With ecclesiastical anxieties leading to the enactment of *De Heretico Comburendo* in 1401, which threatened death to Lollard heretics, and the insecurities of the Lancastrian regime, which persisted even after the Southampton plot of 1415,[10] the textual environment changed drastically. There was far less tolerance for the social satire that motivated Chaucer's finest work, and much more suspicion—even overt hostility—toward precisely the topics that inspired his most ingenious lampoons.

The Knight's Yeoman

"And he was clad in cote and hood of grene"

Though he stands third in the opening roster of pilgrims, the Knight's Yeoman is probably the single Canterbury figure most neglected by modern criticism.[11] Two things stand out prominently in his portrait in the *General Prologue* (I.101–17): he is extremely rustic in appearance, and he travels heavily armed. His rustic identity is emphasized by his green tunic and hood (103), his close-cropped hair and weathered face (109), and his expertise at "wodecraft" (110). The narrator bases his conclusion about the Yeoman's profession on these quite obvious outward trappings: "An horn he bar, the bawdryk was of grene; / A forster was he, soothly, as I gesse" (116–17). The Yeoman is also a somewhat sinister figure literally bristling with weapons. He has a mighty bow and the finest peacock-feathered arrows, a "bracer" or archer's arm guard, a sword and buckler at his side, and a dagger as sharp as the point of a spear. This final simile contributes to the imagination another weapon—a spear—not actually present.

The significance of the Yeoman is tied to the social identity of the Knight and the class he represents. The Cambridge Parliament of 1388 had reasserted the statute forbidding any slander against the grandees of the realm, and this piece of legislation may have contributed to Chaucer's decision to exclude any personage of rank higher than the Knight among the Canterbury pilgrims.[12] William McColly's survey of the historical record concludes that Chaucer's Knight, far from representing the class of poor knights, offered the idealized image of a member of the baronial class, a conclusion that has implications for the Yeoman. "A forester-retainer," McColly notes, "suggests for his master the right to hunt the great beasts of the forest, which was traditionally the prerogative of royalty."[13] When selecting a servant for the Knight, Chaucer probably had in mind a very specific model for the Yeoman, a model that combined this pilgrim's rustic character, his threat of armed violence, and his service to a member of the highest ranking chivalric order of the kingdom, even with connotations of royalty.

Throughout the 1390s, King Richard II surrounded himself with a large number of rustic yeomen of exactly this sort, men who quickly gained a reputation for rough conduct. The Monk of Westminster reported that during Richard's gyrations throughout the northwest in the dangerous year 1387, the king had begun drawing provincial fighting men into his service.[14] Later in that same year, a large force of Cheshiremen faithfully followed Robert de Vere to the disastrous defeat at Radcot Bridge.[15] Rebuilding his power after the humiliation handed him by the Appellants in 1387–88, the king recruited knights from a broad spread of geographical areas to create a true national power base.[16] By 1394 he had turned specifically to Cheshire, however, eventually retaining a company of more than seven hundred of its native sons as knights, esquires, and archers, from whose numbers he selected 312 to form his personal bodyguard.[17] These Cheshire yeomen formed the core of the private army he later summoned to intimidate Parliament in 1397.[18]

The *Brut* described the king's personal engagement in recruiting these Cheshire yeomen for royal service: "And þe kyng hym-self sent ynto Chestirschire, vnto þe Chefteynes of þat cuntre, and þay gagred and brouʒt a grete and an huge multitude of peple, bothe of knyʒtis & of Squyers, & *prynspally of yemen of Chestreschire*, þe which yemen and archers þe Kyng toke yn-to his owne court, & yaf ham bothe boge of court and gode wageʒ, to be kepers of his owne body, both be nyʒt and be day, above alle oþer persons, and most ham loued & best trust."[19]

No sympathizer with Richard II, Adam of Usk reported that the king "kept in his following four hundred unruly men of the county of Chester, very evil; and in all places they oppressed his subjects unpunished, and beat and robbed them."[20] Thomas Walsingham agreed that the king had chosen to surround himself with a bodyguard of Cheshire *malefactores*.[21] In 1397, Richard persuaded Parliament to raise the county palatine of Chester to the status of a principality, on a par with Wales. Augmented with vast Welsh and Shropshire lands recently confiscated from Arundel, the new principality formed "the largest single territorial concentration on the political map of England in the years 1397–99."[22] It was even rumored that Richard intended to make Cheshire his inner citadel of the nation, a bastion from which to rule Wales and Ireland as well as England.

Throughout these dealings, Richard relied increasingly on his Cheshiremen. The Kenilworth chronicler recalled that his bodyguards addressed the king with alarming familiarity: "Et in tantam familiaritatem domino regi annectebantur ut eidem in materna lingua audacter confabularentur: 'Dycum, slep sicurly quile we wake, and dreed nouʒt quile we lyve sestow: ffor zif thow haddest weddet Perkyn douʒter of Lye thow mun well halde a love day with any man in Chester schire in ffaith!'"[23] It is well worth noting that the provincial dialect that the chronicler said these guards spoke—and that Richard apparently had no trouble understanding—was also the *Pearl* poet's language, which scholars have previously tended to consider too provincial for anyone but a Cheshire native to have comprehended.[24] The testimony of the Kenilworth chronicler suggests, then, that the corps of Cheshire yeomen formed the engine by which this northern dialect made a forceful incursion into the powerful circles of Richard's household, probably to the exclusion of Londoners like Chaucer, who had proven unreliable—if not outright hostile in some quarters—to the willful monarch.[25]

The mounting influence of the Cheshiremen at court later in the 1390s, in conjunction with the increasing autocracy of Richard II, would adequately account for Chaucer's decision to exclude the Knight's Yeoman from the tale-telling and, for that matter, from all of the incidents of the roadside drama. *Richard the Redeless* (c. 1399) reported the lethal consequences of running afoul of the Cheshire yeomen who dominated court activities:

> For chyders of Chester / where chose many daies
> To ben of conceill for causis / þat in þe court hangid,
> And pledid pipoudris / alle manere pleyntis . . .
> And ho-so pleyned to þe prince / þat pees shulde kepe,
> Of þese mystirmen / medlers of wrongis,
> He was lyghtliche ylauȝte / and y-luggyd of many,
> And y-mummyd on þe mouthe / and manaced to þe deth.[26]

While the Knight and the Squire return to center stage, their Yeoman is never again glimpsed. It is the Canon's Yeoman—as talkative as the Knight's Yeoman is taciturn—who is introduced to speak on behalf of this servant class, now rendered harmless through gullibility, dimwittedness, and service to someone as politically inconsequential as the alchemist Canon.

It is possible, nonetheless, to detect a grosser version of the Knight's Yeoman later in the collection. In the *Friar's Tale*, a similar sort of rustic yeoman, also dressed in green and carrying a bow and arrows, is invoked only to be subjected to the ultimate form of demonization. He actually *is* a demon. Along with his green attire, this yeoman's admission that he dwells "fer in the north contree" (III.1413) has long been interpreted as contributing to his identity as a devil.[27] While this is certainly true, it also alluded pointedly to the northern origins of the Cheshire yeomen, who were all devils as far as Londoners like Chaucer were concerned. The demon-yeoman's reference to the gold and silver he has stored "in oure shire" (III.1400–01) may conceal another topical reference. Between 1397 and 1399, Richard II transferred a vast amount of coin and jewelry, perhaps worth 100,000 marks, to create a northern treasury at Holt Castle in the new principality of Chester.[28] In the *Friar's Tale*, the northern yeoman's eagerness to offer a bond of "bretherhede" points to what the Kenilworth chronicler identified as the greatest threat of the Cheshiremen: Richard II's willingness to accept them *in tantam familiaritatem*, to treat them with familiarity, to make them part of the *familia regis*, to take them into his "family." By portraying the Yeoman in the *General Prologue* only to exclude him from any further textual presence, Chaucer has effectively taken the opposite tack, dissociating him from the family unit of the Knight and Squire, father and son, while expelling him also from the familiar society of the Canterbury pilgrims.

The Plowman

"He wolde thresshe, and therto dyke and delve"

The Parson and his brother, the Plowman, are usually recognized as the two pilgrims who come closest to representing the ideals of their respective estates.[29] In addition to his strict regard for the traditional duties of a parish priest, the Parson has a puritanical streak shown by his revulsion at the Host's swearing in the Man of Law's Endlink (II.1166–71). Harry Bailey responds by accusing the Parson of being a Lollard (II.1172–77):

> Oure Host answerde, "O Jankin, be ye there?
> I smelle a Lollere in the wynd," quod he.
> "Now! goode men," quod our Hoste, "herkeneth me;
> Abydeth, for Goddes digne passioun,
> For we schal han a predicacioun;
> This Lollere heer wil prechen us somwhat."

The accusation sounds like a humorous jab rather than a savage attack. The Parson's presence among the pilgrims traveling to the shrine of St. Thomas at Canterbury and later his "tale"—a relentlessly orthodox treatise on confession—have long been taken as proof positive that he could not have been a true Lollard but was instead one member of an apparently large population of conservative clerics.[30] In addition to their objections to auricular confession, true Wycliffites became fiercely critical of the abuses of pilgrimage, specifically making offerings to Becket's relics.[31] The rejection of the physical journey in favor of a metaphorical concept, already valorized in texts such as *Piers Plowman* that antedate the emergence of the more radical forms of Wycliffism,[32] had become a topos in the catalogue of Lollard tenets during the period in which Chaucer was composing the *Canterbury Tales*. Almost exactly contemporary with Chaucer's final creative period, *The Sixteen Points on Which the Bishops Accuse Lollards* warned those who might be subject to interrogation of the stereotypical "Lollard" position on pilgrimage: "Also we graunten þat it is leueful and medeful to go on pilgrimage to heuenwarde, doing werkes of penance, werkis of riȝtfulnes and werkis of mercy, and to suche pilgrimage alle men ben boundoun after þer power wile þei lyuen here."[33] The copy of the *Twelve Conclusions of the Lollards* affixed to the doors of Westminster Hall during the session of Parliament in 1395 was more precise in its rejection of pilgrimages as the occasions for idolatry, concluding with a swipe at Becket's status as an authentic martyr.[34] This controversy surrounding St. Thomas of Canterbury might also account for Chaucer's tactful omission of the saint's name from the beginning of his work, where the poet refers to him only vaguely as "the hooly blisful martir" (I.17).

Paul Strohm has proposed that the climate of opinion about Lollardy remained largely a "fractured field" until 1401, when William Sawtry was burned as a heretic.[35] There is evidence to suggest that opinions changed earlier, however, at least for those closest to the royal court. Since Roger Dymmok's *Liber contra XII Errores et Hereses Lollardorum*, which was prompted by the posting of the *Twelve Conclusions*, had addressed its introductory "Epistle" directly to Richard II, it seems clear enough that at the highest official levels the decision to brand Wycliffites as heretics and condemn their position on pilgrimage as error had been made in the 1390s. It is significant, I think, that in 1395 Richard II instructed this inscription to be included on the tomb he had commissioned in Westminster Abbey: "He destroyed heretics and scattered their friends."[36] Though Dymmok's reply to the eighth conclusion deals mostly with venerating saints and making offerings to sacred images, he cites various scriptural examples in support of the practice of pilgrimage by emphasizing the same purpose mentioned by Chaucer: healing the sick. There is one signal difference, however. Whereas Dymmok launches his argument by claiming that pilgrims were miraculously cured by visiting a saint's relics,[37] Chaucer in the line "That hem hath holpen whan that they were seeke" (I.18) implies that the pilgrims travel to Canterbury to give thanks for recoveries already effected at home, without benefit of actual contact with relics.

The testimony of William Thorpe before Archbishop Arundel includes many of the central Lollard positions emerging during the time when Chaucer was working on his *Tales*.[38] Because Thorpe's extended comments on the misconduct of pilgrims have often been cited as a commentary on the activities of Chaucer's pilgrims,[39] his remarks are worth quoting at length: "Also, sire, I knowe wel þat whanne dyuerse men and wymmen wolen goen þus aftir her owne willis and fyndingis out on pilgrimageyngis, þei wolen ordeyne biforehonde to haue wiþ hem boþe men and wymmen þat kunnen wel synge rowtinge songis, and also summe of þese pilgrimes wolen haue wiþ hem baggepipis so þat in eche toun þat þei comen þoruȝ, what wiþ noyse of her syngynge, and wiþ þe soun of her pipinge, and wiþ þe gingelynge of her Cantirbirie bellis, and wiþ þe berkynge out of dogges aftir hem, þese maken more noyse þan if þe king came þere awey wiþ his clarioneris and manye oþer mynystrals. And if þese men and wymmen ben a moneþe oute in her pilgrymage, manye of hem an half ʒeere aftir schulen be greete iangelers, tale tellers and lyeris."[40] Here we find a contemporary complaint against the Miller's bagpiping (I.565–66), the singing of the Summoner and the Pardoner (I.672–73), the jingling bells on the Monk's bridle (I.169–71), and particularly the reputation of pilgrims as great tellers of tales.

What cannot be omitted from critical evaluation, however, is the fact that these complaints, which Chaucer seems to have assimilated into his satirical representations of the pilgrims and, indeed, into the entire dramatic occasion for the tale-telling narrative, had become implicated in the 1390s with the repertory of Lollard invectives. The satire had become freighted, in ways the poet himself probably understood all too keenly, with the topics of social dissidents who were in the process of being stigmatized with charges of heresy by religious writers like Dymmok. It is therefore striking that William Thorpe's opening distinction between "trewe pilgrimes and fals pilgrimes" could just as well have been spoken by Chaucer's Parson: "I clepe hem trewe pilgrymes trauelynge toward þe blis of heuene whiche, in þe staat, degree or ordre þat God clepiþ hem to, bisien hem feiþfulli for to occupie alle her wittis, bodili and goostli, to knowe treweli and to kepe feiþfulli þe heestis of God, hatynge euere and fleynge alle þe seuene dedli synnes and euery braunche of hem."[41] The Host's efforts to poke fun at puritans like the Parson ceased to be a laughing matter after the Lollards had nailed their *Conclusions* to the door of Parliament in 1395. Chaucer seems to have caught the political drift of the decade and decided to cancel the Man of Law's Endlink altogether.[42] That the poet left it in his working papers, however, is evidenced by its survival in the landmark manuscripts Corpus 198 and Harley 7334. But it is missing from the earliest and most authoritative manuscripts, Hengwrt and Ellesmere, as well as from forty-seven later copies of the *Tales*.

The Plowman suffered from a different kind of backlash. His earnest livelihood, unifying as it does physical labor and Christian love—"A trewe swynkere and a good was he, / Lyvynge in pees and parfit charitee" (I.531–32)—set an ideal example for opposing the money-grubbing farmworkers who abandoned their manorial duties in favor of the cash they received as migrant laborers.[43] This was hardly the image Chaucer's contemporaries presented. Intensifying a traditional literary disdain toward *vileins*, for instance, John Gower's *Mirour de l'Omme* (c. 1374–78) complained about lazy day laborers who exploited the manpower shortage to demand triple wages: "Vagabond laborers see the world in need of their services and labor, and they are arrogant because there are so few of them."[44] During the English Rising of 1381, one of the rebels' demands had been the right freely

to negotiate wage-labor contracts.[45] Written in the wake of the English
Rising, Gower's *Vox Clamantis* (c. 1385) lashed out even more savagely
in characterizing casual laborers as sluggish, scarce, uncontrollable, and
grasping.[46]

The Commons' petitions to the Cambridge Parliament of 1388 led to a
renewal of statutes seeking to control the workforce, its movements, and
its wages—so much so that nearly two-thirds of all the Cambridge statutes
spoke directly to labor issues. Thomas Wimbledon's 1388 sermon *Redde
Racionem* began with the parable "liknyng þe kyngdom of Heuene to an
housholdere" (Mt. 20:1–16) interpreting it as a commentary on the nature
of salvation, but also using the opportunity to address himself to the proper
operation of society's three estates of priests, knights and farm laborers.[47]
Even *Pearl*, a poem that seems so innocent of political wranglings, incorporated the Parable of the Laborers for the same dual purpose—to reinforce
the subservience of agricultural workers and to relay a spiritual message
on the rewards of faithful Christian works, both ideally represented by
Chaucer's Plowman.[48]

The spiritual aspect of the Plowman's activities is strongly reminiscent
of the epitome of Christian labor in the literature and culture of late
fourteenth-century England—Piers the Plowman. Nevill Coghill long ago
pointed out that even the phrases in Chaucer's description of the Plowman
echoed Langland's poem. The line "That hadde ylad of dong ful many of
fother" (I.530) recalls the Langlandian line "That lawe shal ben a laborer
and lede afeld donge" (*Piers* B.4.147). And the statement "He wolde thresshe, and therto dyke and delve" (I.536) is even more strongly reminiscent
of Langland's lines "I dyked and I dolue, I do þat he hoteþ; / Som tyme I
sowe and som tyme I þresshe" (*Piers* B.5.545–46).[49] *Piers Plowman* was
relentless in attacking agricultural "wastours" and "lollares," while cele-
brating those workers, particularly the poem's title character, who remained
faithful to their masters. As James Simpson has remarked concerning *Piers*
B.5, "What Langland seems to be doing here is to represent Piers as a peasant loyal to his manorial lord God in perpetuity."[50] These moral judgments
were fortified by precise legal information. Ralph Hanna has made the
compelling argument, based on close textual comparison with the *Statutes
of the Realm*, that Langland's satirical self-portrait in the C-text (5.1–104)
relied point for point on the Statute of Laborers enacted by the Cambridge
Parliament in 1388.[51]

The relationship between Langland's poem and the early history of Lollardy is complicated by a lack of documentation for the movement's early
phase. But as the threat of radical reform began to loom larger, texts like
Piers Plowman became tainted with guilt by association. "Had archbishop
Arundel read the poem around 1396, he would surely have regarded it as

dangerous," Anne Hudson has remarked; "Had [he] scrutinized the poem again after promulgating the 1409 *Constitutions,* he would surely have had to adjudge the poem heretical."[52] The appropriation of the name "Peres Ploughman" as a code word in John Ball's letters urging sedition during the English Rising of 1381 cast an even darker shadow over Langland's poem, especially since Ball was placed on record as a disciple of John Wyclif.[53] Its opponents could doubly condemn the short-lived rebellion as both a revolt against the government of the Crown and a heretical conspiracy against the Church.

Though Chaucer's Plowman shares his brother's innocence because not only is he on pilgrimage, but he is also eager to pay tithes (I.539–40)— which Lollards often complained about[54]—the religious controversy had become sufficiently heated by the later 1390s to account for Chaucer's decision to deprive the Plowman of a tale and to exclude him from any subsequent appearance in the frame narrative. The pilgrim remains exactly as Lee Patterson describes him: "the psychologically opaque and socially quiescent Plowman, whose portrait assiduously effaces the very real economic struggles of Chaucer's contemporary world, struggles that were in other texts expressed precisely by means of the figure of the plowman."[55]

The ideological energies released by Langland's poem continued to flow into and around Chaucer's Plowman, however, with the result that *two* apocryphal tales came to be attached to this pilgrim.[56] The later of the two is the 1,380-line *Complaint of the Ploughman* thought to have been written as a Wycliffite satire around the year 1400, but reworked as the Chaucerian *Plowman's Tale* first printed in Thomas Godfray's black-letter folio edition of about 1532–36. This spurious tale was incorporated into William Thynne's second edition of the *Works* in 1542, where it displaced the *Retraction* and followed the tale of his brother, the Parson, capping the whole collection.[57] This piece of Reformation propaganda was clearly designed to claim Chaucer as a literary champion of Wycliffism. It worked in the opposite direction from fifteenth-century attempts at rendering the *Canterbury Tales* less susceptible to interpretation as Wycliffite or Lollard. The presence of the Plowman, even as Patterson's "psychologically opaque and socially quiescent" character, clearly represented both an opportunity and an irritant.

The solution taken by one early editor of the *Canterbury Tales* was to give this mute pilgrim a tale that was beyond reproach in its orthodox pieties. The complete text of the *Ploughman's Tale* exists only in Christ Church Oxford MS 152 (fols. 228b–231a), dated c. 1450–70. It was written on pages originally left blank at the end of the quire after the unfinished *Squire's Tale,* just before the *Second Nun's Tale.*[58] Apparently the primary scribe had hoped that the missing part 3 of the Squire's Oriental romance would turn up. But when time passed and no conclusion was found, a rhyme-royal Miracle of the Virgin originally written by Thomas Hoccleve (d. c. 1426) was given a linking prologue and inserted in the sequence of narratives. Hoccleve's eighteen-stanza poem, originally entitled "Item de Beata Virgine" in the autograph manuscript Huntington Library HM 744, is also preserved in a scribal copy in Trinity College, Cambridge, MS R.3.21, bringing to three the total number of surviving copies.[59]

What makes the *Ploughman's Tale* implicitly anti-Lollard? Hoccleve himself was a relentless opponent of Lollardy throughout his writings, most famously in his fierce attack on Sir John Oldcastle.[60] This particular narrative praises the devotion of a monk, whereas Lollards stood opposed to the "private religion" of monks as well as canons, friars, and even courtly clerics.[61] The tale recounts a miracle of the Virgin, whereas the Lollards criticized the cult of saints and voiced skepticism concerning any recourse to miracles.[62] The tale's praise of virginity, Mary's and the young monk's, ran counter to Lollard claims that Christ did not actually sanction the virgin life but instead gave his blessing to the married life, even for clergymen.[63] Finally, the exemplum's whole point is that the monk is rewarded by promotion to prior—quite a mercenary payoff in itself—for saying his paternoster in Latin, whereas Lollards maintained that prayers ought to be recited in English and addressed directly to God, without the sort of mediation afforded here by the Virgin Mary.[64] The anonymous interpolator of the *Ploughman's Tale* rejected the possibility of inserting a narrative related in any way to the pilgrim's worldly estate—a tale of village life such as the *Nun's Priest's Tale*, for example, or a subject of rural affairs such as the *Tale of Gamelyn*—and instead imposed on Chaucer's Plowman a pious tale incorporating the most orthodox values and devout practices.

The Five Guildsmen

"Of a solempne and a greet fraternitee"

Many of the Canterbury pilgrims belong to subgroups that formed prior to the assembly of the company in Southwark. The trio of the Knight, the Squire, and the Knight's Yeoman stand at the beginning of the roster, for example, and the duo of the Summoner and the Pardoner bring up the rear. The largest of these organized clusters is composed of the Five Guildsmen—the Carpenter, the Haberdasher, the Weaver, the Dyer, and the Tapestry-maker (I.361–78). The size of this group makes Chaucer's omission of all of its members from the tale-telling remarkable, especially since the Carpenter would have been the natural respondent to the *Miller's*

Tale with its ridicule of a carpenter as a cuckold. Chaucer went through narrative contortions to create an unlikely professional history for the Reeve, whose prior occupation as a carpenter comes as a total surprise and greatly strains the audience's credulity. It would have been far simpler to have called forth the Carpenter to retaliate against the Miller, but Chaucer seems to have felt constrained not to draw this or any other Guildsman into the arena of competitive gamesmanship. Why?

With neither tales nor any subsequent mention in the frame narrative, the Guildsmen have attracted little critical attention. Scholarship over the years has largely attended to defining their corporate status. Chaucer describes them as "clothed alle in o lyveree / Of a solempne and a greet fraternitee" (I.363–64), but he does not give clear indication what kind of fraternity would include five different trades. Efforts at identifying a craft that would admit all five have not been completely satisfying.[65] Something of a critical consensus has emerged that the tradesmen wear matching livery because they belong to a religious fraternity rather than a single craft mystery.[66] Yet the challenge to identification is probably more than a matter of remote historical circumstances. Guilds, whether they operated as "trade unions" or as parish societies, were a matter of considerable controversy in the 1380s and caused some very shrewd political maneuverings in the 1390s.

One of the greatest threats to aristocratic dominance in England during the late fourteenth century came from the craft guilds, particularly in London.[67] These powerful associations pursued their political interests with such fierce determination that their disputes boiled over into Parliament and involved the most influential men of the nation, notably John of Gaunt—the magnate who in many ways came closest to fulfilling the role of Chaucer's patron.[68] The city's political history in the 1380s was played out in the conflict between the forces represented by Sir Nicholas Brembre, who acted on behalf of rich merchants and victualer guilds, and Gaunt's protégé John Northampton, who headed a movement supported by a variety of nonvictualing crafts. Because Chaucer's Guildsmen were drawn specifically from the nonvictualing trades,[69] they would have been aligned with the same Lancastrian faction with which the poet himself maintained such close affiliation during the last quarter century of his life.[70]

Reaction to the civic activism of the craft guilds emerged in the Commons' petitions to the Cambridge Parliament of 1388. One of the petitions asked for the abolition of all liveries assumed since the first year of Edward III's reign so that the uncontrolled formation of liveried bands might no longer threaten public order. Closely related to this move was another petition asking for the suppression of all guilds and fraternities, which were also liveried companies.[71] The resulting Ordinance of 1390 made no distinction among the liveried associations which were to be banned, whether craft guilds, parish fraternities, or retainers of lesser lords.[72]

Liveried parish guilds had risen to prominence during the second half of the fourteenth century, especially in the larger cities. London had nearly fifty fraternities in the 1390s, each hiring its own staff of chaplains and clerks to perform the liturgical function of offering masses for the dead.[73] Some gained considerable social prestige. One signal example is the Tailors' fraternity of St. John the Baptist, which numbered many distinguished individuals among its honorary members, including, from 1385, Richard II.[74] The trend throughout the 1390s was for craft guilds to pretend to greater sanctity by assuming the character of religious fraternities. This strategy succeeded, probably because Richard II was fond of the religious fraternities and effectively exempted them from the Ordinance of 1390 by issuing a royal writ instructing sheriffs merely to demand reports of their statutes, properties, and activities.[75] The effort the craft guilds made to look like parish guilds was not only shrewd; it was also easy enough to do, since craft members tended to live and work in the same quarter and were likely to belong to the same parish.

This blurring of distinctions between craft and parish guilds was not entirely new, but it was exploited more fully for the purposes of camouflage after 1388. Contemporary records had trouble distinguishing between parish fraternities seeking stronger civic influence and craft guilds dedicating themselves to saints—even pursuing benevolent activities and religious observances—while engaging in every manner of urban politics. To the bedevilment of modern scholarship, Chaucer exploited this ambiguity to the fullest. George Unwin concluded that the ambiguity assumed strategic significance in the 1390s: "The Janus-like appearance of the gild, as a craft on one side and as a fraternity on the other, and the difficulty we find in clearly separating these aspects, were not the result of a mere confusion in the medieval mind. It was a more or less conscious device for securing liberty of action."[76]

Since the fraternity element was largely free of ecclesiastical dominance, these liveried companies emerged from insecurity to a position from which they could obtain more than they had ever hoped before: a perpetual commonality for the accumulation of property and social power. "So far as a royal charter could ensure it," Thomas Reddaway has observed, "they had become unchallengeable, self-governing, property-owning bodies."[77] And they owed this new status of power and privilege directly to Richard II.[78] When Chaucer concluded the General Prologue's portrait of the Guildsmen by reporting that their wives would attend vigils with "a mantel roialliche ybore" (I.378), he was drawing attention to the collusion between the guilds and the crown in civic politics.

The parish guilds were also aggressively orthodox.[79] John Wyclif himself opposed them as bodies of Christian indenture that were unnecessary, and their concern for maintaining chantry priests to say prayers for the souls of deceased members became a consistent target of Lollard criticism.[80] In response, the parish guilds became fiercely anti-Lollard. The conduct of the Five Guildsmen, as participants on a Canterbury pilgrimage, was therefore an implicit affront to Wycliffite criticism.

In the struggle for respectability in the 1390s, several older crafts, for example, the Skinners in 1393 and the Salters in 1394, took shelter by rededicating themselves under the auspices of Corpus Christi.[81] Both King Richard and Queen Anne are included in a list of "Foundors and Brethern and Sustern" of the Skinners' fraternity of Corpus Christi.[82] Drawing on what Miri Rubin has called "the iconography of power," their spectacular processions afforded occasions for displaying social hierarchies expressed in an idiom of privilege and lordship.[83] Organized by guilds that served as training grounds for ambitious burgesses such as the Five Guildsmen— "Wel semed ech of hem a fair burgeys / To sitten in a yeldehall on a deys" (I.369–70)—Corpus Christi gatherings permitted the unambiguous inscription of local political meaning by including the city's aldermen in the line of march. When Chaucer notes that each of his Guildsmen "Was shaply for to been an alderman" (I.372), he points to the political ambitions of these liveried men, even when the fraternity to which they belonged was explicitly defined as religious. The irony pervading all of these observations concerning their wealth and civic ambition derives from the fact that the separate guilds of Haberdashers, Carpenters, Weavers, Dyers, and Tapestry-makers were the least politically and socially powerful in fourteenth-century London. The mayor and the aldermen came instead exclusively from the prestigious mercantile guilds of Mercers, Grocers, Drapers, Goldsmiths, Fishmongers, Vintners, Skinners, and Tailors.

The Cook's Tale

"Of this Cokes tale maked Chaucer na moore"

With the Guildsmen travels their hired Cook, one of the few pilgrims clearly identified as a London resident. In the *General Prologue* he is introduced as an expert on "a draughte of Londoun ale" (I.382), and in the first line of his tale's prologue he is described precisely as "the Cook of Londoun" (I.4325). Though he names himself "Hogge of Ware" or Roger of Ware, a town in Hertfordshire some thirty miles from London (I.4336),[84] he seems to be an immigrant from the country to the city. He had come to

London and entered a profession that granted him a civic identity largely superseding his Hertfordshire origins, except in the retention of his home-town as a sort of last name.[85]

The unfinished state of the *Cook's Tale*, breaking off as it does after only fifty-seven lines, seems to have resulted not from the pilgrim's controversial character but from the unsettling contents of his tale. Donald Howard suggests self-censorship: "Possibly it was finished but too scurrilous to be transcribed, and so went underground. Possibly Chaucer or someone else suppressed it, ripped it out of an early copy leaving only what was on the same folio with the ending of the *Reeve's Tale.*"[86] As the first to attempt organizing the fragments of Chaucer's *Tales*, the scribe-editor of Hengwrt left space to add the missing portion of the fabliau of Perkyn Revelour, apparently in the hope that the stray pages would turn up among the author's working papers. But when no additional sections were delivered and it became clear to the copyist that none ever would appear, he made a note in the left margin of the blank half-page that he had previously reserved: "Of this Cokes tale maked Chaucer na moore."[87]

Later copyists struggled with this awkward circumstance as best they could. The incomplete state of the *Cook's Tale* created an obvious rupture between the brilliant continuities of Fragment I and the isolated sturdiness of the *Man of Law's Tale* in Fragment II. In ten manuscripts, the problem was swept under the carpet, as it were, and the *Cook's Tale* was simply dropped to avoid the appearance of a break. The workaday scribe of Rawlinson Poetry 141 (fol. 29a) patched together this grim four-line conclusion:

And thus with horedom and bryberye
Togeder thei used till thei honged hye.
For whoso evel byeth shal make a sory sale;
And thus I make an ende of my tale.[88]

The landmark manuscripts Corpus Christi 198 and Harley 7334, followed by twenty-three later collections, remedied the problem by adding as a continuation the 902-line *Tale of Gamelyn*. This rustic romance was sometimes connected to the end of the authentic *Cook's Tale* by the use of a brief bridge, such as the following couplet in Royal 18.C.ii: "But here-of I will passe as now / And of yong Gamelyne I wil telle yow."

First printed by John Urry in his Chaucer edition of 1721, then again as a spurious piece by Walter W. Skeat in 1884, *Gamelyn* has been largely neglected except by Neil Daniel in his fine doctoral dissertation of 1967.[89] Written in old septenary / alexandrine couplets, the romance is thought to have been composed at some time around the middle of the fourteenth century, though no source has ever been discovered. No copy of *Gamelyn* survives outside the *Canterbury Tales*. The text occurs in the same place in all twenty-five manuscripts, with the exception of one eccentric collection (Rawlinson Poetry 149), so it probably assumed this position at the beginning of the tradition of transmission.[90] Since textual analysis strongly suggests that all copies derive from a single archetype not among the surviving copies, the exemplar was most likely a text discovered among the poet's working papers. The rhyme words suggest a text originally composed in northern dialect but written by a Londoner with some Kentish forms,[91] so it is possible that Chaucer himself copied this single written source. At least two questions have never received adequate attention, however. How did this unique copy of *Gamelyn* establish its fixed position following the fragment of the *Cook's Tale*? And how did *Gamelyn* find such ready acceptance by the early organizers of Corpus Christi 198 and Harley 7334?

I have long been inclined to accept Tatlock's suggestion that the unique copy of *Gamelyn* was inserted into the working papers of the *Canterbury Tales* by Chaucer himself in the position immediately following the Cook's fragment.[92] After deciding not to continue the tale of Perkyn Revelour, the poet began to consider a replacement by doing what he seems always to have done when planning a new piece: he looked for a source text. At some later date, perhaps in the middle 1390s, he came into possession of a copy of *Gamelyn* and decided that it might serve as a source for a replacement tale. So he inserted it tentatively in the position immediately following the *Cook's Tale*, between Fragments I and II, but he never returned to compose a new tale based on this source. Why not? Perhaps time ran out, and Chaucer died before the new tale could be written. Perhaps the frank "Englishness" of the rustic romance dissuaded a poet who had consistently preferred Continental sources. Or perhaps there was something unsuitable about a narrative whose protagonist was an outlaw hiding out in the greenwood.

Part of the growing discontent throughout England in the 1390s seems to have been centered on what was perceived to be the increased threat of outlaws. The kingdom seemed beset by a crime wave, and many considered Richard II indifferent or incompetent to remedy the situation. Jean Froissart, who returned to England for a visit in 1395, was shocked by a criminal threat that had drastically increased since his stay in the 1360s. According to his *Chronicles*, honest men no longer felt safe and no longer expected justice when wronged: "They began to be attacked by a class of people who roamed the country in troops and gangs. Merchants dared not ride about upon their business for fear of being robbed, and they did not know to whom to turn for protection or justice. Such things were most disagreeable to the English people and contrary to their habits and customs."[93] When Chaucer traveled about the country as Clerk of the King's Works in 1390, for example, he was robbed three times of money intended to pay workmen busy on royal construction projects. But justice was not totally inefficient in 1390. The highwayman Richard Brierley and his gang were apprehended, they confessed, and all were jailed or hanged for their crimes.[94]

With an uncurbed outbreak of crime later in the decade and a breakdown in the effectiveness of the judicial system—real or perceived—Gamelyn's sympathetic view of outlawry would have been grossly inappropriate. After all, Gamelyn's gang specialized in religious victims: "Ther was no man þat for him ferde þe wors / But abbotes and priours, monk and chanoun" (780–81). Its disrespect for the law would help to account for Chaucer's neglect of the work as a replacement for the unfinished Cook's Tale. Civil peace under Henry IV and Henry V improved, probably because the outlaws were absorbed back into the army when the wars with France were renewed,[95] and Gamelyn could then find a more comfortable berth in the Canterbury collection. And since Gamelyn's struggles principally concerned the right of a son to claim his inheritance from his father,[96] the story would have resonated with a Lancastrian public whose kings justified their seizure of the crown by the claim that Henry, duke of Lancaster, had been denied his rights of inheritance by Richard II.

In one other attempt at remedying the incompleteness of the Cook's Tale, Oxford Bodley MS 686 (fols. 54b–55b), dated c. 1430–40, padded the tale with thirty-three supplemental lines and gave it a new twelve-line conclusion.[97] Critics have long suspected that Chaucer dropped the story of Perkyn Revelour because its sexual contents were too explicit, too full of "vileynye," and too "lewed." The continuation confirms the anonymous writer's revulsion at this aspect of Chaucer's original. The last authentic line, which describes how Perkyn's companion had a wife who kept "a shoppe, and swyved for hir sustenance" (I.4422)—that is, used her shop as a front for prostitution—was altered to read: "A wife he hadde that helde her contenaunce / A schoppe, and ever sche pleyed for his sustenaunce" (ll. 85–86). Even more obviously, however, the anonymous continuator showed a deep anxiety about another social threat that may have prompted Chaucer to abandon this tale—the threat of the unruly apprentice in late fourteenth-century London.

Employed by the Five Guildsmen, who belonged to five nonvictualing crafts, the Cook begins a tale in which a master "of a craft of vitailliers" (I.4366) becomes the butt of his rambunctious apprentice, Perkyn. The choice of guild recalls the long-standing antagonism between victualers and nonvictualers, seeming to play to the prejudices of the Cook's paymasters. But the narrative involves the apprenticeship system on which all guilds were dependent for their financial success and, indeed, their very survival. Though apprentices provided a source of cheap labor, they also constituted the next generation of masters who would guarantee the future of the guild.[98] The social structure was strictly hierarchic and explicitly patriarchal, in ways benevolent as well as coercive. Chaucer's grandfather Robert, it should be recalled, assumed the family name as a gesture of esteem for his own master, the London mercer John le Chaucer.[99]

Sylvia Thrupp describes a system fully responsive to the dynamics of patriarchal rewards and obligations as part of a larger civic role: "Since everyone knew that the preservation of the local civic liberties hung upon the continuance of orderly behavior, all emotional resources were drawn upon to secure this end. The merchant controlled his staff of apprentices and servants by the help of some of the overtones that were to be found in the ideas of lordship and paternity. A man's authority over his apprentices was always semipaternal in nature. . . . Unruly apprentices were punished in some way that would dramatize the duty of deference."[100] Perkyn's unruliness runs the gamut of misconduct often spelled out in contracts of indenture. An apprentice was forbidden from playing games of chance, visiting taverns, and consorting with women in any capacity.[101] Perkyn violated these rules point for point. He was so much given "to pleyen at the dys" that no apprentice in London was more skillful at gambling (I.4384–86). He preferred to spend his time in taverns rather than in the shop (I.4376). And he was passionately drawn to women of ill repute: "He was as ful of love and paramour / As is the hyve ful of hony sweete" (I.4372–73).

One of the worst offenses that an apprentice could commit was to steal from his master, a customary practice for Perkyn. Not the victim of subtle pilfering, the Master frequently found himself cleaned out completely: "For often tyme he foond his box ful bare" (I.4390). What is extraordinary about the situation in the *Cook's Tale* is the Master's long-suffering patience and final leniency. In historical instances of embezzlement in fourteenth-century London, the offending apprentice was taken into the hall—sometimes the master's hall, sometimes the guild's hall—where he was stripped and beaten until blood flowed, then publicly humiliated by expulsion from the craft, with the loss of all the time that he had already committed as an apprentice.[102] In the Cook's account, the Master has endured this in-house robbery for many years. We are told that Perkyn was "ny out of his prentis-hood" (I.4400) when typically the term of apprenticehood ran for seven to ten years. Only then does the Master reach the conclusion that one bad apple will spoil the barrel—a commonplace that grossly underestimates the gravity of Perkyn's thefts—and decide to punish him by giving him "acquitance," or liberation from his contract of service.[103] Though the Master gives him an angry send-off—"And bad hym go, with sorwe and with meschance!" (I.4412)—Perkyn greets his expulsion more like a welcome release from unwanted restraints. He casts his lot with a companion of his own kind and with the companion's prostitute wife, and the narrative breaks off.

The *Cook's Tale* halts so soon after getting started that few scholars have hazarded a guess at how Chaucer might have proceeded. Earl Lyon's contribution to *Sources and Analogues of Chaucer's Canterbury Tales* scrambled to find likely analogues, offering among other candidates the following tale from Robert Greene's *Blacke Bookes Messenger:* "Two rogues and a prostitute 'cross-bite' a citizen: the prostitute entertains the victim; the one rogue surprises them, accuses the citizen of dishonoring his wife, and calls in a 'constable,' who is the second rogue."[104] An analogue of this sort has a strong appeal, because it suggests how the Master could be drawn back into the story as a continuing character while fulfilling the theme stated in the prologue: "For herberwynge by nyght is perilous" (I.4332). The Master had initiated the action by sacking Perkyn, and so narrative logic would seem to require that the discharged apprentice have his revenge. As in the two preceding fabliaux, the *Miller's Tale* and the *Reeve's Tale*, patriarchal authority would be subverted and the older man tricked, dispossessed, and humiliated.[105] If the narrative strategy of "quyting" was intended to remain operative in the *Cook's Tale*, then it was inevitable that the Master would show up again only to become the victim of Perkyn's vengeful connivance.

Such a tale, whatever its details, would have been told at the expense of a guild master and would therefore have become a provocation to the Cook's employers, the Five Guildsmen. The sense of professional solidarity that motivated the Reeve would have required a firm response from one or more of the offended craft members. Fragment I would have shifted into the arena of London guild controversies—an arena that Chaucer's neglect of the Five Guildsmen suggests he had decided to place off limits. As David Wallace has very perceptively noted, the great anxiety underlying the opening of the *Cook's Tale* becomes legible in Perkyn's efforts to gather about himself a *meynee*, a company or association of other scoundrels (I.4381).[106] The anonymous poet of Bodley 686's continuation expanded this statement with lines owing their vehemence of moral disapproval, as well as their alliteration and personification allegory, to the Langlandian tradition of social complaint (ll. 19–23):

> With Rech-never and Recheles this lessoun he lerys
> With Waste and with Wranglere, his owne pley-ferys,
> With Lyght-honde and with Likorouse-mowth, with Unschamfast;
> With Drynke-more and with Drawe-abak, her thryst is y-past,
> With Malaperte and with Mysseavysed—*such meyny they hight*.
> [emphasis added]

The formation of such a *meyny* would have touched a deep nerve in a London readership during the late fourteenth century. It invoked the threat of secret confederacies and criminal covens that continued to fuel fear in the wake of the English Rising of 1381. A mayoral proclamation of 1383 declared that "noman make none congregaciouns, conuenticules, ne assembles of poeple, in priue nen apert."[107] The lurking insecurity finally emerged in petitions to the Cambridge Parliament of 1388 that targeted every form of civic association, including craft guilds. The early 1390s, therefore, became a time of frantic maneuvering among these "respectable" associations, with efforts that included the isolation, the marginalization, and the demonization of fringe associations. The conclusion of the padded version in Bodley 686 imposes its own severe judgments on Perkyn and his companion (ll. 87–98):

> What thorowe hymselfe and his felawe that sought,
> Unto a myschefe bothe they were broght.
> The tone y-dampned to presoun perpetually,
> The tother to deth for he couthe not of clergye.
> And therfore, yonge men, lerne while ye may
> That with mony dyvers thoghtes beth prycked al the day.
> Remembre you what myschefe cometh of mysgovernaunce.
> Thus mowe ye lerne worschep and come to substaunce.
> Thenke how grace and governaunce hath broght hem a boune,
> Many pore mannys sonn, chefe state of the towne.
> Ever rewle the after the beste man of name,
> And God may grace the to come to the same.

The one scapegrace is jailed while the other is executed, because he had neglected to learn to read while an apprentice and therefore could not claim benefit of clergy for sentencing in an episcopal court, where there was no capital punishment.[108] Their namelessness becomes a marker of their outcast status as condemned men. The concluding apostrophe to "yonge men" displaces the earlier threat to the guilds' status quo by asserting the benefits of faithful adherence to their rules and procedures. From "worschep" comes "substaunce," and from submission to "governaunce" comes the "boune" or reward of professional success. Even a "pore mannys sonn," if he were obedient and followed the rules of craft membership, could achieve the highest reward of guild participation in the political realm by attaining "chefe state of the towne," a success famously attained during this period by Richard Whittington.

Conclusion

If recent theoretical debates have rendered the interpretation of an author's extant writings problematic, the prospect of investigating what Chaucer did *not* actually write may seem altogether chimerical. Yet these absences deserve fuller notice than has lately been granted them. The founders of modern Chaucerian studies, scholars such as Walter Skeat, John Tatlock, and Carleton Brown, showed a willingness to speculate about the poet's creative processes and readily detected evidence of his uncertainties, first shots, makeshift changes, and flagging inspiration. New Criticism, however, required readers to operate on the assumption that a text produced by a literary genius like Chaucer was perfectly accomplished for the purposes of minute analysis and immune to the imputation of any faltering on the writer's part, as well as resistant to outside influences, political or otherwise. This assumption about the faultless stability of the text, even a text as manifestly a work in progress as the *Canterbury Tales*, has proved even more durable than the New Critical methodology that required it.

But these ruptures nonetheless form part of the text's self-declaration legible within the literary system deployed according to the author's own rules. At the beginning he promised four tales from all thirty pilgrims, and at the end he has the Host declare to the Parson "For every man, save thou, hath toold his tale" (X.25). But the author has not, in fact, delivered the goods. I realize all too keenly that *Chaucer the author* has here been constructed to ventriloquize a whole set of intentions concerning omissions and deletions in the intervening fragments. Key to my interpretation of these rhetorical silences is the duplicity by which the achieved text itself stubbornly resists any "respectful doubling of commentary" in its own narrative assumptions and expectations.[109] Any one of my guesses at motivation might be countered with other, equally convincing accounts, including the perennial confidence that each of these gaps would have been mended if only Chaucer had lived long enough to do so. What is more, my narrow concentrations on specific social pressures to account for these silences are offered with a consciousness of the limitations of these or any other historicist "explanations." What has not been fully articulated throughout these discussions—though felt intensely in the writing of almost every page—is what Paul Strohm so brilliantly cultivates in his historical studies as "a considerable receptivity to multiple reference, undecideability, and, especially, the constant instability of relations between what frames and what is framed."[110]

Yet I hold fast to the proposition that these authorial suppressions of material are far more consciously intended than the repressions Strohm has located in "the textual unconscious." Again I propose that the surprise entrance of the Canon's Yeoman and the unexpected insertion of his tale strongly indicate an authorial decision to dismiss as tale-tellers certain pilgrims originally portrayed in the *General Prologue* and to leave unfinished the *Cook's Tale*, the one narrative that shows no signs in the frame narrative of being halted by the Host or other pilgrim. If any of the particulars seems tenuous or even tendentious, my overall argument remains powerfully suggestive, I hope, in exposing a larger field of the poet's social anxieties and the instinctive caution that had safeguarded his prior literary performances (as well as his public career) and in crediting these anxieties with motivating a variety of evasions during the composition of the *Canterbury Tales*. Though Chaucer made the gesture of renouncing any objectionable writings in his "retracciouns," he seems to have made no effort to expunge evidence of these evasions from the textual traces left to be assembled after his death. A deep awareness of social instability formed the very substance of his creativity and afforded the crucial tensions making possible, for example, the dangerous "jokes" that, as Strohm has shown, so steadily complement the restless textual center of his *Tales*. What we are left to witness, in short, is a constant negotiation between the wildly controversial and the politically correct.

Notes

1. Donald R. Howard, *The Idea of the Canterbury Tales* (Berkeley and Los Angeles: University of California Press, 1976), 1.

2. See Derek Pearsall, "Theory and Practice in Middle English Editing," *Text* 7 (1994): 113. "What the evidence of the manuscripts demands that we recognize, though, is that the *Canterbury Tales* are unfinished—never released or even prepared for publication, and with the stages of revision and recomposition manifest in the surviving manuscripts." All citations to the *Canterbury Tales* are taken from *The Riverside Chaucer*, 3d ed., general editor Larry D. Benson (Boston: Houghton Mifflin, 1987).

3. V. A. Kolve pursues a unified reading of Ellesmere Fragments I and II by arguing that Chaucer intended to cancel the *Cook's Tale* entirely (*Chaucer and the Imagery of Narrative: The First Five Canterbury Tales* [Stanford: Stanford University Press, 1984], 275–85).

4. This continues the argument I set forth in John M. Bowers, ed., *The* Canterbury *Tales: Fifteenth-Century Continuations and Additions* (Kalamazoo, Mich.: Medieval Institute Publications, 1992), esp. 1–4.

5. Gabrielle M. Spiegel, "History, Historicism, and the Social Logic of the Text in the Middle Ages," *Speculum* 65 (1990): 77.

6. Fredric Jameson, *The Political Unconscious: Narrative as a Socially Symbolic Act* (Ithaca: Cornell University Press, 1981), 9: "We apprehend [texts] through sedimented layers of previous interpretations, or—if the text is brand-new—through the

sedimented reading habits and categories developed by those inherited interpretive traditions."

7. Anne Hudson, ed., *Selections from English Wycliffite Writings* (Cambridge: Cambridge University Press, 1978), 24–29, 150–55. For a prime witness to clerical alarmism in royal court circles, see Roger Dymmok, *Liber contra XII Errores et Hereses Lollardorum*, ed. H. S. Cronin (London: Wyclif Society, 1922).

8. See two articles in *The Reign of Richard II: Essays in Honour of May McKisack*, ed. F. R. H. Du Boulay and Caroline M. Barron (London: Athlone, 1971); Caroline M. Barron's "Quarrel of Richard II with London, 1392–7," 173–201; and John H. Harvey's "Richard II and York," 202–17.

9. Jean Froissart, *Chronicles*, trans. Geoffrey Brereton (Harmondsworth: Penguin, 1968), 438–42. Richard Maidstone's *Concordia Facta inter Regem Riccardum II et Civitatem Londonie per Fratrum Riccardum Maydiston*, ed. Charles Roger Smith (Ph.D. diss., Princeton University, 1972), offers the most detailed description of the 1392 pageants.

10. The regime had a solid base only from Agincourt in 1415 to the young king's death in 1422. Henry V's strategies for shoring up the Lancastrian regime have formed the subject of a number of recent studies: P. S. Lewis, "War Propaganda and Historiography in Fifteenth-Century France and England," *Transactions of the Royal Historical Society*, 5th ser., 15 (1965): 1–21; Christopher Allmand, *Lancastrian Normandy, 1415–1450: The History of a Medieval Occupation* (Oxford: Clarendon, 1983); G. L. Harriss, ed., *Henry V: The Practice of Kingship* (Oxford: Oxford University Press, 1985); Edward Powell, *Kingship, Law, and Society: Criminal Justice in the Reign of Henry V* (Oxford: Oxford University Press, 1989); John H. Fisher, "A Language Policy for Lancastrian England," *PMLA* 107 (1992): 1168–80; and Christopher Allmand, *Henry V* (Berkeley: University of California Press, 1992), 306–32.

11. This pilgrim's bibliography is far from extensive: Edith S. Knapp, "A Note on Chaucer's Yeoman," *Modern Language Notes* 43 (1928): 176–77; Earle Birney, "The Squire's Yeoman," *Review of English Literature* 1 (1960): 9–18; Stoddard Malarkey, "Chaucer's Yeoman Again," *College English* 24 (1963): 289–95; George A. Test, "Archer's Feathers in Chaucer and Ascham," *American Notes & Queries* 2 (1964): 67–68; and John W. Conlee, "A Yeman Had He," in *Chaucer's Pilgrims: An Historical Guide to the Pilgrims in* The Canterbury Tales, ed. Laura C. Lambdin and Robert T. Lambdin (Westport: Greenwood Press, 1996), 27–37.

12. The ninth statute is included in *Knighton's Chronicon, 1337–1396*, ed. and trans. G. H. Martin (Oxford: Clarendon, 1995), 520–23: "None should be so bold as to speak ill or spread any false report, or lies, or any false matter about the prelates, dukes, earls, barons, or other great nobles of the realm, or of the chancellor, treasurer, clerk of the privy seal, steward of the household of our lord the king, the justices of either bench, or the other great officers of the realm." J. A. Tuck discusses the social background of these statutes ("The Cambridge Parliament, 1388," *English Historical Review* 84 [1969]: 225–43).

13. William B. McColly, "Chaucer's Yeoman and the Rank of His Knight," *Chaucer Review* 20 (1985): 23. Lawrence Besserman suggests that the Yeoman's belt partakes of the symbolism of wealth and opulence ("Girdles, Belts, and Cords: A Leitmotif in Chaucer's *General Prologue*," *Papers on Language and Literature* 22 [1986]: 322–25).

14. *Westminster Chronicle, 1381–1394*, ed. and trans. L. C. Hector and Barbara F. Harvey (Oxford: Clarendon, 1982), 186–87. Background materials on the Cheshire

yeomen, as well as later materials on the guilds controversies, are adapted from John M. Bowers, *"Pearl* in Its Royal Setting: Ricardian Poetry Revisited," *Studies in the Age of Chaucer* 17 (1995): 111–55.

15. Thomas Walsingham, *Historia Anglicana,* ed. Henry Thomas Riley, 2 vols. (London: 1863–64), 1:321; *Historia Vitae et Regni Ricardi Secundi,* ed. George B. Stow, Jr. (Philadelphia: University of Pennsylvania Press, 1977), 112–13; and Adam of Usk, *The Chronicle,* A.D. *1377–1421,* ed. Edward Maunde Thompson (1904; reprint, Dyfed, Wales: Llanerch, 1990), 14–15. See Gervase Mathew, *The Court of Richard II* (New York: Norton, 1968), 19–20, and Chris Given-Wilson, *The Royal Household and the King's Affinity: Service, Politics and Finance in England, 1360–1413* (New Haven: Yale University Press, 1986), 214–15.

16. Chris Given-Wilson, "The King and the Gentry in Fourteenth-Century England," *Transactions of the Royal Historical Society,* 5th ser., 37 (1987): 94.

17. Anthony Tuck believes the king's Cheshire strategy dates from 1394 and was not, as commonly thought, a sudden obsession in 1397 (Tuck, *Richard II and the English Nobility* [New York: St. Martin's, 1974], 180–81).

18. Adam of Usk, *Chronicle,* 24. *Vita Ricardi Secundi* (140) numbered the Cheshire archers at only two hundred, while other sources—like Adam of Usk—ran as high as four thousand; Tuck, *Richard II* (186) places the recruitment target at two thousand.

19. Friedrich W. D. Brie, ed., *The Brut, or the Chronicles of England,* EETS, o. s., 136 (London: K. Paul Trench, Trübner, 1908), 353.

20. Adam of Usk, *Chronicle,* 39. See also James L. Gillespie, "Richard II's Cheshire Archers," *Transactions of the Historic Society of Lancaster and Cheshire* 125 (1975): 1–39.

21. Walsingham, *Historia* 2:224, had harsh criticism for the Cheshire guardsmen: "Interea Rex, sibi metuens, convocavit ad tutelam sui corporis multos malefactores de Comitatu Cestriae, qui noctium vigilias dierumque servarent, et dividerent, circa illum;" see also *Annales Ricardi Secundi et Henrici Quarti,* ed. Henry Thomas Riley (London, 1866), 208.

22. R. R. Davies, "Richard II and the Principality of Chester, 1397–99," in *The Reign of Richard II,* ed. Du Boulay and Barron, 260.

23. Maude Violet Clarke cites BL Add. 35295, fol. 260b ("The Deposition of Richard II," in *Fourteenth Century Studies,* ed. L. S. Sutherland and M. McKisack [Oxford: Clarendon, 1937], 98). V. H. Galbraith discusses the use of *materna lingua* in the promotion of "provincial or regional nationalities" ("Nationality and Language in Medieval England," *Transactions of the Royal Historical Society,* 4th ser., 23 [1941]: 114).

24. For this provincial master's connections with the royal court, see Bowers, *"Pearl* in Its Royal Setting."

25. Michael J. Bennett suggests that the alienation of the London writers Gower and Chaucer may have been prompted by the king's preference in the 1390s for provincial poets ("The Court of Richard II and the Promotion of Literature," in *Chaucer's England,* ed. Barbara Hanawalt [Minneapolis: University of Minnesota Press, 1992], 12, 16). See also Michael J. Bennett, *"Sir Gawain and the Green Knight* and the Literary Achievement of the North-West Midlands: The Historical Background," *Journal of Medieval History* 5 (1979): 63–88, and *Community, Class and Careerism: Cheshire and Lancashire Society in the Age of* Sir Gawain and the Green Knight (Cambridge: Cambridge University Press, 1983), esp. 233–35.

26. The incomplete *Richard the Redeless* from BL MS Add. 41666 was joined with

another fragment from Cambridge University Library Ll.4.14 and published as *Mum and the Sothsegger*, ed. Mabel Day and Robert Steele, EETS, o.s., 199 (London: Oxford University Press, 1936), 21–22 (ll. 317–19 and 334–37). The two fragments are now considered separate works; see Helen Barr, "The Relationship of *Richard the Redeless* and *Mum and the Sothsegger*: Some New Evidence," *Yearbook of Langland Studies* 4 (1990): 105–33.

27. Alfred L. Kellogg, "Chaucer's *Friar's Tale*: Line 1314," *Notes & Queries* 204 (1959): 190–92; D. W. Robertson, Jr., "Why the Devil Wears Green," *Modern Language Notes* 69 (1954): 470–72; and Michael Murphy, "North: The Significance of a Compass Point in Some Medieval Literature," *Lore and Language* 9 (1983): 65–76.

28. Davies, "Richard II and the Principality of Chester," 271–72, and Given-Wilson, *The Royal Household*, 90 and 180–81. See *Annales Ricardi Secundi*, 249: "Holt in quo magna pars fuerat thesauri sui."

29. D. W. Robertson, Jr., "Chaucer and the 'Commune Profit': The Manor," *Mediaevalia* 6 (1980): 239–59, and Elton D. Higgs, "The Old Order and the 'Newe World' in the *General Prologue* to the *Canterbury Tales*," *Huntington Library Quarterly* 45 (1982): 155–73, affirm critical agreement about the ideal representations of the Parson and the Plowman.

30. See, for example, the more recent work of Douglas J. Wurtele, "The Anti-Lollardry of Chaucer's Parson," *Mediaevalia* 11 (1989 for 1985): 151–68.

31. Anne Hudson, *The Premature Reformation: Wycliffite Texts and Lollard History* (Oxford: Clarendon, 1988), 371–74 on oaths, 294–301 on confession, 301–09 on pilgrimage, and 390–94 on Chaucer's Parson.

32. John Burrow, "The Action of Langland's Second Vision," *Essays in Criticism* 15 (1965): 247–68.

33. Hudson, ed., *Wycliffite Writings*, 23. For comments on the manuscript and dating of the text, see 145.

34. Ibid., 27.

35. Paul Strohm, "Chaucer's Lollard Joke: History and the Textual Unconscious," *Studies in the Age of Chaucer* 17 (1995): 29–32.

36. The epitaph is quoted by J. A. Tuck, "Carthusian Monks and Lollard Knights: Religious Attitude at the Court of Richard II," *Studies in the Age of Chaucer, Proceedings, No. 1, 1984: Reconstructing Chaucer*, ed. Paul Strohm and Thomas J. Heffernan (Knoxville: New Chaucer Society, 1985), 153. See also H. G. Richardson, "Heresy and the Lay Power under Richard II," *English Historical Review* 51 (1936): 1–28.

37. Dymmok, *Liber contra XII Errores et Hereses Lollardorum*, 192 (viii, 7).

38. The interrogation preceded the manuscript by some years (see Anne Hudson, ed., *Two Wycliffite Texts: The Sermon of William Taylor 1406, The Testimony of William Thorpe 1407*, EETS, o.s., 301 [Oxford: Oxford University Press, 1993], xlv–liii).

39. For example, Edith Rickert, *Chaucer's World*, ed. Clair C. Olson and Martin M. Crow (New York: Columbia University Press, 1948), 264–65.

40. Hudson, ed., *Two Wycliffite Texts*, 64.

41. Ibid., 61–62.

42. See Ralph Hanna's textual note in *The Riverside Chaucer*, 1126. Lee Patterson attributes this omission to scribal censorship (*Chaucer and the Subject of History* [Madison: University of Wisconsin Press, 1991], 44).

43. Gardiner Stillwell argued that this representation of the ideal peasant shows the poet's antagonism toward the actual peasants of his era (Stillwell, "Chaucer's Plow-

man and the Contemporary English Peasant," *ELH* 6 [1939]: 285–90). See also Joseph Horrell, "Chaucer's Symbolic Plowman," *Speculum* 14 (1939): 82–92. Daniel F. Pigg gauges the political valance of a figure bearing "obvious signs of ideological friction and potential volatility" (Pigg, "With Hym Ther Was a Plowman, Was His Brother," in *Chaucer's Pilgrims*, ed. Lambdin and Lambdin, 264–65).

44. John Gower, *Mirour de l'Omme*, trans. William Burton Wilson, rev. Nancy Wilson Van Baak (East Lansing, Mich.: Colleagues Press, 1992), 347 (ll. 26,425–84).

45. J. L. Bolton, *The Medieval English Economy, 1150–1500* (Totowa: Rowman and Littlefield, 1980), 215. *The English Rising of 1381*, ed. R. H. Hilton and T. H. Aston (Cambridge: Cambridge University Press, 1984), offers two studies especially pertinent here: Christopher Dyer, "The Social and Economic Background to the Rural Revolt of 1381," 9–42, and J. A. Tuck, "Nobles, Commons and the Great Revolt of 1381," 194–212.

46. *The Major Latin Works of John Gower*, trans. Eric W. Stockton (Seattle: University of Washington Press, 1962), 208–10 (5.9–10); by stating "Everyone owning land complains in his turn about these people," the poet places himself in solidarity with landlords over and against laborers: "See how one peasant insists upon more than two demanded in days gone by." For the poet's social alignments see Andrew Galloway, "Gower in His Most Learned Role and the Peasants' Revolt of 1381," *Mediaevalia* 16 (1993 for 1990): 329–47.

47. Nancy H. Owen, "Thomas Wimbledon's Sermon: 'Redde racionem villicacionis tue,'" *Mediaeval Studies* 28 (1966): 178. The homiletic literature of the late fourteenth century is unanimous in its condemnation of lazy laborers; see G. R. Owst, *Literature and Pulpit in Medieval England* (Oxford: Blackwell, 1966), 362–67, 553–74. The parable's farm imagery, however, conveniently allowed the *Pearl* poet to pass in silence over the fact that his fellow clergymen had become very mobile in their own searches for better employment. Chaplains especially were receiving such high stipends that the archbishops considered it necessary to impose restraints. See Bertha H. Putnam, "Maximum Wage-Laws for Priests after the Black Death, 1348–1381," *American Historical Review* 21 (1915): 12–32, and A. K. McHardy, "Ecclesiastics and Economics: Poor Priests, Prosperous Laymen, and Proud Prelates in the Reign of Richard II," in *The Church and Wealth*, ed. W. J. Sheils and Diana Wood (Oxford: Blackwell, 1987), 129–37.

48. See John M. Bowers, "The Politics of *Pearl*," *Exemplaria* 7 (1995): 419–41, esp. 421–27, which provided much of the background material on these labor disputes.

49. Nevill Coghill, "Two Notes on *Piers Plowman*: I. The Abbot of Abingdon and the Date of the C Text; II. Chaucer's Debt to Langland," *Medium Ævum* 4 (1935): 83–94, esp. 89–94; Helen Cooper, "Langland's and Chaucer's Prologues," *Yearbook of Langland Studies* 1 (1987): 71–81, has reopened the case. See also *Piers Plowman: The B Version*, ed. George Kane and E. Talbot Donaldson (London: Athlone Press, 1975); I have chosen different word divisions for B.5.545.

50. James Simpson, "Spirituality and Economics in Passus 1–7 of the B Text," *Yearbook of Langland Studies* 1 (1987): 99. Other studies of Langland's conservative response to economic changes include John M. Bowers, "*Piers Plowman* and the Unwillingness to Work," *Mediaevalia* 9 (1987 for 1983): 239–49; John M. Bowers, *The Crisis of Will in* Piers Plowman (Washington: Catholic University of America Press, 1986), esp. 97–128; Anna Baldwin, "The Historical Context," in *A Companion to* Piers Plowman, ed. John A. Alford (Berkeley: University of California Press, 1988), 70–71; David

Aers, *Community, Gender, and Individual Identity: English Writing, 1360–1430* (London: Routledge, 1988), 20–72; Helen Jewell, *"Piers Plowman*—A Poem of Crisis: An Analysis of Political Instability in Langland's England," in *Politics and Crisis in Fourteenth-Century England*, ed. John Taylor and Wendy Childs (Wolfeboro Falls, N.H.: Alan Sutton, 1990), 59–80, esp. 61–64; and Lawrence M. Clopper, "Need Men and Women Labor? Langland's Wanderer and the Labor Ordinances," in *Chaucer's England: Literature in Historical Context*, ed. Barbara A. Hanawalt (Minneapolis: University of Minnesota Press, 1992), 110–29.

51. Ralph Hanna III, *William Langland* (Brookfield, Vt.: Ashgate, 1993), 16–17, 31–32.

52. Hudson, *Premature Reformation*, 408. See also Pamela Gradon, "Langland and the Ideology of Dissent," *Proceedings of the British Academy* 66 (1980): 179–205.

53. John M. Bowers, "Piers Plowman and the Police: Notes toward a History of the Wycliffite Langland," *Yearbook of Langland Studies* 6 (1992): 1–50, esp. 2–10. See also Anne Hudson, "The Legacy of *Piers Plowman*," in *A Companion to* Piers Plowman, ed. Alford, 251–52; Richard Firth Green, "John Ball's Letters: Literary History and Historical Literature," in *Chaucer's England*, ed. Hanawalt, 176–200; and Susan Crane, "The Writing Lesson of 1381," in *Chaucer's England*, 201–21.

54. Hudson, *Premature Reformation*, 152–53, 342–44.

55. Patterson, *Chaucer and the Subject of History*, 31.

56. Helen Cooper, *Oxford Guides to Chaucer:* The Canterbury Tales (Oxford: Clarendon, 1989), 415–18.

57. Andrew N. Wawn, "Chaucer, the *Plowman's Tale* and Reformation Propaganda: The Testimonies of Thomas Godfray and *I Playne Piers*," *Bulletin of the John Rylands Library* 56 (1973): 174–92, and Thomas J. Heffernan, "Aspects of the Chaucerian Apocrypha: Animadversions on William Thynne's Edition of the *Plowman's Tale*," in *Chaucer Traditions: Studies in Honour of Derek Brewer*, ed. Ruth Morse and Barry Windeatt (Cambridge: Cambridge University Press, 1990), 155–67. This version of the *Plowman's Tale* has been edited for TEAMS by James M. Dean in *Six Ecclesiastical Satires* (Kalamazoo, Mich.: Medieval Institute Publications, 1991), 51–114.

58. Bowers, ed., *Continuations and Additions*, 23–32.

59. Beverly Boyd, ed., *The Middle English Miracles of the Virgin* (San Marino, Calif.: Huntington Library, 1964), 50–55, 119–22.

60. Hoccleve's fierce anti-Lollard stance forms the subject of three recent studies: David Lawton, "Dullness in the Fifteenth Century," *English Literary History* 54 (1987): 761–99; Larry Scanlon, "The King's Two Voices: Narrative and Power in Hoccleve's *Regement of Princes*," in *Literary Practice and Social Change in Britain, 1380–1530*, ed. Lee Patterson (Berkeley: University of California Press, 1990), 216–47; and Derek Pearsall, "Hoccleve's *Regement of Princes:* The Poetics of Royal Self-Representation," *Speculum* 69 (1994): 386–410.

61. Hudson, *Premature Reformation*, 347–51.

62. Ibid., 302–04.

63. Ibid., 357–58.

64. Ibid., 310–13.

65. The argument that Chaucer meant a craft guild has been forwarded by J. Wilson McCutchan, "A Solempne and a Greet Fraternitee," *PMLA* 74 (1959): 313–17, and Peter Goodall, "Chaucer's 'Burgesses' and the Aldermen of London," *Medium Ævum* 50 (1981): 284–92. Other early studies include Thomas Kirby, "The Haberdasher and

His Companions," *Modern Language Notes* 53 (1938): 504–05; Ann B. Fullerton, "The Five Guildsmen," *Modern Language Notes* 61 (1946): 515–23; Sarah Herndon, "Chaucer's Five Guildsmen," *Florida State University Studies* 5 (1952): 33–44; and Peter Lisca, "Chaucer's Guildsmen and Their Cook," *Modern Language Notes* 70 (1955): 321–24. The fullest commentaries on the individual Guildsmen are offered by the series of chapters in Lambdin and Lambdin, eds., *Chaucer's Pilgrims:* Laura C. and Robert T. Lambdin, "An Haberdasher," 145–53; Julian N. Wasserman and Marc Guidry, "And a Carpenter," 154–69; Gwendolyn Morgan, "A Webbe," 170–79; Diana R. Uhlman, "A Dyere," 180–91; and Rebecca Stephens, "And a Tapycer," 192–98.

66. George Unwin, *The Gilds and Companies of London*, 4th ed. (London: Frank Cass, 1963), 110–26; Muriel Bowden, *A Commentary on the* General Prologue *to the* Canterbury Tales, 2d ed. (New York: Macmillan, 1967), 181–85; and D. W. Robertson, Jr., *Chaucer's London* (New York: John Wiley & Sons, 1968), 79–81. Thomas Garbáty has made the case specifically for the parish guild of St. Botolph's in Aldersgate (Garbáty, "Chaucer's Guildsmen and Their Fraternitee," *Journal of English and Germanic Philology* 59 [1960]: 691–704).

67. Antony Black, *Guilds and Civil Society in European Political Thought from the Twelfth Century to the Present* (Ithaca: Cornell University Press, 1984), 66–75. D. W. Robertson, Jr. associates the sudden prosperity of the guilds with post-plague transformation of the English economy (see Robertson, "Chaucer and the Economic and Social Consequences of the Plague," in *Social Unrest in the Middle Ages*, ed. Francis X. Newman [Binghamton, N.Y.: Center for Medieval and Early Renaissance Studies, 1986], 49–74).

68. Unwin, *The Gilds and Companies of London*, 127–54; Sylvia L. Thrupp, *The Merchant Class of Medieval London* (Ann Arbor: University of Michigan Press, 1948), 66–80; Ruth Bird, *The Turbulent London of Richard II* (London: Longmans, Green, 1949), 44–101; May McKisack, *The Fourteenth Century, 1307–1399* (Oxford: Clarendon, 1959), 373–80; and Anthony Goodman, *John of Gaunt* (Harlow, England: Longman, 1992), 97–107.

69. Ernest P. Kuhl proposed that the Five Guildsmen were drawn from crafts that had remained largely neutral during the political wranglings of the period (Kuhl, "Chaucer's Burgesses," *Transactions of the Wisconsin Academy of Sciences, Arts and Letters* 18 [1916)]: 652–75).

70. Paul Strohm clarifies Chaucer's long-time Lancastrian ties (Strohm, *Social Chaucer* [Cambridge: Harvard University Press, 1989], 34–36).

71. Miri Rubin, *Charity and Community in Medieval Cambridge* (Cambridge: Cambridge University Press, 1987), 250–59, "Charitable Activities of Religious Guilds and Fraternities." Unwin reports that "it is extremely unlikely that all the parish fraternities were as innocent of political intentions as they would have had the Government believe" (*Gilds*, 125).

72. Tuck, "Cambridge Parliament, 1388," 234–38.

73. Unwin, *Gilds*, 367–70, and Caroline M. Barron, "The Parish Fraternities of Medieval London," *The Church in Pre-Reformation Society*, ed. Caroline M. Barron and Christopher Harper-Bill (Woodbridge, England: Boydell, 1985), 13–37.

74. Charles Mathew Clode, *Memorials of the Guild of Merchant Taylors of the Fraternity of St. John the Baptist in the City of London* (London: Harrison and Sons, 1875), 3, and W. Carew Hazlitt, *The Livery Companies of the City of London* (1892; reprint, New York: Benjamin Blom, 1969), 265. Britton J. Harwood, "The 'Fraternitee'

of Chaucer's Guildsmen," *Review of English Studies*, n.s., 39 (1988): 413–17, argues that while each of Chaucer's Five Guildsmen belongs to his own separate craft guild, all have become honorary members of a religious society, specifically the Fraternity of Tailors and Linen Armorers of St. John the Baptist.

75. Tuck, "The Cambridge Parliament, 1388," 237–38. Six of the returns are printed in *A Book of London English, 1384–1425*, ed. R. W. Chambers and Marjorie Daunt (Oxford: Clarendon, 1931), 41–60.

76. Unwin, *Gilds*, 108–09.

77. T. F. Reddaway, *The Early History of the Goldsmiths' Company, 1327–1509* (London: Edward Arnold, 1975), 70–71. Unwin, *Gilds* (155–75) charts the transition in 1390–93 to "the immortal collective personality of a corporation" (158).

78. Sylvia L. Thrupp, "The Guilds," in *Cambridge Economic History of Europe*, 8 vols. (Cambridge: Cambridge University Press, 1963–89), 3:230–80, 624–35 (bibliography).

79. Ben R. McRee, "Religious Guilds and Regulation of Behavior in Late Medieval Towns," in *People, Politics and Community in the Later Middle Ages*, ed. Joel T. Rosenthal and Colin Richmond (New York: St. Martin's, 1987), 111.

80. Sylvia L. Thrupp discusses Wyclif's opposition to guilds (Thrupp, "Social Control in the Medieval Town," *Journal of Economic History* 1, supp. [1941]: 41–42). For the reasons underlying Lollard resistance to prayers for the dead, see *Fasciculi Zizaniorum*, ed. Walter Waddington Shirley (London: 1858), 363–64.

81. Hazlitt, *Livery Companies*, 252–53 and 293, and Unwin, *Gilds*, 105–06; John Stevens Watson, *A History of the Salters' Company* (Oxford: Oxford University Press, 1963), 6–8.

82. John James Lambert, ed., *Records of the Skinners of London, Edward I to James I* (London: Allen & Unwin, 1934), 48, 54.

83. Miri Rubin, *Corpus Christi: The Eucharist in Late Medieval Culture* (Cambridge: Cambridge University Press, 1991), 243–71.

84. Edith Rickert, "Chaucer's Hodge of Ware," *Times Literary Supplement*, 20 October 1932, 761, and Earl D. Lyon, "Roger de Ware, Cook," *Modern Language Notes* 52 (1937): 491–94, discovered references in contemporary records to an actual cook by this name.

85. Steven A. Epstein, *Wage, Labor and Guilds in Medieval Europe* (Chapel Hill: University of North Carolina Press, 1991), 197–202.

86. Howard, *Idea of the* Canterbury Tales, 244. M. C. Seymour suggests that Chaucer actually completed a seven-hundred-line version of the story, but the final quire of the author's booklet ending with the Cook was lost before it reached the earliest copyists c. 1405 ("Of This Cokes Tale," *Chaucer Review* 24 [1990]: 259–62). Richard Beadle, "'I wol nat telle it yit': John Selden and a Lost Version of the *Cook's Tale*," in *Chaucer and Shakespeare: Essays in Honour of Shinsuke Ando*, ed. Toshiyuki Takamiya and Richard Beadle (Cambridge: D. S. Brewer, 1992), 55–66, hypothesizes that Selden's lost manuscript *Se2 contained a longer version of the Cook's Prologue.

87. Geoffrey Chaucer, *The Canterbury Tales: A Facsimile and Transcription of the Hengwrt Manuscript*, ed. Paul G. Ruggiers, with an introduction by Donald C. Baker, A. I. Doyle and M. B. Parkes (Norman: University of Oklahoma Press, 1979), 224–25. Doyle and Parkes (xxvii) note that the copyist did not fill the space with an *Explicit*, as done elsewhere in the manuscript; this suggests that he or his director had not given

up hope of receiving additional materials. See also E. G. Stanley, "Of This Cokes Tale Maked Chaucer Na Moore," *Poetica* 5 (1976): 36–59.

88. Bowers, ed., *Continuations and Additions*, 33–34.

89. Neil Daniel, "The *Tale of Gamelyn*: A New Edition" (Ph.D. diss., Indiana University, 1967). On the editorial tradition, see 1–2.

90. Derek Pearsall notes that *Gamelyn*'s placement among Chaucer's *Tales* guaranteed more widespread survival for it than for any other English romance of the period (*Old English and Middle English Poetry* [London: Routledge & Kegan Paul, 1977], 144).

91. Daniel, "*Tale of Gamelyn*," 28–29. For an assessment of textual transmission, see 34–38.

92. J. S. P. Tatlock, "The *Canterbury Tales* in 1400," *PMLA* 50 (1935): 112. Aage Brusendorff also thought that Chaucer placed the *Gamelyn* source in his working papers with the intention of assigning it to the Yeoman, not the Cook (Brusendorff, *The Chaucer Tradition* [Oxford: Clarendon, 1925], 72–73).

93. Froissart, *Chronicles*, 441.

94. Derek Pearsall, *The Life of Geoffrey Chaucer: A Critical Biography* (Oxford: Blackwell, 1992), 213.

95. Edward Powell suggests, "We may suspect that the courtrooms of 1414 had an aura of the recruiting-office about them" ("The Restoration of Law and Order," in *Henry V*, ed. Harriss, 71).

96. Stephen Knight notes that *Gamelyn*'s account of a disinherited gentleman of the knightly class distinguishes it from other stories of heroic outlaws (Knight, *Robin Hood: A Complete Study of the English Outlaw* [Oxford: Blackwell, 1994], 41).

97. Bowers, ed., *Continuations and Additions*, 33–39.

98. Hazlitt, *Livery Companies of the City of London*, 75–76.

99. Lister M. Matheson, "Chaucer's Ancestry: Historical and Philological Reassessments," *Chaucer Review* 25 (1991): 179–81.

100. Thrupp, *The Merchant Class of Medieval London*, 16–17.

101. Ibid., 169.

102. For accounts of these ceremonial floggings, see Thrupp, *The Merchant Class of Medieval London*, 169, and Reddaway, *The Early History of the Goldsmiths' Company*, 83–84, 147.

103. Reginald Call, "'Whan He His Papir Sought' (Chaucer's *Cook's Tale*, A 4404)," *Modern Language Quarterly* 4 (1943): 167–76.

104. Earl D. Lyon, "The *Cook's Tale*," in *Sources and Analogues of Chaucer's Canterbury Tales*, ed. W. F. Bryan and Germaine Dempster (London: Routledge & Kegan Paul, 1941), 151.

105. On the basis of literary and historical analogues, V. J. Scattergood suggests that the completed tale would have involved trickery or actual crime targeting an older victim (Scattergood, "Perkyn Revelour and the *Cook's Tale*," *Chaucer Review* 19 [1984]: 21).

106. David Wallace, "Chaucer and the Absent City," in *Chaucer's England*, ed. Hanawalt, 70–81. Wallace has expanded this discussion in his book *Chaucerian Polity: Absolutist Lineages and Associational Forms in England and Italy* (Stanford: Stanford University Press, 1997), 156–81.

107. H. T. Riley, ed. *Memorials of London and London Life in the XIIIth, XIVth and XVth Centuries, A.D. 1276–1419* (London: 1868), 480.

108. Peter Heath, *The English Parish Clergy on the Eve of the Reformation* (London: Routledge & Kegan Paul, 1969), 119–33.

109. In "Chaucer's Lollard Joke: History and the Textual Unconscious" (24), Paul Strohm acknowledges his indebtedness for this concept to Jacques Derrida, *Of Grammatology*, trans. Gayatri Chakravorty Spivak (Baltimore: Johns Hopkins University Press, 1976), 158.

110. Strohm, "Lollard Joke," 42.

Creating Comfortable Boundaries: Scribes, Editors, and the Invention of the *Parson's Tale*

Míceál F. Vaughan

Editorial Divisions

Once a "text" has gained independence from its surrounding contexts and gains a separate title, is it ever permissible to remove that independent status? Can a text ever be distinguished from its context in any essential or useful way, since all "texts" are constituents of an ongoing discourse, and any titled individuality is a critical construct that betrays questionable assumptions about identity and autonomy? Even if the answers to these, and related, questions were clear, it would still be useful, for the sake of detailing historical processes, to attempt to distinguish one text (or stage in a "text") from another, and to maintain an arguably separate, though no doubt contingent, existence for these texts (or stages). In the case of the dynamic texts of medieval manuscript culture, according particular authority to one manuscript's snapshot of the state of the text may substitute a scribe's interpretation or an editor's judgment for his exemplar's pre-text—or for what the author actually composed.[1] By investigating how and when texts evolved into the forms that have survived, we can also learn something about the reception of the texts by their earliest readers.

Discriminating one state (or stage) in a text's transmission from another, with its additions and subtractions from the preceding stages, is a productive enterprise—even if it cannot, finally, ever claim to have located authorial intentions—or perhaps even authorial texts. But there is something useful to be learned about our modern "texts" and their cultural environments if, say, First Isaiah is distinguished from Second Isaiah, if the C-Text sections of *Piers Plowman* are separated from the A-Text preceding it in Trinity College Cambridge MS R.3.14, or if Chaucer's *Anelida and Arcite* is revealed to be two complete poems (either or both of which may be Chaucer's) rather than a single incomplete poem.[2] At times these scholarly fictions of textual evolution remain safely in the footnotes, while the texts they qualify continue their simpler, unitary existence. In some cases, however, the reverse may be true: the scribal and scholarly fiction of independent textuality becomes imposed firmly on the representation of the text itself, with the result that this independence is established in critical editions and proves very difficult to ignore or reverse.

Not all formal separations of one text from another deserve the acceptance and authority they have achieved, and sometimes applying Occam's razor might (paradoxically) impel scholars to stitch back together texts whose separation produces greater complications and interpretative difficulties than critics are able to resolve—or that they can "resolve" only by ignoring the complicating difficulties. Received opinions, even when nearly unanimous, can be mistaken; and raising fundamental questions about commonplaces is not always a waste of time. I focus here on the texts which today are called the *Parson's Tale* and the *Retractions*, which "most Chaucerians believe . . . Chaucer was responsible for placing . . . at the end of his *Canterbury Tales*."[3] Sketching an argument about the *logical* stages by which the present separation of these texts achieved its consensus position, I emphasize the problems with that consensus. But since it is a consensus that extends back almost to the very first editions of the *Canterbury Tales*, to the earliest manuscripts in which these two texts appear, any argument against maintaining the separation must meet unenviable, and perhaps unattainable, standards. Logical inferences derived from ignored minor details of the extant witnesses may provide the only dependable evidence for my argument, which is that the traditional division of these two texts, a scribal construct, deserves reconsideration, and that a reasonable alternative exists that should be seriously entertained. As Charles Owen has recently made clear, many of these manuscripts "show an uneasiness with the Parson's Tale, expressed mainly at its juncture with the Retraction."[4] This "uneasiness" in the manuscripts may have been ignored, but the evidence is clear and challenges our contemporary comfort with these texts. Owen put it well: "Those troubled by the Parson's Tale have directed their efforts towards assimilating it into a reading of the work as a whole. They have failed to consider the possibility that Chaucer intended it as an independent work, the *Treatise on Penitence*, with the Retraction as a fitting conclusion."[5] And that "possibility" alone should lead us seriously to consider reuniting more completely that *Parson's Tale* and *Retraction*—and, as a result, dissociating them both from the text of the *Canterbury Tales*.

Nothing in the *text* of the *Parson's Tale* and the *Retractions* demands that a division be made between them. The syntax and substance of the penitential treatise and of the penitentially inspired prayers that the *Retractions* comprise do not require that the two be separated. Uninterrupted

by scribal rubrics, the text of the *Retractions* seems quite comfortably continuous with the *Parson's Tale:*

> . . . Thanne shal men understonde what is the fruyt of penaunce; and,
> after the word of Jhesu Crist, it is the endelees blisse of hevene, ther joye
> hath no contrarioustee of wo ne grevaunce; ther alle harmes been passed
> of this present lyf; ther as is the sikernesse fro the peyne of helle; ther as
> is the blisful compaignye that rejoysen hem everemo, everich of otheres
> joye; ther as the body of man, that whilom was foul and derk, is moore
> cleer than the sonne; ther as the body, that whilom was syk, freele, and
> fieble, and mortal, is inmortal, and so strong and so hool that ther may
> no thyng apeyren it; ther as ne is neither hunger, thurst, ne coold, but
> every soule replenyssed with the sighte of the parfit knowynge of God.
> This blisful regne may men purchace by poverte espiritueel, and the glorie
> by lowenesse, the plentee of joye by hunger and thurst, and the reste by
> travaille, and the lyf by deeth and mortificacion of synne. Now preye I to
> hem alle that herkne this litel tretys or rede, that if ther be any thyng in
> it that liketh hem, that therof they thanken oure Lord Jhesu Crist, of
> whom procedeth al wit and al goodnesse. And if ther be any thyng that
> displese hem, I preye hem also that they arrette it to the defaute of myn
> unkonnynge and nat to my wyl, that wolde ful fayn have seyd bettre if I
> hadde had konnynge.[6]

Only when the treatise is assigned to the Parson as his concluding contribution to the series of Canterbury tales do readers become uneasy with the
"I" of the *Retractions*, and this uneasiness about that voice impels them to
distinguish the author of the *Canterbury Tales* from the last in his series of
fictional narrators. What may have been an independent, continuous prose
text could function acceptably as the ending of the *Canterbury Tales* only
if it were divided into two texts, one assigned to the fictional Parson, the
other to the real author. To accomplish this, the continuous text of the
penitential treatise had to be broken in two, with the break marked in an
obvious and uncompromising way. Early manuscripts and recent editions
offer various solutions that allow modern editors and critics (as they did
earlier scribes and readers) the comforts of closure for the *Canterbury Tales.*
Scribal inventions have come to stand for authorial intentions, and potential complications recede before a desire for a satisfactory conclusion to
Chaucer's final great work.

When they are adverted to at all, as happens only infrequently, the
framing rubrics at the beginning and the end of the *Retractions* in modern
editions are (like most of the other rubrics) generally and quite rightly
acknowledged as scribal additions to, and interruptions of, Chaucer's prose.[7]
Manly and Rickert went so far as to exclude virtually all consideration of

manuscript rubrics from their edition: "We have not regarded as proper material for inclusion on the collation cards the Incipits, Explicits, tale or part headings, or page headings (these were often written many years later), except where they were clearly or apparently traditional—i.e. copied by the scribe from his exemplar. In general, it is clear from the MSS themselves that they did not belong to the textual tradition but, whether put in by the original scribe or by a special rubricator, were dictated by the supervisor according to his own taste and judgment."[8] Yet they, like many others who explicitly admit that most rubrics are scribal, nevertheless incorporate many of them into their text, lending them approximate, if not actual, authorial warrant. Critical discussions, which depend on such editions, are at least unconsciously influenced by such warrants.[9] While scholarly opinion is virtually unanimous, then, in attributing these rubrics to scribes (or their supervisors), modern editors continue to present rubrics prominently in their texts, generally without any qualification. If this choice is a conscious one, as it must be, then presumably it issues from some belief that the rubrics they offer are consistent with—if not indeed reflective of—Chaucer's own intentions.[10] It is a belief that has remained virtually unquestioned—except for the period from Thynne to Urry, when the text of the *Retractions* was simply omitted from printings of the *Canterbury Tales*.[11]

While the *Retractions*, including the rubrics as a regularly accepted (even required) part of its text, poses problems for later critics and editors, the rubrics themselves and their history are seldom singled out for attention. But the variation among them in the surviving manuscripts indicates that scribes were not following a single authoritative practice. Modern predilections for particular versions of the rubrics can be imputed to critics' acquiescence in such editorial practice and to their comfort as readers of the *Canterbury Tales*. In most manuscripts and editions, rubrics categorically separate the *Retractions* from what precedes. Readers are distanced from the demands of the unrubricated text, which brings the fictional Parson into uncomfortable proximity to the historical author Geoffrey Chaucer. Modern editorial consensus oversimplifies the widely varying manuscript forms of the rubrics. Those forms indicate a high degree of uneasiness, in exemplars or on the part of scribes, about how they might best meet—or, more often, avoid—the demands of the uninterrupted text. Though modern editors regularly acknowledge the rubrics' scribal origin, they nonetheless retain the rubrics to help readers (including themselves) avoid facing the possibility that if the *Retractions* can be assigned to Chaucer *in propria persona*, then the *Parson's Tale* should also be delivered in his own authorial voice. Few readers of the *Canterbury Tales* would wish to be forced to such a conclusion, and the *Parson's Prologue* proposes a different attribution of the following tale. The choice is clear: either dismiss this entire tale's assignment to the Parson (and deny it a place in the *Canterbury Tales*), or else find an alternative way to resolve the ambiguous attribution caused by the tale's prologue and "epilogue," an alternative that maintains the necessary critical distinction between Parson and poet, fiction and fiction-maker.[12]

As the *Parson's Tale*, this treatise provides a satisfactory and fairly conventional ending to the series of Canterbury tales: a penitential recapitulation of human life as an "allegorical voyage" with its achievements and failings measured against orthodox standards of virtue and vice.[13] Assigning the concluding "vertuous sentence" (I.63) to the "good shepherd" of the *General Prologue*, whose own prologue clearly indicates the approach of an ending and a final judgment (or Final Judgment), provides a relatively safe, orthodox, and generally unproblematic sense of an ending to the *Canterbury Tales*. The *Retractions* offers an effectively personal ending to the treatise on penance, sin, and virtue, and to the tale of a conservative Parson. Since this penitential treatise is, however—in all but one of the manuscripts in which it appears—firmly attributed by the *Parson's Prologue* to the Parson, the last tale-teller on the Canterbury pilgrimage, additional complications arise: does what proves satisfactory as a treatise's ending, or as a single tale's, also successfully conclude the entire *Canterbury Tales*? Addressing the complications raised by the layering of drama and narrative in this collection of tales is far from easy, and most (but *not* all) early scribes resolved the apparently ambiguous attribution by separating the treatise's conclusion from the body of the *Parson's Tale*. Having settled on one scribal version of the rubrics separating the *Retractions* from the preceding text, modern editors continue the practice of these early transmitters of Chaucer's text, and critics continue to grapple with the major ambiguities that arise when the penitential treatise is assigned to the Parson as his concluding tale for the *Canterbury Tales*.

The long-established presence of rubrics in printed editions of the *Canterbury Tales* almost inevitably turns modern readers against any interpretation that excludes these rubrics from consideration. The rubrics that appear in Ellesmere[14] and a few other manuscripts have been elevated in the minds of generations of readers and critics to equal status with Chaucer's prose. These rubrics categorically *constitute* the two texts, having traversed the significant distance from being *possible* interpretations of the texts they mark to being *necessary* signs to and clarifications of the authorial idea. In the minds of readers and critics they have become definitive parts of the texts they frame. But since these clarifications of the Chaucerian text are indeed the work of editors and scribes, should readers not maintain the distinction between the purportedly authorial and the admittedly scribal? Are the texts that lie behind what Ellesmere and other editors have enacted as the conclusion of the *Canterbury Tales* recoverable? Or should modern readers, heirs to six centuries of critical readings of the *Tales*, continue to accept the comfortable fiction that the scribal rubrics simply declare what is implicit in Chaucer's text, a declaration he himself would presumably have made had he lived to revise and publish the ending to his "book of the tales of Caunterbury"? The history of the *Retractions* has been marked by recurrent "solutions" to these problems, some as dramatic as complete excision of the text: the folio containing the *Retractions* was excised from one of the extant manuscripts (Gg), and possibly from a second (Ll²); and the text was clearly omitted from Pynson's first edition (c. 1492)—though not from his second (1526)—and from all subsequent printed editions from Thynne (1532) to Urry (1721).[15] Urry's posthumous edition revealed continuing uncertainty about the *Retractation* by setting it well apart from the *Parson's Tale* and printing it in a distinctive font (213–14). Tyrwhitt later bracketed part of the text as "an interpolation" (3.310). These approaches demonstrate continuing problems with the texts of the *Parson's Tale* and the *Retractions*, and perhaps it is time at last to entertain even more radical solutions.

   Which rubrics, assuming that they have *any* value, should be included in editions as the closest to the archetype(s) discoverable behind the surviving manuscripts? Lending editorial authority to *any* of the rubrics in Chaucerian manuscripts may be suspect. Selecting as correct one small group of scribal additions—however important those scribes may be as witnesses to the author's text—is even more dangerous. Modern readers' comfort should not be a guide to historical or textual authority. The great diversity in the surviving manuscripts' rubrics, as in other textual matters, indicates significant differences in the assumptions and interpretations of the texts these scribes are gathering, organizing, and copying for themselves and their patrons or readers. If Chaucer intended the *Parson's Tale* and the *Retractions* to comprise a single treatise, or if he died before finally making its division into two separate, though related and contiguous, texts in the evolving *Canterbury Tales*, editors and scholars would nonetheless be faced with the same salient facts: none of the rubrics can be safely taken as Chaucer's, and their variety attests to a number of acceptable alternative and nearly contemporary readings of the text(s).

   There may be little reason, then, to reject the principles on which Manly and Rickert decide to exclude collation of *incipits*. And if there are doubts about editorial judgments with respect even to texts derived from a single archetype (which the *Canterbury Tales* is decidedly not),[16] then how much more ought editors hesitate to accept the value and authority of purportedly independent matter such as rubrics? The rubrics and the text should doubtless be handled separately. The rubrics of less good manuscripts may even preserve better evidence of the *form* of the author's text than those of the best manuscripts. Calling for the exclusion of scribal rubrics (or other scribal readings) from authoritative editions is not inconsistent with considering these scribal artifacts as themselves having value: they *can* be useful signs of how scribes understood or read the texts they were copying. While it might be foolhardy to argue that any simple evolutionary process was at work in the scribal reception of texts as complicated as those now comprising the *Canterbury Tales,* the "invention" of the *Parson's Tale* and the *Retractions* can be helpfully illuminated by identifying discrete categories of rubric types and hypothesizing something approximating an evolution of these types based on the evidence of the extant manuscripts.

What the manuscripts show in their rubrics is a continuum running from no separation of the two texts at all to the modern editorial practice of dividing and separately titling them. These diverse ways of handling the ending of the *Canterbury Tales* arguably reveal a progressive hardening of the boundaries between distinct texts,[17] boundaries which today are virtually unassailable. By considering in more detail the available evidence, we can raise productive questions about the permanence or necessity of these accepted boundaries—and touch on the significant implications of their more reasonable answers.

The Five Categories

Three elements mark the juncture between what are generally referred to as the *Parson's Tale* and the *Retractions:* a textual close to the *Parson's Tale;* an *explicit* or equivalent rubric marking that tale's conclusion; and the "titling" of the *Retractions* by what I call a "leave-taking formula."[18] Alone, or in their various combinations, the three elements define distinct "receptions" of Chaucer's text(s): by their presence or absence from the manuscripts, they articulate the stages by which an independent double treatise on penitence and the seven deadly sins became the *Parson's Tale* and the *Retractions.* The thirty manuscripts and Caxton's first printed edition (1478), which can be adduced as witnesses to the *Retractions,*[19] array themselves in terms of these three features and two others—the close of the *Retractions* and its valedictory rubrics—into five groups of varying size and complexity:[20]

CATEGORY 1:   Bo¹, Gl, Ht, Ra³
(no boundaries)

CATEGORY 2:   Ad¹, Cn, En¹, En³, Ha⁴, Ma, Pp, Tk², To
(shorter "leave-taking")

CATEGORY 3:   El, Gg, Ll², Ph¹
(longer "leave-taking")

CATEGORY 4:   Fi, Ha², La, Lc, Mm, Pw, Ra², Ry², Se, Tk¹
(added *explicit* for *Parson's Tale*)

CATEGORY 5:   Cx¹, Ii, Ne, Tc²
(omitted "leave-taking")

Since there are essentially two versions of the close of the *Parson's Tale*, we can divide these five categories into two larger groups. The first—comprising my first three categories—has what is generally taken to be the earlier version (ending with "mortificacioun of synne").²¹ The remaining two categories contain a longer and presumably later version—adding a clause ("to that life . . . precious blood. Amen")—which provides a firmer ending for the tale. (This version is plainly extrapolated from the wording of the *Retractions.*) The larger two groupings are fairly standardized, but the variability in form (and even presence or absence) of *explicit*s and leave-takings is much greater.

My first category ("no boundaries") offers no break at all between *Parson's Tale* and *Retractions.* Manuscripts in the second category contain a short version of the leave-taking formula—"Here takith the maker his leue" (Tk²)—which is expanded in the third, the "Ellesmere Group": "Heere taketh the makere of this book his leue" (El). Categories 4 and 5 present the expanded close of the *Parson's Tale* mentioned above and introduce an *explicit* for that tale. Category 4 retains the leave-taking in an expanded form related to Ellesmere; category 5 drops it.

Despite the assumed individual responsibility of scribes for their rubrics, there are obvious similarities (even identities) in scribes' practices that support categorization. The similarities may not permit the presentation of a full *stemma*, but they can certainly point to groupings and even to stages in the fixing and transmission of the text. If, for instance, Hg and El are the work of the same scribe, there are profound differences between the "individuals" responsible for the two manuscripts—if such individuality is adjudged by their ordering of the tales, their textual readings, and their rubrication.²² A fuller inventory of the main features distinguishing the categories and their constituents appears in the appendix.

The categories, defined and ordered as above, present logically plausible stages by which Chaucer's tract on "penitencia" or "septem peccatis mortalibus"—as the members of category 5 variously title it—could have become the *Parson's Tale* and the *Retractions*. There is no evidence of any revision or "domestication" of the text of that treatise itself to personalize it for the Parson. Its connections with the *Parson's Prologue* depend on little more than the general appropriateness of the subject matter, a few verbal echoes, and the consecutive placement of the two texts. Careful examination of the features that Manly and Rickert left out of their collations can, however, support a hypothetical series of distinct stages through which the "litel tretys" passed on its way to becoming a Canterbury tale. The rubrics that Manly and Rickert, and many others, have ignored deserve more attention in our discussions of the genuinely Chaucerian texts they mark, particularly since, as Norman Blake has suggested, increased rubrication overall can probably be correlated with a manuscript's relative lateness in the text's evolution.[23]

The defining boundary-markers in modern editions, on which so much critical judgment depends, are evidenced by only a handful of the total of thirty-one manuscript witnesses. Since these five included important manuscripts like Ellesmere and Petworth, most editions have used them, often without seriously considering competing rubrics (such as those in Harley 7334). Some have reinforced the Ellesmere division with additional titles—for example, "Chaucer's Retraction"[24]—articulating interpretative presumptions and overriding the text's syntactic continuity.

Identifying and analyzing these stages of the text's rubrication can illuminate the different readings of Chaucer that they enable. Whether *any* of these admittedly scribal contributions to the *Retractions* can finally resolve the interpretative difficulties remains open to question. Since most surviving manuscripts of the *Retractions* offer rubrics rather different from those found in Ellesmere and its descendants, this variety, and the relations among the individual forms, can significantly elucidate the early reception of the *Canterbury Tales*.

The Priority of Category 1

Discussion can usefully begin with the current state of the texts. The concluding portion of the *Canterbury Tales* presented in the most recent Riverside edition of Chaucer reads as follows:

> . . . . / This blisful regne may men purchace by poverte espiritueel, and the glorie by lowenesse, the plentee of joye by hunger and thurst, and the reste by travaille, and the lyf by deeth and mortificacion of synne. /
> (327)

Heere taketh the makere of this book his leve.

Now preye I to hem alle that herkne this litel tretys or rede, that if ther be any thyng in it that liketh hem, that therof they thanken oure Lord Jhesu Crist, of whom procedeth al wit and al goodnesse. / And if ther be any thyng that displese hem, I preye hem also that they arrette it to the defaute of myn unkonnynge and nat to my wyl, that wolde ful fayn have seyd bettre if I hadde had konnynge. / For oure book seith, "Al that is writen is writen for oure doctrine," and that is myn entente. / Wherfore I biseke yow mekely, for the mercy of God, that ye preye for me that Crist have mercy on me and foryeve me my giltes; / and namely of my translacions and enditynges of worldly vanitees, the whiche I revoke in my retracciouns: / as is the book of Troilus; the book also of Fame; the book of the XXV. Ladies; the book of the Duchesse; the book of Seint Valentynes day of the Parlement of Briddes; the tales of Caunterbury, thilke that sownen into synne; the book of the Leoun; and many another book, if they were in my remembrance, and many a song and many a leccherous lay, that Crist for his grete mercy foryeve me the synne. / But of the translacion of Boece de Consolacione, and othere bookes of legendes of seintes, and omelies, and moralitee, and devocioun, / that thanke I oure Lord Jhesu Crist and his blisful Mooder, and alle the seintes of hevene, / bisekynge hem that they from hennes forth unto my lyves ende sende me grace to biwayle my giltes and to studie to the salvacioun of my soule, and graunte me grace of verray penitence, confessioun and satisfaccioun to doon in this present lyf, / thurgh the benigne grace of hym that is kyng of kynges and preest over alle preestes, that boghte us with the precious blood of his herte, / so that I may been oon of hem at the day of doom that shulle be saued. *Qui cum Patre et Spiritu Sancto vivit et regnat Deus per omnia secula. Amen.*

Heere is ended the book of the tales of Caunterbury, compiled by Geffrey Chaucer, of whos soule Jhesu Crist have mercy. Amen.

(328)

With relatively minor changes, these are the text and rubrics that appear in all modern editions of Chaucer since Skeat.[25] It would be necessary to go back to Morris's and Wright's mid-nineteenth-century editions to find significantly different treatment of them, the result of their preferring Harley 7334 as their base manuscript.[26] Through format and rubrics, these editors leave readers in no doubt that they have two distinct texts here. The exact relationship between them may be a little indefinite, but it is clear that they are parts of the same book, whose "makere" takes "his leve" with the final paragraph. And the only things marking this significant moment when the voice of the pilgrim-Parson modulates into that of this "makere" (presumably through the unmarked medium of the pilgrim-narrator of the *Canter-*

bury Tales) are the *editorially supplied* break in the layout of the prose text and the *scribal* leave-taking formula.

The notes in the Riverside edition recognize only one significant textual variant:

1086 XXV] XIX three manuscripts (Cn Ma Ry²) and Skt Rob¹; XV La.²⁷

Editors have taken little notice of variants in the *explicits*, etc., treating them as largely irrelevant (because not authorial), and leaving unquestioned the attribution of the tale to the Parson. Accepting that there is no codicological or editorial reason to omit the *Retractions* entirely, as Thynne and his successors did for nearly two centuries, editors are left with the necessity of distinguishing these two texts. Most feel that the "editor" (or supervisor, as opposed to scribe) of Ellesmere distinguished best between these two texts in his choice of rubrics. Pratt's admiration is evident in his announced decision: "Headings and endings of the tales are from the Ellesmere manuscript" (561). Other editors more often follow Ellesmere in silence.

Although it is a relatively early exemplar, Ellesmere is, I argue, logically posterior to treatments of Chaucer's text in other manuscripts. What its rubrics and the subsequent editorial consensus represent is the end point of a process begun with the first copyists of the *Canterbury Tales*, a process teleologically determined by the scribe's desire to minimize the incompleteness of the "book of the tales of Caunterbury."²⁸ What Ellesmere achieved early in time, however, must not efface the very real probability that texts closer to Chaucer's original treated what now are generally taken as two texts as a single whole, and that the assignment of the treatise to a Canterbury pilgrim introduced complications unresolved, and perhaps unforeseen, at the moment of that assignment—whoever initiated it. Logically (if not temporally) the "Ellesmere Group" stands—in this regard, as perhaps in others—at a significant distance from the inferred textual original. The diverse treatment of tale texts and tale order may also be further testimony to the active editorial intervention of the (Hengwrt) Ellesmere scribe/supervisor and may thereby direct our attention elsewhere for the final authorial condition of, and intentions for, the *Canterbury Tales*. I believe that the manuscripts in my category 1 better represent the author's intention for the *Retractions*.

The category 1 manuscripts can claim to stand logically anterior to the rubricated state of Ellesmere and others. Three manuscripts (Bo¹, Gl, and Ht) do not interrupt the continuous text with *explicits*, leave-takings, titles, or the introduction of new lines.²⁹ They entirely avoid any interruption of the prose text, and they incorporate the *Retractions* as the concluding

paragraph of a single continuous work. No more than a *littera notabilior*—
with or without a preceding paraph mark, usual elsewhere in these manuscripts and frequently used in similar circumstances in this prose treatise—
appears in the manuscript line.

The three complete manuscripts offer a continuous text similar to the
following (transcribed from Bo[1], and retaining its pagination and lineation):

> . . . . ¶ This blisfulle Reame mai men purchas
> bi pouert spirituall / and the glorie bi lownesse / the
> plente of ioye bi hungur and thirst / and the rest by
> trauaile / and the life bi dethe and mortificaciou[n] of
> synne / ¶ Now pray I to theym alle that herkne to
>
> (433)
>
> this litle tretice or reden it / that if ther be any thing in it
> that likith hem that therof thei thanke oure lord ihesu
> crist of whome procedith alle witte and alle goodnes
> And if ther be any thing that displeasith hem I prey
> hem also that thei arrett it to the defaut of myn vnco[n]=
> nyng and not to my wille that wold haue seid bettir
> if I hadde cu[n]nyng / ffor the book seith that alle that is
> writen is for oure doctrine And that is myn intent /
> wherfore I beseche you mekeli for the merci of god
> that ye prey for me that crist haue merci on me and
> foryeue me my giltis / and nameli my translacions
> and enditinges of worldli vanitees which I reuoke
> in my retraccions / as to the book of Troilus / the boke
> also of fame / the book of 25 ladies / the book of the
> Duchesse / the book of seint Valentines day · of the p[ar]=
> liament of birdis / the talis of Cauntirbury thilk þ[at]
> sowu[n] into synne / the book of the leon / and many an
> othir book if thei were in my remembrance and ma=
> ny a song and many a lecherous lay / of the which
> crist of his gret merci foryeue me the synne / But
> of the translaciou[n] of Boice of consolacione / and oþ[er]
> bokis of legendis of Seintes and Omelies and mo=
> ralite and deuociou[n] that thank I oure lord ih[es]u crist
> and his blisfulle modir and alle the seintis in heuen[e]
> beseching hem that thei from hens furth vnto my
> lyues ende send me grace to bewaile my giltis and
> to studie to the saluaciou[n] of my soule and graunt
> me space of veraye penitence confessiou[n] and satis
> facciou[n] to do in this present life thurgh the benyngne
> grace of him that is king of kingis and preest ouer
> alle preestis / that bought us with the precious blode

of his hert / So that I mut be one of hem atte the
day of dome that shalle be saued Qui cum patre & c[etera]

(434)

This manuscript begins the text of the *Retractions* with the second word in
the last line of its penultimate page, the recto of the last sheet in this paper
manuscript.[30] The choice to begin the *Retractions* here speaks volumes for
this scribe's sense of the continuity of his text, since the amount of text
remaining for the verso would not come close to filling that page.[31] The
mere suspicion of some required—or even possible—division would no
doubt have led the scribe to begin the new paragraph at the top of the next
page, a common feature in many other manuscripts and printed editions.[32]
Charles Owen comments that "[o]n the whole Bo[1] shows signs of more
careful production"[33] than its "twin" Ph[2],[34] which is missing the last folio
of the *Canterbury Tales* (PsT 1061ff.). He continues: "It gives a neater appearance, and in the *Parson's Tale* especially it sets off the divisions with
space for multi-lined capitals, entirely missing in Ph[2]. The system breaks
down, however, for the *Retraction*, which begins in midline with a red paraph as its only mark of emphasis." Professor Owen's accepting the *Retractions* as a separate text arguably provides his sole justification for
characterizing this as the only occasion where an otherwise "careful" and
systematic scribe "breaks down"; a reasonable counterargument might ad-
duce this as yet another indication of this scribe's laudable care in presenting his text and its divisions. That his text is not in line with modern
editorial practices ought not lead to its being condemned.

The other three manuscripts in category 1 are more committed to
marking the ends of their texts of the *Canterbury Tales* than is Bo[1].[35] But
Gl and Ht, which we have not yet discussed, offer no greater intrusion
between the *Parson's Tale* and the *Retractions* to help reinforce this sense
of an ending. In Gl the lines containing the juncture are as follows:

> . . . the life by deth[e]
> and mortificac[i]ou[n] of synne *Now praye to*
> *hym alle* that herkene yet this tretise or reden
> þat þ[er]e be . . .[36]

The parallel lines in Ht read:

> . . . þe life by
> deth and mortificac[i]ou[n] of syn[ne] ¶Now prey I to hem all[e] that
> herken[e]
> þis litul tretise or reden þat if þer[e] be . . .

Few editors or textual scholars might happily include any of these category 1 manuscripts high among their most important manuscripts of the
Canterbury Tales.[37] They are not mentioned at all, for instance, in the index
to Blake's *Textual Tradition*, and none of them was written in the first fifty
or sixty years after Chaucer's death. Yet if the scribal origin of the rubrics
is seriously maintained, these manuscripts approximate what may be the
best logical candidate for the *form* of the Chaucerian original of the treatise
that now appears at the end of the *Canterbury Tales*. Though relatively late,
all four of these manuscripts are in this portion of their text closely allied
with two early and important "independent" (in Manly and Rickert's
terms) manuscripts, Hengwrt and Harley 7334 (both part of Manly and
Rickert's first textual "line" for the *Parson's Tale*, which includes the *bcd*
groups and others). Though "minor" manuscripts, they may still be trustworthy witnesses to formal details of the exemplars for an important strain
of manuscripts. For these scribes, and their overseers and readers, the texts
are a single text: the *Retractions* follows without any break after the word
"synne," which usually ends the so-called *Parson's Tale*.

How, then, does this allegedly "early" version of the integrated text
survive in these manuscripts? Is it likely that scribes simply ignored (or
consciously omitted) the line-breaks, rubrics, and spacing that are so prominent a part of most of the other witnesses to the conclusion of the *Canterbury Tales*? Or does their retaining a continuous text more likely attest to
such a text's existing independently for more than fifty years, and so argue
for an autonomous manuscript tradition that points back to Chaucer's own
text? Since we cannot directly identify in extant manuscripts what might
pass for immediate exemplars for these four versions, the question remains
unresolved: was their unbroken text an "original" result of some inadver-
tent scribal mistakes in copying the text from exemplars containing one or
other of the divided and rubricated forms? Against an affirmative answer
to this question stands the following: since scholars have identified two
distinct lines of textual affiliation/association in these four cases, the possible independent coincidence of such marked errors of omission is less
likely than if all four manuscripts arrayed themselves firmly in a single
line of descent. Their agreement in omitting any rubricated division may
therefore not signal an agreement in *error*, but may open up long-closed
windows to the authorial original.

Is this, then, a case where the slighting of editorial attention to Manly
and Rickert's first textual line for the *Parson's Tale* manuscripts—in favor
of El and the other manuscripts of their second group—has led scholars
astray? Hg is, of course, completely silent about the text of the *Retractions,*
but if "the few variants indicate the persistence of the same groups as are
found in PsP and PsT,"[38] then *if* there had been a text of the *Retractions* in

Hg it would likely have been "away" from El and others in the second line, as it is elsewhere in the *Parson's Tale*. If this were so, then our four manuscripts would benefit immensely from sharing the authority of Hg, a text preferred by many (like Owen and the *Variorum Chaucer*) over that in the same scribe's later El. In the absence of stronger positive evidence or more sustained argument, it is useless to attempt a reconstruction of what *must* have been the form of text missing from Hg. But it should remain a distinct possibility—verging even on likelihood—that Hg, on the evidence of the related manuscripts in category 1, may also have presented a text of the *Parson's Tale* and *Retractions* unbroken by rubrics or other text-defining boundary markers. Arguing from silence is a dangerous practice, but let me risk it here: *if* the lost folios of Hg did indeed *not* separate the *Retractions* from the *Parson's Tale*, that manuscript would stand as the authoritative exemplar for the manuscripts in my category 1, and thereby assure the antecedence of their form of the text to any contained in the remaining manuscripts. By the time the same scribe came to copy Ellesmere, in this as in other matters, he saw the need for substantial editorial rearrangement and rubrication to create the "book of the tales of Caunterbury."

To address the matter in more general terms: is it likely that eye-catching divisions and rubrics found in exemplars for these category 1 manuscripts would have been missed, ignored, or consciously omitted by their copyists? Is it not more likely, given usual scribal practice, that any such divisions would have been maintained and that more, rather than fewer, rubrics would have been introduced by other scribes in the textual transmission? There are, for instance, in Ht many *incipits* and *explicits* for tales and prologues quite elaborately marked and spaced,[39] and Bo[1] elsewhere takes care (as already noted above) to mark sections and divisions in its texts, as for example in the *Parson's Tale*. While it would be foolhardy to dismiss as entirely implausible the loss of rubrics and divisional spacing in the relatively long history of textual transmission that issues in these three late manuscripts (the earliest of which, Ht, is unlikely to be earlier than the 1450s), it would be even more suspect simply to assume that such is the demonstrated direction of change. If the text contained in these category 1 manuscripts is not representative, *formally* at least, of an earlier (if not perhaps the earliest) stage in the transcription of this treatise, then more convincing explanations must be provided, detailing how there came to be *no* formal boundaries or boundary marks separating what others repeatedly present as two discrete texts. Has such an explanation already been made? Apparently not. Indeed, there has been little argument, convincing or otherwise, that the two were originally discrete texts: the virtually universal attribution of the rubrics to the scribes, and the *ordinatio* provided by them (or their supervisors), implies the contrary. This same conclusion has been reached by Charles Owen: "It seems likely, then, that the earliest state of the text, the one represented in Hengwrt, Hatton Donat 1, Physicians 388 and Bodley 414, had no division between the treatise and the Retraction. The efforts to separate by rubrics the Retraction from the treatise testify to the uneasiness among early readers, who saw that the Retraction itself could not be part of the Parson's Tale."[40] Can the evidence provided by other manuscripts encourage us to take seriously this radical conclusion? Their varied responses to the uneasiness Owen notes demand it.

Harley 7334 and Category 2

Though the manuscripts in category 1 show no desire to separate the prose they are copying into two separate texts, the other manuscripts do separate them in one way or another. The diversity of means is worth noting. Some do little more than begin a new line (Ra[2], Tk[1], and To) with "Now pray I," while others more firmly separate them into clearly differentiated units, each with its own *explicit*. In addition to those in category 1, a few more manuscripts, which I assign to other categories for various reasons, also do not contain any interruptive rubrics. They do, however, indicate a clear separation of the two texts, starting the *Retractions* with a large initial "N" on a new line, having "closed off" the *Parson's Tale* with, for example, a simple "Amen" (To: category 2). Others provide a more extensive closing formula: "to thilke lif he vs bringe that boughte vs with his preciouse blood amen" (Ra[2]: category 4). A variant of this appears in the closely related Tk[1], which in addition leaves a blank line between the two texts.

The eight other manuscripts in category 2 establish clear boundaries between the texts, usually by providing the shorter version of the leave-taking formula introducing the *Retractions:* "Here takith the maker his leue" (Tk[2]). Omitting the more definitive "of this book" found in Ellesmere and a number of others in categories 3 and 4, this shorter version may be the earlier of the two, appropriate as an ending either for a tale or even for the "tales of Caunterbury" before they later came to be more generally characterized as a book.[41] Most of these nine manuscripts are members of Manly and Rickert's *a* group or (like Pp and To) have close connections to that group in this section of the *Canterbury Tales*. All begin the *Retractions* on a new line (usually with a multi-line initial capital—or at least the space for it; Ma does not really have a multi-line capital, but it is more elaborate than usual). All but one (To) provide a leave-taking introduction to the *Retractions*. Five of the nine add "Amen" after "synne," and this reinforcement (or establishment) of closure makes clear that the following leave-taking formula introduces a separate text. The addition of these various new features (new line, intervening blank line, and leave-taking formula—with variable distribution of "Amen") add progressively more clarity to the division between two texts. This clarity, however, and its defining effect are not accomplished immediately.

The first and perhaps most anomalous manuscript in this category is Ha[4]. A particularly important manuscript, ranking high among the early witnesses to the text and ordering of the *Canterbury Tales*, it is usually placed between Hengwrt and Ellesmere in the chronology of extant manuscripts.[42] Its anomalies might well have warranted its inclusion in category 1[43]—or even assignment to its own category. Unlike the others in category 1, however, it does divide the two texts and presents what may well have been the first "title" given the text called the *Retractions:* "Preces de Chauceres." This decidedly non-authorial title in French presumably takes the first three words of what follows (and the subsequent "preye"s) as its inspiration, identifying the "I" of these prayers as Chaucer—an identification supplied by glossators for many other first-person pronouns in these manuscripts also. A gold-highlighted paraph introduces the title, in a two-line space between "synne" and the blue-and-red-infilled gold initial N. This inserted heading provides the manuscript with its only rubrics in this portion of the *Canterbury Tales:* there are no closing formulae before this rubric, and nothing follows the end of the "Preces," with its concluding "Qui cum patre."

There is indeed no necessary insistence on closure here at all, since prayers may appear in other locations. Like the repeated "Canticus Troili" in *Troilus,* this rubric may be more intent on scribally marking the form/genre of this distinctive passage. Or like the "Lenuoye de Chaucer" at the close of the *Clerk's Tale*—which this scribe also provides in a similarly elaborate script—attributing part of the tale to Chaucer may be scribal recognition of its being a substantively "original" contribution to the text Chaucer is otherwise "translating." Nonetheless, the scribal marking of the *Retractions* in what is likely the earliest surviving witness to that text does little to identify it as the end of the *Canterbury Tales.* It attributes the epilogic prayers of this treatise on sin and penance directly to Chaucer, unmediated by the drama of the pilgrimage narrative that plays so prominent a part elsewhere in the *Canterbury Tales.* This scribe does not regularly insist on providing *incipit*s and *explicit*s for the tales, and so the absence of any firmly enunciated *explicit* for this tale or the *Tales* is not altogether surprising. But this concluding text is one of the very few judged deserving of particular note by this scribe, on a par with "Lenuoye de Chaucer." As Blake notes, compared to Hengwrt, this manuscript is even "less advanced" in its use of "sub-divisions of the tales and rubrics. . . . [and] marginal annotations."[44] The sparing and inconsistent use of such elements in this early manuscript may indicate its exemplar's lack of them. It also reinforces the likelihood that Blake is correct in his view that the elaboration in rubrics is a sign of relative lateness in the hierarchy of transmission. At a minimum it is consistent with marking Ha[4]'s independence from, and potential priority over, El and related category-3 manuscripts.

To the extent that "Preces de Chauceres" might best be characterized as a *descriptive* rather than a *divisive* rubric, Ha[4] can readily be assimilated to its cousins in category 1. The anomalous form of Ha[4]'s treatment of the ending of the *Canterbury Tales*, and particularly its early date in the textual transmission of the poem, encourages us to reconsider the critical and editorial consensus separating the *Parson's Tale* and *Retractions*. The very form in which this important manuscript marks the closing stage of its text reinforces the likelihood that the textual format evidenced in category 1 may have been close to that of Ha[4]'s own exemplar, to which its scribe made his own important contributions. It is considerably easier to imagine the version in Ha[4] deriving from forms of the text like those in Bo[1] or Gl or Ht than the reverse. And it is even easier to dismiss Ha[4]'s derivation from an exemplar closer to the more evolved and definitively separated form found in category 2 or 3. Finally, its failure to share the distinctive leave-taking formula of category 2 might lead us to include it as the final member of category 1, as a transitional manuscript whose formal separation of the two texts was not specifically related to those in category 2, but may have made their scribal insertions possible. If there had been an authorial or exemplary heading—or a marginal note—identifying the concluding "prayer" in the earliest copies of Chaucer's penitential treatise, it is striking that the three earliest surviving witnesses to that heading—Ha[4], El, and La—differ so markedly in their renditions of it. In the textual history of the *Canterbury Tales*, the title in Ha[4] has no close relatives and produced no surviving progeny; it differs radically from the others, and its text may in many important respects stand closer to later manuscripts found in category 1.

Though it has its own complicating features,[45] En[1] represents more fully the characteristic features of category 2: it marks the separation of the *Parson's Tale* and *Retractions* with the shorter leave-taking formula: "Here the makr[e] taketh his leue."[46] The formula, in black ink—as is usual for "rubrics" in this manuscript—is set in a six-line blank between the texts, and the *Retractions* begins with a three-line blue initial N, elaborated with red vinets reaching up to the middle of the folio and down to the bottom. The elaborate initial and the six-line separation leave the reader in no doubt about the initiation of a new text. What is perhaps less clear is the exact identity of the one who is taking his leave. This formulaic leave-taking contains some words familiar from the slightly longer form enshrined in standard editions of the *Canterbury Tales*, words (sometimes reordered, and with or without "of this book" following "maker") that prevail in most later manuscripts. This early group *a* manuscript (listed in Manly and Rickert's second line in the textual tradition of the *Parson's Tale*), therefore, signals another point of no return in defining the boundary and extent of the *Parson's Tale* and the *Retractions*. Chaucer's prayers have now become a maker's taking leave. The absence of the phrase "of this book" perhaps leaves open the possibility that the "makr[e]" being identified here is the one responsible for the tale immediately preceding: that is, Chaucer as author of the penitential treatise, or the Parson as teller of the final Canterbury tale.

Four of the manuscripts in category 2 mark the shift to a new "text" with the leave-taking formula (or "Preces de Chauceres") alone.[47] The remaining five reinforce the closure of the *Parson's Tale* by inserting an "Amen" after "synne." In Cn, for example, this conclusion appears, followed by "Amen"; in the two-line space left after it, we find the introductory formula: "Here takith the maker his leve." The initial *H* of this is a three-line capital in the same (relatively modest) style as the two-line initial *N* (of "Now"). The heading was obviously produced before the scribe wrote the following text of the *Retractions*, since he disposed the words in its first line around the long descenders of the *H*. Clearly this scribe was in no doubt about the separation, or the heading.

Yet Cn does little more to elaborate the closure of the *Canterbury Tales;* its *Retractions* ends elliptically with the Latin closing formula: "Qui cum deo p[at]re [et] c[etera]." Unlike most others in its category, Cn provides no colophon, no formal *explicit:* taking leave is sufficient to mark this text's ending. In the evolution of rubrical forms, the absence of any colophon following the *Retractions* (or the *Canterbury Tales* as a whole) may be invoked to support the priority of category 2 over category 3, which the missing "of this book" may also have suggested. The simpler treatment, on both counts, appears the earlier. It may, of course, signal only differences in taste or style on the part of scribes, but if the more elaborate forms of category 3 did precede those of category 2 in time, they were clearly not perceived as either necessary or decisively authoritative; they did not preempt other (simpler, if potentially ambiguous) treatments of the ending of the *Canterbury Tales*.

Another member of category 2 deserves mention: The Trinity College Oxford manuscript (To), as I briefly noted earlier, altogether omits any titling of the text, which begins on a new line after its midline conclusion: ". . . synne Amen."[48] Though it emphasizes the text with a three-line blue

initial *N* and has space in the blank half-line following its Amen, To does
not offer a leave-taking formula. Although the scribe of To usually provides
initial capitals (or space for them) elsewhere to mark the beginning of new
texts (or sections of works), in this case he does not provide an accompanying section-defining rubric. So some doubt must remain about the exact
status of his "new" text. Whatever he would have called it, however, in this
case there can be little doubt that the scribe intended to set this concluding
section somewhat apart. He may have decided that the Amen, in combination with the following line-initial *littera notabilior*, would provide the required division; and simply omitting the leave-taking formula might avoid
added complications. Alternatively, he may have substituted the Amen for
the formula, for which he judged there not to be quite enough space left in
the line.

He goes on to conclude the *Retractions* with an extended version of the
prayer-closing formula suggested by Cn's "Qui cum deo p[a]tre [et] c[etera]."
Here again, To provides a conclusive Amen, but the "automatic" nature of
his expansion of "ₜc" is made evident by his including the inappropriate
(and, in the surviving *Canterbury Tales* manuscripts, unique) "[et] filio" in
the formula here. His colophon, appearing in the middle of his final folio
(295v), ends the tales, which are not yet a book: "Explicit fabule de
Caunterburi / s[e]c[un]d[u]m Chauchers."[49] While To does not rubricate
the break between the *Parson's Tale* and the *Retractions*, he quite clearly
intends us to read them as two texts, each deserving a closing Amen. His
colophon's referring to the text he has been copying as "fabule de Caunterburi" presumably reflects a consciousness of fictional narrators distin-
guishable from "Chauchers." His running head, "ffabula Rectoris," at the
top of this final folio of the MS reinforces this, but his resisting any alteration of it above the text of the *Retractions* on his final page may suggest
that he (like others) reads this text as no more personally Chaucer's than
any of the other tales.[50]

Three of the category 2 manuscripts discussed (Ha⁴, Cn, and To) have
distinctive differences from the fourth (En¹), which may qualify them as
representing earlier stages in boundary marking. The relations between the
two from the Amen subcategory (Cn and To) introduce genuinely complicating features into any straightforward account of their evolution. Although the manuscripts are fully in agreement in defining a boundary
between what are clearly being presented as two distinct texts, it is less
certain how exactly to name those two texts and assign them to individual
voices. In omitting the leave-taking formula, To appears to be simpler than
Cn (and Ha⁴?), but the specificity of its closing *explicit* arguably marks it
as later in development. If this be so, then the absence of the leave-taking
formula may be the result of its scribe's simply not having written it in

the half-line space available after "synne Amen." The omission may be consistent with the "very hurried and careless" work of this "amateurish" scribe,[51] for though there are many corrections in this manuscript, they have some feeling of randomness, and a number of spaces left for his "few pale blue and red amateurish capitals" are not filled in.[52] A blue *N* begins the *Retractions*, but presumably the leave-taking formula would have been, as similar rubrics are elsewhere, in red. This may have required another "stint" for its provision. Alternatively, John Leche (the To scribe/owner) may have omitted the leave-taking intentionally, because he thought it either unnecessarily redundant or inappropriate to what he took to be still "ffabula Rectoris."[53]

The logic of placing category 2 ahead of Ellesmere and its companions has been suggested a number of times above. An argument based merely on its manuscripts' having simpler rubrics than Ellesmere may not be entirely persuasive, and so it would be worthwhile to consider if there is any other less obviously subjective (or tendentious) evidence in the manuscripts that could be adduced to support this. That such an inference is possible is confirmed by two other manuscripts in category 2, both of which do supply leave-taking formulas for the *Retractions:* En³ ends the *Retractions/Canterbury Tales* with "Here endith the Persounys Tale" and the closely related Ad¹ begins its colophon with "Explicit narracio Rectoris."[54] Their willingness to extend the "narracio Rectoris" to include the "leave-taking" of the "Maker/Autor" mentioned in their "title" for the *Retractions* betrays either an insensitivity (or indifference) to any dramatic distinction between Parson and poet, or an assumption that the voice of their "leave-taking" conclusion to the *Canterbury Tales* is unambiguously that of the Parson. The potentially ambiguous reference to the "maker" (either the Parson *or* Chaucer) in the rubrics of category-2 manuscripts is resolved, of course, in categories 3 to 5, where the added genitive phrase declares the voice to be unambiguously that of the *book's* maker, not simply the final tale's.

Categories 4 and 5

The numerous manuscripts in categories 4 and 5 reveal even more firmly defined boundaries than do those in the other categories (including the Ellesmere group). Their distinguishing features are an expanded closing formula for the *Parson's Tale* (with accompanying Amen) and the introduction of a variety of *explicits* for that tale. Both of these are features infrequently found in categories 2 or 3 (Pp and Ll² providing the only *explicits* to PsT in these categories). The manuscripts in categories 4 and 5 correspond, respectively, with the *c/d* and *b* groups in Manly and Rickert's scheme. The

expanded close of the tale in the two categories, with the regular variant
thilke (or *that ilke*) *life/that life*, suggests their division from an earlier √*bcd*.
This differentiation is maintained in the form of the *explicit* and in the
regular omission of the leave-taking formula by the members of category 5.

La, one of the two earliest manuscripts preserving a text of the *Retractions*, may serve as a representative example of category 4. At the boundary
point being examined, this manuscript reads:

> be trauayle & þe lyf be deþ & mortificacione of sinne. To þilke lif he vs
> bringe þat bouht vs wiþ his p[re]cious blode AmeN
> Explicit ffabula Rectoris
>
> (fol. 254v)
>
> Composito [*sic*] huius libri hic capit licenciam suam
> Now preye I to hem all[e] þat herken þis litel tretis or rede þ[at]
> if þ[er]e bue any þinge in it . . . [55]
>
> (fol. 255)

Variations occur in the form the *explicit* of the *Parson's Tale* takes: Pw
and Mm share the Latin of La; Ry[2] and Fi anglicize it as "Thus (Fi: Here)
endeth þe p[ar]sones tale," while the anomalous Se has "Here enden the
talis of Caunturbury." Ha[2] has an oddly placed "ffinis" (*following* the leave-
taking formula and extending into the margin)[56]; and Lc omits the *explicit*
and shortens the leave-taking, presumably for lack of space. The remaining
two manuscripts (Ra[2] and Tk[1] [*olim* Dl]) offer no rubrics (*explicits* or leave-
takings) to separate the *Parson's Tale* from the *Retractions*. Like To, however, both provide distinct breaks, beginning the *Retractions* on a new line
with a multi-line initial *N*. Tk[1] leaves a full line blank between them (which
may have been intended, of course, to contain some form of *explicit* or
leave-taking—as could the large space remaining in the line after the Amen
in Ra[2]).[57] As was the case with To, the Amen indicates that something is
ending, and starting the *Retractions* on a new line reinforces the sense that
another text is beginning. The absence of any form of the *explicit*, however,
restrains confident assertions about the nature of these two texts. And the
running head—"¶Thee parsonis tale"—of the final folio of the *Canterbury
Tales* in Tk[1] may, as elsewhere, encompass the *Retractions*, which fills the
lower half of the page—or it may simply be a sign of the lack of oversight.
Little additional information about what is ending may be gleaned from
the final *explicits* that close these two manuscripts: for Ra[2] what is concluded here is the enigmatic "fabula script[?a] p[ro][erasure]"; for Tk[1] the
foregoing is the by now more common "book of the talis of Caunterbery."

Category 5 contains representatives of Manly and Rickert's *b* group of
manuscripts (and Caxton's first edition). They share a variant of the ex-

tended conclusion to the *Parson's Tale* ("to þat lif he vs bringe . . .); they have a distinctive Latin *explicit* for that tale (Ne: "Explicit tractatus Galfridi Chaucer . . . vt dicitur pro fabula Rectoris")[58]; and they omit (or, as appears in the case of Ii, erase) the leave-taking. Category 5 divides easily into two pairs, Ii/Ne and Cx/Tc². The first pair calls the "tractatus" of its *explicit* to the *Parson's Tale* "de vij [Ii: septem] peccatis," while Cx/Tc² identify it as "de Penitencia." Ii/Ne conclude with a colophon, reading (in Ii surprisingly at the top of a new folio): "Explicit liber [Ne: Tractatus] Galfridi Chawcer De gestis / Peregrinoru[m] Versus Cantuariam." Cx has no such colophon, nor does Tc² (though there has been an effective erasure of something in the space below its concluded text). Their regular omission of the common leave-taking formula raises questions about what status and genre they conceived the *Retractions* as having, and since they name Chaucer as the author of the "tractatus" usually called the *Parson's Tale*, they complicate the matter of attribution. This is further confused in Ii/Ne, which go on in their concluding colophons to assign the entire foregoing "liber [Ne: Tractatus] . . . De gestis Peregrinoru[m] Versus Cantuariam" to the same "Galfrid[us] Chawcer."

Taken together categories 4 and 5 indicate that even late in the development and transmission of the *Canterbury Tales*, fundamental uncertainties about the exact status of the final text(s) of the work persist. It is hardly surprising that further variations appear in the other early printed editions. The *Retractions* was omitted from Pynson's first edition and partially re-written by Wynkyn de Worde. Though Pynson restored the text in his second edition, Thynne omitted the *Retractions* from his three printings and established a precedent that was followed until Urry restored the text in 1721. While Urry (or, after his death, Timothy Thomas) forcefully separates his text of the *Retractation* from the *Parson's Tale* by printing it on a separate page and in a different font, Tyrwhitt integrated it more into the text of the *Persones Tale*, merely skipping a line after the Amen before printing the untitled *Retractions* (a title he specifically denies it: III:309). Despite the preceding Amen, he remarks (III:310) that "the beginning of this passage (except the words *or reden it* in l. 19.) and the end make to-gether the genuine conclusion of The Persones Tale, and that the middle part, which I have inclosed between hooks, is an interpolation." (The brack-eted lines are those mentioning the specific titles of works being revoked in his "retracciouns," which Tyrwhitt believes to be a separate, "distinct piece.")[59] While later editors removed Tyrwhitt's brackets, many critics (no-tably Wurtele) have notionally retained them in their interpretations of the text, and scholarship has not in this regard progressed much beyond the position he arrived at more than two centuries ago. Tyrwhitt clearly recog-nized a shift in the voice of the *Retractions*, and others (from Speis to Travis) have shared this view. In the absence of any demonstrable textual support for the interpolation, and weighing the remaining difficulties with it *as* an interpolation (discussed briefly in note 11), there is little reason to adopt Tyrwhitt's insight as a guide for editorial intervention.

Possible Conclusions

In one important respect the *Parson's Tale* is by no means unique: not all the texts we know as *Canterbury Tales* were initially conceived as belonging to such a composite collection, as, for instance, was the case with the *Knight's Tale* and the *Second Nun's Tale*.[60] Most would readily agree that the *Canterbury Tales* at the time of Chaucer's death was still in progress. As a result, we may ask the question whether Chaucer had, or would have, designated this double treatise on penitence and the seven deadly sins as his concluding tale, assigned to the Parson.[61] The treatise is clearly Chaucer's work, but Manly and Rickert expressed strong doubts that the "crude combination of the two treatises" (and by implication, at least, the assignment of that combination to the Parson) is Chaucer's.[62] If the individual tales, Groups, or Fragments Chaucer left behind were intended as constituent parts of a yet-to-be-completed series of "tales of Caunterbery" whose final form remained only a glint in its dying creator's eye, then significantly less confidence is warranted about the place of the prose work we call the *Parson's Tale*. As Manly and Rickert put it in discussing the two prose tales, "While Mel is firmly attached to the framework of links before and after, there is nothing to show that Chaucer intended to use the double treatise (I) at the end as PsT" (2.503). Prior to the recent work of Charles Owen, the pragmatic decision of the late E. Talbot Donaldson to drop the tale from his edition is as close as recent Chaucerian scholarship has come to questioning the authority for the tale's assignment to the Parson. His denying the tale a place in the *Canterbury Tales* should be more actively emulated, despite the tale's regular appearance after the *Parson's Prologue* in the extant manuscripts.

An array of difficulties and doubts has been set aside by Chaucerians in the interest of maintaining the transmitted status quo: the *Canterbury Tales* would be inconclusive without its final tale and epilogic *Retractions*. While critics readily accept that others of Chaucer's works (such as *Hous of Fame* and *Legend of Good Women*) are incomplete or unfinished, they do not wish his final masterpiece to be unconcluded, even if it is demonstrably incomplete: its fragmented middle is clearly less unsatisfying than a suspended ending. The *Parson's Prologue* (about whose placement there is no doubt) proposes a *Parson's Tale* at the end of *Canterbury Tales*, but there is nothing to indicate firmly that Chaucer intended to put his double treatise in the Parson's mouth—nothing, that is, except readers' and editors' feelings of its appropriateness, feelings also evidenced by the extant manuscripts. Chaucer could have been intending this assignment (as he could have been considering assigning the *Life of St. Cecilia* to the Second Nun— or using *Gamelyn* to follow the *Cook's Tale*, after it undergoes its "swyvyng" *interruptus*). But scholarship should not proceed on an unexamined probability that the scribal attribution of the treatise to the Parson is correct; nothing demands it. If the treatise, instead, had independent status, its concluding prayer would, as a consequence, have more authorial force— and perhaps be less subjected to ironic or deconstructive readings. But the prayer's authorial status (and authority) becomes more problematic when the autonomous treatise it concludes is translated into the *Parson's Tale*. Such a translation complicates (and is complicated by) the voice(s) of the narrated tale collection it concludes, and it demands the introduction of often quite awkward boundaries in the majority of early manuscripts and their editorial (and interpretative) descendants. Chaucer, of course, may have wished for such ambiguity at the conclusion of an intended book, together with the concomitant breaking of the fictional levels he so carefully and clearly established in the *General Prologue*. But this remains, though widely assumed by readers and critics, nothing more than a possibility; it ought not continue as an unexamined belief, raised virtually to the level of required interpretation. The rubrics of the *Retractions* point to a different conclusion—even if not a clear one.

On the matter of the penitential treatise's place in the *Canterbury Tales*, as on the scribal origin of the rubrics, Chaucerians have insisted on having it both ways: maintaining the comfort of the long-established text while footnoting their doubts, quibbles, hesitations. While I can scarcely hope to reverse the critical and editorial practices of six centuries, I can perhaps give added prominence to the difficulties and contradictions that lie comfortably dormant below the surface of those practices. The attribution of Chaucer's double treatise to the Parson has undoubted manuscript authority, but it is not therefore indisputable. There is nothing in the text of either the prologue or the tale that requires this "tractatus . . . de Penitencia" to be the Parson's tale—or any Canterbury tale. One major difficulty with the voice(s) of the *Retractions* as an integral part of the *Canterbury Tales* is resolved if it stands as the epilogue to Chaucer's (rather than the fictional Parson's) "tretys" on penance and the seven deadly sins.

Attempts to imagine what such a pre–*Canterbury Tales* version of the *Parson's Tale* and the *Retractions* may have looked like can be aided by one well known manuscript: Longleat 29 (Ll²). There the treatise is not preceded by the *Parson's Prologue*; nor, in its present form at least, is it followed by the epilogic *Retractions*. Unlike Pepys 2006, another case where the treatise appears outside the context of a "complete" *Canterbury Tales* collection, Ll²'s text betrays no connection at all with the *Canterbury Tales*, or with Chaucer for that matter. Its text, which is closely related to El, presents a version of what such a double treatise may have looked like pre–*Canterbury Tales*. But Ll², unfortunately, is missing the folio following its conclusion of the treatise, and so we do not know if it ever contained the *Retractions:* including the *Retractions* would have given more personality and context to the treatise than it presently has and might have compromised (as the prologue and any mention of the *Canterbury Tales* would) the ostensible rationale for this text's being included in the Longleat collection. It is a collection of religious works, not of literary or Chaucerian texts. Luckily we are not limited to Ll² as the only example of what this "tractatus de penitencia" might have looked like with its concluding passage attached.

The manuscripts in category 1 remain arguable representatives of the earliest surviving form for the treatise conjoined to the *Canterbury Tales*. As such, they reveal that Chaucer had not (yet?) revised the treatise to take its place in the narrative drama of the Canterbury pilgrimage. The efforts of scribes and editors to make it the conclusion of the *Canterbury Tales* do not, finally, deserve the authority they presently are accorded. Editorial near-unanimity notwithstanding, the manuscripts as they survive simply do not supply complete enough evidence, nor are they closely enough connected with Chaucer, to warrant our continuing to set aside or ignore the obvious problems attending the *Retractions* as an ending for the *Parson's Tale* and for the *Canterbury Tales*. Most of these problems recede if the so-called *Retractions* remains a conclusion to Chaucer's independent treatise on penance and the seven deadly sins. And there is some manuscript evidence, admittedly slight and scattered, which can be adduced in support of this radical departure. Scribal attempts to clarify the situation of the *Retractions* finally fail, revealing themselves as imaginative editorial attempts to solve the wrong problem. Arguing interpolations or otherwise unmarked changes in "voice" overcomplicates the textual "evidence" in a recurrent effort to maintain the status quo. The attachment of the treatise to the *Parson's Prologue* has for centuries invoked creative energies that the text reveals to be misplaced.

In the manuscript history of the *Canterbury Tales*, the installation of progressively more solid boundaries between the *Parson's Tale* and the *Retractions* at last produced a situation in which any authorial responsibility for the *Retractions* was long and forcefully denied. Leaving aside the excision from Gg (and arguably from Ll²), and even the omission from Pynson's first edition, we must with Urry and Tyrwhitt face the fact that from Thynne onward editions of Chaucer excluded the text from the *Canterbury*

Tales and from any position in Chaucer's works. And from Urry to the present, editors have argued (often quietly and indirectly) against full-blooded acceptance of Chaucer's authorship of the text, in whole or in part. The hesitations of editors have found complicated expression in the ambivalences about and repeated reinterpretations of the *Retractions* in the critical literature. The critics have been more forthright in voicing their doubts and hesitations about the meaning and significance of this text. But they have not solved the difficulties.

But the problem is not, finally, a problem with the text or meaning of the *Retractions*, and to let it remain so is a distraction. The difficulties arise from the text's location, its placement at the end of the penitential treatise attributed to the pilgrim-parson as the conclusion of the *Canterbury Tales*. Despite its long history, that location is a scribal construct (one perhaps directly attributable to the Hengwrt [Ellesmere] scribe) and should not remain beyond dispute, though it will be a brave editor who excises the entire work from the text of the *Canterbury Tales* for reasons more substantive than those adduced by Donaldson and Baugh. Editors are trapped by the scribes who transmit the texts to them, but perhaps scholars can divide and conquer those early transmitters of the text(s) by using only those scribes who insist on keeping the *Parson's Tale* and the *Retractions* united in an uninterrupted "tretys." Such actions would serve as a foundation for arguing in favor of disconnecting Chaucer's entire double treatise on penance and the seven deadly sins from the *Canterbury Tales*. It may be a more honest conclusion to the various problems these texts and their accompanying rubrics raise. The established alternative is plausible, but not, finally, persuasive. This "tractatus . . . de penitencia" can confidently take its place with the *Treatise on the Astrolabe* and *Boece* as another undisputed piece of Chaucerian prose, and it casts light on Chaucer's interests, attitudes, and thematic preferences. It does not, however, need to remain part of the *Canterbury Tales*.

Ending the *Canterbury Tales* with the final line of the *Parson's Prologue*—"And with that word he seyde in this manere"—provides no more unlikely an ending than the proleptic "man of gret auctorite" does for the *Hous of Fame;* can we not as easily imagine a "meditacioun . . . in litel space" from the authoritative (or authoritarian) Parson to "knytte up wel a greet mateere"?[63] It is no less conclusive than the teasing "This tale is seyd for this conclusioun" that ends the *Legend of Good Women*. Indeed, the endings of the *Legend* and of its successor series of tales have an almost uncanny similarity: Chaucer leaves his readers expectantly looking for an imminent, decisive "conclusioun" to the preceding ambiguities—and the same might be inferred from the ending of the *Hous of Fame*. In the case of the *Canterbury Tales*, a reader's imagined "myrie tale in prose" may with greater authority "knytte up" the tales of Canterbury than any actual "tretys" could hope or pretend to do.[64] The tale that has been accepted for nearly six centuries is more a tangle than a knot, and it deserves to be unraveled. Its attribution to the Parson should, I maintain, be denied "auctorite." To preserve its integrity as Chaucer's treatise on penance and the seven deadly sins, the text should be untied from the *Canterbury Tales* and its conclusion left in its earlier place as an apt ending for that penitential text. In this way, the *Retractions* will remain undeniably Chaucer's, and the reference to the "tales of Caunterbury, thilke that sownen into synne" will be released from the potentially ironic self-referentiality that comes with its present location. This is a radical solution to the complications attending the disputes examined above, but those disputes have led to such a variety of solutions, all of them unsatisfactory, that more radical action is clearly called for. Examining more fully the details of the scribal and editorial treatment of the boundary lands between the *Parson's Tale* and the *Retractions* encourages a rejection of *any* formal boundaries between the two texts. And the inevitable result of erasing those boundaries will be to reunite a divided text and declare its independence from the text it has "comfortably" concluded for nearly six hundred years. Such actions will bring attendant critical discomforts, of course, but facing these new realities more openly will also bring its own, greater, rewards. It may even relieve the "embarrassment" not long ago expressed by Charles Muscatine at the "inclusion" of the *Parson's Tale* in, and "its nearly crucial significance as the last of," the *Canterbury Tales*.[65] Perhaps it is time for Chaucerians to convene their own high-level diplomatic assembly to settle these disputes over boundaries and textual identities.

Appendix

CATEGORY 1 ($N = 4$)
No Boundaries

Manuscript	Close ParsT	Exp. ParsT	Inc. Ret	Close Ret	Exp. Ret
	synne	*None*	*None*	*saved Qui cum patre*	*None*
Hatton donat. 1 [Bodleian] (Ht) *(with Hg)*	*syn[ne]*			*saved And he that wrote this boke also/ AmeN ~ Qui cum patre ~*	approx. 2/3 blank page follows
Bodley 414 [Bodleian] (Bo¹) *(<√Pyj)*	*synne /*			*saved Qui cum patre [et] c[etera]*	approx. 1/3 blank page follows (filled with later additions)
Rawlinson poet. 223 [Bodleian] (Ra³) *(with Ha⁴)*	(out)	(out)	(out)	*saved and he that wrot this boke also. Qui cum patre et sp[irit]u sancto viuit et regnat deus per infinita secula Ameñ.*	*Deo Gracias* in approx. 1/2 blank page cf. category 2
Hunter 197 (U.1.1) [Glasgow University Library] (Gl) *(with Ha⁴/Ra³)*	*synne*			*saued. Qui cu[m] patre et sp[irit]u s[an]c[t]o uiuit et regnat deus p[er] infinita secula amen.* (further scribal additions in remaining 3/5 of column)	*Orate pro salute a[nim]ar[um] Galfridi Spirleng....*

CATEGORY 2 (N = 9)
Shorter Leave-Taking

Manuscript	Close ParsT	Exp. ParsT	Inc. Ret	Close Ret	Exp. Ret
	synne [Amen]	**None**	**[Here taketh the maker his leue]**	**saved Qui cum [deo] patre**	**[Deo gracias]**
Harley 7334 [BL] (Ha⁴) *(with Ra³)*	*synne;*		*Preces de Chauceres*	*sauyd. Q[ui] cu[m] p[at]re*	
Egerton 2726 [BL] (En¹) *(a-Group)*	*synne ·|·*		*Here the makr[e] taketh his leue*	[later copy: *saved.*] (No *Qui cum patre*)	[later copy: *Deo gracias. here endith the Canterbury Tales compiled by Geffrey Chaucer, of whose soule Ih[es]u Crist have mercy. Amen.*] cf. Ra³/Pp/Tk¹
Pepys 2006 [Magdalene College Cambridge] (Pp) *(with a-Group)*	*synne.*	*Explicit de Satisfact[i]o[n]e*	*Here taketh his lyeue Om[n]e p[ro]missu[m] est Debitu[m]* (followed by approx. 10 blank lines; then new page)	*saved*	*¶Deo gracias*
Takamiya 24 (TK²) *(olim Devonshire MS)* *(a-Group)*	*sinne.*		*Here takith the maker his leue*	*saued Qui cum patre [et] ce[tera]*	*Of your charite praieth for the writer of this book.* EXPLICIT cf. Gl/Ht/Ra³

	synne Amen		savyd	Explicit fabule
Trinity College Oxford Arch. 49 [To] *(with a-Group)*	synne Amen	Begins new line after blank half-line	sauyd. Qui deo patri [et] filio [et] s[pirit]u s[an]c[t]o viuis [et] regnas in secula seculor[um] amen	Explicit fabule de Caunterburi s[e]c[un]d[u]m Chauchers.
Cardigan MS [University of Texas] (Cn)	synne. Amen	Here takith the maker his leve:	sauyd. Qui cum deo p[at]re [et] c[etera])	
English 113 [John Rylands Library, Manchester] (Ma)	synne Amen	here takith þe maker his leue cf. Ra²	saued/ Qui cum p[at]re [et] c[etera]	Expliciunt fabule Cant[er?] Iste liber Constat Joh[ann]i Brode Juniori [et] c[etera] cf Ra²
Egerton 2864 [BL] (En³) *(with a-Group; √Cn)*	synne Amen	here takith the Maker[e] his Leve	savid Qui cu[m] deo p[at]re [et] sp[irit]u s[an]c[t]o viuis [et] regnas deus p[er] omnia secula Amen	here endith the Persounys Tale
Additional 5140 [BL] (Ad¹) *(with a-Group)*	synne Amen	Hic capit Autor licenciam	savid Qui cum deo patre [et] sp[irit]u sancto viuis [et] regnas deus P[er] om[n]ia secula Amen	Explicit narracio Rectoris et ultima inter narraciones huius libri de quibus composuit Chaucer, cuius anime propicietur deus AMEN.

CATEGORY 3 (N = 4)
Longer Leave-Taking

Manuscript	Close ParsT	Exp. ParsT	Inc. Ret	Close Ret	Exp. Ret
	synne	*None*	*Here taketh the makere of this book his leue*	*saved Qui cum patre*	*Here is ended the book of the tales of Caunterbury co[m]piled by Geffrey Chaucer of whos soule Ih[es]u crist haue mercy. Amen*
Ellesmere 26 C 9 (El)	*synne.*		*¶Heere taketh the makere of this book his leue*	*saved ~ Qui cum patre [et] c[etera]*	*¶Heere is ended the book of the tales of Caunterbury co[m]piled by Geffrey Chaucer of whos soule Ih[es]u crist haue mercy. Amen*
Longleat 29 (Ll²)	syn. [et] c[etera]	¶Explicit deo gracias	out	out	out
Gg.iv.27 (1) [Cambridge University Library] (Gg)	synne ~		Here takyt the makere of this bok his leue··	out	out
Philips 6570 [University of Texas] (Ph¹)	synne.		Heere takeþ the makere of this book his leue:	saued. Qui cu[m] patre [et] sp[irit]u s[an]c[t]o [et] c[etera])	Heer[e] is ended þe book of þe tales of Caunte[er]bury Compyled by Geffrey Chaucer of whos soule Ih[es]u Crist haue mercy Amen··

CATEGORY 4 (N = 10)
Added *explicit* for *Parson's Tale*

Manuscript	Close ParsT	Exp. ParsT	Inc. Ret	Close Ret	Exp. Ret
Lansdowne 851 [BL] (La) *(from √Cp)*	**To þilke lif he vs bringe þat bouht vs wiþ his precious blode Amen** To þilke lif he vs bringe þat bouht vs wiþ his p[re]cious blode AmeN	**Explicit ffabula Rectoris** Explicit ffabula Rectoris (+ space)	**Composito huius libri hic capit licenciam suam** (begins new page) Composito huius libri hic capit licenciam suam.	**saved. Qui cum patre** saved. to receyue þe blisse þat eu[er]e schal last wiþ outen ende. AmeN	**Explicit** Explicit
Petworth House 7 (Pw) *(prob. earliest d̲-Group MS)*	To þilk liffe he vs bringe þat bouȝt vs wiþ his precious blode AmeN	¶Explicit Fabula Rectoris	Here takeþ þe maker of þis booke his leue:	saved. Qui cu[m] p[at]re [et] s[piritu] s[ancto] vi[vit] [et] r[egnat] d[eus] [et] c[etera]	Here endeþ þe boke of þe talys of Cant[er]bury compiled by Geffray Chaucer on whoos soule Ih[es]u crist haue m[er]cy // AmeN
Mm.ii.5 [Cambridge University Library] (Mm)	To þilk liffe he vs brynge þ[at] boȝht us w[ith] his p[re]cious blode Amen~	¶Explicit fabula Rectoris	Here takith þe maker of þis booke his leue:	saved. amen. Qui cum p[at]re [et] c[etera])	Here endeth þe book of þe talis of Cauntirbury compilede by Geffray Chaucer of whos soule Ih[es]u criste haue m[er]cy amen.

continued

CATEGORY 4 ($N = 10$) *Continued*
Added *explicit* for <u>*Parson's Tale*</u>

Manuscript	Close ParsT	Exp. ParsT	Inc. Ret	Close Ret	Exp. Ret
Lichfield Cathedral 29 (Lc)	¶To thilk lif he vs bringe þat bought vs wiþ his precious blood. Amen.	omits (no space available?)	Here takeþ þe maker his leue (omits "of this book" —no space available?)	saued. Qui cum deo p[at]re [et] sp[irit]u sancto [et] c[etera]	Here endeth the boke of the tales of Canterbery co[m]piled by Geffray Chaucers of whoos soule Ih[es]u crist haue mercy. Amen: cf. En[1]
Royal 18.C.11 (Ry²)	To thilke lyf he vs brynge þat boughte vs wiþ his p[re]cious blode AmeN	Thus endeth þe p[ar]sones tale//	And here takeþ þe Aucto[ur] of þis book his leue ~//~//~	saved AmeN ~//~	¶ Here endeth the book of the tales of Cau[n]terburye compiled by Geffrey Chaucer of whos soule Ih[es]u Crist haue mercy / AmeN~//~.
Harley 1758 (Ha²)	To thilke lif he vs brynge that boughte vs with his precious blood. ¶ Amen. (¶Amen in margin) (with √Lc)	¶ffinis. (postpositioned in space after Inc Ret?)	Here taketh the Maker of this boke his Leue.	savyd. Qui cum patre. [et] c[etera]	Here endeth the booK of the tales of Cau[n]tirburye-Compyled bi Geffraye Chaucers. Of whos soule Ih[es]u crist haue mercye. ¶AmeN quod Cornhyll[e]∴∴

MS	Last lines of the Parson's Tale				Qui cum patre	Colophon / Explicit
Takamiya 8 (Tk[1]) [*olim* Delamere MS]	¶To that ilke lyif hee vs brynge that bowghtte vs w[ith] his precious blood Amen	omits	(blank line between "Amen" and "Now")	omits	saved ¶qui cvm patre [et] sp[irit]u	¶Here endyht thee book of the talis of Caunterbery compiled by geffrey Chauceris of whos sowle Ih[es]u Crist haue Mercy Amen cf. En[1]
Rawlinson poet. 149 [Bodleian] (Ra[2])	to thilke lif vs bringe that bougte vs with his preciouse blood amen.	omits	(two-thirds blank line after "amen")	omits	saved Amen	Explicunt fabula script[a?] p[ro]....
McClean 181 [Fitzwilliam Museum Cambridge] (Fi)	To that lyfe he us brynge That with his p[re]cyo[us] blode bought.A.M.E.N)	Here endeth the P[ar]sou[n]s Tale:		Here taketh the maker his leve: (omits "of this book" for space reasons?)	saued; Qui cum patr[e] [et] c[etera]	Here endeth the Boke of the Talys of Caunt[er]biry Compiled by Geffrey Chaucers on whose soule Ih[es]u haue m[er]cy A.M.E.N.
Arch. Selden B.14 [Bodleian] (Se) (*c-Group*)	To thilke liff he vs bringe that bought vs with his p[re]cious bloode Amen	Here enden the talis of Caunturbury/		And next thautour taketh leve~ (omits "of this book" for space reasons?) (also cf. Ad[1]/Ry[2])	out	out

CATEGORY 5 (N = 4)
Omitted Leave-Taking

Manuscript	Close ParsT	Exp. ParsT	Inc. Ret	Close Ret	Exp. Ret
	To þat lif he vs brynge þat bouȝt vs with his precious blood Amen	Explicit Tractatus Galfridi Chawcer de septem p[ec]catis mortalibus vt dicit[ur] pro fabula rectoris [et] c[etera]	None?	saved. Qui cum patre	Explicit liber Galfridi Chawcer De gestis Peregrinorum Versus Cantuariam
Ii.iii.26 [Cambridge University Library] (Ii)	*wiser than Salamon* ~ ~~~ (incomplete)	*Explicit Tractatus Galfridi Chawcer de septem p[ec]catis mortalibus vt dicit[ur] pro fabula rectoris [et] c[etera]*	erased: *Inci. . . .*	*savyd Qui cu[m] deo patr[e] [et] spiritu sancto viuit [et] regnat deus p[er]om[n]ia s[e]c[u]la*	*Explicit liber Galfridi Chawcer De gestis Peregrinoru[m] Versus Cantuariam ~* (begins new page)

New College Oxford, D 314 (Ne)	To þat lif he vs brynge þat bouȝte vs with his precious blood. Amen	Explicit tractatus Galfridi Chaucer de vij peccatis mortalib[us] vt dicitur pro fabula Rectoris	None (3–4 blank lines follow Exp. ParsT; "Now" begins new page)	saued. Qui cu[m] p[at]re [et] c[etera] (last three words in bottom margin)	(begins new page) Explicit Tractatus Galfridi Chauser de gestis p[er]egrinorum versus Cantuariam ~~ (rest of page blank)
Caxton 1478 (Cx¹) [and Caxton ?1484 (Cx²)]	To that lyf he vs brynge that bought with his precyous blood/ Amen.	Explicit Tractatus Galfrydi [Cx²: Galfridi] Chaucer de Penitencia vt dicitur pro fabula Rectoris	(begins new page)	sauid. Qui cu[m] patre et sp[irit]u s[an]c[t]o viuit et regnat deus. Per omnia secula seculor[um] Amen.	None (text ends page of Cx¹—but not of Cx²)
Trinity College Cambridge, R.3.15 (Tc²)	To that lyfe vs brynge the bought with his precious blode vpon the rode tree Amen.//	Explicit Tractatus Galfridi Chauces de penitencia vt dicitur pro fabula Rectoris	erasure: 6–7 blank lines	sauyd/ Qui cum patre [et] sp[irit]u s[an]c[t]o viuit et regnat deus. Per omnia secula seculorum / Amen	well erased writing. (end of verso; pasted on)

Notes

1. For some recent stimulating reflections on complexities in these questions, see, for example, Louis Hay's essay, "Does 'Text' Exist?" *Studies in Bibliography* 41 (1988): 64–76.

2. A. S. G. Edwards, "The Unity and Authenticity of *Anelida and Arcite:* The Evidence of the Manuscripts," *Studies in Bibliography* 41 (1988): 177–88. Other examples might also be adduced: for example, John C. Pope, "An Unsuspected Lacuna in the Exeter Book: Divorce Proceedings for an Ill-Matched Couple in the Old English Riddles," *Speculum* 49 (1974): 615–22. And see N. F. Blake, *The Textual Tradition of the Canterbury Tales* (London: Arnold, 1985), 85–86, for the argument that the *Man of Law's Prologue* and the *Man of Law's Tale* were not intended to go together.

3. James Dean, "Chaucer's Repentance: A Likely Story," *Chaucer Review* 24 (1989): 65. The recent important essay by Charles A. Owen, Jr.—"What the Manuscripts Tell Us about the Parson's Tale," *Medium Ævum* 63 (1994): 239–49—anticipated many of my major conclusions and presented them with enviable directness.

An essential bibliography on the *Retractions* would include at least the following: James D. Gordon, "Chaucer's *Retraction:* A Review of Opinion," in *Studies in Medieval Literature in Honor of Albert Croll Baugh,* ed. MacEdward Leach (Philadelphia: University of Pennsylvania Press, 1961), 81–96; Olive Sayce, "Chaucer's 'Retractions': The Conclusion of the *Canterbury Tales* and Its Place in Literary Tradition," *Medium Ævum* 40 (1971): 230–48; Donald R. Howard, *The Idea of the Canterbury Tales* (Berkeley: University of California Press, 1976), 56–61, 210–13, and 376–82; Douglas Wurtele, "The Penitence of Geoffrey Chaucer," *Viator* 11 (1980): 335–59; Gayle C. Schricker, "On the Relation of Fact and Fiction in Chaucer's Poetic Endings," *Philological Quarterly* 60 (1981): 13–27; Robert S. Knapp, "Penance, Irony, and Chaucer's *Retraction,*" *Assays* 2 (1983): 45–67; Rosemarie Potz McGerr, "Retraction and Memory: Retrospective Structure in the *Canterbury Tales,*" *Comparative Literature* 37 (1985): 97–113 (revised in her *Chaucer's Open Books: Resistance to Closure in Medieval Literature* [Gainesville: University Press of Florida, 1998], 131–53); James Dean, "Dismantling the Canterbury Book," *PMLA* 100 (1985): 746–62; Victor Yelverton Haines, "Where Are Chaucer's 'Retraccîouns'?" *Florilegium* 10 (1988–91): 127–49; Peter W. Travis, "Deconstructing Chaucer's Retraction," *Exemplaria* 3 (1991): 135–58; and Jameela Lares, "Chaucer's *Rectractions:* A 'Verray Parfit' Penitence," *Cithara* 34 (1994): 18–33. To these should be added recent discussions of the *Parson's Tale:* Carol V. Kaske, "Getting around the Parson's Tale: An Alternative to Allegory and Irony," in *Chaucer at Albany,* ed. Rossell Hope Robbins (New York: Franklin, 1975), 147–78; Lee Patterson, "The *Parson's Tale* and the Quitting of the *Canterbury Tales,*" *Traditio* 34 (1978): 31–80; David Lawton, "Chaucer's Two Ways: The Pilgrimage Frame of the *Canterbury Tales,*" *Studies in the Age of Chaucer* 9 (1987): 3–40; and Albert E. Hartung, "'The Parson's Tale' and Chaucer's Penance," in *Literature and Religion in the Middle Ages: Philological Studies in Honor of Siegfried Wenzel,* ed. Richard G. Newhauser and John Alford, Medieval and Renaissance Texts and Studies 118 (Binghamton, N.Y.: Medieval and Renaissance Texts and Studies, 1995), 61–80.

4. Owen, "What the Manuscripts Tell Us," 239.

5. Ibid.

6. The text here is taken from Larry D. Benson, general editor, *The Riverside*

Chaucer (Boston: Houghton Mifflin, 1987), 327–28. I have omitted the intervening blank space, page break, and italicized rubrics, which divide the *Retractions* from the *Parson's Tale.*

7. See, among others, John M. Manly and Edith Rickert, *The Text of the* Canterbury Tales *Studied on the Basis of All Known Manuscripts*, 8 vols. (Chicago: University of Chicago Press, 1940), 2:471–73; 3:528–32; M. B. Parkes, "The Influence of the Concepts of *Ordinatio* and *Compilatio* on the Development of the Book," in *Medieval Learning and Literature: Essays Presented to Richard William Hunt*, ed. J. J. G. Alexander and M. T. Gibson (Oxford: Clarendon Press, 1976), 115–41; Blake, *Textual Tradition;* and Charles A. Owen, Jr., *The Manuscripts of the* Canterbury Tales, Chaucer Studies 17 (Cambridge: D. S. Brewer, 1991), 6.

The few instances that Manly and Rickert report (e.g., "The Stag of an hert" after F 346 of the *Squire's Tale*) are recorded because they assist them in determining manuscript agreements and affiliations (2.10).

8. Manly and Rickert, *Text of the* Canterbury Tales, 2:10.

9. Siegfried Wenzel gives a good summary of these matters in the notes to the *Riverside Chaucer* (965). Blake, *Textual Tradition,* includes frequent reference to rubrics. While he and others hold that the exemplars for the early manuscripts probably lacked rubrics (or at least many rubrics), the repeated forms that occur in later manuscripts clearly suggest that scribes felt less free to diverge from their exemplars when they were rubricated. Only when there are few or no rubrics do scribes feel free to create and vary their own. The wide variety of rubrics and the categories into which they fall demonstrate both an early impulse toward rubrication and the hardening of established patterns once rubrics were introduced.

10. Travis, for example, can quite explicitly present the opening "leave-taking" rubric as Chaucer's own words ("Deconstructing," 142).

11. While the omission of the *Retractions* from earlier printed editions may imply that the whole text was considered an interpolation, the theory that the middle section enumerating Chaucer's works may have been editorial was apparently first voiced by Thomas Tyrwhitt (*Chaucer's Canterbury Tales* [London, 1775], 3:309–11). For a recent, more sustained argument, see Wurtele, "Penitence" (aptly criticized as a "tortured attempt" by Travis, "Deconstructing," 141). The point has also been advanced by others. See W. W. Skeat, ed., *The Complete Works of Geoffrey Chaucer*, 6 vols. and supplement (Oxford: Clarendon Press, 1894–97), 3:503; and Norman Eliason, *The Language of Chaucer's Poetry* (Copenhagen: Rosenkilde and Bagger, 1972), 209–14.

There is, of course, no manuscript evidence to support this selective excision of text; and there are not a few difficulties with defining the extent of the interpolation. Wurtele's division (following Henrich Spies, "Chaucers Retractatio," *Festschrift Adolf Tobler zum siebzigsten geburstage* [Braunschweig: Westermann, 1905], 383–94) of the concluding lines (356–57) has syntactic and other difficulties. For instance, the change from third to second person (1081–82, 1084), and the formulaic oddity (to say nothing of the theological irregularity) raised by having the Parson pray "that Crist have mercy on me. . . . and graunte me grace . . . thurgh the benigne grace of hym that is kyng of kynges and preest over alle preestes, that boghte us with the precious blood of his herte" (1084, 1090–92).

12. Cf. Owen, "What the Manuscripts Tell Us," 239.

13. See Dean, "Likely Story."

14. Frederick J. Furnivall and the Chaucer Society gave prominence to Ellesmere

(and Hengwrt) in the last century. Prior to that, of course, and to some extent since, Harley 7334 (Ha⁴) had been a favored early authority. Though the position of El has come under considerable attack in the last decade or so, yet, as Blake notes (*Textual Tradition*, 39), "El is still used as the basis for editions and its order was considered a good order." Despite the continuing critical agreement that "Hg was the earliest manuscript and had the best text. . . . the attempt to work out the relationship between Hg and El so that Hg is given proper recognition is a long and painful one; El still commands the support of sentiment, tradition and some conviction."

15. William Thynne, *The Workes of Geffray Chaucer* (London: Godfray, 1532; and later editions printed by Bonham: 1542 and 1545); William A. Jackson, F. S. Ferguson, and Katharine F. Pantzer, *A Short-Title Catalogue of Books Printed in England, Scotland, and Ireland and of English Books Printed Abroad, 1475–1640*, 2d ed. First compiled by A. W. Pollard and G. R. Redgrave (London: Bibliographical Society, 1976—), 5068, 5069, and 5071 [hereafter *STC*]; John Stow, *The Works of Geoffrey Chaucer* (London: Jhon Kyngston for Jhon Wight, 1561; *STC* 5075); Thomas Speght, *The Workes of Our Antient and Learned English Poet, Geffrey Chaucer* (London: Islip for Bishop, 1598: *STC* 5077; his second edition—Islip, 1602—is *STC* 5080); John Urry, *The Works of Geoffrey Chaucer, Compared with the Former Editions and Many Valuable MSS.* (London: Lintot, 1721).

Blake's implication (*Textual Tradition*, 6 and 8) that both of Pynson's editions omitted the *Retractions* is incorrect. The text does appear in the second edition: *Here begynneth the boke of Caunterbury Tales, dilygently corrected and newly printed* (London, 1526; *STC* 5086). His first edition is *STC* 5084 (London, 1492).

16. Manly and Rickert, *Text of the* Canterbury Tales, 2:41.

17. See Owen, "What the Manuscripts Tell Us," 243–44, for his account of these stages.

18. Ha⁴ precedes the *Retractions* with what we might call a title: "Preces de Chauceres."

19. Twenty-eight manuscripts contain the text of the *Retractions;* they account for a third of all manuscripts containing any of the *Canterbury Tales,* and make up half of those with the "complete" text of the work. There is ample evidence for the loss of other contemporary manuscripts. Any textual inferences imply many more manuscripts than those that survive.

Two further manuscripts, Gg and Ll²—both, as it happens, members of the editorially favored "Ellesmere Group" (category 3)—preserve no text of the *Retractions* proper. Gg has its leave-taking formula clear at the bottom of the last folio of its *Parson's Tale;* the next folio is lost, but it no doubt did contain the text of the *Retractions.* Like Gg, Ll² is also missing the folio immediately following the one on which the *Parson's Tale* concludes. In this case, however, matters are more complicated. Ll² is the one exemplar in which the tale exists in independent form as a tract on "penitencie," without the *Parson's Prologue* or the "epilogue" that accompanies it when it appears at the end of the *Canterbury Tales,* and it may never have contained a text of the *Retractions.* But even though it presently concludes with a more forceful explicit than Gg—putting "¶Explicit deo gracias" in the middle of the next line—it is still an open question whether this unique marking of closure was supplied by the scribe/rubricator after the decision was made to excise the folio containing the (now unacceptable) *Retractions.* We do not know, *pace* Owen (*Manuscripts*, 105–6), absolutely that Ll² never included the *Retractions.* While on the strength of the *explicit* it seems likely that it was never an *approved* part of this manuscript's text, it does not follow that it was not part of the text at all—or of its exemplar. That exemplar was, after all, closely related to El and its tradition, and there is no doubt about the text of the *Retractions* existing there. It is a curious coincidence that two of the surviving early witnesses to a text closely related to El no longer contain the *Retractions*. Like the omitted text of the *Retractions* in Pynson's first edition, this correspondence of Gg and Ll² raises questions not only about textual transmission but also about subsequent editorial deletion of the troublesome folio. While this deletion may be inferred with some certainty for Gg, it still remains possible for Ll², even if its tracks have been more completely obscured. Perhaps at this early stage of transmission of the *Parson's Tale* and the *Retractions*, excision offered as attractive an alternative as inserting categorical rubrics.

20. Further information on the manuscripts identified by these sigla appears in the appendix.

21. This first type of closing for the *Parson's Tale* is sometimes reinforced by a following Amen, which leaves no doubt about the tale's conclusion; the longer version of the tale's close invariably ends that way. While I earlier considered the Amen with the *synne*-ending a more systematically distinctive feature—distinguishing one category (which closes with "synne Amen") from another ("synne" alone)—the use of Amen is simply too fluid and irregular to underwrite such a categorical distinction. It may help distinguish subcategories (as it does in category 2), and although its presence or absence at any given point does not, finally, support stable distinctions between or among groups of texts, it is nonetheless a significant marker of scribal reading and interpretation of the text. It certainly is, at least, a trustworthy sign that one text has ended and that what follows it has an independent textual identity.

22. R. V. Ramsey would add spelling to this list ("The Hengwrt and Ellesmere Manuscripts of the Canterbury Tales: Different Scribes," *Studies in Bibliography* 35 [1982]: 133–55). That point is disputed by M. L. Samuels in "The Scribe of the Hengwrt and Ellesmere Manuscripts of the *Canterbury Tales*," *Studies in the Age of Chaucer* 5 (1983): 49–65.

23. Blake, *Textual Tradition*, 79–80.

24. In their classroom editions neither Albert C. Baugh nor E. T. Donaldson prints the entire *Parson's Prologue* and *Tale*, but both provide the title "CHAUCER'S RE-TRACTION" above the leave-taking formula heading their texts of the *Retractions*. Donaldson, unlike Baugh, omits the closing colophon for the *Retractions*. Baugh explains his omission of the *Parson's Tale* as follows: "The 'myrie tale in prose' which the Parson promises is actually a treatise or sermon on Patience [*sic*] and the Seven Deadly Sins. Since the present volume is limited to Chaucer's poetry, it is not included" (*Chaucer's Major Poetry* [Englewood Cliffs, N.J.: Prentice-Hall, 1963], 532). Donaldson's rationale is that the "piety" of this "enormously long discussion in prose. . . . does not, however, raise it into the realm of literature, and although it has moments of imaginative art it remains on the whole a tract of rather specialized interest" (Donaldson, *Chaucer's Poetry: An Anthology for the Modern Reader*, 2d ed. [New York: Ronald Press, 1975], 1112).

John Fisher similarly titles it "Retraction" at the top of a new page of his edition (John H. Fisher, *The Complete Poetry and Prose of Geoffrey Chaucer* [New York: Holt, Rinehart and Winston, 1989], 397).

"Retract(at)ion(s)" is, as Tyrwhitt pointed out (3.309), *not* a title ever used in any of the manuscripts or early printed editions and is derived only from the purportedly self-referential comment in the text. The first use of this "title" for the conclusion seems to be Thomas Hearne's 1709 letter to Mr. Bagford, in *Remarks and Collections of Thomas Hearne*, 2.200, quoted in Caroline F. E. Spurgeon, *Five Hundred Years of Chaucer Criticism and Allusion, 1357–1900* (1914–24; reprint, New York: Russell, 1961), 1:307–08.

  25. A. W. Pollard, M. H. Liddell, H. F. Heath, and W. S. McCormick, eds., *The Globe Chaucer* (London: Macmillan, 1898); F. N. Robinson, ed., *The Works of Geoffrey Chaucer* (Boston: Houghton Mifflin, 1957); Robert A. Pratt, ed., *The Tales of Canterbury* (Boston: Houghton Mifflin, 1974); and Fisher, *Poetry and Prose of Geoffrey Chaucer*. The same could be said for the earlier editions of Arthur Gilman (*The Poetical Works of Geoffrey Chaucer*, Riverside Edition of British Poets, vols. 11–13 [Boston: Houghton, Osgood, 1879]) and Thomas R. Lounsbury (*The Complete Works of Geoffrey Chaucer*, 2 vols. [New York: Thomas Crowell, 1900]).

  26. Richard Morris, ed., *The Poetical Works of Geoffrey Chaucer*, Aldine Edition of the British Poets, vols. 8–13 (London: Bell and Daldy, 1866); Thomas Wright, ed., *The Canterbury Tales of Geoffrey Chaucer*, Percy Society, vols. 24–26 (London: Richards, 1847–51).

  At the other end of the publication history, Wynkyn de Worde, who offers a widely variant, "modernized" text of the *Retractions,* begins that text at the top of the penultimate page, concluding it (and the book) with a colophon about a third of the way down the second column:

> Here endyth the boke of the tales of
> Caunterbury Compiled by Geffray
> Chaucer | of whoos soule Criste haue
> mercy. Emprynted at Westmestre by
> Wynkin de word þ[e] yere of our lord.M
> CCCC.lxxxxviii.

(The final page has a woodcut print of the pilgrims feasting at a round table.) The *Parson's Tale* he ends six lines from the top of the recto preceding the *Retractions*. He follows this with about four blank lines; the *explicit* "Here endyth the Person his tale"; a print of a well-dressed pilgrim on horseback; and a leave-taking "Here takyth the maker of this boke his leue" about a line from bottom.

  Pynson (1526) introduces the *Retractions* with

> Explicit tractat[us] Galfridi Chau=
> cer de Penitentia | vt dicitur
> pro fabula rectoris"

and follows it with

> Thus endeth the boke of Caunterbury
> tales. Imprinted at London

  Urry ends the *Parson's Tale* in the middle of 213: "Here endeth the PARSON's TALE." Heading the text of the *Retractation* at the top of 214 is the following: "What follows is published out of MS. Ch. [i.e., Tk[1] (*olim* Delamere = Cholmondeley)] with some amendments out of other MSS. where the sense required it."

Tyrwhitt has the extended conclusion for the *Parson's Tale* ("to which life he us bring, that bought us with his precious blood. Amen." ["which" is his emendation]), skips a single line, and proceeds directly with the text of what Urry called *Retractation* (3.276; cf. 309). (The emendation aside, this closely emulates the format of Tk[1].) After about six blank lines following the conclusion of that text, he closes his edition with: "The End of the Canterbury Tales" (3.278).

27. This is not, in fact, completely accurate: the reading "XV" is found only in Mm; in La a second "x" (ergo, "xxv") can be clearly seen in the crease that runs through the middle of the number (and the length of the folio), as Manly and Rickert noted in their variants (*Text of the* Canterbury Tales, 8:546), and as I have confirmed by my own examination. The error derives, apparently, from Robinson, who reports this in the textual notes of his first edition (1015)—and an apparent copyediting error in the second edition's note (898) added further difficulty by attributing this same reading to Ha (Harley 7334). (That manuscript clearly reads "25," which had been earlier misreported in Robinson's first edition as "29"—the result of a not-unprecedented misreading of the leaning 5 as a 9.) Of the manuscripts not cited in the *Riverside* textual notes, Gl offers the only other significant variant at this point: it reads "Twenty."

28. Owen, *Manuscripts*, 6. In "Adam Scriveyn" and at the end of *Troilus*, for example, Chaucer certainly separates the scribal role from his own role as maker of poems and supervisor of scribes. As Donald Howard has convincingly argued, the attribution of "book" to the *Canterbury Tales* in these final rubrics must also be scribal rather than authorial (*Idea of the* Canterbury Tales, 56–60). Chaucer nowhere refers to the *Canterbury Tales* as a book, and critics at least from Brusendorff and Tatlock (Blake, *Textual Tradition*, 34–35) to Charles Owen and Norman Blake would insist that it did not exist as one at Chaucer's death. Even if not qualifying as the book that we know as the *Canterbury Tales*, it is likely that some "tales of Caunterbury" were known in Chaucer's lifetime (cf. Blake, *Textual Tradition*, 51–52), though they may not have been in circulation for copying. The fragmentary nature of the tales' collection supports its not yet having attained book status.

29. The fourth manuscript, Ra[3], is unfortunately missing its penultimate folio and so is missing the transition from *Parson's Tale* to *Retractions;* however, because of its close relation to Gl—and to a lesser extent to Ht—it fits best in this category.

30. Manly and Rickert (*Text of the* Canterbury Tales, 1:58) state that the last quire (#28) is a six; I counted only five paper sheets.

31. There are approximately eight blank lines remaining on this page; they were subsequently filled by notes. Given the absence from this manuscript of a number of multi-lined capitals for which space is left, we can infer that the scribe intended to supply a colophon for the *Canterbury Tales* here. In any case, postponing (and even rubricating) the "Now pray I . . ." would not have come close to using up the available space on the verso.

32. For example, Gg, La (Ll[2], possibly), Ne, and Pp; among printed editions, the move to a new page (with or without accompanying heading or rubric) is found in Cx[2], de Worde, Urry, Skeat, Robinson (second edition), Baugh, Fisher, and *Riverside*.

33. Owen, *Manuscripts*, 80. (The longer quotation following is from the same page.)

34. Manly and Rickert, *Text of the* Canterbury Tales, 1:422.

35. In respect to the text of the *Parson's Tale*, Ht (like Bo[1], though perhaps even more directly) has distinct connections with Hg; the other two manuscripts, Gl and Ra[3],

are affiliated with Ha⁴. Connected with two important early textual traditions, these four manuscripts offer a number of interesting variants. They confirm, for instance, the very close ties between Gl and Ra³ (and perhaps less dramatically those with Ha⁴).

At the end of the *Retractions* there is clear individuality in each of the four manuscripts. Where Bo¹ reads ". . . saved Qui cum patre & c[etera]," Ht reads ". . . saved And he that wrote this boke also. AMEN. Qui cum patre." (The remaining three-fifths of this final verso of Ht are entirely blank—only stubs survive for the remaining three folios of this quire of eight.) Ra³ has an elaborate "Deo gracias" following the same insertion after "saved" and the expanded Latin prayer-close:

> . . . saved and
> he that wrot this boke also. Qui cum patre et sp[irit]u sancto vi
> uit et regnat deus per infinita secula Amen

Gl closes without the added English words but with the identical Latin closing formula, including the "infinita" distinctive to these two manuscripts:

> . . . saved. Qui
> cu[m] patre et sp[irit]u s[an]c[t]o uiuit et regnat deus p[er]
> infinita secula amen.

36. The underlined words are in slightly enlarged script, and, beginning with the very much elongated *N*, are written in red ink like many personal names, quotations, or important phrases (some even as long as three consecutive lines) in Latin and English in this work.

37. Charles Owen indeed grants Hatton considerable importance, derived from its close relation to Hengwrt: "Hengwrt and Hatton Donat 1 reflect the earliest state of the text" ("What the Manuscripts Tell Us," 243). He also asserts that Hengwrt "undoubtedly once included the Retraction" (ibid.).

38. Manly and Rickert, *Text of the* Canterbury Tales, 2:472.

39. Ibid., 1:252.

40. Owen, "What the Manuscripts Tell Us," 243.

41. Cf. ibid., 243–44. Alone in these category 2 manuscripts, the scribe of Tk² concludes his copying of the *Canterbury Tales* (fol. 274) with a prayer "for the writer of this book," reminiscent of those in category 1. (It is *not*, however, "at the end of the MS," as Manly and Rickert claim [*Text of the* Canterbury Tales, 1:120].)

42. Owen, *Manuscripts*, 9–11, and "What the Manuscripts Tell Us," 239 and 243; Blake, *Textual Tradition*, 67–72, 109–19. The other manuscript by this scribe (Corpus Christi 198) is missing the end of the *Parson's Tale*.

43. We saw above the textual associations of Ha⁴ with Gl and Ra³. Ha⁴ and the four category 1 manuscripts share a couple of unique textual readings. At 1087 all read "of the which Crist" where other MSS agree to "that Crist" (or simply replace the "that" with a punctuation mark); at 1085 (Ra³ excluded) they do not have "of" (or "for," as in some manuscripts) before "my translacions." They also agree (along with five other manuscripts—Ad¹, Cn, En³, Ma, and Tk²) in reading "seintis in heven" instead of "seintes of hevene" (1089).

44. Blake, *Textual Tradition*, 70; cf. 113–14, 118–19.

45. The main obstacle to placing it confidently in the present discussion is the loss of the original final folio (271: i.e., 1085b ff.), which was replaced in the early 1700s, perhaps by William Thomas, one of the collaborators on Urry's edition (Manly and Rickert, *Text of the* Canterbury Tales, 1:131). The exemplar for this seems to have been a manuscript (or print) related to Pepys 2006. Or, since such an exemplar would in any case be closely affiliated with En¹, perhaps it was the damaged original folio itself.

46. I have rendered the looping ascender above the *r* as a suspension for *e;* it may simply be an otiose stroke—not unusual in this scribe's hand.

47. Pp reinforces the division more strongly than other manuscripts. It precedes the leave-taking formula with a unique explicit—"Explicit de Satisfact[i]o[n]e"—and follows it with "Om[n]e p[ro]missu[m] est Debitu[m]" and about ten blank lines. The *Retractions* begins at the top of the next page with a two-line initial *N.*

48. Unlike the other manuscripts employing Amen, To's textual affiliations are not altogether clear. The others are closely related. Ma is directly copied from Cn's "immediate exemplar" (Manly and Rickert, *Text of the* Canterbury Tales, 1:350; cf. Owen, *Manuscripts*, 15–22.). En³ and Ad¹ were, according to Owen, considerably influenced by the Cn tradition, and their *Parson's Tale* (with the *Retractions*) "is the only full tale with its text from Cn" (*Manuscripts*, 87).

Manly and Rickert assert (2:472) that the *Retractions* in general provides "little evidence for classification, but the few variants indicate the persistence of the same groups as are found in PsP and PsT." Their one important qualification of this, however, concerns To: "The relation of To [to their Group II] is not *ctm* (cf. 1082, 1087), as in PsT; whether genetic or *acco* it is impossible to say" (2:473). To these two examples, we might well add 1085, 1086, and 1091 as other instances of To's connection with their Group II (which includes *a*, El, Gg, et al.) (For those not intimately familiar with Manly and Rickert's shorthand, *ctm* is "contamination, contaminated" and *acco* is "accidental coincidence" [2:245].)

49. The rubric reads the plural "fabule," not "fabula," as reported by Manly and Rickert, *Text of the* Canterbury Tales, 1:539.

50. For To, "Melibee" is "fabula Chauceris" while Sir Thopas is simply "Thopas" in the running head. If the now separated text of the *Retractions* is assigned to anyone, it remains the Parson's.

51. Manly and Rickert, *Text of the* Canterbury Tales, 1:539.

52. Ibid., 1:536.

53. Owen (*Manuscripts*, 104) notes, in this regard, that "[h]eadings for the prologues and tales are similarly sparse, sometimes omitted (92a), sometimes in a simple 'Explicit' (170b), set off when present in a similar paraph-cradle. . . . Little preparation or forethought and little expense went into the production of To."

54. The rubricator of Tk² may be invoked to support this possibility: his eye-catching running head at the top of the page containing the bulk of the *Retractions* is "[ffabula] Rectoris."

55. The "AmeN" is highlighted with blue ticks, and the "Explicit ffabula Rectoris" is in red (as is the Latin leave-taking following). The final *explicit* (which follows the *Retractions* after one blank line) is also in red, and the remainder of the page (about fourteen lines) is blank.

56. Ha², presumably after the fact, felt the need for some definitive *explicit* and inserted the "ffinis," substituting it, perhaps for reasons of space, for the longer versions found elsewhere. The concluding Amen is wholly in the margin of the preceding line.

It is plausible that since the one-line blank left for the rubrics here was not sufficient for the fuller leave-taking formula, it was (as I suggested was also the case with To) abbreviated by omitting "of this book."

57. The varied evidence of Tk[1]'s textual cousins in my category 4—e.g., Ha[2], Lc, Ry[2]—gets us little closer to determining what, if anything, might have been intended for this blank line in Tk[1].

58. See Owen, "What the Manuscripts Tell Us," 240–41.

59. Tyrwhitt, *Chaucer's Canterbury Tales*, 3:309.

60. The references in the Prologue to the *Legend of Good Women* attest to the independence of these tales: the "storye . . . knowen lyte" of "al the love of Palamon and Arcite" (fols. 420–21) and "the lyf also of Seynt Cecile" (fol. 426).

As Blake points out (*Textual Tradition*, 87), without the rubrics the "life of St. Celia" could not be assigned to any single Canterbury pilgrim, particularly not to a female pilgrim, given the "unworthy sone of Eve" reference (VIII.62). The category 5 predilection for calling the *Parson's Tale* "tractatus Galfridi Chaucer" would point to the existence of a tract separate from and antecedent to the present "fabula (Ad[1]: narracio) Rectoris."

61. Cf. Donaldson, *Chaucer's Poetry*, 1112. The "pro" in the clause "vt dicitur pro fabula Rectoris" of category 5 MSS may mean "in place of; as a substitute for" rather than the simpler "for; as." In such a case the witness of these MSS might well indicate an early appreciation of the surrogate quality of this tale.

62. Manly and Rickert, *Text of the* Canterbury Tales, 2:454–55; as far as I have been able to ascertain, the promised article in *ELH* in which this was to be "argued in detail" never appeared.

63. *Parson's Prologue*, X.69, 71, 28.

64. *Parson's Prologue*, X.28, 46–47.

65. Charles Muscatine, "Chaucer's Religion and the Chaucer Religion," in Ruth Morse and Barry Windeatt, ed., *Chaucer Traditions: Studies in Honour of Derek Brewer* (Cambridge: Cambridge University Press, 1990), 256.

II

DISSEMINATION AND INTERPRETATION

The Fifteenth-Century *Prioress's Tale* and the Problem of Anti-Semitism

MARY F. GODFREY

Once admired by Wordsworth and Matthew Arnold for its pathos and beauty of poetic line, Chaucer's *Prioress's Tale* has become one of the most problematic of all the *Canterbury Tales*. A Marian legend of a child murdered by brutal Jews, it is told by a meticulous, worldly nun whose anti-Semitism goes unremarked by the other pilgrims, the Chaucerian pilgrim narrator, and Chaucer himself. In this century, critics have felt increasingly compelled to defend Chaucer's apparent acceptance of attitudes now abhorrent, and a host of arguments have been made that variously attempt to exonerate him from the anti-Semitic culture of his time, show that he is drawing on centuries of theological and doctrinal arguments in his depiction of Jews or using anti-Semitism as a kind of literary device to explore issues of character or voice.[1]

That the presence of anti-Semitism in literature remains a crucial, even explosive issue is evinced by the uproar greeting two recent studies of T. S. Eliot by Christopher Ricks and Anthony Julius.[2] Reviewers wondered if it was still necessary to attend to bigotry as personal belief or as an element in art. But as one reader commented, "Isn't it obvious that when an author's anti-Semitism is evident, as in Eliot's poetry, those poems are compromised *as poems*? All anti-Semitic (and racist) poetry is in some measure bad poetry, whatever its felicities and ethical concerns."[3] If a certain sanitizing distance may be said to exist between the era of Eliot's prewar poetry and the 1990s, that distance is multiplied manifold by the immeasurably greater gap between Chaucer's fourteenth century and the twentieth—so much so that some medievalists recommend giving up trying to understand the tale's anti-Semitism (and, by implication, the alterity of medieval culture). In Daniel Pigg's cogent argument, "any analysis . . . that attempts to resolve this explicit problem with anti-Semitism will prove only marginally successful and will reflect more about the critic than about Chaucer or the *Prioress's Tale*."[4] Chaucer himself would seem to compound the problem, with that

93

studious avoidance of topical or personal references that makes it difficult to uncover his own investment in the beliefs of his characters.

Robert Worth Frank has reminded us that it is important not "to underestimate how 'alive' the Jew remained in England after the expulsion of 1290" as an imaginative "construct created and validated by [medieval] culture"[5]—not only for Chaucer, but for the fifteenth-century scribes and readers who make up the first significant audience of his verse. If the theological and social discourses that encoded stereotypes and legislated persecutions are increasingly clear to us,[6] what is less well understood is the way in which the cultural construct of the Jew is imaginatively maintained in an England without Jews. These early readings of the tale—in their emendations, annotations, and expansions of Chaucer's text—are a valuable means of understanding how and why such cultural beliefs are either sustained or altered with time.[7]

For indeed, the quality of "aliveness," to borrow Frank's term, changes. Certainly some scribes preserved the vituperative tone familiar to much medieval anti-Semitic literature; one early fifteenth-century manuscript containing an analogue of the *Prioress's Tale* spitefully rails against Jews: "O people favored by the devil only! . . . It does not move them that everywhere they see themselves to be the scandal of mankind and the rejected of men."[8] But the manuscript anthologies studied here that include versions of the *Prioress's Tale*, British Museum MSS Harley 1704, 2251, and 2382— far from enthusiastically preserving older stereotypes about Jews—show little interest in depictions of the Jews as theological bogeymen. These collections reflect an interest in Chaucer as a popular author of erotic lyrics or short verse narratives eminently suitable for the anthologies that might constitute a one-volume library,[9] as well as the popularity of the *Prioress's Tale* in particular as an anthology selection.[10] They also tell us much about late medieval tastes, in which moral or didactic qualities in literature were highly prized,[11] and in which the *Tale's* pathos and anti-Semitism are altered, excised, or otherwise ignored. Modern commentators on the *Prioress's Tale* have uniformly addressed anti-Semitism as it may have existed in Chaucer's fourteenth century, drawing on theological or historical evidence that is centuries older. These alterations of Chaucer's tale offer additional cultural evidence for the ways in which anti-Semitic beliefs had ossified some two hundred years after the expulsion of the Jews from England.

The fifteenth-century portion of Harley 1704 is representative of late medieval anthology compilation in its diversity and simplicity of execution. It contains religious verse and prose pieces such as *The Three Kings of Cologne,* verses on the Seven Penitential Psalms, a prose *Life of Adam, Do Merci bifore thi Judement,* and works associated with Richard Rolle.[12] The manuscript is simply written in single-columned pages, using a thick version of the cursive hand used by fifteenth-century professional scribes and some amateurs;[13] the text's dialect suggests a northern or East Midlands origin, although the exemplar likely originated elsewhere.[14] Like many anthologies, Harley 1704 shows no sign of supervision or correction; it appears to be the work of one or perhaps two scribes.

The poetry in this anthology is overwhelmingly of a devotional or didactic nature, packaging its moralizing themes with the forms and imagery of fashionable secular poetics. One intriguing possibility that the scribe had a complete exemplar of the *Tales* from which he copied is suggested by the rubric following the portion of the MS containing the *Prioress's Tale* (fols. 28r–31r), "alas that euer loue was synne," a line identical, but for another "alas," to D614 of the *Canterbury Tales*, in the *Prologue* to the *Wife of Bath's Tale*.[15] Conceivably the scribe, attracted by what looked like an elegant lament on one's personal sinfulness, intended to copy a portion of the *Wife of Bath's Prologue*, but changed his mind after reading further. Substituting for this canceled entry is an eleven-stanza poem, *As I fared in a frith* or *In thy most helth wisely be ware* (fols. 31r–32v), combining lapidary vocabulary with reminders on the mutability of fortune:

> As I fared in a frith
> In somer to hure fowlis sing,
> I waxe wery and slepid there-with.
> To me was sent a swete thing:
> A lady me brought a fayre gold ring,
> A blisfull worde there-it bare;
> It was this withoute lesyng,
> "In thy most helth wysely be ware!"[16]

The gold ring brought to the narrator, "pight with pereles a-boute, / With saphures and rubies set on the syde" (9–10), warns the recipient always to be ready for changes in fortune, and to govern his behavior accordingly. The poem is a Middle English variation of the French *chanson d'aventure*, using all that genre's conventions: a sylvan setting, a courtly encounter between a drowsy or fatigued narrator and a lady, exchanges of tokens. The Harley poem demonstrates not only the conventionality of this form by the fifteenth century, but its use for didactic purposes in a form at once simplistic and evocative of sophisticated poetics of the previous century.[17] The same interest in deploying fashionable poetic convention is seen in other anthology items: verses on the Seven Penitential Psalms are in ballade stanza, with added introduction and refrain, updating their earlier alternating-rhyme form.[18] The popular *Do Merci bifore thi Judement* (fols.

26v–27v), here immediately preceding the *Prioress's Tale*, uses the same octosyllabic lines as *As I fared in a frith*. *Do Merci* addresses itself to the "Maker of All Creatures" to whom "we make oure mone," offering a reminder of the world's "temptacoñ and stryfe," exhorting the reader to recognize his guilt and atone (fol. 26v, 2, 5; fol. 27v, 12, 14–17). Like the other selections in this manuscript, *Do Merci* stresses that one is never far from sin, that God's mercy is crucial, and that penitence is necessary to obtain such mercy.

The *Prioress's Tale* begins with the rubric "Alma redemptoris mater" (fol. 28r) heading a single-columned, very lightly punctuated transcription. It is not identified as being a work of Chaucer's, nor is any distinction made between prologue and tale. The text is touched with red at the beginnings of lines, but has no visual division into stanzas. Its most significant distinction from fuller versions is the collapse of the first three lines of the Prioress's prologue:

> O Lord, oure Lord, thy name how merveillous
> Is in this large world ysprad—quod she—
> For noght oonly thy laude precious . . .
>
> (B², 1643–45)

These appear as a single line. Lines 1646–56 ("For noght oonly thy laude precious / Parfourned is by men of dignitee . . .") are omitted entirely, moving immediately into the prologue's invocation to the Virgin (1657ff). A reference to the conception of Jesus is abridged, as lines 1661–62 ("Of whos vertu, whan he thyn herte lighte, / Conceyved was the Fadres sapience") are blended:

> O lord thy name how precious_
> hit is in this world how meruelous_
> O moder mayde o mayde & moder free
> O busch vnbrent brent in moyses syght
> That raueshed downe fro the deite
> Through thy humblenesse þᵉ gost in the light
> Of whos v[er]tu conceyued was the faders sapience
> Help me to tell this tale in thy reuerence
>
> (fol. 28r, 1–8)

In conjunction with the other selections in Harley 1704, the removal of the "quod she" tags de-emphasizes the tale's narrator and provenance. It continues the first-person narration and dialogue with God characterizing other selections: the "I" of *As I fared* and the Rollean tract; the "we" addressing a hopefully merciful God in *Do Merci*. The *Prioress's Tale* becomes the articulation of an unnamed narrative voice addressing God, the Virgin, and the thoughtful reader.

This pared-down opening moves almost immediately from invoking God, however, to invoking Mary as mother of God and intercessor with Christ. The prologue retains the later (B², 1674–75) comparison of the speaker to "a child of xii moneþes olde or lesse / Tha kanne vnneth ony worde expresse" (fol. 28r, 19–20), but the omitted lines have removed some of the expressions of humility and inability ("as I best kan or may," B², 1650) that link a passive—even masochistic—narrator with suckling children. Gone are the tale's first references to children as performers of the praise of God, perhaps because the scribe seeks to narrow the depiction of "parfourning." Thus the "laude" that

> not only
> Parfourned is by men of dignitee,
> But by the mouth of children thy bountee
> Parfourned is, for on the brest soukynge
> Somtyme shewen they thyn heriynge
>   (B², 1645–49)

is deferred; performance of the praise of God comes much later in an odd rendering of B², 1797–98:

> O grete god thou p[er]formest thy laude
> by mouth of innocence to here thy myght
> Thy wem of chastite this emerawde
> And eke of martyrdome the rubie bright"
>   (fol. 30r, 9–12; cf. B², 1797–1800).

"Wem"[19] is a unique reading, all other manuscripts supplying "gemme."[20] The choice of "wem" may be an error, perhaps of mistakenly substituting a similar-sounding word during copying. However, recalling that the manuscript's dialect indicates northern influence, *wem*, a northern form for "wame"—belly or abdomen—is a possibility,[21] evocative of the child's mutilated (yet chaste and theologically intact) body. Also unique is the fate of the corpse after the throat is cut; it is not "thrown" into a privy or wardrobe (B², 1762), but "drenchid" (fol. 29v, 7), drowned or even soaked,[22] a delicate detail that maintains a focus on the roughly handled body. Other alterations in the text add nuances to the depiction of the Jews not found in the canonical renderings of the *Tale*, as do several other exemplars. In Caxton's first edition and in Harley 2251, the Jews' ghetto is open at "eu[er]y ende" (fols. 28r/29r) not simply at "eyther ende" (B², 1684; Harley 2382 uses "eyther"),[23] heightening the ghetto's permeability of access

and threat. Harley 1704 also alters B², 1754, Sathanas's argument to the
Jews that the child's incessant singing is "agayn youre lawes reverence"—
here, "a yenst your[e] lawes & reu[er]ence" (fol. 29r). The frantically
searching mother "goth as she were all oute of her mynde" (fols. 29v/29r),
not "half," as elsewhere.

For the copyist of MS Harley 1704, the tale represented an opportunity
to alter the narrative and emotive focus of a Marian miracle, omitting material that portrayed its protagonist as childlike and passive. In constructing
a collection of didactic verse and prose, much of it metrically and imagistically slanted toward a less sophisticated (or an old-fashioned) readership,
the scribe increased the dramatic focus on the chorister as victim and testimony. The tale's Jews remain largely faceless antagonists, although the
scribe's alterations make them at once omnipresent and threatening, yet
easily overcome. They appear in antithesis to the power of God, temporally
potent until defeated by agents of greater spiritual and earthly strength—
God, the Virgin, and the provost who orders them to be drawn by horses
and then hanged. The child remains the unchallenged emotive center of the
tale, not one whose infantile innocence pivots with the narrator's avowed
childishness. The tale ends with a perfect fillip for the anthology's preoccupations with physical and spiritual dangers: A hopeful prayer for God's
mercy (B², 1877–79) is now filled with triumphant certainty: "ffor of his
mercy god is so merciable / On us he his gret mercy will multiplie / ffor
the reuerence of his moder marie / Amen" (fol. 31r, 23–26). Elsewhere in
the anthology, the reader is repeatedly abjured to keep the mutable nature
of the world always in mind. The *Prioress's Tale* also preaches the need
to be ever on guard against the spiritual dangers facing "we synfull folke
vnstable." The moment of death itself, as *Do Merci bifore thi Judement*
reminds its reader, may require the intercession of Jesus and his mother,
and these works urgently stress not only the nearness of death but the
equal closeness of such heavenly aid.

Harley 2251 includes the *Prioress's Tale* in a large and varied collection
of verse nearly three hundred folios long. Most of the works are by Lydgate. The glosses and marginalia of the manuscript, which was profession-
ally produced by two scribes, include items originally by John Shirley and
notations by sixteenth-century owners and readers.[24] Its richness of theme
and subject, rendered largely in rhyme royal or eight-line stanzas, defies
easy description.[25] The works by Lydgate include selections from longer
poems such as the *Testament, Fall of Princes,* and the translation of the
Secreta Secretorum by Lydgate and his follower Benedict Burgh; hymns;
didactic or moralizing pieces such as *Stans Puer ad Mensam;* occasional
works written for court occasions or noble marriages; religious or devotional poems such as *Gaude Virgo Mater Christi;* allegorical and dramatic

works, such as the *Debate between the Horse, Goose and Sheep*. (The category of "courtly" poems is represented here only by *A Gentlewoman's Lament*, on the misfortunes of loving above one's station; none of Lydgate's hagiographic poems is included). Those of Chaucer's works that are included are the *Prioress's Tale, Gentilesse*, the *ABC*, and the *Complaint against Fortune*. Burgh is also represented by a selection from his translation of the *Distichs of Cato*. And Henry Scogan, a contemporary of Chaucer's, is represented by his *Moral Ballade*.[26]

Harley 2251 is a collection representative of its era's tastes and interests. It showcases Lydgate's range as a *maker*, moving from an initial focus on Marian poems and hymns to questions of piety (*On Verbum Caro Factum Est*) and thinly veiled *Fürstenspiegel* written during the late 1420s, while Lydgate was active at the court of Henry VI (*A Prayer for King, Queen, and People, 1429*). It continues the Marian and moralizing themes on the world's and man's mutability (a concern in Lydgate's *Pageant of Knowledge*), the paradox of contraries and the harmony of things drawing to their own likenesses (*Tyed with a Lyne, A Song of Just Measure, Ryme without Accord, Every Thing to His Semblable*). Laments about the world's falseness are matched by the Virgin's lament over her son's suffering on the cross (*Quis Dabit*). Following the lengthy extract from the *Fall of Princes* is a series of pieces on education (*Stans Puer*) and what could best be described as good counsel—the dangers of women, drinking, and age. Scogan's *Moral Ballade* appears here, split into two discrete portions (fols. 156v, 179r) bracketing Burgh's *Disticha Catonis* and other gnomic works.

The first portion of the manuscript comes to a denouement with an excerpt (part 5) from Lydgate's *Testament* (fols. 40r–41r); another section of the manuscript (fols. 42r–78r) in essence begins again, mixing the Chaucerian pieces among works that mull over the transitory, even dangerously unstable, nature of the world—and the rewards meted out to the persevering faithful. Harley 2251's *Prioress's Tale* joins several poems amplifying these thematic preoccupations; that it and other Chaucerian selections appear in some proximity, although not consecutively, suggests a wish to bring together poems by Chaucer and Lydgate that are linguistically and thematically complementary. This section begins with a rhyme-royal stanza, part of a group of English verses and Latin proverbs attributed to Lydgate in Trinity College Cambridge R.3.20 and other Shirley manuscripts.[27] A single stanza at fol. 42r, beginning "Worldly worship is ioye transitory"[28] is followed by *Quis Dabit*, Chaucer's *Fortune*, and *Amor Vincit Omnia Mentiris quod Pecunia*. Very rare for this manuscript, this last poem is given a title and its author identified: "A demawnde by lydgate." Chaucer's *Gentilesse, ABC*, and Lydgate's lengthy narrative *Fabula Duorum Mercatorum* follow, with Lydgate's Marian miracle *The Legend of Dan Jose*,

Chaucer's *Prioress's Tale*, Lydgate's *Praise of St. Anne*, two unique legends of a monk of Paris and of a Wiltshire priest named Wulfryk, and one last item by Lydgate, a three-stanza rhyme-royal poem in which the infant Jesus addresses his mother as a rose.

This manuscript's *Prioress's Tale* distinctively removes the final stanza, in which Hugh of Lincoln, another child reportedly murdered by Jews in 1255,[29] is invoked:

> O yonge Hugh of Lyncoln, slayn also
> With cursed Jewes, as it is notable,
> For it is but a litel while ago,
> Preye eek for us, we synful folk unstable
> That of his mercy God so merciable
> On us his grete mercy multiplie,
> For reverence of his mooder Marie. Amen.
>   (B², 1874–80)

Without this stanza, the poem ends with the bishop's entourage weeping on the church pavement and the little clergeon entombed. The tale's "Amen" is moved up, a gesture of finality: "There he is now. god leue us for to mete · Amen" (fol. 76v, 7). This is no accidental omission on the scribe's part. The remaining space on this folio is used to copy Lydgate's verses on St. Anne, along with a Latin couplet and the final stanza of his *Tretise for Lauandres*. All are in the hand of the first scribe responsible for the tale and the other items, contemporary in appearance, and with little variation in ink density, making it likely that copying was continuous. The scribes of this collection are notable for making excisions from their exemplars, particularly in the earlier portions of the anthology. Besides the two stanzas from Scogan's *Moral Ballade* already noted, portions of Lydgate's *Pageant of Knowledge* appear in two locales: first at fol. 22v, twenty-two stanzas beginning "The world so wyde · the ayre so removable," among items concerned with the transitory nature of the world and man's own mutability; then at fol. 78v, stanzas 11–13 of those already copied, on the humors or "complexiouns," are repeated.[30] *Ryght as a Rammes Horne* (fol. 19r) is represented by only the three last stanzas most pointedly satirizing hypocrisy and other contemporary evils, with the poem's final exhortations to virtue; *Every Thing to His Semblable* (fol. 19v) omits one stanza on God's gifts and comparisons of man to angels or inanimate objects, keeping the poem's focus on the mundane and human; *A Ditty upon Haste* (fols. 26v–28r) skips the broad opening stanza, as well as seven other stanzas in this twenty-stanza poem, eliminating both repetitions of idea or example and the poet's tendency to make sweeping generalizations.

The immediate narrative effect of the canceled stanza in the *Prioress's Tale* is to diminish the accusation of Jews as murderers of Christian children found in longer versions. An intriguing change to the tale is the narrator's invocation to the Jews of the ghetto after the child is murdered: "O cursed folk · of herowdis al newe / What may youre evil trise · yow availe" (fol. 74v, 10–11; cf. B², 1764–65). *Trise* is a unique rendering of what most manuscripts copy as *entente* (or more confusedly, *tent, ente,* or in one instance, *tonge*).[31] *Trise* is an obscure word that the *OED* defines as a form of *trice*,[32] a single act of pulling or plucking, a way or course of action. Either connotation holds out interesting possibilities for the Jews of the tale, whose actions are expressed more mildly than in the language of intention. Instead, they act through a culmination of circumstance and influence. A similar shift in effect occurs at fol. 74r, 23: Sathanas "hath in Jewys · the waspis nest"—given these scribes' habits, this is likely a deliberate softening of the usual "in Jeues herte" (B², 1749).[33]

Certainly the scribes of Harley 2251 avoid the worst expressions of anti-Judaism so frequently seen in late medieval literature, for example, in popular pieces such as the *Northern Homily Passion, The Alphabet of Tales,* and other Marian legends. Even Lydgate's *To St. Robert of Bury,* a poem with clear parallels to the tale, is not included (it addresses another putative martyr as "A sowkyng child, tendre of Innocence, / So to be scourged, and naylled to a tre; / Thou myghtest crie, thou spak no woord, parde").[34] The poems that do mention Jews in this collection—Chaucer's *ABC* (fol. 49r), *The Interpretation and Virtues of the Mass* (fols. 179r–188r), *The Child Jesus to Mary the Rose* (fol. 78), *Gaude Virgo Mater Christi* (fol. 235r,v) and *Criste Qui Lux Es et Dies* (fols. 235v–236r)—refer to the passion or the crucifixion in general terms. Jews are occasionally identified as protagonists in Harley entries: *A Seying of the Nightingale* (fols. 229r–234r) once refers to Jews as Jesus' crucifiers and the recipients of his garments (ll. 253–54). In *Quis Dabit,* Mary complains once in her lament that "the Iewys do me gret vnright / To naylle my sone allas on to a tre" (ll. 23–24). The selection from Lydgate's *Testament* asks the reader to consider Jesus' suffering, in which he describes himself as being "like a lambe offred in sacryfice" by "my enemyes that do me so despice" and "paynemes," to "bysshopes" who "to my deth assented" (ll. 761, 759, 762, 780). "The Iewes which be ther cruel werre, / Han my body vnto the cros I-nayled," but nameless "Iuges" and "people . . . of fals entent" conspire against him, and "knyghtes" play dice for his clothes (ll. 812–13, 803, 806, 842). The many hymns, lyrics, and narrative poems in this anthology avoid sustained reference to Jews as the killers of Christ, or as typological agents of salvation history. It could be argued that anti-Semitic and anti-Judaic material became so internalized by the fifteenth century that the most general references (to "paynemes"

or "enemyes") would suffice. But in this manuscript, and not least in the
section in which the Chaucerian tale appears, such strongly anti-Semitic
material is largely absent.[35]

Instead, the poems falling between the *Testament* and the *Pageant of
Knowledge* excerpt at fol. 78v are connected by a host of parallels. The poem
by Lydgate plays on the courtly language and pious concerns of the Chaucerian pieces, such as *Gentilesse*, in its adjuration that

> He that intendeth · in his hert to seke
> To love the dought[er] of any womman fre
> he must of gentilles · love the moder eke
> (fol. 76v, ll. 8–10).

"A holy man / in his contemplacioun" calls on St. Anne and her daughter,
the Virgin Mary, on his deathbed; they appear and deliver him "from all
aduersite" (fol. 76v, ll. 17, 21). *A demawnde by lydgate*, which Shirley's
Ashmole 59 manuscript explains is a "a questyon, made in wyse of balade /
by þat Philosofre Lidegate daun johan"[36] debates the truth of the saying
"Amor vincit omnia." If Shirley views the poem as a philosophical debate,
Harley 2251's compiler is thinking of the tag's affinities with the description
of the Prioress in Chaucer's *General Prologue* portrait (A 162) and tale.
Chaucer's *ABC*'s invocatory rhetoric and references to Mary's "unwemmed
maidenhede" (l. 91) is reminiscent of the prologue to the *Prioress's Tale*,
with its interest in chastity. In its turn, the prayerful tone of the *Prioress's
Tale* narrator and protagonist is reminiscent of the themes of praise and
supplication found here and throughout the manuscript. Among the poems
nearest to the tale is one of the legends unique to this collection, "The
legend of the monk of Paris." In a bare twenty-eight lines, it tells the story
of a monk whose constant prayers for the souls in purgatory bear fruit
when he is attacked. He is saved when he "sayde De Profundis with entier
diligence" and the bodies of the dead rise from their graves to defend him.[37]
The pious man of *A Praise of St. Anne* also meets a crisis—his death—
with fervent prayer and steadfast devotion.

The clearest connections between Chaucer's and Lydgate's poetry made
in Harley 2251 precede the *Canterbury Tales* selection, Lydgate's *Legend of
Dan Jose*.[38] A Marian legend in rhyme royal, it is a patent imitation of the
Chaucerian poem, from its opening invocation to the Virgin as a "welle of
swetness" to its narrator's request for her aid in relating his tale.

> O Welle of swetnesse replete in euery veyne!
> That all mankynde preseruyd hast from dethe,
> And all oure ioy fro langour dydest restreyne

At thy Natiuite, O floure of Nazareth!
Whan the Holygost with his swete breth
Gan to enspyre the, as for hys chosen place,
For loue of man by influence of his grace . . . [39]

Unlike the infantilized and passive tactics of the Chaucerian tale-teller, Lydgate's narrator proclaims his "rewdenes" and insists that he will not alter a single "poynt" of his tale (ll. 14, 28), but the lengthy appeals to Mary's mercy and direction are very familiar. The story is taken from Vincent of Beauvais' *Speculum Historiale* (l. 29), of an illiterate monk who hears a bishop reciting Latin psalms in honor of Mary, and decides to learn and recite them to please the Virgin. One day, he is found dead in his cell, and the other monks are astonished to find roses growing out of his mouth, eyes, and ears:

Owte of his mowthe, a Roose boothe sprang and sprede,
Fresshe in his coloure as any floure in May,
As other tweyne out of his eyen gray
Of hys eares as many full fresshly flowryng,
That neuer yet in gardyne half so feyre gan spryng.
(ll. 73–77)

A rose in the monk's mouth is inscribed "Marie" in golden letters. The community takes the body into church "with lawde & hye solempnyte, / Beryng the corse that all men myght hit se" (ll. 83–84).

This piece clearly held great appeal for the compiler as another account of the Virgin's intercession on behalf of a devoted follower whose apparent lack of gifts marginalize him from his community. Both protagonists are illiterate (the little clergeon because of his youth); both are roused into action by overhearing the performances of the literate from whom they are separated. Chaucer's infant hears older schoolchildren singing the *Alma Redemptoris;* Lydgate's monk hears the fateful psalms "by a gardeyne as he romyd vp and doune" (l. 32) and memorizes alone and unaided (he "wrote hem in hys mynde," l. 50). The arc of the Lydgatean narrative—the discovery of the miraculously transformed body, the procession to church, the fears and the marveling of the brethren—are familiar elements in the *Prioress's Tale,* a parallel made still stronger in the tale's final stanza, omitted from Harley 2251, about Hugh of Lincoln.

The poems in this section also share a notable Boethian flavor. Lydgate's *Fabula Duorum Mercatorum* is epitomal. The story of the devoted friendship of two merchants depicts the reversals of one, who bewails the world's "woe and werynesse":

Now vp, now doun, as doth a curraunt goute,
So ar we travailed with solicitude:
The world with mowhes so weel can vs delude
(ll. 575, 579–81).

The *demawnde by lydgate* observes, "Eche man folwith his owne fantasye / Liche as it fallith in his oppinioun" (ll. 1–2), that "The world vnsure, fortune is variable" (l. 81). With Chaucer's Boethian meditations on fortune in his *Complaint*, the compilation brings the reader to realize the mutability of earthly emotions and relationships, and the deceptiveness of one's own imaginary life. Pressing the registers of courtly emotion and earthly love into the service of pious worship and philosophical reflection, it envisions a literary history of poetry in the modes and styles of Lydgate. In such a collection, Chaucer has a place not as a competitor, but as an honored literary father. Lydgate's ballade *Amor Vincit Omnia* makes an explicit echo of Chaucer's masterpiece:

Remembre Troye, of Troylus and Creside,
Eche in theyr tyme furtherd to plesaunce;
But whan fille after longe or Troylus deyde?
A false serpent of chaunge and variaunce
Withouten any lengger attendaunce
Put out Troylus, and set in Dyomede.
(ll. 17–22)

The reader is enjoined to direct his thoughts to "that gracious gostly mansion" whose heavenly precinct "excellith in beaute and brightnes / Rome, Cartage, Troye and Ilioun" (ll. 123–24). Even the poem *A Thoroughfare of Woe*, appearing much later (fol. 246v–249v), can combine both exhortations to refuse the earthly life with an admission that the "refreyd" has been taken "Of hym that was in makyng souerayne, / My mayster Chaucier, chief poete of Bretayne" (ll. 186, 187–88).

Harley 2382 demonstrates elements of manuscript production using booklets, probably by an amateur. Its idiosyncratic dialect forms and spelling suggest an East Midlands or Norfolk origin, perhaps as "a book which a country parson might have written for himself."[40] Whether or not the compiler was a Norwich chaplain named William Hert who died by 1504,[41] the manuscript was probably assembled by such a man, educated enough to compose simple Latin glosses and be comfortable with Latin scribal abbreviations. Harley 2382 contains the *Prioress's Tale* and the *Second Nun's Tale* in a single quire; when empty spaces occur between these two tales and elsewhere, they are filled up with lines from Lydgate's *Testament*, carried over from a previous booklet.[42] The contents of this modest miscellany of 128 quarto-sized leaves include Lydgate's *Life of Our Lady;* verses on the Assumption; a prayer in couplets, *Oracio ad Sanctam Mariam* (with the anaphoric tone familiar from the *Prioress's Tale:* "Mary moder, weele thu be! / Mary mayden, thenk on me!")[43]; *De Sancto Erasmo Martire;* one of three versions of the *Charter of Christ,* here called *Testamentum Christi;* and a poem known as *The Child of Bristowe.*[44] With the exception of *Bristowe,* which exists in only one variant,[45] all survive in multiple manuscript copies; some, like the *Oracio,* can be found in dozens of extant collections. This is an anthology of highly devotional works, extremely popular and frequently copied, for which exemplars would be easy to obtain; as Charles Owen observed, it was "a labor of love, evolving as the scribe worked on it."[46]

The collection also presents evidence for the use of manuscript exemplars in copying Chaucer's poetry. Manly and Rickert, describing the Chaucerian works in Harley 2382 as a "bad copy of a good MS," note the *Second Nun's Tale*'s strong Hengwrtian affiliations.[47] No such clear relationship can be found for the *Prioress's Tale,* perhaps because of textual corruption, memorial recovery, or the use of more than one exemplar representing different textual traditions.[48]

Both the *Prioress's Tale* and the *Second Nun's Tale* are lightly glossed— quite unusual in anthology copies of the *Prioress's Tale*—suggesting that these poems were valued not only for devotional purposes, but for their intellectual associations. Despite the textual affiliations of the *Second Nun's Tale* in Harley 2382 with Hengwrt, the glosses for the *Prioress's Tale* are independent of any other manuscript.[49] Ellesmere's glosses of the *Prioress's Tale,* for example, are confined to noting *auctor* (possibly for *auctoritas*)[50] at lines that may have been read as authorial or tale-teller asides, as at B², 1748 ("Oure furste foo, the serpent Sathanas") and 1797 ("O grete God, that parfournest thy laude"). The Ellesmere manuscript also supplies Latin equivalents, glossing "usure and lucre of vileynye" at 1681 as *turpe lucrum,* and defining "flesshly" as *carnaliter,* 1775.[51] Hengwrt's glosses are more complex. Besides sharing *turpe lucrum* and *carnaliter* glosses and the heading *Domine dominus noster* with Ellesmere, Hengwrt (along with several other manuscripts) includes lengthy Latin comments opposite lines 1770 and 1773, citing passages in Revelation (fol. 211v), or noting the image of the grieving Rachel (l. 1817; fol. 212r).[52] Its last gloss (fol. 212v) consists of an excerpt from John of Garland's *Stella Maris.*[53]

The Latin glosses in Harley 2382, by contrast, are brief and modest. The *Prioress's Tale* is labeled ¶*fabula monialis de S[an]c[t]a Maria,* its only indication of its derivation from the larger *Canterbury Tales.*[54] Headings are used on subsequent folios (*de S[an]c[t]a Maria*) and on an *explicit* at the tale's end. While laconic, it is perhaps unfair to label these and other glosses in the manuscript as unimportant;[55] those in the *Prioress's Tale* are unique, documenting the scribe's responses to and shaping of his text. He is interested in the narrator's invocation to the Virgin as a "bush vnbrent, brennyng in Moyses sighte" (fol. 97r, opposite l. 16), reiterating its biblical derivation: *Rubu[m] qu[em] / vid[er]at moy[ses].*[56] He notes moments of impassioned piety, such as the little clergeon's first performance of his hymn,

> "this litell child as he come to & fro
> full merily wold he synge & crie"—*Infans canebat*
> Alma rede[m]ptoris / mater
>   (fol. 98r, opposite ll. 28–30).

The narrator's subsequent invocation, "O gret god that p[er]fomed thi laude" (fol. 99r, 11), is glossed *no[ta] de laude / dei*, in contrast to El's gloss of this and B², 1748, with *auctor*. His last annotation calls attention to the clergeon's explanation of his posthumous singing—"my throte is kut vnto my nekbon[e] / said that child & as by way of kynde"—with *r[espo]nsio pu[eri] occisi* (fol. 99v, opposite ll. 20–21). The compiler is not interested in drawing attention to echoes between the two tales, such as a line in the *Second Nun's Tale* similar to the "burning bush" invocation of the *Prioress's Tale,* or other parallels between the two prologues.[57]

The glosses point to an owner anxious to use his small Latin to frame a reading experience in which the perusal of these selections are moments of scholarly study, reminders of biblical antecedents and connections to the world of intellectual argument and persuasion. He is less interested in identifying the *auctor* Chaucer than in plucking *auctoritates* from these poems—Cecilia, Ambrose, the little clergeon—and formulating their words as exemplary statements of instruction and devotional practice.[58] He is drawn to piously transcendent moments, junctures in which the evidence of speech, either the narrator's or the saintly protagonist's, takes precedence over that of the body. It is significant that his responses are not to the lurid details of the clergeon's murder, to the Jews' culpability, or to the typological functions of Jews as recalcitrant nonbelievers. His one comment on the dénouement of the child's death notes the miraculous ability to speak. He marks the child's singing only during life, after the clergeon has learned the hymn and has his heart so pierced by the "swetnesse" of "Cristes mooder that, hire to preye, / He kan nat stint of syngyng by the weye" (B², 1745–57). The singing after death that reveals his body in the Jewish ghetto and continues while the body lies in the abbey passes without comment.[59]

With the other selections in the collection, the excerpted tales in Harley 2382 form a compendium of devotional reading. The showpiece of the collection is the first item, Lydgate's lengthy *Life of Our Lady*, which takes up more than half the volume. The selections following imply an initial interest in compiling a book specifically of Marian readings; the earliest booklets contained the Lydgate *Life* and the poem on the Assumption; the two Chaucerian pieces followed in a second booklet, and the narrative on Erasmus and the *Testamentum Christi* in a third.[60] Over time, then, the collection's focus shifted from its initial Marian preoccupations to a series of narratives (the Canterbury items, the *Testamentum*, the life of Erasmus, *The Child of Bristowe*) enumerating physical trials undergone by various protagonists. Of these, the *Testamentum Christi* is a representative example. The body of Christ is imagined to be a testament, or charter: His skin is the parchment, the ink is the spittle of his tormentors, the pen the scourges. His blood is a vermilion dye. He is a book to be looked on "with gostly eyen."[61] The inclusion of the *Testament* testifies to a thematic similarity with the depiction of martyrdom. Its depiction of the body of Christ as a document to be read by his followers enshrines a notion of the body as book. Just as martyrs' bodies bear the insignia of their suffering, the little clergeon's body proclaims the Jews' crime and the additional changes wrought on it by the intercession of the Virgin. To cause injury, to destroy the body, to cause pain paradoxically writes the best language, the best orthography. The poems in this anthology offer an entire poetics of the rent body as the best means of conveying meaning to a reader. Such meaning became increasingly common in English devotional lyrics and iconography of the later Middle Ages. But the inclusion of these texts, set against the evidence supplied by the copyist's glosses, is puzzling. It reveals a tension in his work in which the parameters of a religious and didactic collection clashed, perhaps over the span of time when the book was compiled, with a fascination with the intellectual aspects of their interpretation.

•◆•

The scribes and readers who produced the manuscripts excerpting the *Prioress's Tale* had a variety of interests and motivations for their selections. For the copyist of Harley 1704, the tale offered an opportunity to rewrite the narrative and emotive focus of a miracle of the Virgin. Constructing his collection of didactic literature, much of it metrically and imagistically slanted toward a less sophisticated readership, that scribe shaped his exemplar to depict a less childlike and passive narrator in a collection suitable for less advanced adult readers. In Harley 2251, the compiler selected poems displaying fashionable, Lydgatean stanzaic and stylistic forms. The scribe of Harley 2382 wished to gloss his texts, showing a fascination with the apparatus of intellectual commentary and discussion that colored his handling of the tale.

As a work isolated from the rest of the *Canterbury Tales*, the excerpted *Prioress's Tale* enjoyed a remarkable degree of popularity throughout the fifteenth century. The anthologies discussed here demonstrate that Chaucer's work was not yet regarded as unique or better than his contemporaries'. He appears to have been valued as a poet writing in a Lydgatean style,[62] with work also suitable for anthologizing: lyrics, ballades, verse narratives capable of standing outside their original contexts—alone or in new arrangements.[63] The apparent anonymity of anthologized excerpts was probably not due to scribal ignorance. For example, Manchester Chetham's Library MS 6709, a collection of saints' lives, many by Lydgate, contains unidentified versions of the *Second Nun's Tale* and the *Prioress's Tale* taken "almost certainly" from Caxton's second edition, even preserving some of Caxton's apparatus; its *Prioress's Tale*, however, is introduced only as a *mirac[u]l[u]m*.[64] For Chaucer and for other writers popular at this time, anthologies provided contexts for literature in which authorship and the coherence provided by a work's ultimate derivation were less compelling than the impulses governing the construction of a new volume of work and new meanings for appreciating—an aesthetics of reading literature as fragment.

Within these contexts, the *Prioress's Tale* joins dozens of poems and prose tracts that dramatize (Harley 2382 calls the tale a *fabula*) the trials facing the faithful and virtuous in this world and celebrate the rewards to follow. The tale operates as an *exemplum*, trading in stock figures who function to propel the lesson toward the reader.[65] Despite the narrative's violence, Chaucer's Jews are hardly repositories for readers' fears and paranoias, but instead are the emptied-out stock villains of Marian legend, in the same way as the clergy, the Virgin, and the precocious infant. This level of idealization has particular implications for the anti-Semitic content of the *Prioress's Tale*. None of the marginal glosses in the manuscripts discussed here draws attention to the Jews or their murder of the child. (Not until Speght's second edition of 1602 is the tale termed "A Miracle of a Christian child murthered by the Iewes.")[66] That excisions of the tale consistently call attention to other portions of the poem, or remove references to Jews or the reference to the murder of Hugh of Lincoln, suggests that late medieval readers felt little reaction to the presence of Jews *as Jews* in the tale, and that anti-Semitism no longer represented, at least for this small group of readers and owners, a viable reality.

This lack of reaction needs to be placed in the context of a society in which Jews were not only unfamiliar by Chaucer's lifetime, as critics have rightly noted, but nearly unknown in the next century. After the 1290 expulsion, Jews were no longer present in England, at any rate officially. And the number of Jews present in the country by the end of the thirteenth century may have been much smaller than once believed—perhaps two or three thousand, rather than the sixteen thousand once cited (most of these would have lived in urban centers such as London, York, or Winchester).[67] Most late medieval Englishmen probably never saw a Jew. Those living in or passing through London and Bristol might conceivably see a *domus conversorum* or meet a converted Jew.[68] But outside such rare opportunities, Jews would have been even more exotic—even mythical—than the "Asye" of Chaucer's poem. And yet, as familiar: some Jews and Christians believed that an additional expulsion took place during the reign of Edward III.[69]

If Jews were absent from the everyday experience of the English, they nonetheless appeared to be familiar from late medieval texts and images. Felicity Riddy has argued that the *Prioress's Tale* and other examples of "The Marian miracle of the Chorister Killed by Jews" formed a significant part of medieval women's reading culture.[70] While surviving examples are rare, wall paintings of Jews existed, some depicted as despoilers of the Eucharist, some as murderers of Christian children.[71] Yet, the "Jews" who stare down from these paintings look very familiar. One of the most frequently cited, the depiction of William of Norwich in Holy Trinity Church, Loddon, Norfolk,[72] shows a small crowd of men surrounding the trussed-up figure of William, one of whom places a knife to his side and holds a bowl to catch his blood. Yet all are dressed in the fashions of the painting's fifteenth-century day, with no visual hints that these are any but beardless, nearly all fair, Englishmen.[73] If, as Joshua Trachtenberg famously remarked, "The only Jew whom the medieval Christian recognized was a figment of the imagination,"[74] that imagination becomes increasingly inward-turning and self-reflective in the late medieval period. The "Jew" Englishmen saw looked more and more like themselves.

Notes

1. Some recent representative studies include: Emmy Stark Zitter, "Anti-Semitism in Chaucer's *Prioress's Tale*," *Chaucer Review* 24 (1991): 277–84; Richard Rex, "Chaucer and the Jews," *Modern Language Quarterly* 45 (1984): 107–22, and "Wild Horses, Justice, and Charity in the Prioress's Tale," *Papers in Language and Literature* 22 (1986): 339–51; Wolfgang E. H. Rudat, "The *Canterbury Tales:* Anxiety Release and Wish Fulfillment," *American Imago* 35 (1978): 407–18. An important discussion of critical response remains Florence Ridley, *The Prioress and the Critics* (Berkeley: University of California Press, 1965). Sources and analogues of the tale are collected in Carleton F. Brown, *A Study of the Miracles of Our Lady,* Chaucer Society, 2d ser., 45 (London: Kegan Paul, Trench, Trübner: 1910 [for 1906]); W. F. Bryan and Germaine Dempster, eds., *Sources and Analogues of Chaucer's* Canterbury Tales (Chicago: University of Chicago Press, 1941), 447–85; Ruth Wilson Tryon, "Miracles of Our Lady in Middle English Verse," *PMLA* 38 (1923): 340–73.

2. Christopher Ricks, *T. S. Eliot and Prejudice* (London: Faber and Faber, 1988); Anthony Julius, *T. S. Eliot, Anti-Semitism, and Literary Form* (Cambridge: Cambridge University Press, 1995); for a review, see David Bradshaw, "T. S. Eliot and the Major," *TLS*, 5 July 1996, 14–16.

3. Melvin Wilk, "The T. S. Eliot Problem," *TLS*, 4 August 1996, 2; emphasis in original.

4. Daniel F. Pigg, "Refiguring Martyrdom: Chaucer's Prioress and Her Tale," *Chaucer Review* 29 (1994): 65–73, on 66.

5. Robert Worth Frank, "Miracles of the Virgin, Medieval Anti-Semitism, and the *Prioress's Tale*," in *The Wisdom of Poetry*, ed. Larry D. Benson and Siegfried Wenzel (Kalamazoo, Mich.: Medieval Institute, 1982), 177–88, on 187.

6. See, for example, Cecil Roth's "The Medieval Conception of the Jew," in *Essential Papers on Judaism and Christianity in Conflict: From Late Antiquity to the Reformation*, ed. Jeremy Cohen (New York: New York University Press, 1991), 298–309; Zefira Entin Rokéah, "The State, the Church, and the Jews in Medieval England," in *Antisemitism through the Ages*, ed. Shmuel Almog (Oxford: Pergamon Press, 1988), 99–116; Kenneth R. Stow, *Alienated Minority: The Jews of Medieval Latin Europe* (Cambridge: Harvard University Press, 1992).

7. The methodology of this study thus builds on the work in fifteenth-century reception instigated by John M. Bowers, "*The Tale of Beryn* and *The Siege of Thebes*: Alternative Ideas of *The Canterbury Tales*," *Studies in the Age of Chaucer* 7 (1985): 23–50; and Seth Lerer, *Chaucer and His Readers: Imagining the Author in Late Medieval England* (Princeton: Princeton University Press, 1993), among others.

8. *O soli diabolo priuilegiate persone! . . . Nec mouet eos quod vbique terrarum se vident esse obprobium hominum & plebis abieccionem.* Quoted in Frank, "Miracles," 186 (Latin text, 296 n. 53). The manuscript is Sidney Sussex Cambridge MS 95.

9. Julia Boffey and John J. Thompson, "Anthologies and Miscellanies: Production and Choice of Texts,"in *Book Production and Publishing in Britain, 1375–1475*, ed. Jeremy Griffiths and Derek Pearsall (Cambridge: Cambridge University Press, 1989), 279–315; P. Hardman, "A Mediaeval 'Library in Parvo,'" *Medium Aevum* 47 (1978): 262–73.

10. The tale is excerpted in five extant fifteenth-century collections: British Library MSS Harley 1704 (1460–70); Harley 2251 (post-1464); Harley 2382 (1470–1500); Bodleian Library MS Rawlinson C.86 (acaudal; post-1483); and Manchester Chetham's Library 6709 (1490). A leaf in Cambridge University Library Kk.1.3 contains lines B², 1650–1719, but has no apparent physical connection to the manuscript's other items and so does not qualify as an anthologized excerpt. See John M. Manly and Edith Rickert, eds., *The Text of the* Canterbury Tales, *Studied on the Basis of All Known Manuscripts*, 8 vols. (Chicago: University of Chicago Press, 1940), vol. 1; Daniel S. Silvia, "Some Fifteenth-Century Manuscripts of the *Canterbury Tales*," in *Chaucer and Middle English Studies in Honour of Rossell Hope Robbins*, ed. Beryl Rowland (London: Allen and Unwin, 1974), 153–63.

11. Lerer, *Chaucer and His Readers*, 85–116; Silvia, "Some Fifteenth-Century Manuscripts."

12. Harley 1704, 2251, and 2382 were examined at the British Library and on microfilm, Canterbury Tales *Manuscripts from the Manly Collection* (Chicago: University of Chicago Library, n.d.). The contents of Harley 1704 are described in Manly and

Rickert, *Text of the* Canterbury Tales, 1:238, and Carleton Brown, *A Register of Middle English Religious and Didactic Verse*, 2 vols. (Oxford: Bibliographical Society, 1916–20), 1:312.

13. See M. B. Parkes, "The Literacy of the Laity," in *Literature and Western Civilization*, vol. 2, *The Mediaeval World*, ed. David Daiches and Anthony Thorlby (London: Aldus Books, 1973), 555–77, on 563.

14. Manly and Rickert, *Text of the* Canterbury Tales, 1:240.

15. "Allas, allas! That evere love was synne! / I folwed ay myn inclinacioun / By vertu of my constellacioun; / That made me I koude noght withdrawe / My chambre of Venus from a good felawe" (D 614–18); Larry D. Benson, general editor, *The Riverside Chaucer*, 3d ed. (Boston: Houghton Mifflin, 1987). There is no notation of the line in Brown, *Register*, or in Carleton Brown and Rossell Hope Robbins, *The Index of Middle English Verse* (New York: Columbia University Press, 1943); nor do Rossell Hope Robbins and John L. Cutler list this or any similar first line (*Supplement to the Index of Middle English Verse* [Lexington: University of Kentucky Press, 1965]). Manly and Rickert, *Text of the* Canterbury Tales, 1:240, believe this manuscript to be affiliated with two shop-produced MSS of the *Tales*, McCormick (1440–60) and Bodleian Library MS Rawlinson poet. 141 (1450–60), both placing the *Wife of Bath's Prologue* and *Tale* after most of group B².

16. Fols. 31r–32v, unique to this manuscript (Brown and Robbins, *Index*, 345). Helen Estabrook Sandison, ed., *The "Chanson d'Aventure" in Middle English*, Bryn Mawr College Monographs 12 (Bryn Mawr: Bryn Mawr College, 1913), 116–18, on 116, ll. 1–8. Sandison's expansions are silently retained.

17. Sandison, *Chanson d'Aventure*, 2; on didactic *chansons* in the fifteenth century, 81–88. Many objects could participate in a dialogue with a narrator, or, as in British Library MS Cotton Cleopatra C.4, fol. 69, alone: a "voyse ryght mervelus obscure" (Sandison, 123–26); birds; letters written on a wall, ring, ribbon, robe, hood, briar-leaf, or book (82).

18. Derek Pearsall, *Old English and Middle English Poetry* (London: Routledge and Kegan Paul, 1977), 244; John J. Thompson, "Literary Associations of an Anonymous Middle English Paraphrase of Vulgate Psalm L," *Medium Aevum* 57 (1988): 38–55, on 42.

19. See *OED*, s.v. "wem"; as a noun, the word means "moral defilement, stain (of sin)" (1); "material blemish, defect, injury, or stain" (2); "hurt, harm, injury" (2b); "bodily blemish, disfigurement, or defect; also, the mark of a bodily injury, a cicatrix, a scar" (2c).

20. Manly and Rickert, *Text of the* Canterbury Tales, 7:171.

21. *OED*, s.v. "wame" 1, citing examples from 1425 on.

22. Francis Henry Stratmann, *A Middle-English Dictionary*, rev. ed. (Oxford: Oxford University Press, 1974), s.v. "drenchen."

23. Variants collated in Beverly Boyd, ed., *The Prioress's Tale*, vol. 2 of *A Variorum Edition of the Works of Geoffrey Chaucer* (Norman: University of Oklahoma Press, 1987), 129.

24. Manly and Rickert, *Text of the* Canterbury Tales, 1:242–44. The first scribe, responsible for nearly the first half of the MS's 293 folios, worked on British Library MS Add. 34360, which has many items in common with Harley 2251. See Eleanor Prescott Hammond, "Two British Museum Manuscripts (Harley 2251 and Adds.

34360)," *Anglia*, n.f., 16 (1905): 1–28; Aage Brusendorff, *The Chaucer Tradition* (1925; reprint, Oxford: Clarendon Press, 1967), 222–23.

25. A partial list of contents is provided in Brown, *Register*, 1:315–19; see also Hammond, "Two British Museum Manuscripts." On fifteenth-century attributions of Chaucer's poetry to Lydgate, see A. S. G. Edwards, "Lydgate Manuscripts: Some Directions for Future Research," in *Manuscripts and Readers in Fifteenth-Century England*, ed. Derek Pearsall (Cambridge: D. S. Brewer, 1983), 15–26, on 22; these include Rawlinson C.86, which attributes Chaucer's *Legend of Good Women* to Lydgate.

26. Pearsall, *Old English and Middle English Poetry*, 239, 195.

27. The other manuscripts are Fairfax 16, Ashmole 59, Additional 34360, Harley 116, and Harley 7578; Henry Noble MacCracken, ed., *The Minor Poems of John Lydgate*, part 2: *Secular Poems*, EETS, o.s., 192 (1934 [for 1933]; reprint, London: Oxford University Press, 1961), 708–09. Titles of Lydgate's poems will be cited according to this volume and MacCracken's *Minor Poems of John Lydgate*, part 1: *The Lydgate Canon; Religious Poems*, EETS, o.s., 107 (1911 [for 1910]; reprint, London: Oxford University Press, 1961).

28. MacCracken, *Minor Poems*, part 2: 709, l. 22.

29. Joseph Jacobs, "Little St. Hugh of Lincoln: Researches in History, Archaeology, and Legend," in *The Blood Libel Legend: A Casebook in Anti-Semitic Folklore*, ed. Alan Dundes (Madison: University of Wisconsin Press, 1991), 41–71; Gavin Langmuir, *Toward a Definition of Antisemitism* (Berkeley: University of California Press, 1990), 237–62.

30. MacCracken, *Minor Poems*, part 2: 734–38.

31. Manly and Rickert, *Text of the* Canterbury Tales, 7:167; *tonge* is used by British Library MS Sloane 1685.

32. See *OED*, s.v. "trice" sb.^{2}, fifteenth-century examples as a single, sudden pluck or pull (as in *at a trice*); sb.^{3}, "conjectured to be a variant or erroneous form of "trace" sb.^{1} in the sense of 'way, course of action.'" As a verb ("trice" v.^{1}), examples are given from the *Monk's Tale*, Hoccleve, and Lydgate.

33. It is a phrase altered in many manuscripts. Three substitute *hertes;* eight besides Harley 2251 omit *herte;* Trinity College Arch. 48 substitutes *nose.* Manly and Rickert, *Text of the* Canterbury Tales, 7:165.

34. MacCracken, *Minor Poems*, part 1: 138, ll. 11–13; it appears only in MS Laud 683.

35. For a similar discussion of varying references to Jews, see Elisa Narin van Court, "*The Siege of Jerusalem* and Augustinian Historians: Writing about Jews in Fourteenth-Century England," *Chaucer Review* 29 (1995): 227–48, on 238–39.

36. Entitled *Amor Vincit Omnia Mentiris quod Pecunia* in MacCracken, *Minor Poems*, part 2, see 744, n. 1.

37. J. O. Halliwell, *A Selection from the Minor Poems of Lydgate*, Percy Society 2 (London: C. Richards, 1840), 1–271, on 74.

38. MacCracken, *Minor Poems*, part 1: xix, item 64.

39. MacCracken, *Minor Poems*, part 1: 311, ll. 1–7; cf. B^2, 1846, "This welle of mercy" and B^2, 1660.

40. Manly and Rickert, *Text of the* Canterbury Tales, 1:247; on the identity of names in the MS and its possible ownership, see 1:248. On booklet production, see Ralph Hanna III, "Booklets in Medieval Manuscripts: Further Considerations," *Studies*

in Bibliography 39 (1986): 100–11; Pamela R. Robinson, "The 'Booklet': A Self-Contained Unit in Composite Manuscripts," *Codicologica* 3 (1980): 46–69.

41. Manly and Rickert, *Text of the* Canterbury Tales, 1:248.

42. For a full description of quiring and assembly, see Manly and Rickert, *Text of the* Canterbury Tales, 1:246.

43. Frank Allen Patterson, ed., *The Middle English Penitential Lyric* (New York: Columbia University Press, 1911), 139–41, on 139, ll. 1–2. Brown and Robbins, *Index, Supplement,* 2119.

44. *The Life of Our Lady,* Brown and Robbins, *Index, Supplement,* 2574; the verses on the Assumption, Brown and Robbins, *Index,* 2165; the life of Erasmus, *Index,* 173; *The Charter of Christ, Index, Supplement,* 4154; *The Child of Bristowe, Index, Supplement,* 1157, tells the story of a son's efforts to save his father from hell after his death (C. Horstmann, ed., *Altenglische Legenden* [Heilbronn: Gebr. Henninger, 1881], 315).

45. For the variant, see Brown and Robbins, *Index,* 1909; Cambridge University Library MS Ff.2.38, fol. 59r.

46. Owen, *Manuscripts,* 115.

47. For the contents, see Manly and Rickert, *Text of the* Canterbury Tales, 1:245; for textual affiliations, 1:247.

48. On shop production of manuscripts using different shop exemplars, see Ralph Hanna III, "The Hengwrt Manuscript and the Canon of the *Canterbury Tales,*" *English Manuscript Studies, 1100–1700* 1 (1989): 64–84, on 80, n. 7.

49. The glosses for the *Prioress's Tale* are printed and collated in Manly and Rickert, *Text of the* Canterbury Tales, 3:518–19. The *Second Nun's Tale* is at 3:521–22. See also Boyd, *Prioress's Tale,* 63.

50. Boyd, *Prioress's Tale,* 64. The *auctor* glosses at ll. 1748 and 1797 also appear in BL MS Add. 35286, and in Bodleian MS Rawlinson poet. 141 only at l. 1748 (Manly and Rickert, *Text of the* Canterbury Tales, 3:518). For a review of arguments that Chaucer wrote the Ellesmere glosses, see Susan Schibanoff, "The New Reader and Female Textuality in Two Early Commentaries on Chaucer," *Studies in the Age of Chaucer* 10 (1988): 71–108.

51. *The Ellesmere Manuscript of Chaucer's* Canterbury Tales: *A Working Facsimile,* with an introduction by Ralph Hanna III (1989; reprint, Cambridge: D. S. Brewer, 1990).

52. The Canterbury Tales: *A Facsimile and Transcription of the Hengwrt Manuscript, with Variants from the Ellesmere Manuscript,* ed. Paul G. Ruggiers (Norman: University of Oklahoma Press, 1979), fols. 210r–213r.

53. *The Stella Maris of John of Garland,* ed. Evelyn Faye Wilson (Cambridge, Mass.: Wellesley College/Mediaeval Academy of America, 1946), 130–31.

54. Eleanor Prescott Hammond, *Chaucer: A Bibliographical Manual* (New York: Macmillan, 1908), 260, n. 1.

55. Cf. Manly and Rickert, *Text of the* Canterbury Tales, 1:248.

56. Ibid., 3:519, read the last word as *Moyses,* but wear and thinning of the paper make the word now almost illegible. Abbreviations are expanded within square brackets.

57. Compare the *Prologue* to the *Second Nun's Tale,* G 36–42 and *ABC,* ll. 89–94; Benson, gen. ed., *Riverside Chaucer,* 914, n. to ll. 467–72; *Man of Law's Tale,* B 841.

58. At the beginning of the exposition of Cecilia's name in Harley 2382—intro-

duced with a large capital *F* (G 85ff.), "exposicio / no[min]is Ce / cilie" (fol. 101v)—is a far briefer variant of the citation of the *Legenda Aurea* found in allied manuscripts. Other Harley glosses show a consistent view of this saint's life as a moral *exemplum*. Lines in the *Nun's Prologue* on sloth (15–21, fol. 100v) are pointed as *accidia*. A reference to Ambrose at l. 337 is also annotated. The compiler's last gloss comes at fol. 105r, the stanza beginning with l. 337. Cecilia is completing her persuasion of her brother-in-law Tiburce, and compares the threefold Trinity to the "sapiences three"—"[m]emorie, engyn, and intellect also" (338, 339)—which the compiler glosses "versibus argumentum cecilia" (fol. 105r).

59. In the life of Saint Cecilia, the copyist takes no notice of her tortures or beheading, where her fellow Christians must mop up the copious blood with sheets (G 526ff.), or her miraculous survival for three days during which she preaches the faith, which might have suggested a parallel to the clergeon's posthumous singing. Instead, the copyist is interested in the tale's framework of argument and persuasion, with Ambrose's name an explicit reference to the narrative's intertextuality, and Cecilia's reference to the threefold nature of the mind a connection to medieval traditions of philosophy and medicine.

60. Manly and Rickert, *Text of* the Canterbury Tales, 1:246.

61. Frederick J. Furnivall, *Minor Poems of the Vernon MS*, part 2, on 637, l. 2. On literary imagery of Christ's body as a book, see Rosemary Woolf, *The English Religious Lyric in the Middle Ages* (Oxford: Clarendon Press, 1968), 212–13, on 253, n. 2.

62. Lydgate is the only author included in full-scale copies of the *Canterbury Tales*; Silvia, "Some Fifteenth-Century Manuscripts," 154.

63. On the ways in which Chaucerian lyrics were copied, see Boffey and Thompson, "Anthologies and Miscellanies," 303–04, n. 12.

64. Manly and Rickert, *Text of the* Canterbury Tales, 1:83; the rubric, fol. 170r. Chetham 6709 preserves a version of the spurious line 1807 from Caxton's first and second editions, "for which founde the chyld fresshly yette bledynge" (fol. 174r), and many other variants from the second edition; Boyd, *Prioress's Tale*, 153, l. 1807n. On print exemplars of manuscript copies, see Curt F. Bühler, "The *Fasciculus temporum* and Morgan Manuscript 801," *Speculum* 27 (1952): 178–83, and *The Fifteenth-Century Book* (Philadelphia: University of Pennsylvania Press, 1960), 34–35; N. F. Blake, "Manuscript to Print," in *Book Production and Publishing*, 403–32, on 403–04.

65. On the *exemplum* as a driving trope in late medieval literature, see Larry Scanlon, *Narrative, Authority, and Power: The Medieval Exemplum and the Chaucerian Tradition* (Cambridge: Cambridge University Press, 1994); on its persistence into early modern literature, John D. Lyons, *Exemplum: The Rhetoric of Example in Early Modern France and Italy* (Princeton: Princeton University Press, 1989), 3–34.

66. Boyd, *Prioress's Tale*, 126–27.

67. Cecil Roth believed estimates of sixteen thousand were too high (Cecil Roth, *A History of the Jews in England*, 3d ed. [Oxford: Clarendon Press, 1964], 90). Contemporary accounts listed numbers varying from 15,600 to 17,511 (James Shapiro, *Shakespeare and the Jews* [New York: Columbia University Press, 1996], 46). Examinations of poll tax records, however, have led scholars to revise the estimate of the total in England at the expulsion to 2,000–2,500 within a total population of five to six million (Shapiro, 46, drawing on Vivan D. Lipman, "The Anatomy of Medieval Anglo-Jewry," *Transactions of the Jewish Historical Society of England* 21 [1962–67]: 64–67).

68. A *domus conversorum* in London founded by Henry III contained nearly a hundred men and women in 1280 and continued to draw much smaller numbers from England and the Continent through the beginning of the seventeenth century (Roth, *History* 133–34; Michael Adler, "The History of the Domus Conversorum," in *Jews of Medieval England* [London: Edward Goldston, 1939], 277–379, on 306). See also H. E. Salter, "Was There a Domus Conversorum in Oxford?" *Miscellanies*, Jewish Historical Society of England, part 2 (1935), 29–32.

69. Roth, *History*, 132 and 282, n. 6 (a Hebrew chronicle gives the year as 1358).

70. Felicity Riddy, "'Women Talking about the Things of God': A Late Medieval Sub-culture," in *Women and Literature in Britain, 1150–1500*, ed. Carol M. Meale (Cambridge: Cambridge University Press, 1993), 104–27, on 105.

71. See Henry John Cheales, "On the Wall-Paintings in All Saints' Church, Friskney, Lincolnshire," *Archaeologia*, 2d ser., 53/2 (1893): 427–32. One panel depicts the piercing of a host by three figures, which Cheales links to English and Continental legends involving Jews. Cheales also found a similar illustration in BL MS Harley 7206, fol. 13, which he dates before 1408 (432). There are wall paintings at Chalgrove, Oxfordshire and St. Stephen's Chapel, Westminster, as well as wall tiles at Tring, now in the British Library and the Victoria and Albert Museum. All are cited by Colin Richmond, "Englishness and Medieval Anglo-Jewry," in *The Jewish Heritage in British History: Englishness and Jewishness*, ed. Tony Kuhner (London: Frank Cass, 1992), 42–59, on 56.

72. A photograph may be seen in Shapiro, *Shakespeare and the Jews*, fig. 1.

73. Compare the famous caricature on the Tallage Roll of 1233 in the Public Record Office, Exchequer of Receipt, Jews' Roll, number 87, Hilary Term, 17 Hen. III (PRO Doc. Reference E 401 [1565]), reproduced with discussion by Frank Felsenstein, "Jews and Devils: Anti-Semitic Stereotypes of Late Medieval and Renaissance England," *Journal of Literature and Theology* 4 (1989): 15–28. Its male figure has a spiked hat characteristic of medieval Jews, a beard, and a prominent nose. Other examples are reproduced in Moshe Lazar, "The Lamb and the Scapegoat," *Anti-Semitism in Times of Crisis*, ed. Sander L. Gilman and Steven T. Katz (New York: New York University Press, 1991), 38–80.

74. Joshua Trachtenberg, *The Devil and the Jews*, 2d ed., 46–47, quoted in Felsenstein, "Jews and Devils," 11.

Scribal Agendas and the Text of Chaucer's Tales in British Library MS Harley 7333

Barbara Kline

In his discussion of the scribes copying *Troilus*, Barry Windeatt argues that, "Unlike *Piers Plowman*, there is relatively little controversial material in Chaucer's work to invite participation by scribes stimulated by their own prejudices and convictions."[1] The canon scribes of British Library MS Harley 7333 may be the sole exception to the general accuracy of this statement. The variants in Harley 7333's text reveal a pattern of scribal participation in the text of Chaucer's tales spurred by the scribes' prejudices and convictions as Augustinian canons. The text of the *Canterbury Tales* in Harley 7333 provides significant examples of the scribes' critical readings. Seth Lerer has demonstrated that such scribal readings are often interpretive in his discussion of scribal strategies and rewritings.[2] But the interpretive aspect of Harley's variant and "unauthoritative" text has long been unrecognized, yet it is the perfect example of the unreliable manuscript that, instead of establishing an "authoritative" reading of a line, provides reliable evidence about Chaucer's early audience. Perhaps of even greater usefulness, in light of the recent interest in Chaucer's readers, this manuscript gives authoritative evidence of some of Chaucer's fifteenth-century readers' reactions to his tales.

Research on Chaucerian manuscripts and reception has continued to take not only scribal readings but Chaucer's contemporary and later readers into account. Seth Lerer pursued the topic in "Rewriting Chaucer: Two Fifteenth-Century Readings of the Canterbury Tales" and later in his book-length study, *Chaucer and His Readers*.[3] Scholars such as Derek Pearsall, Jeremy Griffiths, Ralph Hanna III, A. S. G. Edwards, Julia Boffey, Richard Firth Green, and Norman F. Blake have provided significant insights and information concerning fifteenth-century audiences and the manuscript tradition.[4] Paul Strohm, in *Social Chaucer*, categorized this audience, arguing that Chaucer's readers included a "core" group of friends, those "within hearing," and a larger, secondary, and later group of imagined "page turners."[5]

An intriguing glimpse of these imagined page turners is seen in MS Harley 7333. The manuscript was copied at Leicester Abbey by Augustinian canons who fit nicely within Strohm's secondary category of readers, those who read silently from the written page, yet continue to interact as audience to Chaucer's tales. Harley 7333 was compiled by these canon scribes and provides tangible evidence of their interaction with the narrative of the *Canterbury Tales*. These scribes' "rewriting" of Chaucer's tales shows not only their attention to Chaucer's subject matter, but a poetic sensibility as well. One brief example of this occurs in Harley 7333's text of the *Reeve's Tale*, where the line describing the Parson's "holy blood" is changed to his "own blood"; the line is changed but the rhyme preserved. Seth Lerer discusses a similar scribal interference in Huntington Library HM 140 and the Helmingham manuscript of the *Canterbury Tales* (now Princeton University Library MS 100).[6] Lerer argues that the scribal rewritings in these manuscripts are proof of scribal interpretation. His approach to scribal alteration is especially applicable to the scribal interaction in Harley 7333. In many ways, Harley 7333 offers an even better example for Lerer's purposes than do Huntington Library MS HM 140 and the Helmingham manuscript. Lerer argues by implication that excised portions of the *Clerk's Tale* in HM 140 are due to scribal rewriting. He shows that the scribe of Helmingham has abbreviated sections of *Melibee*, "paring down the allegorical narrative to highlight the assemblage of Prudence's sententiae."[7] He points out a scribal "strategy" in copying the text based on lacking or abbreviated portions of the narrative in *Melibee* and also in the *Pardoner's Tale*.[8] In the case of Harley 7333, there is physical evidence where lines in the tales are cancelled[9] or omitted and completely rewritten. These variants do not occur in any other extant manuscripts of the *Canterbury Tales*.

Harley 7333 provides a stronger example of the type of scribal rewriting of Chaucer that Lerer attempts to prove from HM 140 and the Helmingham manuscript.[10] The unique changes to the text of Chaucer's tales in this manuscript, most notably the scribal alteration of "cloisterer" to "canon cloisterer" in the *Miller's Tale*, provide strong physical evidence that the manuscript's textual variants are the result not of the scribes' exemplar but of their own reading of the tales. There is no extant exemplar with an edited version of the tales from which the scribes copied their text. And although exemplars are often lost, the unique pattern of ideological editing in Harley's text makes the argument for alterations based on a lost exemplar both implausible and unnecessary.

The independent editing in Harley 7333's copy of the *Canterbury Tales* is evidence not merely of variant versions of the tales, but of scribal manipulation, and attempts to limit critical interpretation, of Chaucer's tales. The Leicester Abbey scribes of Harley are not just copiers; they are readers and rewriters. Their variants are not due merely to copying a text and making predictable and unintentional scribal errors that may or may not change meaning.[11] There can be no doubt that these canon scribes read their copy of the tales, understood Chaucer's intended criticisms of the church, and set out to suppress them.

Like the scribes of *Troilus* discussed by Barry Windeatt, the canons read what they copied and made changes based on their reading.[12] They became not merely copyists but some of the earliest literary critics of Chaucer's texts. Close examination of the manuscript reveals a pattern of "censorship" in the independent scribal "editing" of the *Canterbury Tales*.[13] In a number of places a complete rewriting has taken place. Identifying the nature of these changes to the received text provides important information about the preferences of these fifteenth-century readers and their ideological objections to Chaucer's work. A brief discussion of the manuscript's production and a look at the contents of the Leicester Abbey library will provide the foundation for later discussion of the tastes and agendas of these monastic readers.

The compilation and production of Harley 7333 may be dated as early as twenty-five years after Chaucer's death (1425), with work continuing as late as 1475.[14] Compilation of the manuscript may have continued during the reigns of both Henry VI (1422–61) and Edward IV (1461–83).[15] The vellum manuscript consists of 211 folio leaves.[16] It appears from the manuscript's scribal conventions and characteristics that it was produced in a scriptorium at Leicester Abbey. The ruling of the manuscript is consistent, and it appears that it was marked for rubrication and decoration to be done by a later scribe. This was the common practice in a scriptorium where a number of scribes worked on the same text. The manuscript was compiled by at least eight scribes, all connected to the house of Augustinian canons in Leicester (St. Mary de Pratis).[17] The hands of the text are variations of Anglicana typical of much fifteenth-century book production.[18]

The contents of the manuscript provide a showcase of popular fifteenth-century texts. A partial listing of items includes the *Brut*; selections from Gower's *Confessio Amantis*; a number of Lydgate pieces, including *Verses on English Kings, St. Edmund*, and *Guy of Warwick*; a play titled "Burgh's Christmas Game"; Hoccleve's *Regement of Princes*; *Parliament of Foules*, and some of Chaucer's shorter poems such as "Truth," "Lack of Steadfastness" and "Gentilesse," each attributed to Chaucer in the manuscript.[19] The manuscript contains almost all of the *Canterbury Tales*, lacking only the *Wife of Bath's Prologue*, the *Wife of Bath's Tale* and the *Shipman's Tale*. The *Merchant's Tale* is incomplete, breaking off on fol. 72v. The *Pardoner's Tale* breaks off on fol. 97r, at l. 919 (lacking "The words of the Host").[20] The *Squire's Tale* and the *Friar's Tale* both lack lines at the beginning. The *Tale of Sir Thopas* lacks only the final line (l. 918). The manuscript is composed entirely of literary pieces, almost all written in English.[21] Only four items in the manuscript are not in the English vernacular: an untitled ballade by Charles d'Orléans (French); a poem titled "Versus Memoriales"; a piece titled "Versus" (Latin), and a work titled "Dialogue between Man and Death" (Latin, a version of a pious composition known in Latin as "Dialogus Mortis cum Homine").

The contents of Harley 7333 reflect the literary interests of the canons at Leicester Abbey, interests that are also documented in the catalogue of the abbey library. The catalogue was compiled by the abbey's precentor, William Charyte, who was also involved in the copying and editing of Harley 7333. The latest date of Charyte's "evidence books" containing the Leicester Abbey catalogue is 1502.[22] Charyte arranged the abbey's books under a variety of distinct headings, including medicine, astronomy, and philosophy. The catalogue also lists books of the Bible, psalters in French and Latin, and a large collection of the writings of St. Augustine, Hugh of St. Victor, Peter Lombard, and a number of other scholastics. M. R. James stated that nearly 250 books are listed as belonging to the library and scriptorium, and these are only a portion of the books held by the abbey.[23] He also noted that they represent "a sort of reference library, available to the members of the house, and very likely to the public also, at least to properly accredited persons."[24]

The information from Charyte's catalogue suggests that the Leicester Abbey scribes had a variety of interests, often more secular than religious in nature. They had a great number of books and resources at their disposal, an important factor in considering the canons as readers of Chaucer's tales. Harley 7333 was compiled for the Leicester Abbey scribes' reading pleasure, as is apparent from the variety of secular and religious literature, both in prose and poetry, that it contains. Chaucer's tales account for the bulk of the manuscript (fols. 37r–118r). Significantly, none of the other literature in the manuscript has the kind of extensive editing that occurs in the text of the *Canterbury Tales*; the scribes seem to have been most interested in Chaucer's tales.

The available details of book production in the fifteenth century provide, at best, only a rough sketch of publishing activity. Since the bulk of the manuscript was most likely produced under Henry VI, it is possible that some of the texts in Harley 7333 were acquired during his 1459–60 Christmas visit to Leicester Abbey. Burgh's "Christmas Game" is one example of a text that could have been obtained during the king's visit or might have been copied by the canons for his entertainment. There is evidence in Trinity College Cambridge R.3.20 that Lydgate wrote for such an occasion. In "A Christmas Mumming," Lydgate states that he wrote the piece for the entertainment of Henry VI at Hertford.[25]

Historical records of Leicestershire show that the abbey was frequented not only by the court but by many Londoners as well. The variety of texts in Harley 7333 may be due to these visits by royalty and nobles. A. I. Doyle mentions that members of a number of families, including the Beauchamps and their retainers, "moved more or less frequently between their country seats and the royal court."[26] The possibility of exemplars moving from the court to outside London would be strong in this atmosphere, which coincides with the probable time of Harley 7333's production (1425–75). This lateral exchange of literary pieces seems to best explain the variety of literature present in Harley 7333.

Harley 7333 has a long history of being ignored by textual scholars. Although a wealth of information on scribal readings and fifteenth-century literary tastes can be gleaned from it, the manuscript's text of the *Canterbury Tales* was corrupted and labeled "unauthoritative"[27] by Manly and Rickert. They designated most of the tales in Harley 7333 as part of group *b*, although group affiliations were not consistent within tales.[28] Charles Owen, in his study of the manuscripts of the *Canterbury Tales*, provides a helpful discussion of Manly and Rickert's textual groupings and the place of Harley 7333 (H³). He argues that Harley 7333 uses an exemplar "very close to the one earlier used by Cambridge Gg (if not actually the same)."[29] As Ralph Hanna III has shown, however, Manly and Rickert's technique of manuscript grouping by genetic "family" or "stemmatic recension" is not reliable.[30]

The importance of Harley 7333 in the study of *Canterbury Tales* manuscripts is not the authority of its text, but the information it provides concerning Chaucer's readers. Owen points out that Harley 7333 is representative of manuscripts of the *Canterbury Tales* in the 1460s, when "irregularity became a kind of standard among the eleven manuscripts ascribed by Manly-Rickert to that period."[31] These irregularities, viewed by earlier scholars as "textual vices," make the manuscript invaluable to more recent studies of scribal practices and to literary studies engaged in identifying and more adequately determining the reactions of Chaucer's early readers.[32] *The New Ellesmere Chaucer* is a good example of the benefits this more recent approach to manuscript studies provides. The editors' discussion of authorship and authoritative texts of Chaucer's tales does not focus on textual stemmatics and manuscript groupings, but emphasizes the combination of scribe and author in producing an "authentic" text.

Martin Stevens argues that, "in short, the editor is embraced in the term 'authorship.'"[33]

An apt example of the editor/scribe who becomes part of the author's text as it was later received is John Shirley (1366?–1456). His involvement in fifteenth-century manuscript production and specifically in Chaucer and Lydgate texts has been well documented.[34] In Harley 7333's text of the *Canterbury Tales* there are a number of Shirleian notes ("nota per Shirley") and headings that appear to be copied from an exemplar or annotated manuscript by this well known and prolific scribe. Given Leicester Abbey's extensive relations with the court and London, Shirley's exemplars would have been easily accessible to the Leicester Abbey scribes. The *incipit* to the *Canterbury Tales* in Harley 7333 (fol. 37r) is attributed to Shirley and reads as follows (I have modernized some spelling and wording for clarity):

> O ye so noble and worthy prince and princesse
> other estates or degrees whatever ye be that have
> disposition or plesaunce to read or hear the stories
> of old times past to keep you from idleness
> and sloth in eschewing other follies that might
> be cause of more harm following vouchsafe,
> I beseech you, to find your occupation in the reading
> here of the tales of Canterbury which are
> compiled in this book following first imagined,
> and made both for disport and learning
> of all those that have been gentle of birth or of condition
> by the poet laureate and most famous poet that ever
> was before him in the embellishing of our rude
> mother's English tongue. Named Geoffrey Chaucer
> of whose soul God for his mercy have pity of his
> grace. Amen

The influence of Shirley as scribe and editor of Chaucer's texts is evident throughout Harley 7333. The frequent phrase "nota per Shirley" and the Shirleian annotations become a part of the received text. In some places Shirley's glossing informs the Leicester scribes' reading of the tale. This occurs in the *Clerk's Prologue*, where Shirley makes a note comparing Lydgate's education and poverty to the Clerk's. None of the other Shirleian manuscripts has the kind of extensive editing evident in Harley's text of the *Canterbury Tales*. The manuscript also contains independent glosses for the tales, primarily the *Knight's Tale*, the *Miller's Tale*, and the *Reeve's Tale*.

Before the alterations to Harley 7333's text can be accurately identified as scribal, it is important to consider some of the details of the manuscript's production and the hands involved in copying the *Canterbury Tales*. The

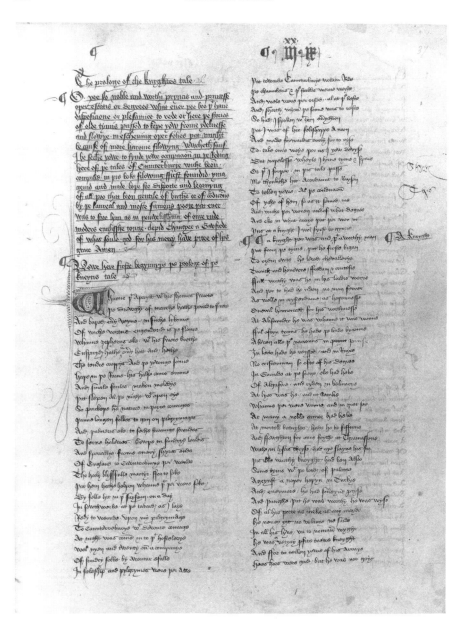

MS Harley 7333. By permission of the British Library.

text of the *Canterbury Tales* in Harley 7333 is copied by three hands, identified by Manly and Rickert as hands #1, #3, and #4.[35] Hands #1 and #3 copy most of the *Canterbury Tales* with hand #4 appearing only in a small section of the *Miller's Tale*. Hand #1 is responsible for the bulk of the texts in the manuscript, including all of the short poems attributed to Chaucer: the *Parliament of Fowls*, "The Complaint of Mars," *Anelida and Arcite*, "Lak of Stedfastnesse," "Gentilesse," "Truth," and "The Complaint of Chaucer to His Purse." The text by hand #3 is of primary interest to this discussion because of the heavy editing and censorship in its text of Chaucer's tales. Hand #3 is responsible for the first part of the *Canterbury Tales*, including the *General Prologue*, the *Knight's Tale*, the *Miller's Tale*, the *Reeve's Tale*, the *Cook's Tale*, and the *Man of Law's Tale*. Hand #3 also copied *Guy of Warwick* (fols. 33–35, with a heading attributed to John Shirley), "Evidens" by Richard Sellyng (fol. 36), and a ballade by Charles d'Orléans (fol. 36). The text of *Guy of Warwick* has a number of corrections, with words and entire lines crossed out in red ink, but not the kind of substantive changes made in hand #3's copy of the *Canterbury Tales*.

The decoration and the correction of the text in Harley 7333's copy of the tales indicate scribal supervision. In hand #3's section of Chaucer's tales the decoration is carefully planned, with red and blue ink work and headings for each tale.[36] This pattern of decoration and heavy glossing is most consistent in the *General Prologue* and the *Knight's Tale*. Later tales have less decoration and fewer notes.[37] It seems that the decorative scheme for the first part of the *Canterbury Tales* was better planned than that for the later tales. The *General Prologue* is carefully decorated with the names of the pilgrims underlined in red, and with alternating red and blue paraphs (fols. 37r–41v). There are light brown outlining marks on the pages, and in some places decoration is rubbed out, evidence that the decorative scheme was outlined and later corrected by another scribe. The *Knight's Tale* continues this pattern (fols. 41v–53v). In the *Miller's Tale* (fols. 53v–57r) there are more corrections, as well as some disruption of the earlier decorative pattern. Paraphs are missing, and words or entire sentences are crossed out and rewritten. The section of the *Canterbury Tales* copied by hand #3 has the most corrections in red ink. These types of corrections provide clear evidence of supervision in the copying and decorating of these texts. On fol. 57r, there is a change in hand; a new hand finishes the copy of the *Miller's Tale* (which ends on fol. 57r and is followed immediately by the *Reeve's Tale*). The later tales have less decoration and little or no glossing. The exception to this is the *Tale of Melibee*, where the decoration is carefully planned; this text may have been of special value to the Leicester scribes because of its subject matter.[38]

The pattern of increased decoration and glossing in the first tales is significant because it is consistent with an increased number of alterations in these earlier tales. The shift of textual type to hand #4 occurs in the *Miller's Tale* at fol. 57r and at fol. 57v, ll. 1–20. Hand #4 is tentatively identified by Manly and Rickert as the hand of William Charyte. My own comparison of the hand in this section of the tale with Charyte's hand shows a close resemblance.[39] As Charyte was precentor of Leicester Abbey and wrote a catalogue of the abbey's books, it would be natural for him to be involved in supervising the production of manuscripts such as Harley 7333.[40] This shift in hand correlates with what seems to be a shift in exemplar; there are no further Shirleian notes from this point in the manuscript to the end of the tales. Hand #3 resumes copying at fol. 57v, l. 21, and continues uninterrupted to the end of the *Man of Law's Tale* on fol. 65v.

Concomitant with the heavier correction and more careful decorative scheme found in the tales copied by hand #3 are more frequent and obvious scribal variants from the standard copies of the *Canterbury Tales*. The other two hands responsible for the text of the tales contain a number of scribal alterations and omissions but the variants are fewer than the text copied by hand #3. The Leicester Abbey scribes worked in collaboration to correct their copy and began their copy of the *Canterbury Tales* with careful corrections most likely made by a supervising scribe.[41] The first stint of tales was the most heavily "edited" by the scribes. It is important to substantiate this collaborative "editing" with textual evidence, because it is crucial to the argument that these scribes were working together as a participatory audience of Chaucer's tales. Although it is often difficult to accurately identify scribal changes to a text, in the case of Harley 7333 the changes can consistently be attributed to the canons' own agenda in reading Chaucer's narrative.

The Canon scribes' "editing" does not affect all the tales evenly. There are more changes to tales with ecclesiastics and fewer to tales not involving clerics or church doctrine. The majority of variants in both the *General Prologue* and the *Knight's Tale* are not substantive and can be identified as typical scribal errors, primarily eyeskip. The scribes are not heavy-handed in their alterations of the tales. They do not change the description of the Monk in the *General Prologue,* as one might expect. (They may not have found the Monk's tendencies toward hunting too offensive considering the Abbey's history of owning hunting hounds.)[42] The line describing the Pardoner's glaring eyes is cancelled on fol. 41r, but it would be difficult to classify this as an ideological change, since it is the only substantive change to the *General Prologue;* it is more likely an error.

The most conclusive variant in Harley 7333's text of the *Canterbury Tales* is found in the *Miller's Tale.* In contrast to the *Knight's Tale,* this tale centers on salvation history (the Flood), and ecclesiastics play a significant role in the narrative's development. The change to the text occurs where Absolon questions a canon concerning the whereabouts of John the Carpenter. Unlike the standard reading: "And axed upon cas a cloisterer" (*RC* A 3661), the Leicester Abbey scribe rewrites the line and specifies a canon cloisterer (fol. 56v): "And axed of A Chanoune cloystere." The variant reading of "cloisterer" to "canon cloisterer" is unique to Harley 7333 and is obviously the work of a Leicester Abbey canon scribe.[43] It is important to note that this cloisterer in the *Miller's Tale* is the only cleric in the tale without some moral defect. The fact that the Leicester canons added the detail of "canon" cloisterer shows their personal touch in transcribing the text. They add a detail to reflect well on their own calling.

This pattern of scribal editing continues in the *Reeve's Tale*. Harley 7333's scribe makes the Miller's wife the daughter of a *swanherd*, not the Parson, and she is brought up in a *dairy*, not a nunnery. These alterations change one of the central narrative designs of Chaucer's tale and show the canon scribes' censorship of some material in the tales to maintain a more positive image of the church. It is clear that the change is scribal. When a second reference is made to the daughter being taught in a nunnery, the reference is left unaltered. Since being taught in a dairy would make no sense, the scribe has left the word nunnery in the second reference. It would be hard to confuse the word "nonnerye" with "dayrye,"[44] so this type of error is not due to scribal miscopying. It is also unlikely that this variant came from the exemplar, as there are no other manuscripts of the *Canterbury Tales* with this variant. Clearly the scribe is rewriting portions of his copy.

The crux of Chaucer's criticism of the church in the *Reeve's Tale* rests on the Miller's wife's "holy lineage" from her father, the Parson. Since Harley 7333 makes her the daughter of a swanherd instead of the Parson, the puns on "holy blood" that appear later in the standard text would be pointless. In Harley's text these lines (*RC* A 3983–86) are completely rewritten. The reference to the Parson's holy blood (3983) is changed from "Therefore he wolde his *hooly* blood honoure," to the following: "The fore he wolde his *oune* blood honoure." The word "holy" is again omitted in the description of the Parson's regard for his holy bloodline (3986). The standard reading of line 3986 is as follows: "Though that he holy chirche sholde devore." In Harley the line is completely rewritten as follows (fol. 58r): "þough þt men þer of speke harome and loure." The line has been altered, but the scribe cleverly retains the rhyme with "devore." This is a sophisticated change to the very nature of the text's meaning, yet the scribe skillfully maintains the original sound of the poetry. The pun on "holy blood" and the illegitimacy of the Parson's daughter elicited a strong response from the Leicester Abbey scribe, who rewrites the lines and cuts all references to "holy blood" and its accompanying double entendre. There are no further alterations of this type (changing the entire meaning of a line and destroying the intended irony) in the *Reeve's Tale*. Other substantive changes to the *Reeve's Tale* are minor shifts in word order and some changes and standardization of dialect. These types of textual variants are problematic to any discussion of scribal agendas. They cannot be securely attributed to the canon scribes at Leicester, as they may have occurred in their exemplar. They should not be completely overlooked, however, since they are consistent with the canons' personalization of Chaucer's tales. A few interesting variants include a change to first person plural in the reference to the two students in the *Reeve's Tale*. The students are pleading with their warden to give them leave: "To yeve *hem* leve, but a litel stounde" (*RC* A 4007). In Harley 7333 the line reads: "Nowe geve *us* leve fir but a litell ſtounde" (fol. 58r). There are also some interesting minor changes to the text that further personalize the tale. In Harley 7333's text, fol. 58r, "the warden" is changed to "their warden" and "their corn" is changed to "oure corn." On the same folio, marks of erasure are visible where "*the* milner" is changed to "*ther* milner."

Perhaps the most significant variant in the *Reeve's Tale* is the scribe's avoidance of the word "swyve." This word is crucial to the tale's description of the students' rape of the Miller's wife and daughter. In Harley 7333 the scribe substitutes the word "dight" for "swyve" (fol. 59r) even though the rhyme scheme is disrupted: "Yf that I may þe wenche here welle I dyght." The standard reading of the line is: "If that I may, yon wenche wil I swyve" (*RC* A 4178). The following line (4179) which ends with "us" remains unchanged. The scribe again avoids the term at line 4266. Unlike "swyve," the word "dyght" is not limited in meaning only to copulation. It has a number of meanings unrelated to sex, among them arranging or preparing. It can refer to sexual intercourse, but it also means "to deal with" or "treat (in a certain way)" often with the sense of abuse or treating badly.[45] The standard reading of the line is: "swyved the milleres doghter bolt upright"(*RC* A 4266). In Harley 7333, the scribe uses the word "pleyed" (fol. 59r): "pleyed wᵗ þe mylners dowter bolt vp ryght." The use of "pleyed" is more ambiguous and not as strongly sexual as "swyve." The significance of using a less violent sexual term to describe what has happened to the Miller's wife and daughter brings up a number of interesting issues in the Leicester Abbey scribes' "editing" of their text. Perhaps the violence of the episode was offensive to the scribe. Since the precise significance in meaning between the two words in Middle English usage is unclear, it is difficult to make a conclusive argument based only on this substitution of "dight" for "swyve."[46] But it is these types of scribal alterations to Chaucer's tales that point toward complex and perhaps unresolvable questions concerning Chaucer's early readers and their reactions to, and interpretations of, this kind of sexual episode.

Following the *Reeve's Tale* there is less editing of Chaucer's tales. The lack of glossing and alterations may reflect a shift in exemplar or a scribe (perhaps Charyte) less prone to alter the text.[47] From fol. 70v through the end of the quire there are no more corrections in red ink, and from fol. 74 to the end of the *Canterbury Tales* there are virtually no further corrections. The *Merchant's Tale* breaks off at l. 2119. Although there are fewer changes to the later tales in Harley 7333's text, those that do occur are no less significant.

The pattern of scribal variants in Harley 7333's text of the *Canterbury Tales* reflects the scribes' Augustinian bent. This bias in their reading of Chaucer appears more than once in their editing of Chaucer's tales. The *Miller's Tale* is a telling example of this agenda in the canons' reading and rewriting of the text. When Nicholas plans to trick Old John, the carpenter, into believing that a second Flood is on its way, he disappears and feigns a stupor in his chamber. When the carpenter, already nervous about bad omens ("I saugh today a cors yborn to chirche"), finds Nicholas, he fears the worst. Full of superstitious fears and finding Nicholas in a stupor, the Carpenter covers all his bases, both Christian and pagan. He cries out to Saint Thomas, Saint Frideswide, Christ, the cross, and as an added protection, recites a charm against "wightes" and "elves":

'Awak, and thenk on Cristes passioun!
I crouche thee from elves and fro wightes.'
Therwith the nyght-spel seyde he anon-rightes
On foure halves of the hous aboute.
(*RC* A 3479–81)

While the reference to "wightes" and "elves" remains, the "nyght-spel" is lacking in Harley's copy of the tale. In Harley's text, the Carpenter does not recite a "nyght-spel" charm but states: "And god in þis house beo to nyghtes" (fol. 55v). The scribe has carefully rewritten the text, maintaining the rhyme, while removing the superstitious charm and substituting a prayer to God. The reason for the incantation, however, a superstitious belief in "elves and wightes" (*RC* A 7934) is not changed. This revision of the text brings up a number of questions concerning medieval superstition and the church's attitude toward it.

On the other hand, the scribal rewriting is not always consistent with greater piety. Although it is less trustworthy textual evidence, the omissions in Harley 7333's copy of the *Franklin's Tale* may offer a similar example of the Leicester Abbey scribes' unique editing agenda. In Harley's text Dorigen's contemplation of her own suicide is omitted: "I wol conclude that it is bet for me / To sleen myself than been defouled thus" (*RC* F 1422–23). Lines 1423–27 are omitted as well (fol. 85v).[48] The scribes retain the sense of the passage with its classical examples of suicides. If they censored Dorigen's conclusion that it is best to take her own life, their censorship does not disrupt the integrity of the story's narrative. They do not omit Dorigen's hope to die (fol. 85v[b]) by altering the later line, "Purposynge evere that she wolde deye" (*RC* F 1458). Without the earlier reference to her plans for suicide, the line can be read as simply a wish to die, not necessarily by her own hands. Although both suicide and magic were forbidden by the church, the theme of magic so integral to the tale is not tampered with. Only the magician's knowledge of astrology is omitted; the four lines concerning "the moones mansioun" are missing in Harley's text on fol. 85r (*RC* F 1286–89). It is interesting that the Leicester Abbey scribes would leave the tale's discussion and clear examples of magic untouched, yet edit the reference to suicide. This scribal alteration shows the difficulty in determining a consistent scribal agenda based on the canons' ideology. The scribes do not remove *all* objectionable material from Chaucer's tales. This is not the only tale dealing with magic that they leave untouched.

In the *Reeve's Tale* the Leicester Abbey scribes rewrite the narrative to change a reference to the devil "feend" (*RC* A 4288) to "goblynne." In the *Canon's Yeoman's Tale*, mention of the "feend" is again omitted. This tale is copied by a different scribe (hand #1) and shows no other independent editing, even though the tale concerns a canon's use of alchemy. At *RC* G 704–09, the Canon has fled and the Yeoman is about to begin his tale, exposing his master's "pryvetee," or forbidden experiments with alchemy. There are a number of significant omissions in the scribe's copy of this text. The Yeoman's admission that the Canon brought him into the game of alchemy is omitted (708). The Yeoman's curse directed at the Canon: "Syn he is goon, the foule feend him quelle!" is omitted (705). The Yeoman's hope for the Canon's ruin is omitted: "Er that he dye, sorwe, have he and shame!" (709). The omission of these lines condemning the Canon to the devil are especially relevant as they concern not only a canon, but most likely a canon Regular of St. Augustine, or black canon. This is the same monastic order as the canon scribes at Leicester Abbey.[49] There are clear reasons for the Leicester Abbey scribes to omit these lines. They have already shown a tendency to personalize Chaucer's tales, as the examples from the Miller's and the Reeve's tales show. What could be more personal to these scribes than an alchemist canon? One doubts that they would be tempted to make this canon a "canon cloisterer." In fact, it is surprising that the tale was not suppressed. The pattern of scribal variants in Harley 7333 reveals both a religious agenda on the part of the canons and at the same time a seemingly contradictory secular agenda of preserving material of personal interest to them as readers.

There are compelling historical reasons for the Leicester canons to be sensitive to a tale about a canon involved with alchemy.[50] In 1420 John Sadyngton was elected abbot, and in 1440 it is recorded in the *Diocesan Visitations* that Sadyngton was suspected and accused of practicing sorcery during the visitation of Bishop Alnwick.[51] This visitation in 1440 is close to the probable date that compilation of Harley 7333 began. Based on the visitation records, Leicester Abbey was scarcely free from corruption; the devotion of the canons may have been lax and their interests more secular than religious.[52] This is substantiated by the predominance of secular texts in Harley. The Leicester canons' reading interests, as shown by Charyte's catalogue, were not strictly religious. Many Austin houses during this period included not only canons regular, but canons secular, who were able to converse with the world and did not have to follow the strict rule.[53] These canons may be more representative of Chaucer's general audience than their religious calling suggests.

A possible explanation for the presence of this tale in Harley 7333 with only a few alterations is that the copyist (hand #1) was less involved in editing the text. He may have been less supervised than hand #3 of the earlier tales. Scribe #1 seems to have paid less attention to the material copied, particularly since his alterations are sporadic. But it is also possible that this was not considered a problematic text by the scribe, or that the material it contained was of interest to the scribes at Leicester Abbey, and they did not want to remove it. This would be consistent with the scribes' treatment of the *Franklin's Tale* and its central theme of magic. A tale concerning alchemy would not be inconsistent with at least one canon's interests. Since the manuscript anthology was most likely compiled only for the canons' own reading, this material would pose no threat to outside readers.

The *Canon's Yeoman's Tale*, left intact but with the reference to the fiend omitted in its prologue, provides a telling example of the scribes' double agenda. The devil is given little dramatic weight in the canons' version of Chaucer's tales. Another significant example of this type of religious editing in Harley 7333 includes the omission of the Friar's statement, in the *Summoner's Tale*, that he would pledge brotherhood with the Yeoman even if he were the devil himself (which, of course, he is [*RC* D 1527–30]). But the most telling example of the personal editing agenda of the Leicester Abbey scribes occurs in the *Summoner's Tale*. The following lines referring to those living in a convent are rewritten: "We lyve in poverte and in

abstinence, / And burell folk in richesse and despence" (RC D 1873–74). In
Harley the last line is changed to: "In poverty clennes and paciens." This
change reflects the canon scribes' subtext since poverty, chastity, and obedience, or patient endurance, were part of their rule.[54] In other tales lines
demeaning poverty have also been omitted. One example occurs in the
Clerk's Tale, where Griselda is not recognized because of her poor array (RC
E 1020); the line is omitted in Harley. In the Man of Law's Tale, lines describing the poor man's days as wicked and containing a warning are omitted: "Be war, therfore er thou come to that prikke! / If thou be povre, thy
brother hateth thee" (RC B¹ 117–20). These lines on the painfulness of
poverty are omitted in Harley, but the line damning the parsimony of the
rich man is left unaltered: "His tayl shal brennen in the gleede" (RC B¹
111). This must have been enjoyable reading for the canons. The fact that
they change the Summoner's Tale to reflect their own vows as canons shows
the personal level of their editing. They have made Chaucer's narrative
their own. In many ways this reflects the scribes' response to Chaucer's
text. They respond to the narrative play between Chaucer's pilgrims and
their tale-telling, becoming a part of the pilgrimage themselves. Their censorship of Chaucer's tales is not completely straightforward. They edit their
copy of the tales with great sophistication and exhibit a complex reading of
the text, both as canon scribes rewriting the tales to reflect better on their
church, and as interested fifteenth-century readers with their own secular
interests.

   These canon scribes also collaborated in their effort to alter the text
and rewrite it to suit their own needs. This can be seen in the many corrections to the copy of hand #3's text of the Canterbury Tales (the hand responsible for copying Fragment I [A] and Fragment II [B¹]). It appears that hand
#3's work was carefully checked against an exemplar, as there are numerous
corrections in red ink to his copy, but none of the censorship which hand
#3 freely indulges in for his portion of the tales is corrected. Hand #3's
changes to the text would be clear to the corrector, as words are crossed out
in brown ink and rewritten above the line, or next to it in the same ink.
There would be no doubt that the text had been tampered with on any close
examination against the exemplar. Therefore, the supervising scribe or corrector must have been aware and approving of these changes.

   In conjunction with the internal evidence of substantive variants, further evidence of the scribes' editing agenda can be gleaned from external
textual evidence. Offensive tales are missing, but a didactic tale like Melibee
is given special decorative attention. It is carefully written on clean pages,
with pen work on fols. 106v and 107r. One cannot argue too strongly from
negative evidence, but it is tempting to speculate that a few of the tales

lacking from Harley 7333 were excised due to the canons' continued censorship of objectionable material. The pattern of scribal censorship earlier in the tales and the physical evidence of the manuscript, including lacunae, gives some weight to such a claim. A few examples of lacunae are interesting to note. The *Shipman's Tale* is an appropriate tale for the canons to leave out, since the narrative revolves around monetary and sexual exchanges implicating a monk.[55] The end of the *Pardoner's Tale* is lacking, breaking off at *RC* C 919, a crucial point in the text where the Pardoner solicits funds from the pilgrims and incurs Harry Bailey's wrath.

Manly and Rickert note the lack of these texts and briefly state that their absence is predictable as part of the Leicester Abbey scribes' removal of unsuitable material in Chaucer's tales. They do not, however, discuss the missing end to the *Merchant's Tale* and the lack of the entire *Wife of Bath's Tale*. These lacunae are also attributable to removal of inappropriate or offensive material. The *Merchant's Tale*, like the *Pardoner's Tale*, breaks off at a telling point (*RC* E 2119), immediately before May tricks her husband in the garden while she enjoys another man in broad daylight. The text of the *Merchant's Tale* shows evidence of deliberate removal of the offensive section; stubs are visible at fol. 72v, where the following pages have been cut out of the manuscript, and an entire quire is lacking. Catchwords appear at the bottom of the page, so the rest of the tale was available to the scribe. Fragment III (Group D) follows IV (Group E, with the Squire's tale first instead of the Clerk's) in Harley's ordering of the tales, so the *Wife of Bath's Tale* should follow the *Merchant's Tale*. A complete copy of the *Merchant's Tale* is missing from the manuscript, with a quire of eight leaves lacking. Thus lacunae include the three hundred lines missing from the *Merchant's Tale* and a lacking quire that could easily have contained the missing *Wife of Bath's Prologue* and *Tale* with room to spare.

Both of these tales may have been displeasing to the canons. The *Merchant's Tale* shows a woman clearly tricking her old husband and participating in adultery, while the prologue to the *Wife of Bath's Tale* portrays a woman freely interpreting scripture and providing exegesis on a number of Pauline epistles concerning marriage and celibacy. These last two topics are especially dear to the heart of any canon. That some scribes found the Wife of Bath's "preaching" offensive is clear from Susan Schibanoff's study of glosses in the Ellesmere and Egerton manuscripts. Schibanoff argues that the Wife of Bath draws the Egerton glossator's "heaviest fire" from her "insistence on the right to interpret Scripture."[56] Again, however, it is impossible to determine whether these tales are missing from Harley 7333 because of the Leicester scribes or because of a faulty exemplar. Their absence would be consistent with the scribes' agenda as monastic readers (the

Wife of Bath's Prologue being especially offensive), and it seems reasonable to ascribe the lack of these tales to the canon scribes.

These scribes' agenda in their copying of Chaucer's tales leaves us with a number of clues about fifteenth-century readers. Since, as canons, they represent a religious audience, it is perhaps surprising that none of the bawdy bits of Chaucer's tales are tampered with, nor have all subjects hostile to church doctrine been censored. They read Chaucer's tales with distinct secular instincts. What remains consistent throughout the manuscript and is fully substantiated by the textual evidence is the Leicester Abbey scribes' interaction with their copy of the text of Chaucer's tales. The Leicester canons should be listed as another example of what Schibanoff termed the "new readers"; the more educated readers of the fourteenth and fifteenth centuries who engaged in private readings of manuscripts, leaving hints of their reactions to the text in glosses or annotations. The canon scribes of Harley 7333 are not merely copiers of Chaucer's tales, but interested readers who have left a record of their own interaction with the text, not just as glossators but as rewriters and, in some instances, censors. Perhaps these Leicester Abbey readers took the Shirleian heading that introduces Chaucer's tales in their manuscript seriously (see p. 122). They may have read the tales to avoid "greater follies" of idleness and sloth. Both are sins strongly warned against in the monastic literature. But they leave behind evidence that they read primarily for "disport" and "learning," as Shirley also advises. The editing of these scribes, as private readers, is one form of interpretation and provides a glimpse of a few fifteenth-century readers' critical responses to, and rewriting of, Chaucer's *Canterbury Tales.*[57] Since they serve as Augustinian canons, perhaps the best description of these readers' interaction with the text is that they indulge in their own responsory to Chaucer's grand lection, the *Canterbury Tales.*

Appendix: Contents of British Library MS Harley 7333

The following catalogue numbers correspond to those used in my descriptive catalogue of MS Harley 7333, which is still in progress. Entries record the item number and folios; titles; authors, if known; languages, if other than English; and first and last lines of poetry or first and last ten words of prose. Folio numbers given for items refer to the modern arabic numbering in the manuscript. The original foliation of the manuscript is in roman numerals, and all original folio numbers are given in roman numerals. Modern pages inserted at the beginning or the end of the manuscript are designated by lowercase roman numerals.

My transcriptions follow M. B. Parkes's principles of transcription (*English Cursive Hands, 1250–1500* [1969; Berkeley: University of California Press, 1980], xxviii–xxx). Punctuation and spelling are that of the manuscript. Lowercase "r" and "v" refer to the recto and verso sides of a folio; superscript "a" and "b" designate the first and second columns, respectively, of applicable texts. "Q" refers to quire.

For easier reference, I have provided line numbers from *The Riverside Chaucer* (*RC*) for items from the *Canterbury Tales*.

A complete listing of the manuscript's contents follows, with the catalogue numbers and first and last lines of texts. In the contents, "H" refers to Harley 7333. "H1" refers to the first item in the manuscript, "H2" to the second, and so on.

H1   fols. 1r^a–24v; *Chronicle of England* [also known as the *Brut*].

      [imperfect; first ten words]
      him privelyche vnto Southehampton to mete þere þe too bretherin

      [imperfect; last ten words]
      Crifte a iij c iiij [xx is written above iiij] xj wher of þe peple were
          fore agafte

      [with the catchwords]:
      7 dred þat wengeans shold come sone

H2   fols. 25r–30v; *Cato*; Burgh [Latin and English].

      [first line]
      When I aduertise in my remembraunce

      [last line]
      Noght caufith me but fympleneffe of witte

H3   fols. 30v^a–31r; *Lament of a Prisoner against Fortune*; Lydgate.

      [first line]
      FOrtune alas · alas what haue I gylt

      [last line]
      But rew on me · and helpe me when I dey

H4   fols. 31r–32v; "Pedigree of Henry VI"; Lydgate.

      [first line]
      TRouble hertis to sette in quyete

      [last line]
      Of mercy þere.for to haue a place

H5   fol. 32v[b]; "Roundel of Henry VI upon coronation"; Lydgate.

[first line]
¶Reioice ye Reames of englond 7 of ffraunce

[last line]
Stable in virtue withoute variaunce

H6   fols. 33r[a]–35v[b]; *Guy of Warwick*; Lydgate.

[First line]
Frome Criestes birthe complete nyen.C.yeere

[last line]
Put all þe wyte / ffor dulneſſe on lydegate

H7   fols. 36r[a]–36v[b]; "Evidens to beware"; Richard Sellyng.

[first line]
¶Whilist I hade youþe I wist nouȝt what it was

[last line]
Off fernyeeris Alſoo oure talis renuwe

H8   fol. 36v[b]; "Ballade"; Charles d' Orléans [French].

[first line]
¶Mon cuer chaunte Joyeuxſement

[last line]
Pour menz que soit deſoubz le firmament / Joux a la mort Je
     naynerys que lui

H9   fols. 37r[a]–41v; *General Prologue* to *The Canterbury Tales*; Chaucer.
       fols. 41v–53v; The *Knight's Prologue* and *Tale*. [The title and *incipit*
       for the *Knight's Tale* head the *General Prologue*.]

[first line]
Whanne þt Aperyll w[t] his ſhoures ſwoote

fols. 53v–57r:	*Miller's Prologue* and *Tale*.
fols. 57r–59v:	*Reeve's Prologue* and *Tale*.
fols. 59v–60r:	*Cook's Prologue* and *Tale*.
fols. 60r–65v:	*Man of Law's Prologue, Tale,* and *Epilogue*.
fols. 65v–68v:	*Squire's Tale* [acephalous, with no words of the Franklin].
fols. 68v–72v:	*Merchant's Prologue* and *Tale* [breaks off at RC 2119].
fols. 73r–74r:	*Friar's Tale* [acephalous; begins at RC 1377].
fols. 74r–77r:	*Summoner's Prologue* and *Tale*.

fols. 77r–82v: *Clerk's Prologue, Tale,* and the Host's stanza.
fols. 82v–86v: *Franklin's Prologue* and *Tale.*
fols. 86v–89r: *Second Nun's Prologue* and *Tale.*
fols. 89r–93r: *Canon's Yeoman's Prologue* and *Tale.*
fols. 93r–94r: *Physician's Tale.*
fols. 94r–97r: *Pardoner's Prologue* and *Tale* [breaks off at
                  RC 919, wanting "The Words of the Host"].
fols. 97r–98r: *Prioress's Prologue* and *Tale.*
fols. 98r–99v: Prologue and *Tale of Sir Thopas* [last lines of
                  Prologue wanting RC 709–11; tale breaks off
                  at RC 918].
fols. 99v–108r: *Tale of Melibee.*
fols. 108r–112r: *Monk's Prologue* and *Tale* [different ending].
fols. 112r–114v: *Nun's Priest's Prologue* and *Tale.*
fols. 115r–116r: *Manciple's Prologue* and *Tale.*
fols. 116r–118r: *Parson's Prologue* and *Tale.*
fols. 118v–119v: Blank.

[last line]
alle his lyf / ffor truſt wel he ſhalle yeve [RC 250.7].

H10 fols. 120r–129v; *Confessio Amantis;* Gower [seven tales
     beginning with Tereus, Book 5].

[first line]
Ther was a Rialle noble kynge

[last line]
I set nouʒt of his vizete

H11 fols. 121vᵇ–122r; "Proverbs"; Impingham [Inserted after first tale
     from *Confessio Amantis*].

[first line]
Next þe derke nyght þe gray morow

[last line]
Lo ſuche A caſt A woman can pleye /
[continuation of *Confessio Amantis* with the following title]:
The tale of conſtance what ffelle
of Enuye and of Bakbytinge (fol. 122rᵃ)

H12 fols. 129vᵇ–132v; *Parliament of Fouls;* Chaucer [gap at RC 679].
[first line]
The lyff ſo ſchort the crafte so longe to lerne.

[last line]
the next vers as I now have in mynde /

[at end an additional stanza beginning]:
maiſter gefferey Chauucers þᵗ now lith graue [fol. 132vᵇ]

H13   fols. 132vᵇ–133vᵃ; "Complaint of Mars"; Chaucer [unfinished; ends
        at fol. 133v, RC 178].

[first line]
Gladith yee floures on this morow grey

[last line]
Of lufe pley and benynge humbilneſſe /

H14   fols. 134rᵃ–135rᵇ; Anelida and Arcite; Chaucer.

[first line]
Yow fiers god of armes Mars the rede

[last line]
haþe thrilled with þe poynte of Rememberaunce /

H15   fol. 135rᵇ–135vᵇ; "Complaint against Hope"

[first line]
As that I me stoode in studeyng loo a loone

[last line]
hope in hope owte þus caus offte fooles feede

H16   fols. 135v–136rᵇ; "Complaint d'Amours"; Chaucer.

[first line begins 136rᵃ]
I which þat am þe ſorowfulleſt man

[last line]
And love hir beſt alle thowhe ſhee do me ſterue

H17   fols. 136r–146v; St. Edmund and St. Fremund; Lydgate.

[first line]
þe noble ſtory to put in rememberaunce

[last line]
And I ſuppoſe by grace which is devyne

H18   fols. 147r–147v; Complaint of Christ; Lydgate.

[first line]
Man to reforme þyne exile and þi loſſe

[last line]
þan ofte thenkynge on Criſtes paſſioun

H19   fol. 147v^a–147v^b; "Lack of Steadfastness"; Chaucer.
[first line]
Svme tyme this worlde was ſo ſtedfaſte 7 ſtable /
[last line]
And drive thi peple Ageyne to ſtedfaſtneſſe

H20   fol. 147v^b; "Gentilesse"; Chaucer.
[first line]
þe ffirſte fadir 7 fynder of gentilneſſe
[last line]
Al were he mytre / corone or dyademe /

H21   fol. 147v^b; "Truth"; Chaucer.
[first line]
Fle ffrome þe pes And dwelle w^t ſothefaſtneſſe
[last line]
And trowthe the shalle deliu*er* it is noo drede

H22   fols. 147v^b–148r^b; "Purse"; Chaucer.
[first line begins fol. 148^r]
To yowe my purſe 7 to noon' o*þer* wyght
[last line]
Haþe mynde vppon' my supplicacion'

H23   fol. 148r^a; "Two ballades"; John Halsham.
[first line]
The worlde so wyde, þe ayer so remuable
[last line]
þaughe I goo looſſe / I tyed am w^t a leygne.

H24   fol. 148r–148v; "A Dialogue between Man and Death"; Latin.
[first line]
Quis es tu quem Video hic ſtare in figura
[last line]
Que credebant ſe ſtabiles / et erant valde pravi

H25   fol. 148v; *Pilgrimage of the Soul.*
[imperfect; a section from book 1 only].
[first line]
I haue long tyme Abiden þee here old ffoule Sathanas
[last line]
wight ſkylfulle may lette me /

H26   fol. 148v; "Versus Memoriales"; Latin.
[first line]
Sunt tria que / vere faciunt / me sepe dolore [for dolere]
[last line]
Quid sisquid fucris quid eas semper memoreris

H26a   fol. 148v[b]; "Versus"; Latin.
[first line]
Da tua dum tua sunt post mortem tunc tua non sunt
[last line]
Nescio sunt cuius mea nunc cras huius 7 huius

H27   fol. 149r[a]–149v[a]; *Verses on English Kings;* Lydgate.
[first line]
Th myghty willem duke of Normandey
[last line]
Longe to reioiſe and regne here in myght

H28   fols. 149v[b]–150r[b]; *A Christmas Game;* Benedict Burgh.
[first line]
Petir petir · prynce of apoſteles alle
[last line]
Come and reioice thyne owne inheritaunce

H29   fols. 150r–203r[a]; *Gesta Romanorum.*
[first line]
Felician regnyd emperour in the cyte of Rome
[last line]
bring vs to his bliſſe That neuer ſhall myſſe Amen

H30   fols. 204r–211v; De Regimine Principum; Hoccleve [imperfect;
       introduction only].
[first line]
Mvſyng' up on the reſtlee' beſineſſe
[last line]
vn to my lorde the p⟨r⟩⟨i⟩nce thus I wrote

Notes

I wish to express special thanks to the staff at the British Library and at the Huntington
Library for making available manuscripts and plates of Chaucerian manuscripts.

1. See Barry Windeatt, "The Scribes as Chaucer's Early Critics," *Studies in the Age of Chaucer* 1 (1979): 122.

2. Seth Lerer, "Rewriting Chaucer: Two Fifteenth-Century Readings of *The Canterbury Tales*," *Viator* 19 (1988): 311–26.

3. Seth Lerer, *Chaucer and His Readers* (Princeton: Princeton University Press, 1993).

4. For a helpful overview of the topic, see Derek Pearsall, *The Canterbury Tales* (London and New York: Routledge, 1985), 1–51; *Book Production and Publishing in Britain, 1375–1475*, ed. Jeremy Griffiths and Derek Pearsall (Cambridge: Cambridge University Press, 1989); Ralph Hanna III, "(The) Editing (of) the Ellesmere Text," in *The Ellesmere Chaucer: Essays in Interpretation*, ed. Martin Stevens and Daniel Woodward (San Marino, Calif.: Huntington Library, 1995), 225–243; A. S. G. Edwards, "Chaucer From Manuscript to Print: The Social Text and the Critical Text," *Mosaic* 28 (1995): 1–12; Julia Boffey, "Proverbial Chaucer and the Chaucer Canon," *Huntington Library Quarterly* 58 (1996): 37–47; Richard Firth Green, *Poets and Princepleasers* (Toronto: University of Toronto Press, 1980); On Chaucer manuscripts see Norman F. Blake, "Editing the *Canterbury Tales:* An Overview," in *The* Canterbury Tales *Project Occasional Papers*, vol. 1, ed. Norman Blake and Peter Robinson (Oxford: Office for Humanities Communication Publications, 1993), 5–18. See also Blake's "Geoffrey Chaucer: Textual Transmission and Editing," in *Crux and Controversy in Middle English Textual Criticism*, ed. A. J. Minnis and Charlotte Brewer (Cambridge: D. S. Brewer, 1992), 19–38.

5. Paul Strohm, *Social Chaucer* (London: Harvard University Press, 1989), 47 and 51. Strohm defines the medieval use of the word *audience* as "those within hearing." In his discussion of audience in chapter 3, Strohm differentiates between the primary readers or "core" audience of Chaucer's works, comprising "social equals or near-social equals," and identifies the later audience of Chaucer's written works as "the imagined page turners." Chaucer writes for both types of audience, addressing a core circle of friends and imagining a later group of readers.

6. See Lerer, "Rewriting Chaucer."

7. Ibid., 318–319.

8. Ibid., 320–322.

9. I use the term "cancelled" in the strict textual sense of cancellation: a word or words deleted by the scribe by means of crossing them out.

10. Although Lerer does not discuss the problem, the scribal strategies he points out in his discussion of the changes in the text of *The Clerk's Tale* in HM 140 (the lack of the Petrarchan stanza and ending of the tale with the ballad "Truth") may stem from variants in the scribe's exemplar. Lerer's efforts are problematized by a manuscript anthology like HM 140, which contains numerous blank pages and might have been put together as two separate books. For a discussion of the compilation of HM 140 see C. W. Dutschke, *Guide to Medieval and Renaissance Manuscripts in the Huntington Library*, 2 vols. (San Marino: Henry E. Huntington Library and Art Gallery, 1989), 1: 189–90.

11. For a complete discussion and classification of scribal errors, see George Kane, ed., *Piers Plowman: The A Version* (Berkeley: University of California Press, 1988), 1:115–72.

12. Windeatt, "The Scribes as Chaucer's Early Critics," 122.

13. Although this term is laden with problematic meanings and political weight,

in its simplest sense of suppressing objectionable material it is appropriate to the type of alterations made in Harley 7333.

14. See Albert E. Hartung, ed., *A Manual of the Writings in Middle English, 1050–1500*, 8 vols. (New Haven: Archon Books, 1967–89), 6:[XVI]42.

15. John M. Manly and Edith Rickert, *The Text of the* Canterbury Tales, 8 vols. (Chicago: University of Chicago Press, 1940), 1:207–18. Manly and Rickert give a later date of 1450–60 for the beginning of work on the manuscript (1:209).

16. The manuscript has the largest page size of any manuscript containing the *Canterbury Tales,* as Charles Owen notes in *The Manuscripts of the* Canterbury Tales (Cambridge: D. S. Brewer, 1991), 69, n. 2. Owen gives the dimensions of the manuscript as 17.75″ x 13″.

17. Manly and Rickert, *Text of the* Canterbury Tales, 1:209, list nine scribes, but the hand they identify as #9 is very similar to #1. Based on a number of test words and the fact that the drawings of #9 also appear in the sections copied by #1, I believe that #9 is best described as a variation in the style of hand #1.

18. I follow the standard nomenclature used by M. B. Parkes in *English Cursive Book Hands, 1250–1500* (1969; Oxford: Oxford University Press, 1980), xiv–xvi.

19. See the appendix for a complete listing. The contents of Harley 7333 were first given in *A Catalogue of the Harleian Manuscripts in the British Museum* (1808), 3:526. Based on my findings, the following corrections should be made to that list: After item 4, the roundel of Henry VI should be added (fol. 32v); after 5, Sellyng's "Evidence to be ware" (fols. 36r^a–36v^b), Charles d'Orléans' "ballad" (fol. 36v^b) should be added. Item 6 is not the *Knight's Tale* but the *General Prologue* (fols. 37r–41v). Item 28 can be identified as *Confessio Amantis.* After item 28, Impingham's proverbs should be added (fols. 121v–122r). After item 35, the "Halsam Squire" (*sic*) ballads should be added (fol. 148r), as well as the "Dialogue between Man and Death" (fols. 148r–148v) and a section from the Middle English translation of Deguilleville's *Pilgrimage of the Soul* (fol. 148v).

E. P. Hammond gives a brief description of the manuscript and a list of its contents (*Chaucer: A Bibliographical Manual* [New York: Peter Smith, 1908]). Hammond identifies the Shirleian heading to the *Canterbury Tales* but does not note that, although the heading is titled as the *incipit* to the *Knight's Tale,* it actually heads the *General Prologue.* She lists the *Confessio Amantis* (unidentified in *A Catalogue of the Harleian Manuscripts in the British Museum*), and she notes the insertion of Impingham's proverbs after the *Confessio Amantis,* although she does not number the proverbs. I have given Impingham a separate item number in my catalogue. Hammond lists the ballad "by John Halsham" (21), and the "Dialogue between Man and Death" (22), but gives no other information on the pieces. She notes a "bit from Deguilleville's Pilgrimage." I have been able to identify this as the anonymous Middle English prose translation of Deguilleville's *Pilgrimage of the Soul.*

A brief description of the manuscript is also given by J. A. Herbert (*Catalogue of Romances,* vol. 3 [London: Printed by order of the Trustees of the Department of Manuscripts in the British Museum, 1910]).

Manly and Rickert give a brief description of the manuscript in *Text of the* Canterbury Tales. They group the manuscript's contents into seven books. A number of corrections should be made to their listing. They do not list the roundel to the "Pedigree of Henry VI," listing it as "Pee deugre" (book 2). In book 5 they list "three bits of Latin verse and two of English prose." These are the "Dialogue between Man and Death" and the section from the Middle English *Pilgrimage of the Soul.* Manly and Rickert do not include "Lack of Steadfastness" in their list of Chaucer's minor poems (book 5), nor do they give the minor poems in the order in which they appear in Harley 7333. Their listing should be corrected to "Lack of Steadfastness" (fol. 147v), "Gentilesse" (fol. 147v), "Truth" (fol. 147v), "Purse" (fol. 148r). Because neither E. P. Hammond, Manly and Rickert, nor Herbert identify and number every item in Harley 7333, I have devised a new numbering system to avoid confusion. These numbers correspond to those used in the descriptive catalogue of Harley 7333 and appear in the appendix.

M. C. Seymour gives a brief listing of Harley 7333's contents (*A Catalogue of Chaucer Manuscripts* [Aldershot, England: Scolar Press, 1995], 21–23). A few corrections should be made: the "Roundel of Henry VI" is not identified (fol. 32v^b), and the break in the text of the *Merchant's Tale* occurs at RC E 2119. Daniel Ransom provides corrected line numbers from Skeat's edition (review in *Studies in the Age of Chaucer* 19 [1997]: 301). The Latin verses that precede *Pilgrimage of the Soul* on fol. 148r are "A Dialogue between Man and Death" (see appendix, H24). Two items precede Lydgate's "Kings of England," and "Versus Memoriales," (see appendix: H26 and "Versus" H26a).

20. Line numbers refer to Larry Benson, general editor, *The Riverside Chaucer* (Boston: Houghton Mifflin, 1987; hereafter *RC*).

21. See Derek Pearsall's discussion of the rise of manuscripts containing English "literature" in the fifteenth century, "The Ellesmere Chaucer and Contemporary English Literary Manuscripts," in *The Ellesmere Chaucer: Essays in Interpretation*, ed. Martin Stevens and Daniel Woodward, 263–80).

22. The catalogue of Leicester Abbey was first printed by John Nichols in *The History and Antiquities of the County of Leicester* (1815; reprint, Publishers Limited, 1971), vol. 1, pt. 2: 101–8. See M. R. James for a more thorough discussion of the catalogue (*Transactions of the Leicestershire Archaeological Society*, vol. 19 [Leicester: W. Thornley and Sons, 1936–37], 121–30).

23. James, *Transactions*, 120.

24. Ibid.

25. See E. P. Hammond's publication of this poem from Trinity College Cambridge R.3.20 ("Lydgate's Mumming at Hertford," *Anglia* 22 [1899]: 365).

26. See A. I. Doyle, "English Books in and out of Court from Edward II to Henry VII," in *English Court Culture in the Later Middle Ages*, ed. V. J. Scattergood and J. W. Sherborne (London: Gerald Duckworth, 1983), 163–66. Doyle also discusses the use of abbeys for travelers going to and from London.

27. See Manly and Rickert, *Text of the* Canterbury Tales, 1:211. According to Manly and Rickert, the *Monk's Tale* is in the Bo^1 subgroup of *d*. The manuscript is paired with Cambridge University Library Gg.4.27. In section A of the tales, Harley 7333 is part of group *d* except for the *Reeve's Tale* (which Manly and Rickert identify as from a *b* manuscript). The *b* affiliation resumes in the *Miller's Tale* and continues through the tales of the Squire, Merchant, Franklin, Summoner, Clerk (sections G and C), and tales of the Prioress, Sir Thopas, and Melibee.

28. Manly and Rickert, *Text of the* Canterbury Tales, 1:211.

29. See Charles Owen, *Manuscripts*, 70. Owen argues that Harley 7333 "continues its close association with Gg through the *Nun's Priest's Tale*, the *Manciple's Tale* and the *Parson's Tale*. It thus confirms the survival of Gg-derived exemplars" (70).

30. Ralph Hanna III, "(The) Editing (of) the Ellesmere Text," 225–43. See also Martin Stevens's introduction to *The Ellesmere Chaucer*. Stevens summarizes Hanna's

argument that "Manly and Rickert's evidence is inconclusive because it was derived from too many manuscripts," and they "failed to discriminate early manuscripts from clearly derivative ones in determining authentic lections," 21–22.

31. Owen, *Manuscripts,* 65. The other manuscripts have irregular orderings of the tales. Owen lists the manuscripts with regular orderings as: Harley 7333, Royal 17, Phillips 6750, and New College D. 314.

32. For an important discussion of textual "vices," see Kate Harris, "John Gower's *Confessio Amantis:* The Virtues of Bad Texts," in *Fifteenth Century Manuscripts and Readers,* ed. Derek Pearsall (Cambridge: Cambridge University Press, 1983), 28–40.

33. Martin Stevens, introduction to *The Ellesmere Chaucer,* 22.

34. See A. I. Doyle, "More Light on John Shirley," *Medium Ævum* 30 (1961): 93–101; Seth Lerer, *Chaucer and His Readers,* 17–46; Julia Boffey and John J. Thompson, "Anthologies and Miscellanies: Production and Choice of Texts," in *Book Production,* ed. Griffiths and Pearsall, 279–315. Boffey and Thompson note that almost every manuscript in Shirley's hand was an anthology. A number of texts in Harley 7333 are common to these Shirley anthologies. Harley 7333's compilation in the fifteenth century places it within the period of rapidly growing book production in English, which, as Boffey and Thompson point out, "encouraged the compilation of various new kinds of anthologies." Unfortunately, the most recent study of Shirley was not available before the final stages of this essay. See Margaret Connolly's *John Shirley: Book Production and the Noble Household in Fifteenth-Century England* (Aldershot: Ashgate Publishing, 1998).

For a listing of Shirley manuscripts, see Jeremy Griffiths, "A Newly Identified Manuscript Inscribed by John Shirley" *The Library* 14 (1992): 83–93. See also A. S. G. Edwards, "John Shirley and the Emulation of Court Culture," in *The Court and Cultural Diversity: Selected Papers from the Eighth Triennial Congress of the International Courtly Literature Society, the Queen's University of Belfast, 26 July–1 August 1995,* ed. Evelyn Mullally and John Thompson (Suffolk, U.K.: D. S. Brewer, 1997), 309–317.

35. Manly and Rickert, *Text of the* Canterbury Tales, 1:209.

36. The decoration pattern is the same as that for *Guy of Warwick.*

37. A complete study of the glosses of the *Canterbury Tales* by Stephen B. Partridge is forthcoming. For further information on the glosses, see Partridge, "Glosses in the Manuscripts of Chaucer's *Canterbury Tales:* An Edition and Commentary" (Ph.D. diss., Harvard University, 1992).

38. The *Manciple's Tale* (fols. 115r–116r) is decorated only at the beginning and the end of the text, with no glosses. This lack of decoration continues for the *Pardoner's Tale* (fols. 94r–97r) and the *Tale of Sir Thopas* (fols. 98r–99v). The *Tale of Sir Thopas* is given only rhyme marks. The lack of decoration changes with the *Tale of Melibee* (fols. 99v–108r), which is ornamented at the beginning of the prologue and at the beginning of the tale. It seems that special effort was made to provide some decoration for this text.

39. My study is based on a comparison of the hand on fols. 57r–57v, ll. 1–20, in Harley 7333 to the plate of Charyte's hand in John Nichols, *History and Antiquities,* vol. 1, pt. 1, plate VI. A close comparison shows that the proportions of the hand and the structure of the letter forms appear to be the same as Charyte's hand.

40. See John Nichols, *History and Antiquities,* vol. 1, pt. 2: 101–8, for Charyte's catalogue of "evidence books." Nichols also gives plates of Charyte's hand: xvii, fig. 6 and 1. no. VI.

41. The supervision and corrections to the text of the tales are fewer beginning at

the point in the text where hand #3 shifts to hand #1. Hand #1 copies the *Squire's Tale* and continues to the end of the quire. Only a few corrections are made in hand #1's section of the tales. These occur in the *Merchant's Tale*, where a word is crossed out, and at fol. 69r, where a line is added in red ink (fol. 69r). There are almost no further corrections from fol. 74 in the *Friar's Tale* (fols. 73r–74r) to the end of the *Canterbury Tales*. The *Friar's Tale* has no red or blue decoration in its text, only paraphs at the tops of columns at fols. 72v and 73r. From this type of evidence it appears that the text copied by hand #3 was most heavily supervised.

    42. The Latin text of Bishop Alnwick's visitation of the Abbey in 1440 states: "Seculares seruientes domus custodiunt canes venaticos ad numerum excessiuum." See A. H. Thompson, ed., *Diocesan Visitations* (Hereford: Printed for the Lincoln Record Society by the *Hereford Times*, 1940), 184–85, and "Monasteries of Leicestershire in the Fifteenth Century" in *Transactions of the Leicester Architectural Society*, vol. 11 (Leicester: Satchell and Sons, 1855–1955), 97–103.

    43. Manly and Rickert, *Text of the* Canterbury Tales, 1:216, first identified this variant but give it scant discussion.

    44. Harley 7333, fol. 57v.

    45. See Hans Kurath et al., eds., *Middle English Dictionary* (Ann Arbor: University of Michigan, 1952–), which lists seven usages of "dighten" v., only one with a sexual meaning.

    46. The term "swyved" does occur unchanged in the last line of the *Cook's Tale*. This tale, however, was copied by hand #4, the same hand mentioned earlier (in the shift of hand at fol. 57r) which includes lines 1–20 of the *Reeve's Tale* (fol. 57v). The copy by this hand correlates with a lack of glossing, which begins with the *Reeve's Tale* and continues through the remaining tales (copied by hand #1).

    47. The hand shifts back to hand #1 at fols. 65v–72v (the *Squire's Tale* and the *Merchant's Tale*), continuing to the end of the quire. Once again, the text by hand #1 has a number of scribal corrections made in red. Missing lines are added and marked with + or + + (fol. 63v), and extraneous lines are crossed out in red ink. The *Merchant's Tale*, also copied by hand #1, has some minor changes in wording and some corrections (examples include corrections in red on fol. 69r and a word crossed out in red at fol. 70v).

    48. Manly and Rickert, *Text of the* Canterbury Tales, 6:651, list four other manuscripts that omit these lines.

    49. Marie P. Hamilton, "The Clerical Status of Chaucer's Alchemist," *Speculum* 16 (1941): 103–08. See also E. A. Webb, *The Records of St. Bartholomew's Smithfield* (Oxford: Oxford University Press, 1921), 1:20. Webb provides a description of the black cape and hood that formed the habit of the canons regular of St. Augustine. For information on monastic orders, see David Knowles, *The Religious Orders in England* (Cambridge: Cambridge University Press, 1957). For a detailed account of Augustinian canons, see A. Hamilton Thompson, *Bolton Priory*, Thoresby Society, vol. 30 (Leeds: J. Whitehead and Son, 1928).

    50. In "Chaucer's *Canterbury Tales*—Politically Corrected," above, John Bowers has explored the intriguing possibility that the canon was a "politically inconsequential" figure. In the context of Harley 7333, of course, the canon becomes tremendously important.

    51. Thompson, "Monasteries of Leicestershire," 97–103.

    52. Alnwick's visitation revealed generally poor conditions at the abbey. The number of canons was low, only fifteen being present at the visitation. The visitation record

states that the sixteenth canon was away at university. See Thompson, "Monasteris of Leicestershire." It was not uncommon for abbeys to send canons to university, another means by which canons may have gained access to texts and books.

53. Webb, *St. Bartholomew's Smithfield*, 1:19–21. Webb states that canons secular were bound by rules of obedience, poverty, and chastity but were not under as strict a rule as the monks. "Canons regular could not undertake cure of souls without dispensation as secular canons could. In individual cases they were allowed to serve the parishes impropriated to their houses which was not allowed to monks" (19). Canons secular could converse in the world and did not have to follow the rule. They had separate dwellings and a separate stipend or prebend.

54. Ibid., 19–21, 245. Webb describes the rule of the Augustinian canons and the connection of St. Bartholomew's, Smithfield, to St. Mary de Pratis.

55. See Thomas Hahn, "Money, Sexuality, Wordplay and Context in the *Shipman's Tale*," in *Chaucer in the Eighties*, ed. Julian Wasserman and Robert J. Blanch (Syracuse: Syracuse University Press, 1986), 235–49.

56. Susan Schibanoff, "The New Reader and Female Textuality in Two Early Commentaries on Chaucer," *Studies in the Age of Chaucer* 10 (1988): 71–108, on 84.

57. See Schibanoff's discussion of "new readers" and glossators of the Ellesmere and Egerton 2874 manuscripts. She provides a thorough list of recent criticism on the subject of glosses and readers' responses to Chaucer's texts ("New Reader," 71, n. 1). See also Jesse M. Gellrich, *The Idea of the Book* (Ithaca: Cornell University Press, 1985). For a thorough discussion of private readers and religious orders, see A. I. Doyle, "Publication by Members of the Religious Orders," in *Book Production*, ed. Griffiths and Pearsall, 109–23.

Geoffrey Chaucer and Other Contributors to the *Treatise on the Astrolabe*

EDGAR LAIRD

I

It has been said of modern school textbooks that they are not so much written as they are assembled. The same could be said, with the same degree of exaggeration, about medieval instructional books of the scientific and technical sort. Once a treatise of that sort has been assembled, moreover, it becomes material out of which further such treatises can be put together. Chaucer's *Treatise on the Astrolabe* (hereafter *Astrolabe*) is such an assemblage, put together out of materials that were themselves assemblages,[1] and it was, in the fifteenth and sixteenth centuries, subject to some further assembling and disassembling as it was reproduced in manuscript. If it is viewed in relation to the flux of astronomical and astrological materials of which it is a temporary coalescence, then one sees the justice in the remark by the historian of science George Sarton that "the study of Chaucer's scientific knowledge is important not so much from the point of view of the history of science stricto sensu, but rather for understanding of the popular diffusion of scientific ideas in his time."[2] Similarly, a study of the manuscripts of the *Astrolabe* is of interest as revealing something of the evolution of such ideas—particularly the astrological turn they sometimes took in the century or so following Chaucer's death.

The *Astrolabe*, as the remarks above have suggested, is a *compilatio*. The sword with which Chaucer slays envy is his accurate claim to be no more than a "compilator of the labour of olde astrologiens."[3] What we have learned in recent years about medieval compilations and compilators[4] applies in a special way to technical and scientific writing, for several reasons: the writers' recognition that scientific knowledge is cumulative; their urge to put together in one book an ordered account of what has accumulated in each scientific subject; and their recognition that the book must be usable as a reference, since memory cannot hold all. The tenth-century Arab astronomer and astrologer Alchabitius, in his prologue to a work Chaucer evidently had in mind when he wrote the *Astrolabe,* expresses his own sense of what he is doing.[5] He says that, in looking at old books assembled from ancient authors, he saw that some had not diligently sought out all things necessary to his science, some had smothered necessary things in unnecessary, and none of them had in their ordering ("in ordinatione," "in ordinacioun," "en l'ordre des choses") followed the way of discipline. Seeing these things, he says, he began to make his own book, and has collected ("collegi," "gadered togidre," "conqueulli") what was necessary for his science from the sayings of ancient authors.

Pélerin de Prusse, a contemporary of Chaucer and, like him, a compilator of a vernacular treatise on the astrolabe, makes clear in a prologue to one of his works why the role of compilator should be so necessary in science.[6] He says that life is short, science ("la science") is long, experience is fallible, and judgment is very hard, so that sages of ancient times have at the ends of their lives left their experiences, observations, and considerations for those who come after. Hence there are many books, and some are very long, involuted, and difficult to understand. Therefore he, Pélerin de Prusse, will write briefly and clearly in French a little book in which he will assemble ("assembleray") the basic and most necessary parts of his science, and he will order it ("ordeneray") so that it is complete in itself and divided ("distingué") into appropriate parts. He will add nothing of his own ("ne metray de nouvel ne de ma teste") except his understanding of the books of his masters. Of the astrolabe in particular he says that the uses and considerations associated with it are so many that no one, no matter how learned and well informed, can hold them in memory; he has, therefore, briefly and simply put the essential ones into a little book and divided it into numbered chapters, which he lists in order.[7]

The remarks just cited sketch an idea of scientific writing according to which virtually everyone who made an instructional scientific book—including Chaucer, his authorities before him, and the scribes after him—was to some degree or in some sense a compilator. This is almost necessarily the case in the science of the Middle Ages, when so much attention was paid to literal books, as opposed to the "book of nature." Chaucer, for his part, shows an awareness that there is already much astrolabe material in existence, as when he speaks in his prologue of "any commune tretys of the Astrelabie" and "any tretis of the Astrelabie that I have seyn." He proposes to select and collect "certain conclusions" into one treatise because the conclusions pertaining to the astrolabe are not borne in ordinary memory—"ben unknowe parfitly to any mortal man in this regioun." His business, therefore, is to compile a treatise from this existing material, excerpting matter according to his own method and dividing and disposing it according to his own sense of order, after the approved fashion of a scientific compilator.[8]

There is a treatise on the stars (not an astrolabe treatise) dating from shortly before Chaucer's time that quite clearly specifies its character as a scientific compilation and thereby establishes the nature of the class of writing to which, I think, the *Astrolabe* belongs. It is the *Compilatio de Astrorum Scientia*, written by Leopold of Austria in the late thirteenth century and translated into French as *Li Compilacions de le sciences des estoiles* sometime before 1324.[9] In his prologue Leopold says that after long study in astronomy he intends to put what he has learned on the subject into a single volume. He knows of no one who has put the whole science into one book. Therefore, he says, students of the subject are required to search in many books. He remarks that it is not important to name an author of the book because the authors have been not one but many, and he is their faithful and diligent compilator ("je suis leurs loiaus compileres et diligens"). He spells out the titles he intends the sections of his work to have and the order in which they are to appear. Having thus identified his matter and ordered his treatise, he insists that certain requirements be carried out, the first of which is that each proposition begin at the beginning of a line so that it can be numbered in the margin for ease and precision of reference. By laying out his matter, his *ordinatio*, and even the *mis en page*, Leopold has done all a compilator can do to protect the integrity of his compilation.

Sometimes scribes respected that integrity, and sometimes they either did not or were unable to do so, employing what stratagems they could. The scribe of one manuscript of the *Compilacions*, apparently working from an incomplete exemplar, reproduces the first eight of the ten sections described in the prologue.[10] The eighth section of Leopold's work is then followed by a French version of book 7 of Haly Abenragel's *De Judiciis Astrorum*, under the title "The Ninth Part of the Complete Book of Judgment of Stars." Is it called the ninth part because it follows the eighth part of the *Compilacions*? Apparently it is, and it looks very much as if the scribe were exercising some of the prerogative of a compilator, if only in attempting to execute the *ordinatio* of the earlier compilator, Leopold. Lacking Leopold's ninth part, the scribe supplies an equivalent excerpted from Haly Abenragel. At this point, however, his resources fail him and, having written out the substitute from Haly, he concludes, "Explicit. And cursed be the thief who stole the end of part 9 and all of part 10."[11] One final point to make about this copy of the *Compilacions* is that it occurs in an "omnibus on astrology and astronomy for some prospective client or for some rich collector."[12]

2

I have briefly described Leopold's compilation and its presentation in manuscript because of analogies with the *Astrolabe*. Chaucer's compilation too lacks the concluding sections, though in Chaucer's case the lack is apparently caused by his never having got around to writing them. He did, however, represent in his prologue that essential part of a compilator's work, an *ordinatio*, in the form of an outline or table of contents describing the five parts into which his treatise was to be divided and arranged.[13] The same urge for completeness that shows itself at the end of the Leopold manuscript appears to have led some copyists of the *Astrolabe* to make various gestures, at least, toward completing Chaucer's work.

Indeed, such is the variety among the thirty-two extant *Astrolabe* manuscripts that it has been difficult to decide just how far toward completion Chaucer actually progressed. Modern editors all agree that, of the five parts projected in the prologue, Chaucer wrote all of part 1 and a portion (probably most) of part 2. He may also have produced some fragments intended for incorporation into later parts. In the now standard numbering of the subsections ("conclusions") in part 2, there are forty that are generally believed to be by Chaucer (2.1–40) and six that are possibly his (2.41–46). Skeat's reflections in the matter have largely established its terms.[14] He accepts as authentic 2.1–40 (on astronomy), 2.41–43 (on taking altitudes of terrestrial objects), and 2.44–45 (on the mean position of planets). He regards 2.46 (on tides) as "possibly" Chaucer's, and he (like his successors) rejects as "certainly spurious" a group of conclusions that he nevertheless prints under the numbers 2.41a–42b. P. Pintelon rejects 2.46 on stylistic grounds and doubts Chaucer's authorship of the other conclusions after 2.40, saying that "the exact point where Chaucer left off his work is still an unsolved little problem."[15] John Fisher prints only conclusions 1–40 of part 2, on the grounds that 2.41–46 are not present in "good" manuscripts and are not in Chaucer's style; he adds that 2.44–45 indicate a very late date (1397), whereas he regards the remainder of the treatise as belonging to 1391.[16] John Reidy, in the *Riverside Chaucer*, accepts 2.1–40 as Chaucer's but doubts the authenticity of the rest, generally on stylistic grounds, though he also notes the scanty manuscript attestation for 2.46 (only two manuscripts) and the late date indicated in 2.44–45.[17] J. D. North, in a substantial study of the *Astrolabe* in *Chaucer's Universe*, casts doubt on all the later conclusions by noting, as the text's editors had also done, that the manuscripts begin to break down in quality and consistency at 2.39.[18] We are, then, given 2.1–40 as authentically Chaucer's, 2.41–46 as supplementary propositions of doubtful authenticity, and 2.41a–42b as spurious conclusions.

In about 1555, one Walter Stevins produced a manuscript of the *Astrolabe* after having, as he says in a preface, "happenyd to looke vpon the conclusions of the astrelabie compiled by Geffray Chawcer and founde the same corrupte."[19] Stevins altered Chaucer's compilation and in the preface made explicit the types of alteration he made. He has, he says,

1. Worked by altering individual words ("amendinge of verie manie wordes")
2. Reordered conclusions ("displaced some conclusions")
3. Completed or augmented the sense ("wheare the sentences weare imperfite, I haue supplied and filled them")
4. Altered whole conclusions ("altered them")
5. Rejected and omitted ("cleane put oute") conclusions found to be false, namely 2.17, 2.35, and 2.40.[20]

All of these procedures—plus one other, the wholesale addition of large elements—had been employed by Chaucer in compiling his treatise from his chief source, the *Compositio et Operatio Astrolabii* attributed to Messahalla.[21] All or some of them were employed on the *Astrolabe* by various copyists before Stevins, resulting in the scribal, editorial, and compilator-like variations that are the object of the present study.

Three special factors would have encouraged copyists of the *Astrolabe* to alter their texts. First is the incomplete state of Chaucer's compilation, obvious at 2.40, where it breaks off in midsentence. Three manuscripts (including that of Stevins) simply complete the sentence, grammatically if not very intelligibly.[22] Second is the fragmentary state of portions of part 2. Part 2 is not continuous throughout but, especially toward the end, contains breaks and gaps, bits that are not clearly related to the whole and were probably written on separate sheets and possibly by someone other than Chaucer.[23] The third factor is Chaucer's table of contents in his prologue, which encourages a copyist to add to the incomplete treatise (as did the scribe of the incomplete Leopold text, described above) or reorder or dispose it so that it will do, or seem to do, what the prologue promises. The simplest expedient for achieving this end is the one adopted by the scribe of Oxford's MS Bodley 68, who divides the unfinished text that came to him into five parts, marked by the section titles indicated in Chaucer's prologue.[24] The text thus divided has, of course, only the appearance of completeness, for its five parts do not contain what the prologue says they will.

What the prologue promises is something in the nature of an "omnibus on astronomy and astrology" similar to the manuscript mentioned above containing Leopold's *Compilacions*. In Chaucer's case the first two parts were to be a compilation on the astrolabe, and the three unwritten parts were to be on related matters. As North succinctly says, "All the signs are that the *Treatise on the Astrolabe* is an unfinished part of an unfinished compendium."[25]

The prologue says that part 1 will do what in fact it does do, which is to "reherse the figures and the membres of thyn Astrelabie." *Reherse*, as used by a compilator, means to repeat without personal intervention.[26] This part, accordingly, Chaucer took fairly directly from a brief description of the astrolabe that introduces part 2 of the Messahalla treatise (part 2 being the *operatio* portion of the *Compositio et Operatio Astrolabii*).[27] There is comparatively little variation among manuscripts in part 1 of the *Astrolabe*, just as there is comparatively little variation between part 1 of the *Astrolabe* and its source. A good description is a good description, and there is no reason to change it if that is what one wants.

The second part, says the prologue, will teach the use, the "verrey practik," of the astrolabe. It too is compiled chiefly from the *operatio* (headed *Practica astrolabii*) of the Messahalla treatise. But in part 2 Chaucer does not follow his source so closely as he did in part 1. He begins submissively enough by translating Messahalla's first three conclusions, but then he begins adding, omitting, and reordering. By the time he leaves off he seems to have ceased continuous, ordered composition and begun to write separate fragments, some taken from Messahalla and some not. Such procedures on Chaucer's part give scribes scope for their own additions and variations. For what we do *not* have in part 2 is Chaucer's *ordinatio* in the sense of a complete, author-revised text in the form in which he wants it to circulate.[28]

Part 3 was supposed to contain tables of various sorts, rather breathlessly listed as if in a jacket blurb: "diverse tables of longitudes and latitudes of sterres fixe for the Astrelabie, and tables of the declinacions of the sonne, and tables of longitudes of citees and townes; and tables as well for the governaunce of a clokke, as for to fynde the altitude meridian; and many anothir notable conclusioun after the kalenders of the reverent clerkes, Frere J. Somer and Frere N. Lenne." One gets the impression that Chaucer had not completely thought out just what tables he would include but intended to have lots of them—of diverse sorts.[29] Looking at the contents of various manuscripts in which the *Astrolabe* occurs, one is struck by how many of the materials in them are tabular and fall more or less within the confines of Chaucer's list.[30] Almost certainly the presence of these materials in the manuscripts is due not directly to Chaucer but to others, who may have seen them as called for in Chaucer's prologue. Chaucer identifies precisely only two of the works he intended for inclusion in part 3, the *kalendaria* of Somer and Lynn, and both occur in manuscripts containing the *Astrolabe*.[31] Chaucer's idea of putting together an omnibus including both an astrolabe treatise and astronomical tables is not unreasonable since, as he points out, one can achieve greater range and accuracy of results by supplementing an astrolabe with tables (Prologue, ll. 73–76; part 2.32). Nor is his idea particularly innovative, for Latin astrolabe treatises are frequently placed in the same manuscripts with tables.[32] Makers of manuscript books might have put Chaucer's treatise together with tables even if his prologue had not suggested the plan, but the suggestion certainly encouraged them to do so.

Chaucer's description of part 4 as a "theorike to declare the moevynge of the celestiall bodies" is not definitive, but it irresistibly suggests writings of a known type, the *theoricae planetarum*.[33] These are simplified (but still highly sophisticated and rather demanding) accounts of Ptolemaic astronomy, without the proofs Ptolemy gives in the *Almagest*. Latin examples of the type from the thirteenth century include the *Theorica Planetarum Gerardi* and Campanus of Novara's *Theorica Planetarum*.[34] An English example probably contemporary with Chaucer, called the "Newe Theorike of Planetis . . . after the Almagest of Ptholome," is preserved in Trinity College Cambridge MS 0.5.26, a compendium of astronomical and astrological works in English.[35] Much of the matter and method of *theoricae* are compiled in book 2 of Leopold's *Compilacions*.[36] Chaucer's plan is not especially innovative, for *theoricae* were often bound with astrolabe treatises.[37]

No full-fledged "theorike" to explain the motions of planets occurs in extant *Astrolabe* manuscripts, but it is possible that Chaucer or the scribes were, in the non-astrolabic sections of the *Astrolabe* now designated 2.40, 44, and 45, making progress toward supplying other materials promised for part 4. Besides a "theorike" of celestial motion, part 4 was to contain a table of lunar motion and a "canon," or set of directions for using a table, not only for tracing the moon's motion in the zodiac but also for determining what zodiacal point it rises with and as well for determining the rising of any planet according to its latitude from the ecliptic. Conclusion 2.40 answers this last element of the description exactly: it is a canon by which "To knowe with which degre of the zodiac that eny planete ascendith on the orizonte, wheither so that his latitude be north or south [of the ecliptic]." It is not compiled from Chaucer's usual sources, Messahalla or Sacrobosco, and opinion on its Chaucerian authenticity is generally but not entirely positive. Conclusions 2.44 and 45, both having to do with the "mene mote" (mean position) of planets, constitute a floating fragment. So clearly do they answer to the character of the promised part 4 that Skeat considered printing them not as 2.44 and 45 but as 4.1 and 2. He restrained himself only because he did not wish to impose his views.[38] The 2.44–45 fragment occurs in only half a dozen manuscripts, of which Bodleian MS Digby 72 (from which both Skeat and F. N. Robinson take it, since it is not in their base texts) is especially interesting in this connection. Not only does it contain the conclusions that are, as Skeat writes, "alternate *canons,* shewing how certain tables may be used"; it also contains the tables themselves—tables of roots of "mene motes" for the "anni collecti" mentioned in 2.44, as well as tables of latitudes of planets and tables for finding the moon's place.[39] In the same manuscript there is a variant in Chaucer's prologue that calls added attention to the tables by noting that an astrolabe yields results less precise than the minutes and seconds of an arc as "calkelid in tabelis of astronomye."[40] The standard modern numbering of conclusions tends to obscure the progress that Chaucer and the scribes were making toward fulfilling the prologue's "bihestes" concerning part 4.

The canons of part 4 are, in and of themselves, purely astronomical. But with their emphasis on locating planets in relation to the ascendant, they lend themselves to astrological purposes, for as Chaucer says in 2.4, "The ascendent sothly, as wel in alle nativities as in questions and eleccions of tymes, is a thing which that these astrologiens gretly observen." It was reasonable therefore for Chaucer to ordain part 5 as a treatment of astrology proper. This last part too was to be a compilation, "an introductorie, after the statutes of oure doctours" containing "a gret part of the general rewles of theorik in astrologie." Its astrological character is certified by the promise to include tables of "equaciouns of houses" and "dignitees of planetes," both of which are strictly astrological in function.

Chaucer did not identify sources for the fifth part, but given that he was working as a compilator of *auctoritates,* both modern readers and early scribes can make certain speculations. One shrewd modern guess is that in planning his "introductorie" to astrology Chaucer was thinking of a work mentioned above, Alchabitius's *Introductorius ad Magisterium in Judiciis Astronomie,* one of the principal authorities for medieval astrology and, as Alchabitius says in his prologue, itself compiled from the statutes of men learned in astrology.[41] Alchabitius's treatise was translated into English in the late fourteenth century as the "Introductorie of the Domes of Sterris" and put into French slightly earlier as the "Introductoires de maistrie des jugemens des estoiles." It does not occur in any extant *Astrolabe* manuscript, but chapter 5 of *Chaucer's Universe* is largely based on the English version and thus can, as North says, "stand proxy for that unwritten fifth part of the *Treatise.*"[42] Chaucer may have intended to include in part 5 tables derived from those of John Walter or Nicholas of Lynn.[43] Nicholas's *Kalendarium,* mentioned above in connection with the planned part 3 of the *Astrolabe,* also contains tables exactly fitting Chaucer's description of tables for part 5: "tables of dignitees of planetes" and "tables of equaciouns of houses after the latitude of Oxenford." Directions for using an astrolabe for equation of houses are given in *Astrolabe* 2.36 and 37, which, as Skeat says, on account of their astrological character "ought certainly to have been reserved for Part V."[44] In a number of manuscripts they are in fact reserved for the end of the treatise. Among the remarks above are modern speculations on how the *Astrolabe* might have looked if it had been completed. The early scribes, too, had their ideas about how, for the sake of completeness, the treatise might be shaped or eked out or both. They employ every sort of textual manipulation by way of moving toward a product that from one point of view or another will seem more satisfactory. They add conclusions to the *Astrolabe* (or suppress ones deemed inappropriate), they reorder conclusions, and they join the *Astrolabe* in manuscripts with other works that seem to belong with it. In some cases they appear to be guided by Chaucer's plans as announced in his prologue; in others their decisions can be better explained as attempts to modify the treatise in ways that would appeal in general to the interests of the times.[45]

By way of substantive additions there are, besides the "Spurious Propositions" printed by Skeat, five others that have not in modern times been seriously considered as Chaucer's but that occur in one or more manuscripts. The first, in the order of the text, is an insertion between 2.2 and 2.3 that occurs in five manuscripts.[46] It is, Skeat says, "clearly spurious" and "merely repeats section 1" of part 2.[47] It specifies that one is to use the "rewle" or pointer on the "baksyde" of the astrolabe. In this it differs from its source (Messahalla), which does not so specify, but agrees with *Astrolabe* 2.1 and also with its French counterpart, Pélerin de Prusse's *Practique de astrolabe* 2.1, and with a marginal note in a copy of Messahalla that Chaucer may have seen.[48] Early Islamic astrolabes had but one rule, but by Chaucer's time European astrolabes had one on each side, so that it was necessary to say which one was referred to.[49] We seem to be seeing, then, a common response by compilers, scribes, and readers to developments in the instrument.

A second addition, attested in one manuscript, occurs after 2.3 and describes the locating in the sky of stars marked on the astrolabe.[50] One should note concerning this conclusion that, like so many of the genuinely Chaucerian ones, it is taken from Messahalla. This is fairly clearly a case of a scribe's improving a writer's text by going to the writer's source.[51] There are some signs that he tried to imitate Chaucer's diction, as in the use of "Nota" to claim the reader's attention and the use of the unusual but Chaucerian word "mediacioun," which an early reader saw a need to gloss in the margin as "mene."[52] I should interject here that although John Selden, in 1621, was the first commentator to notice Chaucer's dependence on Messahalla, from the beginning some scribes would have been well aware of it.[53] The rather clumsy and ill-attested floating fragment on taking terrestrial altitudes (2.41–43), which is also based on Messahalla, may be another scribal mining of Chaucer's source.

The three remaining additions under consideration are intrinsically and in their relation to other astrolabe material the most interesting. They all concern the equation of houses—the dividing of the sky into astrologically significant segments based on the ascendant. One of them is a curiosity, a Latin guide to equating houses, occurring in a manuscript of the sixteenth century.[54] It is attributed to Chaucer in the manuscript and is based on *Astrolabe* 2.36 and 37. Another addition is a second version, in English, of 2.36, in a late fifteenth-century manuscript.[55] The third is an addition to (as if it were a continuation of) 2.36, occurring in an important early manuscript, Brussels, Royal Library, 4862/69.[56]

It begins, "Now for the more openere declaracioun I wole make an ensaumple to the forseide conclusioun of the equacioun of houses." There follows an establishment of houses, taking 6° Leo as ascendant. None of this is in any other extant copy of the *Astrolabe*, nor is it in 2.37 of the Messahalla treatise, which is the source of *Astrolabe* 2.36. An equivalent to it, however, appears in the *Livret de eleccions*, written in 1360 for Charles, Duke of Normandy, later Charles V of France, by Pélerin de Prusse. In that treatise, too, it follows a translation of Messahalla's 2.37. In other words, both the Brussels manuscript and the *Livret* subjoin to a translation from Messahalla a worked example of how to take the next step in casting a horoscope. Pélerin supplies an actual horoscope chart carrying the data from the worked example. The Brussels addition to the *Astrolabe* ends with the words, "right as ye may se by this present figure next folowyng." The figure is absent, but there can be no doubt that the blank space that follows was to have been filled by a horoscope chart.[57]

Pélerin, in his astrolabe treatise (*Practique* 2.16), retranslates the same passage from Messahalla, prefacing it with the remark that "This chapter is the most important and the most often necessary of all the chapters." He thus expresses the view that in the end the main use of the astrolabe is in casting horoscopes. The same view is expressed in relation to Chaucer's *Astrolabe* by John Lydgate,[58] who represents Chaucer as a compiler of elements ("Sette hem in Ordre with ther divisions") into a treatise that proceeds through equation of houses ("Domefying of sondry mansyons") to pronouncement in judicial astrology ("Iuggement"). A comparable view must have been held by those scribes who added horoscope-casting instructions to the *Astrolabe*, as well as by those who reordered the *Astrolabe* with an astrological end in view.

The order of conclusions now accepted as standard was established by the early, good manuscripts that modern editors have used as base texts.[59] There are, however, substantial groups of manuscripts that shift the conclusions about in various ways. The shift that is most obviously considered and deliberate is the one that places discussions of equation of houses at the end of the treatise. Chaucer himself had, it should be recalled, written not one but two conclusions on this astrologically essential topic, 2.36 and 2.37. Five manuscripts, ranging from very early to late fifteenth century, place them at the end of the treatise, following both the supplementary propositions and the spurious conclusions.[60] Three others, one early and the others later, simply omit everything after 2.36 (including 2.37, perhaps because, since both 2.36 and 2.37 give methods for equating houses, 2.37 was felt to be redundant).[61] The earliest of these bears the word "Explicit" after 2.36, and one of the others is even more emphatically conclusive in adding the remark, "To fynde the house by the astrolaby, that is wretin suffyse. Explicit tractatus astrolabii secundum chausers, factus filio sue ludowyco."[62] The point seems to be that what has been written is sufficient in connection with the astrolabe, though more could be said about the equation of houses in general. Indeed, the topic is a complicated one about which a great deal could be written (and was, during the later Middle Ages). North notes that in dealing with it Chaucer showed that he "had mastered what was one of the most difficult of the arts of the astrologer."[63] By deferring it until the end, the scribes are treating it as the goal toward which proficiency with an astrolabe is directed. They are also concurring with the prologue's plan to treat astrology last. Notwithstanding Chaucer's denial, in *Astrolabe* 2.4, of "feith" in and "knowing" of the "judicial matere" of astrology that he calls "rytes of payens," he nevertheless left plenty of scope, even inducement, for exploring and expanding on astrology by anyone who cared to see his work carried forward. These reorderings of conclusions, as well as the additions mentioned earlier, show that some people did want it carried forward.

3

Makers of manuscript books affected the shape and meaning of the *Astrolabe* through binding it with other works into one book. In a few cases the act seems more or less random, as in Cambridge University Library MS Dd.3.53, where the *Astrolabe* is bound with French and Latin grants, warrants, and Signet letters.[64] But in most cases the bringing together appears to be genuinely a "contextualizing gesture,"[65] as when the *Astrolabe* is made to form a part of a compendium or omnibus on astronomy and astrology. We have already alluded to manuscripts in which the *Astrolabe* is placed alongside tables of various sorts, and there are several in which it is joined with other treatises on the stars.[66] One of them, Trinity College,

Cambridge, MS R. 15.18, is an especially instructive example of what became of the *Astrolabe*, of how it came to be seen and contextualized, toward the end of the fifteenth century.[67]

The first item in the manuscript is a not quite complete copy of the *Astrolabe* as Chaucer left it, ending with 2.34 (preceded, however, by 2.36). The second item is a table like the one described in Chaucer's prologue as showing "longitudes and latitudes of sterres fix," although, with seventy-two stars, it is somewhat longer than the usual list provided, as Chaucer says, "for the Astrelabie." Third is a table of equations of houses of the sort Chaucer planned to include in part 5 of his treatise. The tables locate, as was common, the beginnings of only six of the twelve houses (1, 2, 3, and 10, 11, 12) because, as Chaucer explains in 2.36 and 37, the opposites or "naders" of these are the beginnings of the other six, which are therefore, in effect, already located by locating the first six.

The next item is a canon for using planetary tables called "effymeridis." The item is actually an English translation of a Latin canon for the *Ephemerides* of Regiomontanus that appeared in the edition of that work published in 1474 by Regiomontanus's press.[68] The Trinity *Astrolabe* manuscript does *not* contain Regiomontanus's tables, which run to 896 printed pages and at least 300,000 numbers.[69] The canon's opening sentence asserts, however, that its application is general: "We shal shortly manyfest and shew the use of every effymeridis." (The Latin reads "ephemeridis cuiuslibet" but refers only to the ephemerides in the volume in which the canon appears.) At the end is an announcement that further widens its appeal: "And from thence it shall playnly be declared in a propre commentory what commodityse these thingis gyfe to the monyfold experimentis and exercise of lechis or fecisions and the generacion of man and his revolucion; also the mutabill operacions of the ayr to the begynnyngis of workis, which among the pepill be calde eleccions or chosyngis of the best, and to other civyle and necessary usis innumerabill."

No such commentary was forthcoming in the *Ephemerides* of 1474, but in 1481 Erhardt Ratdolt published an edition of the *Ephemerides* to which he added an astrological exposition by one Bartholomaus Mariensüss that served the purpose.[70] That exposition, translated into English, is the next, and in relation to the *Astrolabe* the most interesting, of the items with which the *Astrolabe* is bound in the Trinity manuscript.[71] The first chapter cites "Aristotill . . . in hys boke *Of Generacion and Corrupcion*" for the authoritative doctrine, fundamental to medieval astrology, of the obliquity of the zodiac as "causyng alteracion in these inferiors."[72] Chapter 2 explains the "signes mobil, fix, and comune," repeating in simple terms the doctrines that it says are "sufficiently expowned in Alkabicis [Alchabitius's] *Introductarie.*" Chapter 3 is "an exposicion of the xii signes" that incorporates something the *Astrolabe* promised to include in part 5, a table of dignities of planets, in which numbers indicate the amount of influence each planet has in each sign. Chapter 5 is on "aspectis of the planetis." Chapter 6 "remembrith of the sterrys fixed" and includes another item the *Astrolabe* promised, a table of fixed stars, this one giving not only locations but also astrological significances of stars. Chapter 7 prognosticates "alteracion of the ayre" by bringing together the previously described effects of signs, planets, aspects, and their relations. With this discussion, the English tract ends, although the Latin has two more chapters and three canons on bloodletting, giving medicines, and planting trees, vines, and seeds.

Mariensüss's Latin treatise had a varied history that touches the *Astrolabe* only slightly. It began by promoting sales of Regiomontanus's *Ephemerides* through increasing its appeal to people interested in astrology. It accompanied the *Ephemerides* when that more respectable work was used in monasteries and when it was studied in universities (by, among others, Copernicus).[73] It was carried on voyages of discovery by mariners, including Christopher Columbus, who navigated by Regiomontanus's tables and forecast weather by Mariensüss's astrology.[74] In the mid-sixteenth century it was again translated into English and published as *The pryncyples of Astronamye, the whiche diligently perscrutyd is in maner a pronosticacyon to the worldes end, compyled by Andrew Boord, of physick doctor.*[75] In 1990 Borde's translation was modernized and printed and is on sale in bookstores specializing in the occult.[76] This history suggests the work's character, but it is also true that its character changes with its historical setting. The original Latin version, as part of the *Ephemerides*, explained the astrological uses to which astronomical tables could be put. The English version that was collocated with the *Astrolabe* functioned as or in lieu of Chaucer's (unwritten) part 5, an "introductorie" to the "general rewlis of theorike in astrologie."

4

The manuscript in which the translation from Mariensüss occurs dates from the late fifteenth century,[77] and indeed most if not all of the surviving copies of the *Astrolabe* were made after Chaucer's death and were part of a general late medieval burgeoning of vernacular science.[78] Chaucer himself, in his last years, seems to have lost interest in astronomy and astrology,[79] but others evidently did not. More copies of the *Astrolabe* survive than of any other of Chaucer's works except the *Canterbury Tales*. Moreover, the characteristics of the surviving manuscripts imply a diverse audience. The Bodleian's Rawlinson D. 3, for example, is handsome enough to suggest

courtly or aristocratic patronage,[80] whereas there is a definite air of frugal-
ity about Ashmole 393, a collection of astrology and astronomy in which
the *Astrolabe* is reduced to a brief epitome of part 1 and the beginning of
part 2, closely written on paper in a small, careless hand.[81] Bodley 619
clearly has connections with the learned world: its marginal notes in Latin
correct one of Chaucer's technical misstatements, demonstrate recognition
of Chaucer's dependence on Messahalla, and compare the astrolabe as described by Chaucer with an actual astrolabe in Merton College, Oxford.
This comparison has occasioned the conjecture that the manuscript was
written by a Merton astronomer.[82] Such a diversity of audience suggests a
protean quality in the *Astrolabe* itself.

A modern comparison of real astrolabes with Chaucer's representation
of an astrolabe has revealed a highly interesting connection between an
Astrolabe manuscript and its historical setting.[83] One of the most characteristic elements of an astrolabe is its "rete" or star-map (described in *Astrolabe* 1.21). It now appears that the diagram of a rete in one of the most
important *Astrolabe* manuscripts, Cambridge University Library Dd.3.53,
was drawn from a real astrolabe still extant in a private collection. There is
also still extant a somewhat later astrolabe that may have been designed
after the diagram in the manuscript. What we are seeing here is but one
more example, though an especially impressive and tantalizing one, of
the links that manuscripts can point to between the *Astrolabe* and a late-
medieval scientific culture that may be only intermittently and very
sketchily present to the mind when we read Chaucer's poetry.

The existence of that culture, with its broad strain of astrologism, explains the continued currency and frequent recopying of the *Astrolabe*.[84]
The appeal of vernacular scientific writing seems to have been felt in diverse
social and economic settings, and the *Astrolabe*, as variously presented in
manuscript, could meet various demands that Chaucer himself may not
have contemplated. Some of the manuscript books, such as Trinity's R.
15.18, have a loose unity and a dimly visible mind behind them, a mind
that is quite other than Chaucer's. They have a status somewhere between
that of a *compilatio*, which has an orderly arrangement of parts, and a *col-
lectio*, which does not. In such works Chaucer's own compilation is absorbed
and assimilated. Their contents vary, but most contain other scientific materials. None contains any of Chaucer's poetry. Chaucer does not quite dis-
appear in them, but since he is "but a lewed compilator" to begin with, his
personal voice and vision may have been of less interest than were astrolabes and stars. In the fifteenth century—even as Chaucer was "becoming
a national monument" and as there was being established "'a cult of personality' in which Chaucer, in his very person, embodied the idea of a

national literary tradition"[85]—there remained an audience for scientific compilations. For this audience the person of the compiler was relatively unimportant. In the matter of astrology, whatever Chaucer's views and however he might have treated the topic if he had written part 5 of the *Astrolabe*, the scribes treated it according to their own ends. They could use Chaucer's overall plan as a rough guide; they could ignore it; or they could interpret it so as to accommodate such material as the translation from Mariensüss, a piece of work more mechanical, unphilosophical, and toneless than anything Chaucer could have borne to write.

The characteristics of the *Astrolabe* as Chaucer left it were what made it so adaptable and so attractive a candidate for adaptation. Its status as an incomplete technical or scientific compilation made it subject to further compilator-like operations, both in the assembling of additional materials and in the reordering of what was already there. Its intimations in the prologue and in some of the later conclusions of potential lines of development are sufficiently indeterminate to allow wide interpretation. Its subject, the stars, could be understood astronomically, astrologically, or (as was quite conceivable, indeed usual, at the time) both ways at once. These characteristics help explain the continued interest of a variety of late medieval readers in a work that, if it were not by Chaucer, would interest most modern readers hardly at all.

Notes

1. Chaucer's chief source, known in the Middle Ages as the *Compositio et Operatio Astrolabii* and attributed to the eighth-century Arabic writer Messahalla, appears actually to have been a joining of one western Latin compilation to another, and the two parts may have been "conceived independently and merely put together later by readers or scribes" (Paul Kunitzsch, "On the Authenticity of the Treatise on the Composition and Use of the Astrolabe Ascribed to Messahalla," *Archives internationales d'histoire des sciences* 31 [1981]: 56). It was re-edited in the thirteenth century, with corrections and additions that assured its status as the principal corpus of Latin astrolabe literature (E. Poulle, "L'Astrolabe médiéval d'après les manuscrits de la bibliothèque nationale," *Bibliothèque de l'école des Chartres* 112 [1954]: 85). Chaucer's second most important source is the thirteenth-century *Tractatus de Sphera* by John of Sacrobosco, whose commentators regarded him as a compiler. Michael Scot calls him "compilator huius tractatus," and an anonymous commentator calls him "huius libri compilatore" (Lynn Thorndike, ed., *The "Sphere" of Sacrobosco and Its Commentators* [Chicago: University of Chicago Press, 1949], 249, 413).

2. George Sarton, *Introduction to the History of Science* (Baltimore: Carnegie Institute, 1948), 3/2:1422.

3. *Astrolabe*, Prologue, ll. 61–62. This and subsequent citations of Chaucer's works

are, unless otherwise noted, from Larry D. Benson, general editor, *The Riverside Chaucer* (Boston: Houghton Mifflin, 1987; hereafter *RC*).

4. M. B. Parkes, "The Influence of the Concepts of *Ordinatio* and *Compilatio* on the Development of the Book," in *Medieval Learning and Literature*, ed. J. J. G. Alexander and M. T. Gibson (Oxford: Clarendon Press, 1976), 115–49; A. J. Minnis, "Late-Medieval Discussions of *Compilatio* and the Role of the *Compilator*," *Beiträge zur Geschichte der deutschen Sprache und Literatur* 101 (1979): 385–421; A. J. Minnis, *Medieval Theory of Authorship* (Philadelphia: University of Pennsylvania Press, 1984), esp. 94–103 and 194–97; R. H. Rouse and M. A. Rouse, "*Ordinatio* and *Compilatio* Revisited," in *Ad Litteram: Authoritative Texts and Their Medieval Readers*, ed. Mark D. Jordan and Kent Emery, Jr., Notre Dame Conferences in Medieval Studies, vol. 3 (Notre Dame: University of Notre Dame Press, 1992), 93–111.

5. Chaucer quotes from Alchabitius's *Introductory to Astrology* at *Astrolabe*, 1.8. I paraphrase from the twelfth-century Latin version as represented in Oxford Bodleian MS Selden Supra 78; from a fourteenth-century English version in Trinity College Cambridge MS 0.5.26; and from a fourteenth-century French version in St. John's College Oxford MS 164. The Bodleian manuscript, which also contains the astrolabe treatise of Messahalla, may have been in Chaucer's hands as he wrote the *Astrolabe* (Michael Masi, "Chaucer, Messahalla and Bodleian Selden Supra 78," *Manuscripta* 19 [1975]: 36–47). The St. John's manuscript is a collection of astrological and astronomical works prepared for Charles V of France. (See Edgar Laird, "Astrology in the Court of Charles V of France as Reflected in Oxford, St. John's College, MS 164," *Manuscripta* 34 [1990]: 167–76). On the Trinity manuscript, which is also a collection of astrology and astronomy, see Kari Anne Rand Schmidt, *The Authorship of the "Equatorie of the Planetis"* (Cambridge: D. S. Brewer, 1993), 187–206.

6. *Livret de eleccions*, St. John's College MS 164, fol. 33v. The relevant passage is printed in appendix C of Edgar Laird and Robert Fischer's *Pèlerin de Prusse on the Astrolabe: Text and Translation of His "Practique de astrolabe,"* Medieval and Renaissance Texts and Studies, vol. 127 (Binghamton, N.Y.: Center for Medieval and Early Renaissance Studies, 1995).

7. *Practique de astrolabe*, Prologue. See note 6, above.

8. Cf. Minnis, "Late-Medieval Discussions of *Compilatio*," 390: the literary activity of *compilatio* "entails both the *modus excerptoris* . . . and the *ordinatio* of material excerpted from *auctores*."

9. F. J. Carmody, ed., *Li Compilacions de le science des estoilles, Books I-III*, University of California Publications in Modern Philology, vol. 33 (Berkeley: University of California Press, 1947), 37–101.

10. There are many manuscripts of the *Compilacions* and at least two printed editions. I refer here to Paris, Bibliothèque Nationale, MS French 613, described by Carmody, *Compilacions*, 47–51.

11. "Mauldyt soit le larron qui a desrobé la fin de 9ᵉ traicté et le 10ᵉ tout entier" (fol. 86r).

12. Carmody, *Compilacions*, 47.

13. Cf. Minnis, "Late-Medieval Discussions of *Compilatio*," 404–08, on the compilator's arrangement of materials by topic and his provision, in a prologue, of an analytical table of contents.

14. Walter W. Skeat, ed., *A Treatise on the Astrolabe; Addressed to His Son Lowys*

by *Geoffrey Chaucer* EETS, 1st ser., 29 (London: N. Trübner, 1872), xviii; and *A Treatise on the Astrolabe* in *Complete Works of Chaucer*, ed. W. W. Skeat (Oxford: Clarendon Press, 1894), 3: lxviii. Hereafter page references to Skeat's edition are given for the EETS publication only.

15. P. Pintelon, ed., *Chaucer's* Treatise on the Astrolabe: *MS. 4862–4869 of the Royal Library in Brussels* (Antwerp: De Sikkel, 1940), 57.

16. John H. Fisher, ed., *The Complete Poetry and Prose of Geoffrey Chaucer* (New York: Holt, Rinehart and Winston, 1989), 971. A date of 1391 is widely accepted because of its use in examples in authentic conclusions.

17. John Reidy in *RC*, 1092–93.

18. J. D. North, *Chaucer's Universe* (Oxford: Clarendon Press, 1988), 76.

19. The Stevins manuscript (British Library MS Sloane 261) is the base text for A. E. Brae, ed., *The Treatise on the Astrolabe of Geoffrey Chaucer* (London: John Russell Smith, 1870). For Stevins's preface, see pp. 9–10 of that edition or Caroline F. E. Spurgeon, *Five Hundred Years of Chaucer Criticism and Allusion, 1357–1900* (New York: Russell & Russell, 1960), 92–93.

20. Stevins indicates in the preface that he is omitting these three, but in fact he modifies 2.40 and retains it.

21. Comparison of the *Astrolabe* with the Messahalla treatise is greatly facilitated by the notes on the *Astrolabe* in *RC* and by those in Sigmund Eisner's forthcoming edition of the *Astrolabe* for the *Variorum Edition of the Works of Geoffrey Chaucer*. Professor Eisner has kindly made portions of his edition available to me in typescript.

22. All manuscripts that contain 2.40 break off except the Stevins "edited" manuscript, Columbia University Library MS Plimpton 254, and Cambridge University Library MS Dd.12.51, which according to Reidy (*RC*, 1102) have a common ancestor that supplied the empty clause, "thou shalt do wel ynow."

23. If 2.41–45 are Chaucer's, then they "shew him to have been a fragmentary worker" (Skeat, xix). Even 2.38–40, more certainly authentic, occur in only nine manuscripts and "were probably on sheets detached from the rest" and "became disordered" (*RC*, 1092).

24. This is a very early manuscript, dated 1400 by F. Madan and H. H. E. Craster, *A Summary Catalogue of Western MSS. in the Bodleian Library at Oxford* (Oxford: Oxford University Press, 1922), 1:228.

25. North, *Chaucer's Universe*, 85.

26. Minnis, *Theory of Authorship*, 194.

27. Additions from John of Sacrobosco, *Tractatus de Sphera*, are at *Astrolabe* 1.17 and 1.21. A few modern critics have underestimated the dependence of the *Astrolabe's* part 1 on Messahalla because they have looked for correspondences in Messahalla's part 1 rather than in the little preamble to part 2.

28. It was probably Skeat who suggested anonymously, in a letter to the *Athenaeum*, Sept. 19, 1868, that Cambridge University Library MS Dd.3.53 was corrected by Chaucer. Pintelon, *Chaucer's Treatise*, 15, n. 3, calls the suggestion "alluring," but he notes that it has "nowhere an argument in its support," and it has been allowed to die quietly.

29. North, *Chaucer's Universe*, 46 and chapter 3, argues from calculations Chaucer can be seen in other works to have performed, that he possessed and used such materials but never put them together for his treatise.

30. Examples follow: Bodleian MS Ashmole 391; see Pintelon, *Chaucer's* Treatise, 20–21, and Sigmund Eisner, ed., *The Kalendarium of Nicholas of Lynn* (Athens: University of Georgia Press, 1980), 43–44. Royal Library, Brussels, MS 4862/69; see Pintelon, 37–43, and Eisner, 37. Bodleian MS Digby 72; see Skeat, xiv and xx. Trinity College Cambridge MS R.15.18; see M. R. James, *The Western Manuscripts in the Library of Trinity College* (Cambridge: Cambridge University Press, 1901) 2:356–57.

31. See Eisner, *Kalendarium*, 43–44.

32. The very numerous copies of the Latin "Messahalla" astrolabe treatise have not yet been fully described, but one gets the impression that they are often, perhaps usually, bound with tables, and indeed in some versions have been edited to include tables as an integral part of it (Ron B. Thomson, *Jordanus de Nemore and the Mathematics of Astrolabes: De Plana Spera* [Toronto: Pontifical Institute of Mediaeval Studies, 1978], 53–54).

33. Olaf Pedersen, "The Theorica Planetarum-Literature of the Middle Ages," *Classica et Mediaevalia* 23 (1962): 225–32. See also North, *Chaucer's Universe*, 134–37.

34. The *Theorica Planetarum Gerardi* has been edited by F. J. Carmody (Berkeley: University of California Press, 1942) and Campanus of Novara's *Theorica Planetarum* by Francis S. Benjamin and G. J. Toomer (Madison: University of Wisconsin Press, 1971).

35. The "Newe Theorike" is printed in Schmidt, *Authorship*, 213–74.

36. Carmody, *Compilacions*, 41–44.

37. Of the sixty-odd manuscripts of Campanus's *Theorica* surveyed by Benjamin and Toomer, eleven are bound with copies of Messahalla's astrolabe treatise.

38. Skeat, xix–xx and n. 1.

39. Ibid., xx and xiv.

40. *RC*, 1095.

41. North, *Chaucer's Universe*, 192, points out that Chaucer cites Alchabitius less than a hundred lines after describing the projected contents of part 5. See note 5, above.

42. North, *Chaucer's Universe*, 46.

43. J. D. North, "'Kalenderes enlumyned ben they': Some Astronomical Themes in Chaucer," *Review of English Studies* 20 (1969): 436–37.

44. Skeat, xxii.

45. Pintelon, *Chaucer's* Treatise, 57: "Considering . . . the keen interest of [Chaucer's] time in astronomical and astrological matter, we may readily understand that many a scribe should have been tempted to try his hand at completing the treatise."

46. Printed by Skeat, in his notes to *Astrolabe* 2.3, from BL MS Add. 23002.

47. Skeat, 80–81.

48. See Masi, "Chaucer, Messahalla, and Bodleian Selden Supra 78," 42.

49. William H. Morley, *Description of a Planispheric Astrolabe* (London: Williams and Norgate, 1856), 15–16; reprinted in R. T. Gunther, *Astrolabes of the World*, vol. 2 (Oxford: Oxford University Press, 1932).

50. Printed by Skeat, 80–81, and by R. T. Gunther, *Chaucer and Messahalla on the Astrolabe*, Early Science in Oxford, vol. 5 (Oxford: Oxford University Press), 182–83, from Oxford MS Bodley 619.

51. The case is similar to the scribes' (and Caxton's) improvement of *Boece* by consulting Boethius's Latin, as reported by Tim William Machan, "Scribal Role, Authorial Intention, and Chaucer's *Boece*," *Chaucer Review* 24 (1989): 153–54, 156–57.

52. Both words are used in *Astrolabe* 2.26, which is where, in Oxford Bodleian MS Rawlinson D. 913, the gloss on "mediacioun" occurs.

53. The manuscript that contains this addition (Bodley 619), dating from the second quarter of the fifteenth century, incorporates direct quotations from the Latin Messahalla, reproduced by Skeat, x–xi.

54. British Library MS Sloane 446. See *RC*, 1194.

55. Alnwick Castle, Duke of Northumberland MS 460. See *RC*, 1194.

56. Edited by Pintelon, *Chaucer's* Treatise.

57. The manuscript has spaces for nineteen figures, none of which has been supplied.

58. *RC*, 1098, citing Lydgate's *Fall of Princes* 1.298–301.

59. Skeat and Fisher use Cambridge University Library MS Dd.3.53. Bodleian MS Rawlinson D. 913 (formerly Rawlinson Misc. 1370, then Misc. 1262), which Skeat uses for *Astrolabe* 2.39, garbled in his base text, bears marginal section numbers agreeing with the modern standard numbering. Pintelon uses Brussels, Royal Library, MS 4862/4869. Both Mark H. Liddell in *The Globe Chaucer* (*The Works of Geoffrey Chaucer*, ed. Alfred W. Pollard, Henry Frank Heath, Mark Harvey Liddell, and Sir William Symington McCormick [New York: Macmillan, 1898]) and F. N. Robinson (*The Poetical Works of Chaucer* [Boston: Houghton Mifflin, 1933]) (and thence Reidy in *RC*) use Bodley 619. Pintelon, *Chaucer's* Treatise, 2, names these as the nearest representatives of the original.

60. St. John's College Cambridge MS E.2, perhaps the earliest extant *Astrolabe* manuscript (see *RC*, 1193); Bodleian MS Digby 72; BL MS Egerton 2622, which is "arranged in an orderly fashion, with capital initials and numerous paragraph marks" (Pintelon, *Chaucer's* Treatise, 33); Bodleian MS E Museo 116; and BL MS Add. 23002.

61. Bodleian MS Bodley 68, which shifts 2.38 as well, dated 1400 in the catalogue (see note 24, above); Corpus Christi College Cambridge MS 424, late fifteenth century; BL MS Sloane 314, end of fifteenth century (Skeat, xii); also Bodleian MS E Museo 54, but Schmidt, *Authorship*, 59, shows its present order to be the result of a modern error in rebinding.

62. The remark, quoted by Skeat, xii, from Corpus Christi College Cambridge MS 424, is also in BL MS Add. 23002, where, however, it lacks the *explicit* and is followed by 2.37. Raymond of Marseilles (12th c.) similarly ends his account of equating houses by astrolabe by saying that though he will write more on house equation elsewhere, for purposes of his astrolabe treatise "ad presens ista sufficiant." (Emmanuel Poulle, ed., "Le Traite de astrolabe de Raymond de Marseille," *Studi Medievali*, 3d ser., 5 [1964]: 894).

63. North, *Chaucer's Universe*, 85. See note 62, above, on Raymond of Marseilles. On competing systems of house-division, see J. C. Eade, *The Forgotten Sky: A Guide to Astrology in English Literature* (Oxford: Clarendon Press, 1984), 42–45.

64. Schmidt, *Authorship*, 151. The present binding is postmedieval, and it is not clear when the materials were brought together.

65. The odd but useful phrase is from Ralph Hanna III, "Producing Manuscripts and Editions," in *Crux and Controversy in Middle English Textual Criticism*, ed. A. J. Minnis and Charlotte Brewer (Cambridge: D. S. Brewer, 1992), 123. On "booklet compilation" of English scientific treatises, see Linda Ehrsam Voigts, "Scientific and Medical Books," in *Book Production and Publishing in Britain, 1375–1475*, ed. Jeremy Griffiths and Derek Pearsall (Cambridge: Cambridge University Press, 1989), 353–56.

66. Bodleian MS Ashmole 391; BL MS Add. 23002; Bodleian MS Ashmole 360, "a big volume containing eight different treatises on astrology and similar matter" (Pintelon, *Chaucer's* Treatise, 29); Columbia University MS Plimpton 254; Bodleian MS Ashmole 393; Bodleian MS Bodley 68; Brussels, Royal Library MS 4862/4869, the contents of which are described fairly fully by Pintelon 254, 37–43; Bodleian MS Digby 72; Trinity College Cambridge MS R.15.18.

67. Skeat, xii, calls it "a curious and interesting volume, as it contains several tracts in English on astrology and astronomy, with tables of stars &c." To show "the nature of the old astrology," he quotes generously from this manuscript in his notes to *Astrolabe* 1.21, and he reproduces from it, as his figure 19, a picture of a "zodiac man." See also Voigts, "Scientific and Medical Books," 365, 382–83.

68. The canon, which begins "Vsum ephemerides cuiuslibet breviter exponemus," is reprinted by Felix Schmeidler, ed., *Joannis Regiomontari Opera Collectanena* (Osnabrück: Otto Zeller, 1972), 537–38, 564.

69. Ernst Zinner, *Regiomontanus: His Life and Work*, trans. Ezra Brown (Amsterdam: Elsevier, 1990), 118.

70. Ibid., 119.

71. Following it are tables and *kalendaria* of the usual sorts and a copy of John of Sacrobosco's *Sphere*. The *Sphere* certainly, and perhaps some of the tables as well, are late additions.

72. See S. J. Tester, *A History of Astrology* (New York: Ballantine Books, 1989), 160. Mariensüss's citation is indirect, through Sacrobosco, whom he cites in the next sentence for the etymology of "zodiac." In *Astrolabe* 1.21 Chaucer gives the same etymology from the same source.

73. Zinner, *Regiomontanus,* 118–19.

74. Ibid., 119–25; Donald W. Olson, Russell L. Doescher, and Edgar S. Laird, "Columbus and the Sky of January 17, 1493," *Sky and Telescope* 81 (January 1991): 81–84.

75. Reprinted in facsimile in *The English Experience*, number 570 (New York: Da Capo Press, 1973).

76. Edited and published by David Francis, Austin, Texas, as *The Principles of Astronomy.*

77. The translation of the Mariensüss treatise makes the claim that its star positions have been "verefied" for the year 1486, a likely date for the translation. (The Latin claims verification for 1476.) The copy of the *Astrolabe* in the manuscript may be slightly earlier: mid-fifteenth century according to Voigts, "Scientific and Medical Books," 382.

78. H. S. Bennett, *Chaucer and the Fifteenth Century* (Oxford: Clarendon Press, 1947; reprint, 1965), 196; also H. S. Bennett, "Science and Information in English Writings of the Fifteenth Century," *Modern Language Review* 39 (1944): 1–8; see also Laura Braswell, "Utilitarian and Scientific Prose," in *Middle English Prose*, ed. A. S. G. Edwards (New Brunswick: Rutgers University Press, 1984), 337–84; and Voigts, "Scientific and Medical Books," 380–84, 386.

79. North, "Kalenderes," 442–44; M. Manzaloui, "Chaucer and Science," in *Writers and Their Backgrounds: Geoffrey Chaucer*, ed. Derek Brewer (Athens: Ohio University Press, 1974), 238, 241–42; *RC*, xxviii.

80. Skeat, xiii, describes it as being on vellum "with rich gold capitals, beautifully ornamented; in a large clear handwriting with red rubrics." Pintelon, *Chaucer's* Treatise, 25, calls it "a beautiful MS., written in a large and highly formal hand."

81. Skeat, xv.

82. The conjecture originates with Liddell in the *Globe Chaucer*, liii, and is repeated by Pintelon, *Chaucer's* Treatise, 22, and Robinson, *Poetical Works of Chaucer*, 867. It is discussed by J. D. North, ed., *Richard of Wallingford: An Edition of His Writings, with Translation and Commentary* (Oxford: Clarendon Press, 1976), 3:133–35, and also by North in *Chaucer's Universe*, 39 and n. 2.

83. Owen Gingerich, "Zoomorphic Astrolabes and the Introduction of Arabic Star Names into Europe," in David A. King and George Saliba, eds., *From Deferent to Equant*, Annals of the New York Academy of Sciences, vol. 500 (New York, 1987), 89–93. The article is reprinted in Owen Gingerich, *The Eye of Heaven: Ptolemy, Copernicus, Kepler* (New York: American Institute of Physics, 1993), 98–114.

84. E. T. Donaldson speculates, by way of explaining the large number of surviving *Astrolabe* manuscripts, that perhaps "scientific translations were not so avidly read as creative works" and hence were not worn out ("The Manuscripts of Chaucer's Works and Their Use," in *Writers and Their Backgrounds: Geoffrey Chaucer*, ed. Brewer, 93–94). Manuscript marginalia, however, indicate a readership with interest in the stars. See, e.g., Schmidt, *Authorship*, 156, on marginalia in Cambridge University Library MS Dd.3.53.

85. Derek Pearsall, "Hoccleve's *Regiment of Princes:* The Poetics of Royal Self-Representation," *Speculum* 69 (1994): 399, 402.

Bodleian MS Arch. Selden. B. 24 and the "Scotticization" of Middle English Verse

Julia Boffey and A. S. G. Edwards

The transmission of Middle English texts from England to Scotland and the linguistic implications of such transmission have not hitherto attracted much study. That this is so is in part a consequence of the paucity of surviving materials.[1] Angus McIntosh has opened some fruitful lines of enquiry in his examination of the language of the *Scottish Troy Book* fragments,[2] but his analysis has not led to much wider discussion of the issues raised by such "translation." The observations that follow are a very preliminary attempt to look at the most substantial surviving evidence of the circulation of Middle English poetic texts in Scotland and to attempt to identify the distinctive features that are the result of the Scottification of these works.

The manuscript that is now Bodleian Library MS. Arch. Selden. B. 24 was prepared in the late fifteenth or early sixteenth centuries in Scotland, probably for the Sinclair family, whose arms it contains. Its contents are exclusively verse: it includes copies of a number of Chaucer's works (*Troilus & Criseyde, The Legend of Good Women, The Parliament of Fowls*), together with poems by Lydgate, Hoccleve, and Walton, as well as a number of Scottish poems, most notably the unique copy of *The Kingis Quair*.

The Middle English poems were all, with one exception, copied by a single scribe, whose hand has been identified in other Scottish manuscripts, where it is responsible for a number of prose texts: in the "Abbotsford" manuscript of works by Gilbert of the Hay, now Edinburgh, National Library of Scotland MS. Acc. 9253; in a collection of Latin and Scottish works now owned by the earl of Dalhousie; and in a copy of a printed Rouen edition of Mirk's *Festial*, now St. John's College, Cambridge, MS G. 19. While this last offers some indications of the scribe's practice in copying Middle English prose and of his orthographic habits, only the Selden manuscript preserves any evidence of his practice with regard to Middle English verse.[3]

Physical details of the manuscript's construction suggest that it was copied in several stages and systematically upgraded over time. The first stage was the transcription of *Troilus & Criseyde,* followed—probably at some interval—by the rest of the major Middle English contents of the manuscript. The Scottish poems that conclude the transcription were seemingly a later project, copied mostly by a second scribe who took up the transcription near the end of *The Kingis Quair,* and they lie outside our present concerns.

As a collection the Middle English texts in Selden offer evidence simultaneously for the cohesiveness and growing fluidity of Chaucerian transmission at this period. At one level, the collection confirms the authority of the so-called Oxford group of Chaucerian manuscripts represented centrally by Bodleian Library MSS Fairfax 16, Tanner 346, and Bodley 638.[4] In its contents Selden bears a striking affiliation to the first booklet of the earliest of these collections, the Fairfax manuscript. It reproduces eight of the sixteen texts that occur in that booklet, including *The Legend of Good Women, The Parliament of Fowls,* and the *Complaints of Mars* and *Venus.* In this respect it reflects a degree of relative compilational stability that extended through the second half of the fifteenth century and encompassed Chaucer's dream visions, lyrics and other shorter poems.

More unusual is the collocation of this group of texts with the work that seems to have generated the initial stage of the manuscript's compilation: *Troilus & Criseyde.* This work virtually never occurs elsewhere in manuscript in collocation with any significant number of Oxford-group texts.[5] Such a conjunction in Selden would therefore seem to confirm that the scribe was able to acquire more than one Chaucerian exemplar. This point is itself of some interest in the light it sheds on the apparent availability of a range of such exemplars in northern Britain by this stage in the transmission of Chaucer's works.

But although Selden exhibits a high degree of compilational orthodoxy in the bulk of its Middle English contents, in other respects it seems to reflect new attributional and regional pressures. Selden includes five texts—two anonymous lyrics, and one poem each by Hoccleve, Lydgate and Walton—that do not regularly appear in Oxford-group collections, and are here spuriously ascribed to Chaucer. Some of these seem to have a distinctively Scottish circulation as Chaucer texts.[6]

Indeed, while Selden is the last major Chaucerian manuscript collection, it is also virtually the only substantial indication of the manuscript circulation of Chaucer's works in Scotland. Its distinctiveness is not limited to its attributional eccentricity. It poses some largely unexamined questions to do with the transmission of Middle English literary texts into Scotland and the nature of Scottish vernacular literary language at the end of the Middle Ages, a language that has recently been characterized by Derrick

McClure as variously "the same language as English, one dialect of which, Metropolitan English was another dialect, or a distinct language."[7] Most particularly, we wish to consider the question of the extent and nature of the Scotticization of Middle English verse texts as evidenced by Selden, and to seek to discover what happened as these texts passed over the border. What, if anything, did copyists attempt to do to such texts to make them more accessible or acceptable to a Caledonian audience? And what indications are there of the systematic "translation" of Middle English texts into Scots, a process that has sometimes been seen as a component of the linguistic flavor of *The Kingis Quair* and in other Middle English works that were subsequently copied in Scotland?[8]

To address such questions we begin with some examination of the major Chaucer texts that appear in the manuscript, *Troilus & Criseyde, The Legend of Good Women,* and *The Parliament of Fowls.* The Selden copies of all these collectively raise problems about the possibility of generalizing about the treatment of Selden's Middle English texts as transmitted in Scotland.

In *Troilus,* the separate transcription of which constituted, as we have said, the distinct first stage of the manuscript's construction, Scotticization occurs at the level of orthography, whereby Scottish spellings are regularly substituted for English ones. The general orthographic texture can be represented in the presentation of the treatment of a single stanza:

> And think quhat wo there hath betid or this
> For making of auantes as men rede
> And quhat mischief зit in this worlde there is
> From day to day rycht for that wikked dede
> For quhiche thise wis clerkes þat ben dede
> Haue euer зit prouerbed to vs зong
> That first vertue is to kepe the tong
> (fol. 45r, III:288–94)[9]

Root noted many years ago that "the text of S[elden] has superficially a Scottish cast"[10] and this seems to be so. He notes predictably the substitution of *quh-* for *wh-* and of *su-* for *sw-*.[11] One can add to these the substitution of yogh for *g* or *y,* and occasional systematic lexical substitutions like "thame" for "hem/hym/them,"[12] and "thair(e)" for "hyr(e)/her(e)."[13]

But in comparison with the treatment of some of the other Middle English texts in the manuscript what is striking in the text of *Troilus* is a consistent failure to insert forms of orthographic adjustment that do occur in these other texts and which are manifestly Scottish. The retention of forms like "she," which elsewhere in the manuscript is usually "sche," or of those involving *gh* (e.g., "myght" I:638; "nyght" I:951) where Middle English forms are preferred to Scottish forms ("micht," "nicht") or plural forms in *-es* rather than *-is*, are obvious indications of what seems to be an initial unwillingness to tamper with the exemplar.

That such a rendering could become more thoroughgoing is demonstrated by some of the Chaucer texts that were added later, notably the *Legend of Good Women* and the *Parliament of Fowls*. The treatment of orthography in the *Legend* offers an instructive contrast. This preserves the obvious Scottish orthographic features of *Troilus* and adds a number of further systematic changes. Once again, a representative passage gives some sense of the texture:

> Quhan the wynd was good and gan thame lye
> Out of his contree called Thesalye
> Til In the Ile of lennon arryved he
> Al be this nocht reherced of guydo
> ȝit seithe Ouide In his epistlis so
> That of this Ile lady was & quene
> The fair ȝong Isiphilee the schene
> That quhilom was Thoas doughter the king[14]
>
> (fol. 173r, 1460–68)

Apart from the obvious Scottish features already noted there is a general tendency to substitute *sch-* for *sh-*; *-cht* replaces *-ght*; "schall" appears for "shall"; plural forms are in *-is*; "thaim" or "thame" appears for "hem." Elsewhere, "she" is used interchangeably with "sche"; *su-* forms generally replace *sw-* ("suore" 683); "thair(e)" for "hir" or "theyr" (729); forms occur like "maid" for "mad(e)" (669); "airly" for "erly" (771); *-ce(y)ue* rhymes become *-ssaue* (752–53). The obvious effect is to make the Scots texture of the *Legend* quite pronounced in comparison to *Troilus*.

Although the situation in the treatment of the *Parliament of Fowls* has much in common with that of the *Legend,* it is in certain respects unusual. For reasons that remain obscure, Selden's version of the *Parliament* departs from all other surviving texts at l. 600 and offers a unique and much more resolute conclusion to the birds' debate, recommending plainly to the formel eagle the first of the suitors who speaks for her hand. The language of the grafted-on conclusion is in many of its features more insistently Scottish than that of any of the other Chaucerian texts in the manuscript. On the evidence of the pronounced Scots cast of the orthography and lexicon of this section, one might be justified in supposing it to be a fully Scottish ending, written by a Scot and put into circulation in Scotland, perhaps as a somewhat flamboyant act of linguistic appropriation. The neat technique

by which the final stanza of the new ending is made to recall an earlier
section of the Chaucerian part of the poem affords a good opportunity to
compare the linguistic cast of the two parts. The first time we have this:

> For out of olde feldis quhere sowen sede is
> Commyth all this new corne fro 3ere to 3ere
> And out of olde bookis as men redis
> Cummyth all this new science þat men lere.[15]
> (fol. 142, 22–25)

But the concluding stanza reads:

> For out of olde feildis as men seis
> Cummys all this new corn fro 3ere to 3ere
> And out of olde bookis quho thame viseis
> Cummys all this new science þat men now lere.
> (fol. 152, 673–76).

There is a noticeable intensification of Scottish features: "feildis"; -ys verb
endings (as in "cummys"); and a new formulation that affords a Scots
rhyme word in "as men seis" / "quho thame viseis."

At the same time, though, it would be misleading to talk of the first
part of the *Parliament* in this manuscript as anything other than a Scots
translation, albeit one of variable thoroughness. There remain distinctly
fewer Middle English forms than we noted in Selden's text of *Troilus and
Criseyde*, and those that are there—like the English verb endings in the
first passage just quoted—coexist beside others of Scottish cast (for example, "redis"). The following passage helps to clarify the point:

> The gentill faucon þat with his feet distreyneth
> The kingis hand / the hardy spere hauk eke
> The qualis foo / the merlion þat peyneth
> him self full oft the lark forto seke
> There was the douue with hir eyen meke
> The Ielouse swan before hir deth þat singis
> The oule þat of the deth bodeworde bringis
> (fol. 146v, 337–43)

The Middle English rhyming endings "distreyneth" and "peyneth" occur
in the same stanza as the Scots "singis" and "bringis." Certain orthographic
features that are either absent from or unsystematically presented in Selden's text of *Troilus* (*sch-* for *sh-*; substitutions like "thair" for "hire,"

"quhill" for "till," "ilke" for "any" or "every"), are seemingly routine in the *Parliament*. The Scottish substitutions "ȝa" for "ye" and "ȝett" for "gate" occur more than once (52, 594; 121, 154); and there are several instances where the text is effectively reconfigured as, for example, to incorporate Scottish locutions such as "but more," "but were," "but drede" (17, 21, 28); or to adapt the rhyme scheme to Scottish spellings, as "the hardy asshe / to whippes lasshe"[16] becomes "the hardy esche / to quhippis fresche" (176–78); or perhaps to replace unfamiliar Chaucerian usages with more recognizable dialectal forms, as "the cok that Orlogge ys of thropes lyte" emerges as "The cok that orloge is to folk on nyght" (350).

Systematic rewriting of this sort occurs most densely in the *Parliament* in end-of-line positions, where it would seem to be connected with the exigencies of maintaining a rhyme scheme subject to changes in orthography. At ll. 183–85, for example, where other texts agree on rhyming something along the lines of "blosomed bowis" with "ynowh is," Selden's text, constrained by the Scottish spelling of "blossomyt bewis," supplies in the rhyming position "euermor anewis," substituting the Scottish third-person verb form. Again, at ll. 274–76, the possibility of the rhyme of "sauours swoote" and "hunger boote" (as in Fairfax 16) is lost with the Scottish spelling of "sauouris suete," and the rhyming line is completely recast: instead of "and Ceres next that dooth of hunger boote" Selden offers "And Ceres next þat can the hungir bete."

How is one to account for the variation in the density of Scottish forms between *Troilus* and these other poems? The initial unwillingness to adjust the text may be explained by saying that *Troilus* was a first attempt at rendering Middle English verse for a Scottish audience. The later texts suggest a more intensive application of principles of dialectal translation that had developed over time through greater reflection or greater proficiency in such translation. Superficially this seems a plausible argument; but it is not without its problems. One is that the texture of subsequent Scotticization varies from text to text; other texts in the main Middle English section of the manuscript, such as *The Complaints of Mars* and *Venus* show, like *Troilus*, an equally perfunctory level of Scottish orthographic adjustment. Another problem is that the codicological cohesiveness that appears to link Selden to the earlier Oxford-group manuscripts may be somewhat deceptive. Perhaps Selden reflects the contents of smaller booklets in different stages of transmission within Scotland, demonstrating not varying levels of engagement with the texts but relative degrees of fidelity to a number of different exemplars.

It is hard to muster evidence to assess such an hypothesis. One argument that might be advanced against it is the relative consistency in *Troilus*, the *Legend,* and the *Parliament* of certain changes that seem peculiar to this manuscript and are quite consistent in kind.

The unique variants in Selden for all of these texts suggest a recurrent preoccupation with metrical questions that seems to be an extension of other linguistic concerns. In *Troilus,* for example, many of these variants involve the insertion of additional syllables into the line. These insertions constitute more than half the unique variants in Books I and V[17] (which we used as a sample) and clearly stem from some uncertainty as to what value, if any, could be afforded to final -*e*. For example (taking Corpus Christi College Cambridge MS 61 as the lemma):[18]

How deuel maistow brynge me to blisse] How deuel than maistow bring me to blisse
(fol. 9v, I:623)

And also thynk and ther-with glade the] And also think ther withall glade the
(fol. 13v, I:897)

Al this drede I and ek for the manere] All this drede I and eke of for the manere
(fol. 15v, I:1021)

"ȝe, haselwode," thoughte this Pandare] ȝe hasell wode thocht than this pandare
(fol. 98v, V:505)

Trusteth wel and vnderstondeth me] Trusteth ryt wele and vnderstondith me
(fol. 104, V:887)

But often was his herte hoot and colde] But often tyme was his hert hoot and cold
(fol. 107, V:1102)

These unique variants have very much the feel of deliberate adjustments by a scribe keenly conscious of syllabic norms from which his received text diverged and which needed to be tidied. Uncertainties about the grammatical and metrical value of final -*e* are, of course, common enough in the late fifteenth century. But the activities of the Selden scribe suggest a greater degree of systematization than is evident in other aspects of his translating.

A tendency to metrical smoothing in the text of the *Legend of Good Women* in Selden has likewise been noted by its recent editors, and their text provides a full corpus of the unique Selden variants that can be adduced in support of this conclusion.[19] Our own examination can situate their conclusions in the wider context of the scribe's activities in the manuscript. We have taken as our sample the first and last three hundred lines. Once again, about half the variants involve substitutions that have manifest syllabic significance. For example:[20]

But god forbede but men shulde leve] Bot god forbede bot if þat men schold leue
(fol. 152v, 10)

As dooth the tydif for new fangelnesse] As dooth the tydyf for his newfangelnesse
(fol. 154v, 154)

Therfore I passe shortly in thys wyse] Therfor I pas rycht schortly In this wise
(fol. 188v, 2458)

But I wote why ye come nat quod she] Bot I wote quhy þat ȝe cum nocht quod sche
(fol. 189v, 2520)

And on hir handes faste loketh she] And on hir handis fast than lokith sche
(fol. 191, 2688)

Most of these changes in Selden seem, once again, the consequence of uncertainty as to whether any metrical value can be ascribed to final -e and a
consequent quite systematically expressed desire to eliminate any possibility of metrical ambiguity or infelicity.

That such uncertainties are more pronounced in this manuscript than
is generally the case in the copying of Chaucer in the later fifteenth century
is confirmed in the *Parliament of Fowls*. The first surviving line of Selden's
text of the *Parliament* shows an instance of this smoothing, with the line
padded as if to compensate for what was assumed to be an unsounded final
-e at the end of "vsage." While other manuscripts agree along the lines of
"Of vsage what for luste what for lore" (15), Selden offers "Of vsage olde
quhat for loue quhat for lore." Similar instances recur. Where the other
manuscripts tend to agree on a reference to nature as "This noble emper-
esse ful of g[r]ace" (Fairfax 16), Selden inserts a syllable so that the line
reads "That ryght noble Emperice full of grace" (319). Some of the changes
are more systematic than is the case in other texts. For example, Selden
here regularly suppresses all verbal *i/y*- prefixes and makes corresponding
metrical adjustments:

That hym fro ioy in Armes hath ynome] And him / for Ioye In armes hath he nomen
(38)

How Aufrikan hath hym Cartage ishewed] How Affican hath him Cartage schewit
(44)

That loveth comvne profyt wel ythewede] That loue is cummyn profyte wele thewit
(47)

And ouer the gate with letres large ywroght] And ouer the ȝet with lettres large wele wrocht
(123)

These vers of golde and blak ywryten were] Thir verse of gold and blak wele writen were
(141)

Ywrought aftir hir crafte and hir mesure] Wrocht after hir craft / and hir owne mesure
(305)

What is perhaps surprising is that this sensitivity and ingenuity does not seem to have extended to matters of lexicon. Apart from the substitution of Scottish pronominal forms there is little indication in most of these texts of systematic substitution of Scottish forms for English words. One instance that is notable is the word "couenaunt," which appears several times in the *Legend of Good Women* (688, 693, 790, 2139) and is invariably rendered in the Scottish manner as "counand." In *Troilus,* where the established text reads "and casten to be wroken" (I:88), Selden reads "and shoop for to be wroken" seemingly substituting a Scottish equivalent at a point that troubled many scribes.

The exception to this generalization is the ending of the *Parliament of Fowls,* in which one can point to words and phrases attested only, or mostly, in Scots: the words "orpes orpes," which begin the cock's contribution to the debate (603); his claim that he will "lay wed my hat and hood" (607); and elsewhere, "thir" (612); "in a thrawe" (662); "anerly" (665); "suppose" (679). Furthermore, some of these words occur, significantly, in rhyming positions: "Sauf anerly an oule þat hie gan ʒout / Was leuit behind than of all that rout" (664–65). There are few indications outside the unique concluding portion of this poem of lexical substitutions: the Scots word "gormawe" replaces "cormeraunt" (362), and the expression "this is nat worth a slo" replaces "this nys worth a flye" (500). But in general in the manuscript the process of Scottification does not significantly address matters of lexicon.

Other poems in the manuscript—the Walton stanza and Chaucer's lyric "Truth," and two longer ones, Hoccleve's "Mother of God" and Lydgate's *Complaint of the Black Knight*—are good candidates for analysis because, in addition to their English circulation, they all survive in other contemporary or nearly contemporary Scottish copies whose treatments of the Middle English originals provide some basis for comparison with Selden. Such a comparison might lead to some further conclusions about the Selden scribe's handling of his exemplars.

The extract from Walton's translation of Boethius consists of a single moralizing eight-line stanza, which has acquired the title "Walton's Prosperity":

Richt as pouert causith sobirnes
And febilnes enforcith contenence
Rycht so prosperite and grete riches
The moder is of vice and negligence
And powere also causith insolence
And honour oft sis changith gude thewis

Thare is no more perilous pestilence
Than hie estate gevin vnto schrewis
(fol. 119)

This stanza survives independently in at least nine other manuscripts, of which two—British Library Cotton Vitellius E. xi, fol. 4v, and the sixteenth-century Bannatyne manuscript, Edinburgh, National Library of Scotland, Advocates Library 1.1.6, fol. 75v[21]—are of Scottish provenance and may be profitably compared with the Selden text.[22] Interestingly, in both of these other Scottish manuscripts the language has a more generally Scottish cast: verb endings in -is, for example, replace the English forms used by the Selden scribe. This is perhaps only to be expected in the Bannatyne manuscript, which postdates the other two Scottish copies by some half century or more, but it is notable that the Selden scribe offers a much less Scotticized text than the copyist of the stanza in the Cotton Vitellius manuscript, the bulk of which is occupied mainly by the *Scotichronicon*. Despite their textual differences, though, these two roughly contemporary Scottish copies of the Walton stanza are linked by their attribution of it to Chaucer, an association that is implied in some English manuscripts (notably John Shirley's in Huntington EL 26 A 13) but is never made quite so plain. The Selden scribe seems somehow to have found and exploited the Chaucer connection for his anthology.

"Truth" or "Chauceres counsaling" as it is called in Selden, can be compared to the copy in Cambridge University Library Kk.1.5, fol. 4v, which is the only other surviving occurrence of a Scottish text of Chaucer.[23] Some characteristically Scottish forms are common to both versions: "nocht" (8, 12), "doith" (12), "warld" (16). But the Cambridge text seems to introduce a further layer of Scotticisms, particularly those that substitute -w- for -v- as vowel or consonant: "enwy" (4), "spwrne" (11); Kk.1.5 regularly substitutes "sal(l)" for Selden's "schall" and "dreid" for "drede" (both in 7, 14, 21), though both use "schall" in rhyme positions (5); "hath," the Middle English form that occurs in Selden, is represented as "haith" (3, 4); this copy also has "fra" for Selden's "from" (1).

These indications of what is, in relative terms, a less pronounced degree of Scotticization in Selden lack any particular evidential weight in so short a text. What is more suggestive is the fact that such indications are noticeable elsewhere in longer texts, where contemporary Scots exemplars are available for comparison. Hoccleve's "Mother of God" offers unusual opportunities for study in these terms. A prayer to the Virgin Mary in twenty rhyme-royal stanzas, it survives in only three manuscripts, one of which is Hoccleve's holograph, Huntington HM 111, fols. 34–37. The other two

copies are both of Scottish provenance, Selden (fols. 130–31) and Edin-
burgh, National Library of Scotland (NLS) MS 18. 2. 8, fols. 112v–115 (in
which it is incorporated into the text of John of Ireland's *Opera Theologica*).
In addition to their close textual relationship, these copies have other com-
mon distinctive features. Both can be located within Scottish courtly circles.
Selden, as we have noted, contains the arms of the Sinclair family while
NLS has a note at the beginning "hoc opus compilata est pro honore domini
Jhesu & instructione illustrissimi principis Iacobi quarti Scotorum regis."
Equally striking is the fact that both manuscripts ascribe this poem to
Chaucer. Both were evidently copied quite closely in time. Selden was produced over a period that could have extended from the late 1480s to the
early years of the sixteenth century. The NLS manuscript has a colophon
(fol. 358v) dating it to 1490, but this seems more likely a date of composition than of transcription (paper evidence suggests that it cannot be before 1492).[24]

These two copies seem textually very close and vary significantly from
Hoccleve's holograph. We do not presume that the copyists of the Scottish
versions had direct access to the holograph, but the holograph is the only
extant reference against which to assess the nature of the changes in these
later copies.

Both copies characteristically substitute Scottish forms for a number
of English ones, evidenced in Hoccleve's holograph. Such substitutions
include forms like "Quhan"/"Quhen" for "When"/"whan" (16, 59);
"quich(e)" for "which" (114); "quherefore/quhar(e)for/quhare" for
"wherfore" (45, 116); "tham"/"þame" for "hem" (102); "nocht" for "nat"
(56, 119); "thocht" for "thoght" (35); "mycht" (noun) for "might" (20);[25]
"mycht" (verb) for "mowen" (110); "waurld" (87) for "world"; "wambe"
for "wombe" (71); "saulis" (10, 70) for "soules";[26] "saluioure" for "sau-
ueour" (25); "ʒettis" for "yates" (86); "wikkitnes(se)" for "wikkidnesse"
(32). In addition, both Scottish copies regularly substitute yogh for *y*- in
such forms as "ʒour(e)" for "your" (108, 112, 121),[27] "ʒe" for "yee" (120)
and "ʒow/ʒou" for "yow" (116, 123, 124, 128, 129, 131, 134); "suich"/
"suych" for "swich" (26) (40).

Such regular substitutions confirm the evidence of dialectal transfer.
But there are other changes, less obviously aspects of such transfer, that
are undertaken in highly consistent ways. Chief among these is the treatment of second-person singular pronominal forms, notably the substitution of "thou"/"þou" for "thow" on at least eleven occasions[28] and the
substitution of "the" for "thee" some twelve times.[29] Such changes may be
significant particularly when seen in relation to other smaller, less obvious
systematic changes seemingly of like kind, particularly those involved in
the treatment of possessive pronouns: both regularly spell the first person

plural "oure"[30] (25, 30, 32, 41, 42, 50, 53, 70, 71, 74, 82, 108, 109, 117, 119, 120, 132) in contrast to Hoccleve's "our" and prefer "thy/þi" to "thyn"[31] (33, 59, 60,[32] 98), and, less conclusively, "my" to "myn" (139).[33] These substitutions without substantive or quasi-substantive (for example, metrical) effect suggest a systematic attempt to impose a distinctive and consistent orthographic texture on the transmitted text. This tendency to employ a repertory of common lexical forms regularly seems to indicate the possibility of some common training for these scribes. Little is known about the forms of such training, but the scribes in the Selden manuscript may have been either notaries public, a class of trained writers that became increasingly prominent in Scotland from the late thirteenth century,[34] or possibly clerics within the Sinclair household, figures who generally seem to have been increasingly employed in administrative roles.[35] A number of these were evidently scribes of some competence.[36]

But if it is possible to discern a high level of consistency in orthography and Scotticization between the two Scottish texts of Hoccleve, there are also some indications that these texts reflect different levels or stages of such a process, one that is somewhat more thoroughgoing in NLS than in Selden, and so consistent with our sense of the Selden scribe's relatively conservative treatment.

This can be seen in some of the variations between Selden and NLS, variations that are related to the appearance of some distinctive Scotticisms in NLS alone. The scribe generally, but not invariably, writes "ws" for "vs" (15, 21, 38, 74, 77, 83, 84, 112, 132)[37] and makes equivalent transpositions elsewhere involving w- in initial positions as both vowel and consonant— "wn to" (25, 49, 73, 134), "woce" (30), "wertu" (88). In addition, NLS introduces a number of seemingly Scottish forms where Selden does not: "ane" (40) (omitted in Selden, "an" in Hoccleve's holograph); "quaik" for "quake/qwake" (54); "waurld" for "world" (87); "saulis" for "soulis/ soules" (91); "hartis" for "hertes" (133); "soraw" for "sorow" (57);[38] "madene" for "maiden" (28); "lichtis" for "lightis/lightes" (107); "ouchtene" for "aughten" ("oghten" in the holograph) (64); "saif" for "saue" (62); "precius" for "preciouse" (54).

The textual transmission and language of the longest of the pseudo-Chaucerian texts added to the anthology, Lydgate's *Complaint of the Black Knight*, to some degree confirms the tendencies revealed in the Hoccleve text. This poem survives in nine manuscripts (including Fairfax 16 and others of the Oxford group), of which Selden is among the later ones, together with another Scottish copy, the Asloan manuscript, now NLS 16500, copied in Edinburgh by the notary John Asloan, close in time to Selden.[39] It is also extant in three early prints. One of these, produced by Chepman and Myllar in Edinburgh in 1508, is like the Selden and Asloan manuscripts in entitling it "the mayng or disport of chaucer," and is, on the basis of other evidence, possibly based on Selden's text. As Krausser demonstrated a century ago, the witnesses fall into relatively distinct groupings. Selden, the Chepman and Myllar print,[40] the text in the Asloan manuscript, and London, BL MS 16165 form one such grouping.[41]

That the first three of these should be related is, in the light of their clear and common Scottish provenance, unsurprising. The possible processes of transmission by which Selden came into the hands of Edinburgh printers—and the printed copy in turn became available to the Edinburgh resident Asloan—are not hard to reconstruct and are supported by chronological pointers locating the activities of the Selden scribe and of Asloan roughly to the same two decades. The orthography of the Selden scribe's copy substitutes Scottish for English forms in many of the ways we have already discussed. *Qu-/quh-* spellings are substituted for Middle English *wh-*, and *-ch-* for Middle English *-gh-*, as in the opening stanza

> In maye quhan fflora the fresche lusty quene
> The suyl hath cladde in rede quhite grene aricht
> And phebus gan to sched his stremes schene
> Amydde the bule with all his bemes brycht
> And lucifer to chace aweye the nycht
> Aȝeyne the morow our orisont hath take
> To bid loueres out of thair slepe awake.

"Thair" generally replaces "her" (as at 7, 32, 61, 83, 382, 633, 650), and among other substitutions (taking Fairfax 16 as the lemma) we find commonly "suich" for "suche" or "such" (191, 210), "schall" for "shul" or "shal" (193, 195, 217), along with scattered instances like the following: "suyl" for "soyle" (2, quoted above), "gudely" for "goodly," "buskes" for "busshes" (146), "schade" for "shade" (387), "schap" for "shappe" (498), "bewis" for "bowes" (583), and "ilke samyn" for "eche same" (537).

The relative conservatism of Selden's Scotticizing of this text is thrown into relief by comparison with the copies in the Chepman and Myllar print and the Asloan manuscript, where time and/or the proclivities of different scribes and compositors seem to have allowed for some intensification of the Scottish flavor. Selden's retention of a rhyme on "sprede"/"brede," for instance, emerges in the printed text and in Asloan as "spreid"/"breid" (32–33), and there are a number of similar orthographic substitutions: "doith" in the print and Asloan for "dooth" (68); "taist" in the print and Asloan for "taste" (108); "gleide" in the print for "glede" in Selden and Asloan (231); "kouth" in the print for "coud" in Selden and "couth" in Asloan (144). Even so, the process does not seem to have been thorough, and inconsistencies remain: Asloan's Scottification of a rhyme on "quaike"/ "saike" appears in Chepman and Myllar as "quake"/"saik" (181–82). Interestingly, the Selden scribe demonstrates sporadically here the same taste for metrical smoothing that we noted in his copies of Chaucer's poems. Asloan, in contrast, was seemingly comfortable with less regular lines, and on several occasions seems either to reproduce a common exemplar more faithfully, or—if indeed he was copying Selden's text at the remove of Chepman and Myllar's print—to have deftly removed the padding.

To some degree, then, comparison with other Scottish exemplars serves only to confirm the earlier conclusions we reached from the examination of the major Chaucer texts in Selden. The Scottishness of the manuscript is both variable and relative, open to extension and intensification as and when—as in the case of the Chepman and Myllar *Black Knight*—the texts were transmitted in further stages.

We began this discussion with the suggestion that Selden's assortment of Chaucerian texts may have owed something to the precedent of manuscripts such as Fairfax 16, where some of the dream visions appear in conjunction with attempts at Chaucerian emulation such as *The Letter of Cupid* and *The Complaint of the Black Knight*. Krausser's classification of the manuscripts of the *Complaint*, however, does not support any hypothesis of close textual affiliation between the Scottish witnesses—Selden, Chepman and Myllar, Asloan—and the Oxford-group manuscripts. Instead, and rather surprisingly, they seem closely related to the text in BL MS Add. 16165, copied by the London scribe John Shirley, and very probably the earliest surviving manuscript of Lydgate's poem. Shirley's copy of the poem lacks ll. 610–51 of other texts, a gap not explicable by any hypothesis of lost leaves, and the fact that Selden, Chepman and Myllar, and Asloan were able to make good the omission suggests that Add. 16165 was not their precise exemplar, or at least that they had access to another copy to supplement it. But the close textual relationship is demonstrable in a corpus of common readings that occasionally involve Shirley's own distinctive orthographic habits[42] and his characteristic confusion over the names of classical heroes and deities. A reference to what is in Fairfax 16 and most other manuscripts "the smothe wynde / Of Zepherus" (58–59) is in Shirley's version "feyre Phebus"—contracted in Selden, Chepman and Myllar, and Asloan to "Phebus" alone. Fairfax's "Atteon with his hondes felle" (97), retained more or less by most other manuscripts, is in Shirley's version "Akoun," in Selden "Arceon," in the print "anceon," and in Asloan "anteon." "Tereus, rote of vnkyndenesse" (374), as invoked in Fairfax and several other manuscripts, becomes "Theseus" in Add. 16165, Selden, and Asloan (and also in Pepys 2006 and Thynne's print), and "thecius" in Chepman and Myllar's hands.

The influence, albeit possibly at some remove, of Shirley's exemplars
may also underlie the Selden manuscript's inclusion of "Walton's Prosperity," of which at least four of the extant copies are associated with Shirley
in some way: the texts in Huntington EL 26 A 13 and BL MS Royal 20.
B. xv are copied in his hand, and those in BL MSS Harley 2251 and Add.
29729 derive clearly from his exemplars (as we have already noted, the
association of the stanza with Chaucer's name may derive from Shirley's
copy in the Huntington manuscript). Scottish history seems to have been
among Shirley's many interests, and he made a translation of a now lost
Latin account of the murder of James I that survives in two copies. The
routes offering him access to this material may well have been two-way,
allowing transmission of English texts from a range of sources to Scottish
readers.[43]

At this point it is appropriate to mention a text we have not discussed
hitherto. This is the copy of Hoccleve's *Letter of Cupid* that appears on fols.
211v–217 of Selden. This text is unusual in several respects. It is the only
substantial manifestly Middle English text in the hand of the second scribe
in the manuscript, who began copying near the end of the *Kingis Quair*
and was responsible for the main contents of the rest of the manuscript—
poems that are uniquely or peculiarly Scottish, notably the *Quare of Jelusy*
and *The Lay of Sorrow*. Its situation in such a context is made all the more
distinctive by the general affiliations of Hoccleve's poem elsewhere with
commercially produced or derived booklet manuscripts of the type identified with the Oxford group. Indeed, it appears elsewhere in Bodleian Fairfax
16, Bodley 638, and Tanner 346, as well as in Digby 181 (another booklet
manuscript related to the Oxford group) and CUL Ff. 1. 6 (the Findern
manuscript), which clearly derives from such commercial exemplars, at
least in part. Its relocation to the distinctively more Scottish body of material copied by the second scribe of Selden may, once again, suggest that the
booklet transmission of the texts behind the manuscript was quite fragmented. In addition, it seems noteworthy that this poem also occurs in
Trinity College Cambridge R.3.20, a manuscript in Shirley's hand. This fact
has an obvious potential relevance to our earlier point about the Shirleian
affiliations of Lydgate's *Complaint of the Black Knight*. The textual relationships of Hoccleve's poem have, however, yet to be clarified.

For the present it is the linguistic usages of this scribe that warrant
attention. Why did this scribe, who was otherwise occupied in the transcription of Scottish verse, copy a substantial chunk of Middle English?
One might expect him to transcribe in a more thoroughly Scottish manner
than did the first scribe, who was engaged exclusively in the transcription
of Middle English until his copying of the bulk of *The Kingis Quair*. Once

again, a sample passage from Hoccleve may give some indication of his usage:

> This wordis ben spokyn generaly
> With so pitous a chere and countenance
> That euery wicht þat meneth trewly
> Demith in hert that thai haue such greuance
> They seyne so importable is thare pennance
> That but that lady list to schew thame grace
> Thai richt anon most steruen in that place
> (fol. 211v)

Certainly the text conforms to the Scottish orthography elsewhere in the manuscript in its *sch-* and *-cht* forms, the *-is* plural, and usage of "thai," "thare," and "thame" for their Middle English equivalents. It is our impression that the texture of Scotticized spellings is, in overall terms, somewhat more consistent here, an impression borne out by the evaluation of this scribe's spellings in the most recent edition of *The Quare of Jelousy*.[44]

Selden's texts of the *Complaint of the Black Knight* and the *Letter of Cupid* reinforce the possibility that the compilers of the manuscript had access to a range of exemplars, available possibly in booklet forms: Chaucerian poems, genuine and apocryphal, grouped in collections related to Fairfax 16 and the Oxford group of manuscripts; a copy of the *Parliament of Fowls*, either incomplete or already concluded by a Scottish Chaucer neophyte, which bears no resemblance to any other of the surviving texts; a manuscript of the *Complaint of the Black Knight* deriving, probably at some remove, from a Shirleian exemplar. The activities of the Selden scribe may then have been crucial to the processes by which this range of English texts was made available for wider transmission in Scotland. This is not to say that the scribes or their associates and employers were necessarily directly responsible for introducing the texts into Scotland in the first place. It has been argued that James I must have brought back from his imprisonment in England a number of English manuscripts,[45] and it is certainly not unlikely that copies should have been in limited circulation relatively early in the fifteenth century. But the compilation of the Selden manuscript seems to have served as an occasion, or, more properly, a series of occasions to draw together a number of texts, some of which subsequently became available for wider Scottish transmission.

The differences we have noted between the dialectal and orthographic practices of the manuscript's principal scribe and those of other Scottish scribes copying the same texts may, in relation to this point, be explicable by chronology. It seems entirely comprehensible, indeed to be expected, that the degree of Scottification in these texts should intensify over time and with the processes of transmission. Selden may constitute an early stage in these processes. It may be, too, that the first Selden scribe had some interest in deliberately preserving the English flavor of what he saw taking shape as an anthology of writings by England's major poet, causing him to limit the extent of his translation. It seems clear that the prime impulse behind his activity is orthographic; metrical concerns are secondary. Only rarely does lexicon become a factor, and then primarily as the substitution of Scottish synonyms for English equivalents. There is no indication of any wider, more radical process of Scotticizing apart from the unique ending to the *Parliament*, which may, as we have said, relate to what was available in an exemplar.

A. J. Aitken has written with characteristic authority of the Angliciza-tion—the adoption of Southern English forms and usages—in poetic con-texts that has come to be characterized as "Anglo-Scots."[46] He concludes that Scots poets who wrote in this idiom were "adapting . . . to the partially Scotticized Scots copies of the English classics" available in collections like Selden. B. 24.[47] C. D. Jeffrey's work on *The Kingis Quair* and *Colkelbie Sow* has further clarified some of the processes by which "the vogue for 'Chau-cerian' poetry in Scotland in the fifteenth century led Scottish anthology compilers to copy out English Chaucerian poems in a kind of Anglo-Scots spelling and Scottish poets to write their own works in a kind of Anglo-Scots literary language."[48] The importance of such perceptions makes all the more desirable some fuller understanding of the nature of the earliest and most substantial of these surviving copies, MS Arch. Selden. B. 24, and the ways in which it signals its distinctive transmission of Chaucer to a northern audience.

Notes

1. Outside the manuscript that forms the basis for our present discussion there survive few instances of Middle English texts being translated into Scottish ones. Such texts, for example, those in Cambridge University Library MS Kk.1.5, have been little studied.

2. A. McIntosh, "Some Notes on the Language and Textual Transmission of the *Scottish Troy Book,*" *Archivum Linguisticum*, n.s., 10 (1979): 1–19; reprinted in *Middle English Dialectology: Essays on Some Principles and Problems*, ed. A. McIntosh, M. L. Samuels, and Margaret Laing (Aberdeen: Aberdeen University Press, 1989), 236–55.

3. Fuller details of the contents and construction of the manuscript and of the activities of this scribe are set out in the introduction to our facsimile of this manuscript

(Julia Boffey and A. S. G. Edwards, introduction to *Bodleian Library MS Arch. Selden. B. 24. A Facsimile* [Cambridge: Boydell & Brewer, 1997]).

4. On the Oxford group, see E. P. Hammond, *Chaucer: A Bibliographical Manual* (New York: MacMillan, 1908), 333–40, and A. Brusendorff, *The Chaucer Tradition* (Oxford: Oxford University Press, 1925), 182–207. For facsimiles of all these manuscripts see *Bodleian Library, MS Fairfax 16*, with an introduction by John Norton-Smith (London: Scolar Press, 1979); *Manuscript Tanner 346: A Facsimile*, with an introduction by Pamela Robinson (Facsimile Series of the Works of Geoffrey Chaucer 1 [Norman, Okla.: Pilgrim Books, 1980]) and *Manuscript Bodley 638: A Facsimile*, with an introduction by Pamela Robinson (Facsimile Series of the Works of Geoffrey Chaucer 2 [Norman, Okla.: Pilgrim Books, 1982]).

5. Bodleian Library MS Digby 181 includes the *Parliament of Fowls*, Lydgate's *Complaint of the Black Knight*, and Hoccleve's *Letter of Cupid* with *Troilus*, while the *Letter of Cupid* and *Troilus* appear together in Durham University Library MS Cosin V. II. 13; but these are unusual instances of such collocations.

6. For some discussion of these texts see A. S. G. Edwards, "Bodleian Library MS Arch Selden. B. 24: A 'Transitional' Anthology," in *The Whole Book: Cultural Perspectives on the Medieval Miscellany*, ed. Stephen J. Nichols and Siegfried Wenzel (Ann Arbor: University of Michigan Press, 1996), 53–68, and Julia Boffey, "Proverbial Chaucer and the Chaucer Canon," *Huntington Library Quarterly* 58 (1996): 37–47.

7. See J. D. McClure, "Scottis, Inglis, Suddroun: Language Labels and Language Attitudes," in *Proceedings of the Third International Conference on Scottish Language and Literature (Medieval and Renaissance), University of Stirling, 2–7 July 1981*, ed. R. J. Lyall and Felicity Riddy (Stirling and Glasgow: Culross, 1981), 207–24.

8. See, for example, the discussion of "Language" in J. Norton-Smith, ed., *The Kingis Quair* (Oxford: Clarendon Press, 1971), xxvii–xxx, and W. A. Craigie, "The Language of the *Kingis Quair*," *Essays and Studies* 35 (1939): 22–38.

9. Extracts from the text of Selden are printed in *Specimen Extracts from the Nine Unprinted MSS. of Chaucer's Troilus*, ed. W. S. McCormick and R. K. Root, Chaucer Society, 1st ser., 89 (London: K. Paul, Trench, Trübner, 1914), 2–29. Throughout we have silently expanded contractions apart from the ampersand; this procedure is not without implications for our argument. For example, the form we expand as "nocht" appears not infrequently in a contracted form "noᵗ" in Selden. We have silently expanded it in accord with the scribe's general usage, but some of the Chaucer Society transcripts render it as "noght."

10. R. K. Root, *The Textual Tradition of Chaucer's Troilus*, Chaucer Society, 1st ser., 99 (London: K. Paul, Trench, Trübner, 1916), 27.

11. E.g., "suere" (III:269), "suich" (I:619, III:286), "suorn" (III:312).

12. E.g., III:318, 320; IV:718, 721.

13. E.g., IV:724, 730.

14. The full text of Selden is in *A Parallel-Text Edition of Chaucer's Minor Poems*, ed. Frederick J. Furnivall, Chaucer Society, 1st ser., 58 (London: N. Trübner, 1879), 245–405 (odd pages only). Here, as throughout, we have silently corrected transcriptional errors.

15. The full text of Selden is in *Supplementary Parallel-Texts of Chaucer's Minor Poems*, ed. Frederick J. Furnivall, Chaucer Society, 1st ser., 22 (London: N. Trübner, 1871), 2–26. Line references for the spurious ending are to this text.

16. We use Fairfax 16 as the point of comparison in our discussion of the text of the *Parliament*.

17. We have noted twelve unique variants (out of nineteen) in Book I relating to metrical questions. These are I:88, 95, 184, 263, 380, 623, 744, 897, 917, 948, 985, and 1081. In Book V we have noted forty-eight (out of eighty-five) unique variants: V:15, 37, 50, 171, 184, 224, 228, 276, 288, 352, 498, 505, 596, 648, 775, 794, 825, 830, 845, 868, 887, 906, 919, 954, 969, 981, 1082, 1102, 1129, 1160, 1189, 1209, 1215, 1285, 1290, 1401, 1428, 1528, 1531, 1550, 1585, 1628, 1661, 1662, 1718, 1724, 1755, and 1769. We derive the information and figures from Barry Windeatt, ed., *Troilus and Criseyde: A New Edition of the* Book of Troilus (London: Longmans, 1984).

18. We follow the text and lineation of Windeatt's edition.

19. Janet Cowen and George Kane, eds., *The Legend of Good Women*, Medieval Texts and Studies, no. 16 (East Lansing, Mich.: Colleagues Press, 1995), 105–09; see also E. F. Amy, *The Text of the* Legend of Good Women (Princeton: Princeton University Press, 1918), 8–9.

20. We give the text in Bodleian Fairfax 16 as the lemma rather than using the heavily emended critical text of Cowen and Kane.

21. For a facsimile of the text in the Bannatyne MS, see *The Bannatyne MS: National Library of Scotland, Advocates' MS 1.1.6*, with an introduction by Denton Fox and William A. Ringler (London: Scolar Press, 1980); and W. Tod Ritchie, ed., *The Bannatyne Manuscript*, 4 vols., Scottish Text Society, n.s., 22, 23, 26, and 3d ser., 5 (Edinburgh: W. Blackwood and Sons, 1928–34), 1:186–87.

22. For the most recent listing of the manuscripts and a transcription of the text from BL Cotton Vitellius E. xi, see Julia Boffey, "Proverbial Chaucer and the Chaucer Canon."

23. Both copies are presented together in *Odd Texts of Chaucer's Minor Poems*, ed. Frederick J. Furnivall, Chaucer Society, 1st ser., 60 (London: N. Trübner, 1880), 290–91.

24. We are indebted to Dr. Sally Mapstone for her advice about this manuscript.

25. NLS has "my^t."

26. The word is not in the holograph at l. 10.

27. NLS has "30^r" in these instances.

28. In ll. 22, 24, 41, 49, 50, 58, 61, 69, 83, 88, 92.

29. In ll. 17, 51, 64, 66, 69, 76, 78, 85, 87, 89, 96, 103.

30. NLS generally expresses this form by a final flourish after the terminal -r; at a few points the scribe does use the possibly equivocal contraction "o^r" (25, 41, 50, 71, 133).

31. NLS does have "thyn" at two points (70, 126).

32. Hoccleve's holograph has the nonsensical "this" here.

33. This is not invariable; at l. 36 both Scottish texts have "my."

34. Julia Boffey and A. S. G. Edwards, "Bodleian MS Arch. Selden. B. 24: The Genesis and Evolution of a Scottish Poetical Miscellany," Proceedings of the Eighth International Conference on Medieval and Renaissance Scottish Language and Literature (forthcoming). On notaries see Grant G. Simpson, *Scottish Handwriting, 1150–1650* (Edinburgh: Scottish Academic Press, 1973), 7–8; Lyall, "Books and Book Owners," and John Durkan, "The Early Scottish Notary," both in *The Renaissance and Reformation in Scotland: Essays in Honour of Gordon Donaldson*, ed. Ian B. Cowan and Duncan Shaw (Edinburgh: Scottish Academic Press, 1983), 244–50, 22–40.

35. Simpson, *Scottish Handwriting*, 7.

36. Ibid., 13, fig. 3.

37. He writes "us" at ll. 44, 97, 104, 105.

38. But he writes "sorow" at l. 60.

39. W. A. Craigie, ed., *The Asloan Manuscript: A Miscellany in Prose and Verse*, 2 vols., Scottish Text Series, n.s., 14, 16 (1923–24), 19. See also I. C. Cunningham, "The Asloan Manuscript," in *The Renaissance in Scotland: Studies in Literature, Religion, History and Culture Offered to John Durkan*, ed. A. A. MacDonald, Michael Lynch, and Ian B. Cowan (Leiden: E. J. Brill, 1994), 107–35. On Asloan himself, see C. C. van Buuren-Veenenbos, "John Asloan, an Edinburgh Scribe," *English Studies* 47 (1966): 365–72, and her edition of *The Buke of the Sevyne Sages*, Germanic and Anglistik Studies of the University of Leiden 20 (Leiden: Leiden University Press, 1982), 5–73.

40. On this edition see *The Chepman and Myllar Prints: A Facsimile with a Bibliographical Note by William Beattie* (Edinburgh: Edinburgh Bibliographical Society, 1950).

41. E. Krausser, "The Complaint of the Black Knight," *Anglia* 19 (1897): 211–90. This manuscript shares a distinctive lacuna with Selden and Chepman and Myllar from l. 113 through l. 126.

42. Shirley's "that lykly beon" (292), for "that lykly ar" in most other witnesses, is transmitted in Selden, Chepman and Myllar, and Asloan as "That lykly bene." Asloan's possible dependence on the print is not, however, a matter that can be conclusively resolved.

43. On Shirley's interest in Scottish matters, see M. Connolly, "The Dethe of the Kynge of Scotis: A New Edition," *Scottish Historical Review* 71 (1992): 46–69.

44. J. Norton-Smith and I. Pravda, eds., *The Quare of Jelusy*, Middle English Texts 3 (Heidelberg: Carl Winter, 1976), 22–35 (on "graphy"). They conclude that "the spelling systems of scribe II would seem to show a more standard application of Scottish spelling forms than would the evidence provided by the copying of hand I."

45. Gregory Kratzmann, *Anglo-Scottish Literary Relations, 1430–1550* (Cambridge: Cambridge University Press, 1980), 35–36.

46. A. J. Aitken, "The Language of Older Scots Poetry," in *Scotland and the Lowland Tongue*, ed. J. D. McClure (Aberdeen: Aberdeen University Press, 1983), 26–31.

47. Aitken, "Older Scots Poetry," 31.

48. C. D. Jeffery, "Anglo-Scots Poetry and the *Kingis Quair*," in *Actes du 2ᵉ Colloque de Langue et de Littérature Ecossaises (Moyen Âge et Renaissance)*, ed. J.-J. Blanchot and Claude Graf (Strasbourg: University of Strasbourg, 1978), 207–21, and "*Colkelbie Sow*: An Anglo-Scots Poem," in *Proceedings of the Third International Conference on Scottish Language and Literature*, 207–24. See also P. J. Frankis, "Notes on Two Fifteenth-Century Scots Poems," *Neuphilologische Mitteilungen* 61 (1960): 203–13.

Scottish Chaucer, Misogynist Chaucer

Carolyn Ives and David Parkinson

> *. . . the verity of God is of that nature that at one time
> or at other it will purchase to itself audience. It is an odor
> and smell that cannot be suppressed; yea, it is a trumpet
> that will sound in despite of the adversary. It will compel
> the very enemies to their own confusion to testify
> and bear witness of it.*

So wrote John Knox in 1559, apparently without conscious irony, in his *First Blast of the Trumpet against the Monstrous Regiment of Women*.[1] Polemic against women in power has at times a headlong, unreflective quality in later sixteenth-century Scotland. In ways that sometimes run counter to its makers' purposes, it turns and returns to particular topics and authorities. One authority for misogyny repeatedly cited and alluded to in sixteenth-century Scotland is Geoffrey Chaucer. The point is worth a moment's reflection: When one thinks now about Chaucerian influence on Scottish writers, praise of the master poet himself, not vilification of women, still tends to come first to mind. After all, these writers often continue to be thought of as the "Scottish Chaucerians," with high courtly style and aureation their defining characteristics for many.[2] As testimony to their devotion, there is the *Kingis Quair* manuscript (Bodley Arch. Selden B. 24; c. 1488), itself a strikingly inventive *tombeau de* Chaucer. Students of late medieval Scottish poetry have known for some time that Robert Henryson, William Dunbar, and Gavin Douglas were strong readers of Chaucer;[3] what remains to be investigated is the range and development of Scottish responses to Chaucer in the sixteenth century.

The grounding for this development can be seen in the *Kingis Quair* manuscript. This courtly collection does more than simply display ardent devotion to the master poet: it alters, revises, and completes "Chaucerian" texts, texts derived from Chaucerian precedent.[4] In her *City, Marriage, Tournament*, Louise Fradenburg has offered a sophisticated contextualization of this definitively Scottish Chaucerian manuscript as "an important contribution to the arts of marriage in late medieval Scotland." For Fradenburg, the rewriting in this manuscript of the ending to Chaucer's *Parliament of Fowls* "denudes" the poem "of its changefulness," and, by depriving the formel, who is bestowed upon the royal eagle, of freedom of choice, the Selden reviser silences voices other than that of the sovereign.[5] Even more resonant is Fradenburg's discussion of the *Kingis Quair* itself, a poem akin to this manuscript's *Parliament of Fowls* in its celebration of "an ultimately certain choice, the authority of sovereign love and of the sovereign word," but also one that refers to an anxiety of influence, English as well as queenly, on Scottish sovereignty.[6] Fradenburg's investigation of Scottish motives for Chaucerianism has brought the issue a long way from inventorying allusions and echoes; as has Fradenburg, R. James Goldstein finds anxiety of influence a useful concept in coming to terms with Scottish poets' use of Chaucerian conventions to mark their writing as literary.[7]

Study of Scottish responses to Chaucer has progressed in recent years, but getting past preconceptions about the "Scottish Chaucerians" still requires effort. Instead of transmission and reception of Chaucer by a Scottish readership being treated as a supplement to Chaucer studies, that readership must become the matter of central importance. With this reorientation, what emerges is an inventive, independent-minded Scottish construction of the English author, one that links the Scottish literary tradition to the English tradition by means of Father Chaucer (as A. C. Spearing has argued), but also one that separates the responses of these two traditions to this figure of paternity.

By the 1550s and 1560s—the period of Lindsay's *Satire of the Three Estates*, the Bannatyne MS, and Knox's *History of the Reformation*—Scottish writers, it might be supposed, needed rely no longer on such figures. During a long, embattled regency and the short but no less embattled reign of Mary Stewart, seeking English authority for grandly conclusive cultural gestures would hardly have been timely. After all, as every Scottish reader knew, the absolutist ambitions of James I had ended in disaster, as had the triumphalist ones of James IV. What, then, is the significance of Chaucerian attributions in the literary manuscripts of these decades, in Bannatyne above all? Why should these attributions converge in the context of the argument about women? As can be seen with special clarity in Scottish manuscripts of the later sixteenth century, Scottish writers and readers are keen to shape their Chaucer into an authority on this subject. This is to be an author directly relevant to their own divisive political and social concerns, a Chaucer for whom discontents of gender offer prime ground for expressing—and perhaps diverting—such concerns.

The evidence for Scottish reception of Chaucer is rather more complex and extended than critical commonplaces allow. Given the recurrent fascination in Scottish writings of the earlier sixteenth century with curious, unstable, and problematic combinations of genres and voices, the Chaucer who emerges (and is copied and reprinted through the century) is predictably often the one whose authority compels doubt ("Quha wait gif all that Chauceir wrait was trew?"),[8] and whose affiliation with the threateningly deceptive suggests he may be just as untrustworthy: "he was evir (God wait) all womanis frend."[9] This appropriation of Chaucer and Chaucerian themes invokes literary authority, compromises it, and dismisses it. Criticizing and improving on English literary tradition, Henryson and Douglas claim Chaucer as a source of their own literary tradition; they are quick to alter, "re-vision," and complete the Chaucerian texts they appropriate.[10] A crucial example of this Scottish disposition is Douglas's "attempt to rehabilitate Virgil, to recuperate the auctoritas which the Aeneid had lost at Chaucer's hands."[11] Claiming to be children of Father Chaucer, criticizing him, and claiming higher fathers, the "Scottish Chaucerians" undermine the power of English literary authority. These poets search for guarantees of paternity but also for figures of masculinity both in their acknowledgment of Chaucer's authority and in the undermining of the tradition he embodies. With the notable exception of the *Kingis Quair*, this search also figures in the foregrounding of authorship in these poets' most markedly Chaucerian texts.

"Every woman's friend" Chaucer may notoriously be, but he is used as a tool for depicting women in a far from friendly way. Circa 1550, a character in John Rolland's *Court of Venus* demands that women learn the truth about themselves by reading the authorities for misogyny:

Of your fals luif this is ay the commend:
Reid Gower ouir, and Bocchas to the end.
All Chronikles that ony man of reidis,
Ye sall not find a taill ane vther mend,
Bot to the werst it will ay condiscend.
With euill entent your luif burgeonis and breidis,
And euer mair sa furth it ay proceidis.
Quhat sayis Chaucer? All Christin men may kend
Your euil mind thair, and eik your cruell deidis.[12]

Even more emphatically than the last stanza of Henryson's *Testament of Cresseid*, this passage falls into the topic of unedifying advice. It would appear impossible for a Scottish woman in the sixteenth century, or any woman, for that matter, to reflect profitably on such reading. Here, under the authority of Gower, "Bocchas" (Lydgate of the *Fall of Princes*), the Chronicles ("that ony man of reidis") and especially Chaucer, women are fixed into damning categories. All these categories have ready Chaucerian precedent. There is the coy, deceptive mistress who plays hard to get, as Criseyde supposedly does while being cajoled and threatened by her uncle Pandarus. There is the fickle, too complicit woman, as Criseyde is taken to be when she accepts her fate, first as Troilus's and then as Diomede's lover. There is the domineering wife unafraid of her sexuality and wanting to control her own life and her husband's, with the Wife of Bath as precedent. Criseyde is allowed to be neither resistant nor complicit; similarly, the Wife of Bath is mocked for her unabashed sexual knowledge, which translates into sexual power.

Where Chaucer's versions of Criseyde and the Wife of Bath have otherwise been read as subtle and open for lively debate, the Scottish versions are often—well into the sixteenth century—reductive, stereotypical, and misogynist. Why should this be? Perhaps writers like John Rolland continued to see and use Chaucer as an authority in their combat against a fear more acute and general than that of English hegemony, a fear of being unmanned and rendered illegitimate, politically and culturally. It is a fear that underlies Knox's writings, and indeed comes frequently to the surface there, often in the form of misogynist outbursts.[13] Prevalent across sixteenth-century Europe, with Galen's concept of the fundamental oneness of sex still dominant,[14] fear of women takes acute and prominent forms in Scotland. Popular and learned attacks on female rulers in Scotland (notably the regent Marie de Guise and her daughter Mary Stewart) manifest this fear repeatedly.[15] As writers without enough genealogy in their own tradition, Scottish writers, notably the "Chaucerians," presented women in this unflattering way as a manifestation of their own fears of being feminized, of being bastardized. Perhaps the struggle they present is more about gender than it is about sex. Fear of being rendered feminine or powerless becomes understandable in a culture that not only still believes in Galen's one-sex model, but that must also rely on a foreign literary tradition—one that is perceived as possessing a clear masculine lineage—to construct its own genealogy.[16]

The reductive categories adduced by Rolland and other Scottish writers are not to persuade women to mend their ways; they are not for female readers at all. Like the four encompassing categories in the Scottish book of wicked women (maids, widows, and nuns, as well as wives), *The Spectakle of Luf,*[17] they are presented to men for men's own profit, ostensibly as remedies. As it goes in the preface to the *Spectakle,* reading misogyny cures a man from love, "for in it appeiris and schawis sum evillis and myshappis that cummys to men thairthrow as the filth or spottis of the face schawis in the myrrour of glas."[18] Reading the *Spectakle* is meant to be curative, even purgative, recreation.

Topically far more variegated than the *Spectakle*, Gavin Douglas's *Palis of Honoure* offers ironic versions of such recreation: In *The Palis of Honoure* (reprinted in Edinburgh in 1579), even Venus cannot avoid the topics of misogyny when she attempts to justify her sudden lenience to the clerkly dreamer:

> A lady—fy!—that usis tirrane
> No woman is, rather a serpent fell.
> A vennamus dragon or a devill of hell
> Is na compare to the inequyte
> Of bald wemen, as thir wyse clerkis tell.[19]

Serpent, dragon, devil, and (elsewhere, as in Kennedie's second innings in *The Flyting of Dunbar and Kennedie*) cockatrice, the terms of invective against powerful women are hardly unique to Scottish writings. What is worth noting is the extent to which this topic is given Chaucerian context in these writings.

From this view, Criseyde and the Wife of Bath are mirrors of woman as traitor and predator. With obvious reductions of these two characters for its principal models, it may not be surprising that antifeminist discourse in Scotland often tends to veer between tragedy (of the *de casibus* type) and farce. It is striking that each of the Scottish poets most admired as Chaucerians today attains peculiar intensity of response to Chaucer in depicting a wayward widow: Henryson's Cresseid, the Wedo of Dunbar's *Tretis*, and Douglas's lustful Dido—particularly unforgiving revisions of Chaucerian widows. Of course, widows were the perfect target for masculine aggression: they were the only women not under the direct control of husbands, fathers, or brothers, and were, therefore, considered the direst threats to masculine power.

The positioning of Chaucer at the head of misogynist discourse in Scotland is not simply a matter of making germane allusions. In the sixteenth century, Scottish readers had their own set of Chauceriana against women. A few items in this set are preserved only in Scottish sources. In rhyme royal, often with heavy alliteration, these poems are likely now to seem un- (or sub-) Chaucerian, sometimes strikingly so. In associating these poems with Chaucer, Scottish readers and writers are embroidering on what for them was the defining feature of their author's identity—his involvement in the argument about women.[20] A complex appropriation is taking place here, with a distinctively Scottish discourse "aganis evill wemen" being grounded in the authority of a transformed, Scottified Chaucer.[21] What deserves to be asked, then, is whether this appropriation answers to particular circumstances of time and place—sixteenth-century Scotland, especially Edinburgh of the 1560s and early 1570s.

In their books, Scottish writers and readers of the mid-sixteenth century sought confirmation of fears and consolation for them. The vast majority of these writers and readers were men; those women (a growing minority) who were able to read, and the few who were able to write, were (as in England) the "daughters, wives and widows of professional men and of the nobility and gentry."[22] Prominent among the vast male majority of the literate were those of some standing—burgesses, clerics (with varying degrees of affiliation with the newly reformed Kirk), and gentry—worthy, substantial men living in a realm without much of the machinery of central authority.[23] Few of them absolutely wealthy, Edinburgh merchants typify this readership: "Part-ownership of ships and shares in cargoes, money-lending, including advances to government officials, sub-letting of burgh property, the holding of land in security from debtors, selling merchandise to retailers, provisioning the households of nobles and lairds and the predominance in their stock of expensive cloths and wine, characterize them as a group."[24] For such men, the history of their community often comes down to "a story of family feuds."[25] As they saw it themselves, much depended on these men. As heads of households, they sustained the "basic form of obligation" in Scottish society: agnatic kinship, "dependent on an ancestor, whether real or mythical, in the male line, and recognized as a bond between male relatives. Females—mothers, sisters, daughters—were not part of this bond; they were added to, or removed from, the kingroup by marriage."[26] In this society, the recreation of literature tended to celebrate the legitimacy of the male bond and to treat with suspicion bonds between men and women, and women and women.

Evidently family can be a source of vulnerability as well as security. While Scottish readers often return to texts about death, hell, disorder, and dearth, they also—given their sense of the potential for conflict within and around the family—have a keen taste for writings about sex and marriage, and about women—wives and widows above all—as creatures of appetite, malice, and treachery. In Scotland, experience in sex and marriage often gets written about as if it were deathly, hellish, disorderly, and impoverishing.

In their engagement with topics of misogyny, Scottish male readers do not seem at first glance much different from their counterparts in various other times and places. In fact they are aware of their bond to tradition, and in predictable ways they derive authority from it. One of the consolations of misogyny is belief in the stability and applicability of its old tales and philosophers' sayings. By declaring its indebtedness to the tradition of such books elsewhere, Scottish misogynist writing invites its reader to refer the particulars of his own experience to the permanence of types.

Unsurprisingly, misogyny has a way of arising in reaction—immediate and subsequent—to a woman who assumes prominence in Scottish history.[27] Sixteenth-century chronicles replay the topic of vicious women shaming princes and kingdoms. In divorce or widowhood, queens reveal their true masterfulness and lechery: Margaret Logie, Mary of Gueldres, Margaret Tudor, Marie of Guise, Mary Stewart.[28] The late sixteenth-century chronicler Robert Lindesay of Pitscottie epitomizes the process when he fabricates a precedent for the fall of Mary Queen of Scots.[29] According to Pitscottie, shortly after the death of her husband James II (1460), Mary of Gueldres

> tuik Adame Hepburne of Haillis quho had ane wyffe of his awin and committit adultrie witht him, quhilk caussit hir to be lichtlieit witht the haill nobilietie of Scottland that scho saw sa money nobill men in Scottland, lordis souns and barrouns fre of marieage that scho wald not desyre them to have susteinit hir lust, bot tuik ane wther wyffis husband to satisfie hir gredie appetyte. Thairfoir we may sie in tymes bygaine presentlie and to cum quhair weomen hes ovir mekill of thair awin will but correctioun or guid counsall garris thame oftymes fall frome god and tyne the hartis of thair best lowearis to thair avin gret schame and turpitude.[30]

> [took Adam Hepburn of Hailes (who had a wife of his own) and committed adultery with him, which caused her to be scorned by all the nobility of Scotland. Though she saw so many unmarried noblemen in Scotland, lords' and barons' sons, she had no desire for such as they to cater to her longings. Instead she took another woman's husband to satisfy her greedy appetite. Therefore we may see in time past, present, and future that wherever women have too much according to their own will without correction or good counsel, it generally makes them fall away from God and lose the hearts of their most fervent supporters, to their own great shame and degradation.]

Images of womanly monstrosity were ready to hand to use against past and present queens. Within a year of her coronation, walking in a garden with English ambassador Sir Henry Sidney, Mary Queen of Scots received "a byll" from a Captain Hepburn; in this "byll" were "iiij as shamfull— and, saving your honour, as ribbalde verses as anye dyvleshe wytte coulde invent, and under them drawne with a penne the secreat members bothe of men and women in as monstrous a sorte as nothynge could be more shamfullye dyvisede."[31] For one historian, this is a highly revealing event: "Mary's reputation and prestige were already so low that she was not just the object of scandal spread about her, but the personal recipient of a direct gesture which was profoundly humiliating and insulting."[32] Misogynist texts, a source of recreation, affiliation, even consolation when shared among men in sixteenth-century Scotland, could also be devised to strip power from the women to whom they are directed. In this regard, one may recall Chaucer's *Wife of Bath's Prologue*, in which Jankin uses misogynist texts (his book of wicked wives) in an attempt to control his wife; misogyny becomes discipline for a potentially powerful woman.

In turn, advice to Scottish princes on ruling well by avoiding feminine influence becomes indicative of domestic power struggles. The problem of male suspicion of female power is by no means restricted to the court. In a Scottish burgh, wives and widows of prosperous husbands pushed at the boundaries of a problematic, as yet inadequately studied space in economic and social life.[33] Despite growing evidence that women participated in various aspects of public life, it remains possible for a historian to summarize that "The area of the market, the household and the well, or the event of childbirth were all mainly female preserves."[34] A widow's scope and independence were greater, and hence more problematic, than a wife's: a wife's power to own and dispose of property was circumscribed by her husband, but a widow could carry out transactions "effectively on a par with men"[35]—again perhaps a reason that widows were depicted in such an unfavorable manner by Scottish poets. Perhaps a widowed queen was not the only threat to male sovereignty in Edinburgh. However successful, even a well-off woman who survived her husband and continued his business was in some sense masterless—not quite a member of the community of burgesses, and yet a challenge to the privileges of that community.[36]

Edinburgh in the 1560s was a maze of conflicts and accommodations, many of which involve Holyrood Palace and the kirk, Catholic and Protestant, burgh and queen. Sometimes conflict plays out at the center of a household. A list of those accused of attending Mass at Holyrood in August 1563 includes the names of three women, Katherine Bryce, Isobel Curror, and Helen Johnston, pledged by their husbands: "These men must have been particularly embarrassed by their wives' indiscretion; they were all at least nominal protestants."[37] Even on the burgh council sat uprightly protestant men "who had catholic relations and even catholic wives," and whose households were "incubator[s] of catholicism."[38] In that privileged stratum of the Edinburgh community inhabited by merchants and wealthier craftsmen, Protestantism "frequently represented social or political choice rather than religious conviction."[39] Wives were also asserting themselves politically, and on both sides of the religious debate.[40] Now women held a new power to embarrass their husbands, the power of religious choice.

Here, but also in the economic sphere, were opportunities for female initiative and independence—opportunities dire perhaps to some, if Sir Richard Maitland's invectives against the wastefulness of women can be said to have moved beyond antifeminist convention in their pointedness.[41] As the exceptionally successful career of "wad-wyfe" (female money-lender) Janet Fockart indicates, women held their own during or after marriage, but were not always honored for doing so.[42] Such women were not afraid to speak out against kirk or burgh. Euphemia Dundas, widow of a successful merchant and a successful merchant in her own right, made a memorable accusation against John Knox himself: "Ewfame Dundas, in the presens of ane multitude, had spokin diuers injurious and sclandarous wordis bayth of the doctrine and ministeris, and in speciall of Jhonne Knox, minister, sayand that within few dayis past the said Jhonne Knox wes apprehendit and tane furth of ane killogye with ane commoun hure, and that he had bene ane commoun harlot all his dayis."[43]

Dundas uses the main theme of Scottish sectarian controversy, in which illegitimate relations with women characterized one's opponents: for Protestants, idolatry is akin to fornication, while, for Catholics, the Reformed clergy, "particularly those who married, were lustful libertines," and Protestant women were harlots.[44] Citing occasion and event, however, in public, with calculated insult, and being a woman herself, Euphemia Dundas oversteps various bounds. Her accusation of John Knox has been damned with the inaudible praise of being "not simply the malice of a 'gossiping woman.'"[45] Women's words, like women's beliefs, indeed like any dealings a man might have with a woman, have peculiar power to injure men, or so men fear; hence those words are to be discredited. The disarming of a woman's condemnation is signaled by its being treated as illicit (slander) or trivial (gossip). Even if it could "provoke bitter discord," mere gossip, after all, merely "reaffirmed conformist behaviour and identified the boundaries of deviance."[46]

It may be argued that Mary's controversial reign and the embattled Protestant ascendancy provide the context for a heightened sense of the challenge posed to men by women in Scotland in the late 1560s and early 1570s, and that this context deserves to be taken into account in reading the many complaints against "wo that is in mariage" in Scottish manuscripts, such as Bannatyne (National Library of Scotland Advocates' MS 1.1.6, c. 1568) and the Maitland Folio (Magdalene College Cambridge, Pepysian Library MS 2553, c. 1570). Still, the practice of making and excerpting verses against women is a convention of medieval misogyny.[47] Even in Scotland, this practice substantially antedates the 1560s. Such verses appear in fifteenth-century manuscripts of *Scotichronicon*.[48] The Book of the Dean of Lismore (National Library of Scotland Advocates' MS. 72.1.37, c. 1512–

42) also contains plenty of misogynist verse, mostly in Gaelic but also in Scots.[49] In it appear various passages against women extracted from Lydgate, Henryson, and Dunbar, among them two stanzas ascribed to "chawschir."[50] In their attributions, indeed (to Chaucer but also—for a stanza from Henryson's *Testament of Cresseid*—to "bocas þat wes ful gwd"),[51] the MacGregor scribes of the Book of the Dean extend the claim to authority away from the local and immediate and toward poets dignified by their distance, or, better, by their centrality to literary tradition.[52] In attributing these stanzas to famous old authors, these scribes are augmenting popular misogyny.[53]

The poem (beginning "The beistlie lust, the furius appetyte") from which the two "chawschir" stanzas in the Book of the Dean are taken is also to be found, anonymously, in Bannatyne and Maitland. In both those manuscripts, it ends with what appears to be a warning to men against frequenting prostitutes.[54] As a whole, the poem does not lead one to expect such focus of attack. In Bannatyne, the penultimate stanza goes thus:

> And possible war in till ane cumly cors
> Wyiss Salamonis wit and his hie sapience,
> Arristotillis clergy, Sampsonis strenth and fors,
> Hectoris proves, and Achillis excellence,
> Yit wemen sould with wylie influence
> Cawis all thair vertewis to be of non availl
> With thair sle serpent wrinkis and fals taill.[55]

> [And if it were possible that in a single handsome (male) body to find sage Solomon's wit and great wisdom, Aristotle's learning, Samson's strength and power, Hector's prowess, and Achilles' excellence, even so, women with their wily manipulativeness would use their sly snaky tricks and deceitful tale/tail to make all those manly virtues of no use.]

These sentiments are not directed exclusively against kinds of women—all "wemenkynd" is characterized as "subtill."[56] From "clerkis awld" and other "folkis wyis of gud discretioun" we learn "quhat skaithis and offens / That wemen dois be cullorit eloquens."[57] Nor are these sentiments uniquely Scottish: The topic of womanly wiles overcoming the worthiest of men is firmly established both in English and Scottish verse of the fifteenth century.[58]

In the Book of the Dean of Lismore, the attribution to Chaucer of two stanzas from "The beistlie lust" offers a basis for speculation about the sentiments an early sixteenth-century Scottish cleric like James MacGregor, titular Dean of Lismore, might have read into the *Prologue to the*

Wife of Bath's Tale or *Troilus and Criseyde.* This attribution also reveals
something about that cleric's concept of Chaucer as author. His Chaucer
deserves respect as a wise old clerk, full of sayings and exemplary tales
about the perfidy of women. In effect, this bit of evidence suggests that
MacGregor would remember and identify Chaucer by latching on to, excerpting, and even contributing to his antifeminist saws.

Misogyny serves as an index of authorship in Scottish manuscripts.
Here, and especially but not uniquely for Chaucer, ascriptions to an old
author increase and flourish for precisely those poems that vilify women.
In the *Kingis Quair* manuscript, for instance, the *explicit,* to "Devise prowes
and eke humylitee," reads "Quod Chaucere quhen he was rycht auisit."[59]
The point, then, may be that this convention of authorship gains new mo-
mentum in the Scotland of Mary Queen of Scots, John Knox, and George
Bannatyne—Bannatyne, in whose manuscript has most recently been
found "a humanism that was concerned with the 'common weill' . . . and
with . . . the underlying notion that 'men were born for the sake of men.'"[60]
Such men's fear of the challenge women pose to them gives a new edge to
the old conventions. In turn, the conventions and their old authors grant
prestige to the male response in this time and place.

To be sure, in his celebrated manuscript George Bannatyne goes further
than any of his contemporaries, English or Scottish, to present a Chaucer
through whom he can articulate and authorize largely pessimistic views
about love and marriage. In effect, he devises a Chaucer for a readership of
prosperous Edinburgh men. As a revered, familiar authority, one whose
Englishness has been elided since the late fifteenth century in Scottified
texts and Scottish imitations, and who is easily recognizable for his bringing together of grave and scurrilous discourse, Chaucer is sufficiently dis-
tant, yet accessible enough, to bear responsibility for (among other things)
the misogyny of Bannatyne and his readers.[61]

Many but by no means all of Bannatyne's Chaucerian versions are independent-minded, purposeful reworkings of texts in Thynne's printed
1532 collection, *Chaucer's Workes.*[62] Taken as a group, these Chaucerian
poems—those ascribed to Chaucer, but also neighboring poems written in
Chaucerian style and in rhyme-royal stanzas[63]—offer the male reader a
pattern of love, from Petrarchan intensity of experience, to vilification of
the beloved (and hence women in general), to defense of women, to renunciation of love. Couched in a largely Chaucerian sequence, the Chaucer
ascriptions mark the stages in the process of disillusionment traced through
the fourth part of the manuscript, blandly entitled "ballatis of luve."[64]

Eight of the nine poems Bannatyne ascribes to Chaucer are in the
fourth part. First comes "The song of troyelus"; it is one of Bannatyne's

only two canonical bits of Chaucer (the other, a version of "Lack of Stead-fastness" with an extra stanza, is anonymous among the "ballatis full of wisdome and moralitie," even though Thynne's edition contains this poem).[65] Of the eight Chaucerian ascriptions among the "ballatis of luve," four appear in the subsection entitled "Ballatis of remedy of luve . . . and to the reproche of evill wemen," two in the subsection "to the reproche of fals vicius men And prayis of guid wemen" (fol. 268v), and one (ll. 302–434, 456–69 of Lydgate's *Complaint of the Black Knight*) in the subsection on "the contempt of Blyndit Luve" (fol. 280v).[66] Taken as a group, these eight Chaucerian poems trace male sexual experience from fervent experience of romantic love to renunciation of it.

The extent of Bannatyne's role in the presentation of Chaucer as a misogynist authority cannot be fully realized until we examine Bannatyne's choice and placement of poems, as well as his deviations from his sources. Bannatyne uses the 1545–50 printing of Thynne's Chaucer as copy-text for most of his Chaucer ascriptions;[67] however, he does not simply copy Thynne. Two of his ascriptions are in fact unique to Scottish sources: "Devyce, proves, and eik humilitie" (also in Bodley Arch. Selden B.24 and the Chepman and Myllar prints), and "O wicket wemen, wilfull and variable" (only in Bannatyne). Even where Bannatyne does use Thynne, we receive selected bits and pieces of Scottified poems that sometimes diverge widely from their English source. For example, Bannatyne's "This work quha sa sall sie or reid" is derived from Thynne's "Remedy of Love." Bannatyne's version consists of a mere eleven stanzas (largely given to a racily exemplary story told by a disillusioned lover), where Thynne has eighty-one. Between stanzas ten and eleven in Bannatyne, eight stanzas that appear in Thynne are missing. Similarly, Thynne's version of the *Complaint of the Black Knight* consists of ninety-seven stanzas, while Bannatyne's redaction, "Quhat meneth this quhat is this windir vre," comprises twenty-one—matter devoted to Bannatyne's topic in this part of the manuscript, "contempt of Blyndit Luve."[68] Again the order is not precise. Between stanzas nineteen and twenty in Bannatyne, three stanzas are absent that occur in Thynne. Bannatyne has chosen specific sections and stanzas from these pieces to fit Chaucer to the misogynist purposes of this part of his collection.

Aside from the *Troilus* excerpt, "Lack of Steadfastness" is Bannatyne's only bit of Chaucer accepted today as canonical. It is typical that Bannatyne does not ascribe it to Chaucer. Nor does Maitland, for his copy of the poem, nor any English scribe save one. [69] Neither the Maitland scribe nor Bannatyne slavishly copies his text from Thynne; for one thing, they both include a new fourth stanza (here quoted from Bannatyne):

Falsheid that sowld bene abhominable
Now is regeing but reformatioun.
Quha now gifis lergly ar maist dissavable,
For vycis ar the grund of sustentatioun.
All wit is turnit to cavillatioun,
Lawtie expellit and all gentilnes,
That all is loist [for lak of steidfastnes].

Bannatyne does not recognize this poem as Chaucer's. It had been "part of
the verbal inheritance of late-medieval English literary culture" for over a
century.[70] By 1568, perhaps, it had taken the same place in Scottish literary
culture. Whether Bannatyne or his source has naturalized "Lack of Steadfastness" within political advice in Scotland, it is a poem (like "Truth" in
Cambridge University Library Kk.1.5)[71] for which ascription to an English
author should by rights be omitted. "A Ballat of Steidfastnes" is thus listed
without ascription in the table of contents to the Asloan MS. (The poem
itself is no longer extant in that manuscript.) It would seem that the name
of Chaucer carries less weight for Scottish moralizings on good and bad
government than it does for Scottish denigrations of women. Assuming
Bannatyne is actively constructing ("re-visioning") Chaucer as an authority (with Thynne's inclusion of Henryson's *Testament* in Chaucer's *Workes*
a striking precedent), it would serve his purpose to name his author at
strategic places in the manuscript and to omit that name elsewhere.

   Distinctions between politics and gender are not easy to maintain in
talking about Bannatyne's handling of Chaucer. In the stanza quoted above,
eloquence (wit) has turned into sophistry (cavillatioun), and the ordered
world has turned upside down. The topic of disorder has the masterful wife
as one of its common tropes. It is no surprise, then, that several words and
phrases that appear in Bannatyne's "Lack of Steadfastness," especially in
the uniquely Scottish fourth stanza, give a political edge to Bannatyne's
misogynist Chauceriana. For instance, two of these words, "dissavable" and
"abhominable," appear in "O wicket wemen," there as barbs in an attack
against a "perrellous," unstable womankind that is always liable to
"treichery" and "fellony," and apt to turn against its masters.

   With its alliterating volleys of abuse, "O wicket wemen" may read like
anything but humor; reading or hearing it, a querulous husband may learn
to curse his wife by the letter, or may celebrate a convivial solidarity with
his fellows. As its first stanza shows, its satire is built on vicious, biting lists
of adjectives:

O wicket wemen! wilfull and variable,
Richt fals, feckle, fell, and frivolus,
Dowgit, dispytfull, dour, and dissavable,

Vnkynd, crewall, curst, and covettus,
Ouirlicht of laitis, vnleill, and licherus,
Turnit fra trewth and taiclit with treichery,
Vnferme of faith, fulfillit of fellony.

This is a fierce, noisy scolding, mimicking the very kind of speech of which women are being accused. In fact, for his collection of misogynist poems, Bannatyne offers the authority of a Chaucer who "acts like the woman he censures."[72] The very language of misogyny cannot escape being that "wulgare and matarnall toung," the vernacular.[73] By using the venomous power of words against women, the misogynist poet falls into the trap of being feminized. Seeking to raise a rumblingly apocalyptic vision of an upside-down world in which men are ruled by women, Bannatyne's Chaucer may (like an unwitting John Knox, quoted at the outset) be giving vent only to wind. Whether taken as expression of fear of the regiment of women or as carnivalesque play, misogyny cannot prevent its gaze from turning to bodies—male and female—and their irrepressible functions.

The Chaucer of late sixteenth-century Scotland is a complex, equivocal creation. This is an author both Scots and English, naturalized and markedly foreign, one whose presence in the Bannatyne MS and other Scottish manuscripts of the mid-sixteenth century has been ingeniously derived from English printed sources (notably Thynne) as well as Scottish sources in manuscript and print. Thought of solely in terms of its textual antecedents, this Scottish Chaucer shows evidence of reflection on the status of language and literature in Scotland, connected to, yet distinct from, these activities from their counterparts to the south. Bannatyne's Chaucer is thus selected largely from, but not merely supplementary to, Thynne's. Thought of in terms of its primary subject matter, the subjection of men to women in the experience of love, this Chaucer comes to seem no less problematic. Ostensibly a powerful voice to free men from their subjection and restore them to mastery, this Chaucer speaks of the irresistible, largely destructive power of women, or, more specifically, the feminine, a topic of some relevance to factionalized burgh and court in the Scotland of the 1560s.

Notes

1. John Knox, *First Blast of the Trumpet against the Monstrous Regiment of Women*, in *The Political Writings of John Knox*, ed. Marvin A. Breslow (Cranbury, N.J.: Associated University Presses, 1985), 40.

2. Cf. A. J. Aitken, "The Language of Older Scots Poetry," in *Scotland and the Lowland Tongue*, ed. J. D. McClure (Aberdeen: Aberdeen University Press, 1983), 21–23, 33–37, 45–48.

3. See for instance, Denton Fox, "The Scottish Chaucerians," in *Chaucer and Chaucerians*, ed. Derek Brewer (London: Nelson, 1966), 164–200; Gregory Kratzmann, *Anglo-Scottish Literary Relations, 1430–1550* (Cambridge: Cambridge University Press, 1980), 1–32; A. C. Spearing, *Medieval to Renaissance in English Poetry* (Cambridge: Cambridge University Press, 1985), 59–120; Priscilla Bawcutt, *Dunbar the Makar* (Oxford: Clarendon, 1992), 22–25.

4. Louise Fradenburg, "Scottish Chaucer," in *Proceedings of the Third International Conference on Scottish Language and Literature (Medieval and Renaissance), University of Stirling, 2–7 July 1981*, ed. R. J. Lyall and Felicity Riddy (Stirling and Glasgow: Culross, 1981), 183–89.

5. Louise Fradenburg, *City, Marriage, Tournament: Arts of Rule in Late Medieval Scotland* (Madison: University of Wisconsin Press, 1991), 129–30.

6. Fradenburg, *City*, 133–34.

7. R. James Goldstein, *The Matter of Scotland: Historical Narrative in Medieval Scotland* (Lincoln: University of Nebraska Press, 1993), 257.

8. Robert Henryson, *Testament of Cresseid*, in *The Poems of Robert Henryson*, ed. Denton Fox (Oxford: Clarendon Press, 1981), l. 64.

9. Gavin Douglas, *Eneados* I. Prol. 445–46 in *The Poetical Works of Gavin Douglas*, ed. John Small (Edinburgh: W. Paterson, 1874).

10. Fradenburg, "Scottish Chaucer," 185–89; Ruth Morse, *Truth and Convention in the Middle Ages: Medieval Rhetoric and Representation* (Cambridge: Cambridge University Press, 1991), 241.

11. A. J. Minnis, with V. J. Scattergood and J. J. Smith, *Oxford Guides to Chaucer: The Shorter Poems* (Oxford: Clarendon Press, 1995), 241.

12. John Rolland, *The Court of Venus*, ed. Walter Gregor, Scottish Text Society, o.s., 3 (Edinburgh: William Blackwood, 1884), III:604–12; (cf. 458–62).

13. Jasper Ridley, *John Knox* (Oxford: Clarendon Press, 1968), 131–32, 455, 474–75.

14. Thomas Laqueur, *Making Sex: Body and Gender from the Greeks to Freud* (Cambridge: Harvard University Press, 1990), 52- 62, 125.

15. George Buchanan, *The Tyrannous Reign of Mary Stewart*, trans. W. A. Gatherer (Edinburgh: Edinburgh University Press, 1958), 85; R. D. S. Jack, "Mary and the Poetic Vision," *Scotia* 3 (1979): 38–39.

16. Laqueur, *Making Sex*, 25–28.

17. In the Asloan Manuscript, National Library of Scotland Additional MS 16500; c. 1515.

18. *The Asloan Manuscript*, ed. William A. Craigie, Scottish Text Society, n.s., 14, 16 (Edinburgh: Blackwood, 1923–25), 1:29.

19. Gavin Douglas, *The Palis of Honoure*, ed. David Parkinson (Kalamazoo: Western Michigan University, 1992), ll. 983–87.

20. Francis Utley, *The Crooked Rib: An Analytical Index to the Argument about Women in English and Scots Literature to the End of the Year 1568* (Columbus: Ohio State University Press, 1944; reprint, New York: Octagon, 1970), 55–56.

21. W. Tod Ritchie, ed., *The Bannatyne Manuscript*, Scottish Text Society, 3d ser., 5 (Edinburgh: Blackwood, 1928–34), 32.

22. R. A. Houston, *Scottish Literacy and the Scottish Identity* (Cambridge: Cambridge University Press, 1985), 60.

23. Michael Lynch, *Edinburgh and the Reformation* (Edinburgh: John Donald,

1981), 208; Jenny Wormald, *Court, Kirk, and Community: Scotland, 1470–1625* (Toronto: University of Toronto Press, 1981), 13–14.

24. Margaret Sanderson, "The Edinburgh Merchants in Society, 1570–1603: The Evidence of Their Testaments," in *Renaissance and Reformation in Scottish Society: Essays in Honour of Gordon Donaldson*, ed. Ian B. Cowan and Duncan Shaw (Edinburgh: Scottish Academic Press, 1983), 184.

25. Denis McKay, "Parish Life in Scotland, 1500–1560," in *Essays on the Scottish Reformation*, ed. David McRoberts (Glasgow: Burns, 1962), 96.

26. Wormald, *Court, Kirk, and Community*, 30.

27. Cf. R. Howard Bloch, *Medieval Misogyny and the Invention of Western Romantic Love* (Chicago: University of Chicago Press, 1991), 196–97.

28. See, for instance, John Mair (Major), *A History of Greater Britain*, trans. Archibald Constable, Scottish History Society, vols. 10–11 (Edinburgh: Edinburgh University Press, 1892), 388; Knox, *Monstrous Regiment of Women*, 60.

29. Jenny Wormald, *Mary Queen of Scots: A Study in Failure* (London: George Philip, 1981), 44–45; cf. Fradenburg, *City*, 80.

30. Robert Lindesay of Pitscottie, *The Historie and Cronicles of Scotland*, ed. Aeneas J. G. Mackay, Scottish Text Society, o.s., 42 (Edinburgh: William Blackwood, 1898), 157.

31. Wormald, *Mary*, 136.

32. Ibid., 136, 145.

33. Elizabeth Ewan, "Scottish Portias: Women in the Courts in Mediaeval Scottish Towns," *Journal of the Canadian Historical Association* 61 (1992): 27–43.

34. R. A. Houston, "Women in the Economy and Society of Scotland, 1500–1800," in *Scottish Society, 1500–1800*, ed. R. A. Houston and I. D. Whyte (Cambridge: Cambridge University Press, 1989), 138.

35. Houston, "Women in the Economy," 129.

36. Christina Larner, *Enemies of God: The Witch-Hunt in Scotland* (Baltimore: Johns Hopkins University Press, 1981), 101; M. Lynch, "Continuity and Change in Urban Society, 1500–1700," in *Scottish Society, 1500–1800*, ed. R. A. Houston and I. D. Whyte (Cambridge: Cambridge University Press, 1989), 108.

37. Lynch, *Edinburgh*, 189.

38. Ibid., 43, 190; see also 181.

39. Theo van Heijnsbergen, "The Interaction between Literature and History in Queen Mary's Edinburgh: The Bannatyne Manuscript and Its Prosopographical Contexts," in *The Renaissance in Scotland: Studies in Literature, Religion, History, and Culture Offered to John Durkan*, ed. A. A. MacDonald, Michael Lynch, and Ian B. Cowan (Leiden: E. J. Brill, 1994), 213.

40. Ridley, *John Knox*, 132.

41. *The Maitland Folio Manuscript*, ed. W. A. Craigie, Scottish Text Society, n. s., 7, 20 (Edinburgh: William Blackwood, 1919–1927), poem nos. xxxi, xxxiv, xciv; Utley, *Crooked Rib*, 81.

42. Margaret Sanderson, *Mary Stewart's People* (Tuscaloosa: University of Alabama Press, 1987), 91–102.

43. *Extracts from the Burgh Records of Edinburgh* (Edinburgh: Scottish Burgh Records Society 1869–92), 3:162.

44. Ridley, *John Knox*, 131.

45. Lynch, *Edinburgh*, 33, 194.

46. Houston, "Women in the Economy," 140.

47. Utley, *Crooked Rib*, 168, 270.

48. Roderick J. Lyall, "The Lost Literature of Medieval Scotland," in *Bryght Lanternis: Essays on the Language and Literature of Medieval and Renaissance Scotland*, ed. J. Derrick McClure and Michael R. G. Spiller (Aberdeen: Aberdeen University Press, 1989), 37.

49. William Gillies, "Courtly and Satiric Poems in the Book of the Dean of Lismore," *Scottish Studies* 21 (1977): 45–46.

50. Henryson, *Poems*, xcvii.

51. Ibid., xcvi.

52. Donald Meek, "The Scots-Gaelic Scribes of Late Medieval Perthshire: An Overview of the Orthography and Contents of the Book of the Dean of Lismore," in *Bryght Lanternis*, ed. McClure and Spiller, 388–89, 401.

53. Sally Mapstone, "The *Testament of Cresseid*, lines 561–7: A New Manuscript Witness," *Notes and Queries*, n.s., 32 (1985): 310.

54. William Dunbar, *The Poems of William Dunbar*, ed. John Small, Aeneas J. G. Mackay, and Walter Gregor, Scottish Text Society, o.s., 2, 4, 16, 21, 29 (Edinburgh: William Blackwood, 1883–93), 2:266–68.

55. *The Bannatyne Manuscript, National Library of Scotland Advocates' MS. 1.1.6* (London: Scolar Press and the National Library of Scotland, 1980), fol. 262r.

56. Ibid., ll. 4, 35.

57. Ibid., ll. 15, 19–21.

58. Utley, *Crooked Rib*, 44, 49–50, 55–56; Evelyn Newlyn, "Luve, Lichery and Evill Women: The Satiric Tradition in the Bannatyne Manuscript," *Studies in Scottish Literature* 26 (1991): 283–93.

59. Bodley Arch. Selden B.24, fol. 120r.

60. Van Heijnsbergen, 214, quoting John Durkan.

61. Utley, *Crooked Rib*, 82.

62. The edition used by Bannatyne is c. 1545–50.

63. E. g., Bannatyne's "As Phebus bricht in speir meridiane" (fol. 230r–v), Stewart's "Furth ouer the mold at morrow as I ment" (fols. 265r–266r), Wedderburn's "Ballat of the Prayis of wemen" (fols. 239v–242v) and "My luve was fals and full of flattry" (fol. 260r–v), and the anonymous "Thankit be God and his appostillis twelf" (fols. 263v–264r).

64. *Bannatyne*, fol. 211r.

65. *Bannatyne*, fol. 230r, contains ll. 400–34 of *Troilus and Criseyde*, The Bannatyne version of "Lack of Steadfastness" can be found on fol. 67r. See fol. 43v for the description of the ballads.

66. *Bannatyne*, fols. 249v, 268v, 280v.

67. Denton Fox and William A. Ringler, introduction to *Bannatyne*, 158.

68. *Bannatyne*, fol. 281r.

69. Seth Lerer, *Chaucer and His Readers* (Princeton: Princeton University Press, 1993), 124.

70. Ibid.

71. *Ratis Raving and Other Early Scots Poems on Morals*, ed. Ritchie Girvan, Scottish Text Society, 3d ser., 11 (Edinburgh: William Blackwood, 1939), fols. 4v–5r.

72. Bloch, *Medieval Misogyny*, 66.

73. *Asloan*, vol. 1, l. 31.

The Rewriting of the
Wife of Bath's Prologue in
Cambridge Dd.4.24

·•·

Beverly Kennedy

There is an extraordinary amount of textual variance in the *Wife of Bath's Prologue*, even among the earliest extant manuscripts. In comparison with other parts of the *Canterbury Tales* which Chaucer lived to complete, it is unique in this regard.[1] The major variants consist of five interpolated passages[2] and five lines in which the Wife's husbands have been renumbered.[3] They always occur together in the *a* and *b* groups of manuscripts of the *Canterbury Tales*, and they make their earliest appearance in the manuscript tradition in Cambridge Dd.4.24, the oldest extant representative of the *a* group.

Dd is a small book made up of unruled and irregularly sized sheets of vellum and paper and copied in a practiced but unprofessional hand. Its amateur status is further confirmed by the absence of illumination and signs of supervision and by the presence of marginal comments of a personal nature. All of this suggests that the scribe was a highly educated man making a copy of the *Canterbury Tales* for his own reading pleasure. Despite its amateur status, modern editors have granted limited authority to Dd, precisely because of some of its variants.[4] Indeed, its five variant passages in the *Wife of Bath's Prologue*, like the major variants in the *Nun's Priests's Tale* (which also appear for the first time in this manuscript), have been accepted by all but one recent editor of the *Canterbury Tales* as late authorial revisions.[5] On the other hand, no Chaucer editor has ever taken its renumbered husband variants in the Wife's *Prologue* to be anything but a particularly puzzling series of scribal errors. Yet, the two sets of variants clearly entered the manuscript tradition together—and just as clearly reinforce one another in rewriting Dame Alys in accordance with a familiar antifeminist stereotype, the sexually voracious and unfaithful wife.

In this essay I propose an alternative hypothesis, namely, that both sets of variants are the result of very early scribal interference by well-educated clerics. The "horizon of expectation" of this community of readers would have been shaped by their many years of university education.[6] As a consequence, their "cultural literacy" would have been informed by antifeminist "clerical assumptions" regarding woman's moral capacity.[7] The central moral question they would have asked regarding any woman was whether or not she was chaste according to her degree, as virgin, widow, or wife, and they would have expected an answer in the negative. Indeed, when the clerical authors of Estates Satire thought to include women at all, as a kind of "Fourth Estate," they invariably portrayed nuns as wayward and wives as lascivious and unfaithful to their husbands.[8]

That being the case, the first clerical readers of the *Wife of Bath's Prologue* must have been shocked by the moral ambiguity of Chaucer's portrait of Dame Alys, in particular its apparently deliberate ambiguity with regard to her chastity as wife and widow. Given their horizon of expectation, it is unlikely they could have received this morally ambiguous text without protest. And a means of protest was ready to hand. Late medieval manuscript culture, with its imprecise boundaries separating the functions of author, scribe, and reader, tended to encourage the sort of reading that was also "a kind of rewriting: a way of engaging with the text by commenting, recasting, and in some sense re-inscribing it."[9] Even Chaucer texts were not spared this kind of rewriting by fifteenth-century readers. Thus it is reasonable to hypothesize that one or possibly more than one irate cleric, offended by the poet's ambiguity with regard to such an important moral issue as a woman's chastity (and blessed with a good ear for verse), might have chosen to register his protest by reinscribing Chaucer's text with his own clerical assumptions.

The *A*-Group Variants' Rewriting of the Wife's Chastity

The two major sets of variants in the *Wife of Bath's Prologue* strongly reinforce each other in rewriting the Wife as stereotypically lascivious and adulterous. On the one hand, the renumbered husband variants transform all of her husbands into attractive and sexually potent men and herself into a seemingly much younger women obsessed with their sexual behavior. On the other, the five variant passages, particularly the first one, reinforce this transformation and also attribute to her the qualities of sexual aggression and promiscuity. As a consequence, Dame Alys appears much like the stereotypical wife of traditional Estates Satire.[10]

The renumbered husband variants are not errors at all. Rather, they are the means of effecting a coherent revision of the third and last part of the Wife's *Prologue*. Whereas in Hengwrt and Ellesmere the Wife gives a detailed account of her relations with husbands number four and five at this point (after she has told us how she handled her three old husbands), in Dd she begins again with husband number one and briefly describes each of her five husbands as individuals. After the "first" (452, 453), she tells us about the "secund" (480), "thridde" (503), and "fierthe" (525) husbands. She also tells us about Jankyn, who eventually becomes her fifth husband, but is never so numbered (see appendix A).

There are two major consequences of this revision. First, it restructures the narrative into a series of brief vignettes, punctuated either by vivid reminiscences or proverbial wisdom, thereby erasing the false starts and repetitions of what we take to be Chaucer's original. This effects a remarkable change in the representation of the Wife's character, transforming the garrulous, disorganized old woman of the original into an apparently much younger woman, in much better control of her narrative, and obsessed with the sexual behavior of all her husbands. Second, this revision describes all her husbands as either virile or attractive men: The first was a revelour; the second had a "paramour"; the third beat her regularly but was great in bed; the fourth, the clerk from Oxenford, she married for love; and young Jankyn, whom she selected to be her fifth husband, had such shapely legs that she gave him "al [her] hert" (599).[11]

The variant passages reinforce both of these effects (see appendix B). The first passage, 44a–f (a particularly noticeable interpolation between the Wife's thanking God that she has "wedded fyue" and welcoming "the sixte whan þat euere he shal"), actually anticipates the effect of the renumbered husbands revision, largely by means of the crude puns on "cheste" and "nether purs," which likewise suggest that the Wife was obsessed with the attractiveness and sexual prowess of all her husbands. The second passage (575–84) does not emphasize the Wife's lechery so much as her deceptive nature when dealing with men; however, the third passage (609–12) certainly emphasizes her "likerousnesse," adding to that quality a "marcien" heart and "sturdy hardynesse." And the fourth passage (619–26) asserts that she is so sexually insatiable that she has exercised no "discrecioun" whatsoever in satisfying her "appetit," caring nothing about wealth, status, or even physical appearance, so long as the man pleased her. This passage makes it seem certain that the Wife has repeatedly committed adultery.

The last of the variant passages does not affect the representation of the Wife's moral character at all, but it does confirm the misogyny inherent in the other four. Not content that Eve and all women should shoulder the blame for man's loss of Paradise, this passage blames them for the death of Christ as well, concluding with an accurate translation of the misogynous clerical commonplace so egregiously mistranslated by Chauntecler in the *Nun's Priest's Tale: Mulier est hominis confusio.*[12]

Two further effects of the variant passages in the Wife's *Prologue* strongly suggest that they are not authorial revisions. The first is the number of times that their content contradicts that of other, universally attested, parts of Chaucer's text. By representing all five of the Wife's husbands as either attractive or sexually potent men (as the renumbered husbands revision does also), the first variant passage (44a–f) contradicts the Wife's subsequent description of her three old husbands as scarcely able to pay the marriage debt.[13] By attributing to her imagination a fictive dream suggesting that she looks forward to a sado-masochistic relationship with young Jankyn, the second passage (575–84) contradicts her epicurean love of pleasure.[14] It also contradicts what we know to be true of the couple's relative economic standing by suggesting that *she* rather than he will be enriched by their marriage. Finally, by having her boast of a lifetime of promiscuity, the fourth passage (619–26) contradicts her earlier assertion that she would not commit adultery "of [her] body, in no foule menere" (485), not even to be revenged upon a philandering husband.[15]

The second effect which suggests that the variant passages are not authorial is their erasure of the otherwise perfect ambiguity of Chaucer's text regarding the Wife's sexual morality. Chaucer went out of his way to raise the issue of her chastity in the *General Prologue* by asserting that the Wife had five husbands, "Withouten other companye in hire 30uth" (461). The ambiguity of this qualifying prepositional phrase appears to be both deliberate and irresolvable. On the one hand, it may mean that she had *no* friends or lovers in youth other than her husbands, *withouten* in this case bearing its normal negating sense. On the other hand, if one thinks that five husbands is a very large number, it may mean that she also had many friends or lovers in her youth, since in the context of extremely large numbers *withouten* can take on the sense of "not counting." Chaucer's text gives the reader no help at all in deciding which of these contradictory meanings to choose.

Chaucer continues to be deliberately ambiguous whenever the subject of the Wife's sexual morality comes up, not only in the rest of the *General Prologue* portrait, but also throughout the Wife's own *Prologue*.[16] Moreover, the final instance in this extended pattern of textual ambiguity is as witty and audacious as the first. It is the couplet in which the Wife admits that she could "nat with drawe / [Her] chaumbre of venus fro a good felawe" (617–18). Largely because of the presence of the third and especially the fourth added passages (609–12 and 619–26), modern editors have not been able to see the ambiguity of "chaumbre of venus." In fact, it could be a metaphorical reference either to her "hert," which the Wife has just told us she gave to Jankyn, or to her *queynte*. Chaucer leaves it up to the reader to decide which of these two meanings she intends.[17]

The misogynous impact of these revisions, the internal contradictions they generate, and the disambiguating effect they have on the text all suggest that it was not Chaucer who made them. Nevertheless, with the exception of the first passage (44a–f), which, because it was omitted by the Ellesmere scribe, has in the past been taken by some editors to be an authorial cancellation,[18] the variant passages have been accepted into the text of critical editions as late authorial revisions, while the renumbered husband variants have been corrected as scribal errors.

The Attestation of the *A*-Group Variants in the Manuscript Tradition

The evidence of manuscript attestation does not strongly support this traditional editorial consensus, as we can see from the following table, where the earliest extant manuscripts of the *Canterbury Tales* are listed in approximate chronological order and identified by the manuscript sigla employed by Manly and Rickert.[19]

	44a–f	*575–84*	*609–12*	*619–26*	*717–20*	*Husbands Renumbered*
Hg						
Ha⁴						
Cp						
La						
Dd	X		X	X	X	X
El		X	X	X	X	
Gg		X	X	X		
Pw						

The pattern of limited and erratic attestation seen here continues throughout the manuscript tradition.[20] Thirty-two of the remaining fifty *Canterbury Tales* manuscripts containing texts of the *Wife of Bath's Prologue* are like Hengwrt (Hg), Harley 7334 (Ha⁴), Corpus Christi (Cp), Lansdowne (La) and Petworth (Pw) in having none of the added passages and none of the renumbered husband variants.[21] Eight of the fifty (Manly and Rickert's *a* and *b* groups) have inherited both sets of variants from the same source as Dd, while another six have acquired one set or the other by what editors call "contamination," that is, by copying from a manuscript other than their immediate copy-text.[22] Finally, four manuscripts are like El and Cambridge Gg in having acquired only some of the added passages and, with one exception, none of the renumbered husband variants.[23]

The apparent selectivity of these four manuscripts, taken together with that of El and Gg, suggests that, at some point in the transmission process, scribes had a choice. In most instances we cannot be certain what exemplar a particular scribe had before him. Both El and Gg, the two earliest manuscripts in this group, appear to be the result of a conscientious effort to preserve Chaucer's work in its entirety: all of the *Canterbury Tales* in the case of Ellesmere, and, in the case of Cambridge Gg, all of the *Canterbury Tales*, plus *Troilus and Criseyde*, the *Legend of Good Women*, and many of the shorter poems, including the *Parlement of Foules*. In each case there are grounds for supposing that their scribes may have had access to more than one copy-text.

Certainly the Ellesmere scribe appears to have been copying from a different exemplar, an *a*-group text, throughout the last part of the *Wife of Bath's Prologue*.[24] If this exemplar was typical of all extant *a*-group manuscripts it must have included the renumbered husband variants as well as all five of the variant passages in the Wife's *Prologue*. Why, then, did the Ellesmere scribe ignore the renumbered husband variants and, even more important, why did he not include *all* of the variant passages in his own text? The first question is fairly easy. Any scribe as careful as the Ellesmere scribe appears to have been could have seen that the renumbered husband variants contradict the Wife's description of her three old husbands as nearly impotent. Moreover, if he had simultaneous access to two complete texts of the Wife's *Prologue*, an unrevised Hengwrt-like text as well as the *a*-group text, he would have been able to see through the rather clever stratagem of the renumbered husbands revision, which is to divide the philandering fourth husband into two (the first who was a philanderer, and the second, who had a paramour) and the fifth husband, Jankyn, the wife-beating clerk from Oxford, into three (a wife-beater, a clerk from Oxford, and Jankyn). Therefore, it is not surprising that the Ellesmere scribe omitted the renumbered husband variants. What is surprising, and much more difficult to explain, is why he omitted the first of the five added passages.

It may be, of course, that the *a*-group exemplar used by the Ellesmere editor was not typical of the extant *a* group but included only the four passages he copied, either because 44a–f had not yet been added to the *a*-group text or because the scribe of Ellesmere's *a*-group exemplar had omitted it. In fact, either the Ellesmere scribe or his predecessor might have omitted 44a–f because, like the renumbered husbands revision, it contradicts the Wife's description of her three old husbands as nearly impotent.[25] But if the Ellesmere scribe had simultaneous access to an unrevised text of the Wife's *Prologue* that enabled him to see through the stratagem of the renumbered husband variants, he might have been prompted to question the other variants in his *a*-group exemplar as well.[26] If so, then the important question is no longer why he omitted the first of these variant passages, but rather why he included the other four. If the Ellesmere scribe had simultaneous access to two complete texts of the *Wife of Bath's Prologue*, one of them a typical *a*-group manuscript and the other a Hengwrt-like manuscript, there is no way to avoid the conclusion that he was willing either to "edit out" a passage possibly written by Chaucer himself, or to "edit in" four passages possibly written by someone else.[27]

Later scribes incorporated anywhere from one to four of the variant passages, though none made precisely the same choice as El or Gg.[28] Again, we have no way of knowing what these scribes were working with by way of copy-texts; however, a space marked out for a third passage that was never actually copied into the margins of Harley 1758 (Ha[2]) shows that midcentury scribes sometimes knew about passages for which they could not obtain a copy-text. Nevertheless, the inclusion of only one or two passages in some of these later manuscripts strongly suggests the exercise of scribal choice at some point in the transmission process, if only because none of the earliest extant manuscripts contains so few. It may be significant, therefore, that the most frequently "selected" were 609–12 and 619–26, which effectively disambiguate the "chaumbre of venus" couplet (617–18) by making the Wife boast of her sexual aggressiveness and promiscuity.

On the basis of such evidence, it is difficult to argue convincingly that Chaucer himself added the variant passages to the Wife's *Prologue*. Taking into account their limited and erratic manuscript attestation (and also tacitly acknowledging their un-Chaucerian content), John M. Manly and Edith Rickert hypothesized that Chaucer inserted the passages into a single manuscript very late, after the Wife's *Prologue* was already in circulation, "perhaps to meet the taste of some friend."[29] Manly and Rickert's hypothesis rests on the assumption that Chaucer allowed parts of his work to circulate during his lifetime. This assumption, though still accepted by some textual critics, for example, Ralph Hanna III and Charles Owen, has been rejected by others, among them Norman Blake and John Fisher, who find it more likely that all fifteenth-century copies of the *Canterbury Tales* derive from Chaucer's own copy. According to Fisher's scenario, the author's copy would have consisted of a pile of "foul papers," interlined and interleaved, from which "different scribes" would have "elicited different texts" after the poet's death.[30] But if we accept Fisher's scenario, and if we then further accept that Chaucer added the variant passages to his own copy (rather than that of a friend), it is exceedingly difficult to explain why the passages did not achieve wider manuscript attestation, in particular why they were not copied into very early texts like Hg, Cp, and Ha[4].

This difficulty has led some textual critics to seek alternative hypotheses. Norman Blake has suggested that the variant passages in the Wife's

Prologue are all scribal interpolations, probably added by the Dd scribe, in whose book they first appear.[31] On the other hand, Peter Robinson has recently suggested that they are all authorial cancellations.[32] Both hypotheses would require editors to remove the passages from the text proper of any future critical edition. However, John Fisher, editor of the forthcoming Variorum edition of the *Wife of Bath's Prologue and Tale*, is not willing to go so far. In his critical apparatus, Fisher draws attention to a number of reasons for regarding the authenticity of the added passages as doubtful (including the fact that removing all of them does not impair the continuity of expression of Chaucer's text in the slightest), but he will conclude that "in the present state of our knowledge, no final decision can be reached."[33]

The Probability That the *A*-Group Variants Are the Result of Early Scribal Intervention

In practical terms it is necessary to reach something like a final decision regarding the authenticity of these *a*-group variants, since modern readers are introduced to Chaucer through the medium of critically edited texts. The decision of almost all past editors, to include the variant passages in the text proper, is no longer tenable given that the *a*-group variants change the meaning of Chaucer's text in ways that are most un-Chaucerian and that late medieval manuscript culture permitted, perhaps even encouraged, the creative rewriting of vernacular texts by interested readers. In order to support a different editorial decision, however, we must cast the evidentiary net a bit further to take into account the reception history of the *Wife of Bath's Prologue*. We must ask, then, what sort of early fifteenth-century readers might have wanted to rewrite the Wife according to the familiar antifeminist stereotype? And what sort of readers would have been, on the one hand, as well versed as Chaucer in the antifeminist literary tradition, including Estates Satire, and on the other, either unwilling or unable to accept Chaucer's comic subversion of that tradition in his morally ambiguous representation of the Wife of Bath? The most likely answer to both questions is the same: well-educated celibate clerics. Among this community of readers, in the words of Alcuin Blamires, "there was a continuous recycling of received misogyny" that, despite the "facetious spirit" of some of it, may be viewed "as a form of individual or group therapy in support of celibacy."[34]

In fact, the *a*-group variants in the *Wife of Bath's Prologue* reflect both the high educational level and the misogynous bias of this community of readers, all but one of the variant passages being drawn from the antifeminist literary tradition in either Latin or French. Of course, Chaucer himself was well acquainted with this tradition. In the *Wife of Bath's Prologue* he echoes or alludes to many of its most popular texts: Jerome's treatise against marriage, *Epistola adversus Jovinianum*; Matheolus's *Lamentations*, available to him both in the original Latin and in Le Fèvre's French translation; Jean de Meun's encyclopedic conclusion to Guillaume de Lorris' *Roman de la Rose*; and possibly Deschamps' *Miroir de mariage* as well. But Chaucer resituates these texts in the Wife's *Prologue* in ways that work to question antifeminist stereotypes rather than reinforce them.[35]

Chaucer was also familiar with the tradition of Estates Satire; it clearly lies behind the entire *General Prologue* to the *Canterbury Tales.* However, his representations of most of the pilgrims, especially the two female pilgrims, make it clear that he was not interested in simply replicating the traditional stereotypes of this clerical genre, certainly not the antifeminist ones. Whereas Estates Satire commonly accused wives of being lecherous and unfaithful to their husbands and nuns of being wayward, Chaucer's representations of the Wife and the Prioress in the *General Prologue* are deliberately ambiguous with regard to their sexual morality.[36]

The intention to rewrite Chaucer's Dame Alys in conformity with clerical antifeminism is most noticeable in the stereotypical qualities of lechery and sexual promiscuity attributed to her in 609–12 and 619–26. The other qualities emphasized by the *a*-group variants, for example, coarseness and lasciviousness (44a–f), and deviousness in dealing with men in a courtship situation (575–84), are also commonplaces of the clerical antifeminist tradition. Line 575 actually echoes a line in Jean de Meun's continuation of the *Roman de la Rose*, in which La Vieille advises Bel Acoeil to flatter potential lovers by pretending that s/he has been "enchanted" by them.[37] And ll. 717–20 contain an accusation commonly leveled at Eve by biblical scholars, namely, that she is responsible for the crucifixion of Christ as well as the fall of man.[38] Moreover, l. 720 is an accurate translation of "mulier est hominis confusio," itself the opening line of a very popular work in clerical circles, the *Life of Secundus.*[39]

In sum, whoever authored these *a*-group revisions was well acquainted not only with Estates Satire and the larger antifeminist literary tradition, but also with scholarly Latin works, including biblical exegesis. That means that he had spent several years at university exposed to the antifeminist and antimatrimonial propaganda of the curriculum.[40] It also means that he was a very learned clerk, perhaps a university don, canon, or friar, possibly a well-educated monk or parish priest. It is less likely, though still possible, that he was a civil servant or, like the Wife's fifth husband, had left university without taking holy orders, had married well, if not happily, and still enjoyed reading his student commonplace book of excerpts from favorite antifeminist texts.

As it happens, the *a* group of manuscripts can be linked to a clerical community of readers. Charles Owen has shown that, with the exception of the very late Ds, the manuscripts of this group are all small and plain and were not shop manuscripts copied by professional scribes, but private manuscripts copied by well-educated amateurs, in other words, most probably by clerics of some kind.[41] What is more, the ongoing research of Estelle Stubbs strongly suggests that these well educated amateur scribes were Augustinian friars. The scribe of Cambridge Dd.4.24, the earliest extant *a*-group manuscript, identifies himself several times in the margins as "Wytton" and may have been the friar of this name attached to the priory at Lincoln.[42] Two other Wyttons have also been found living in the very early fifteenth century, an Oxford don and a Cambridgeshire priest, either of whom might also have copied this manuscript.[43] We can be fairly certain, then, that whoever he was, the Dd scribe was a highly educated cleric whose reading of Chaucer's work would have been informed by traditional anti-feminist clerical assumptions. Even though he would have been a "recreational" reader of the *Canterbury Tales,* he would still have brought with him the habits of a "scholarly professional" reader.[44]

If Wytton was the author of the *a*-group variant passages, he must have had a good ear for verse, because the passages are written in a very creditable Chaucerian style. In fact, it is this ostensibly genuine style that has hitherto prevented every modern Chaucer editor, with the exception of Norman Blake, from seriously considering the possibility of scribal origin. Manly and Rickert even preface their discussion of the passages with the observation that Chaucer's authorship of them, except for the first, "has for stylistic reasons never been questioned."[45] Yet, as Blake has recently reminded us, there is no foolproof way to distinguish between the work of an author and that of a talented imitator.[46] Another reason Chaucer editors have long refused to consider the possibility of scribal origin is the supposition that all fifteenth-century scribes were poetic dunces. Yet, as Stephen Knight has observed, this assumption is not borne out by the evidence, either, for "by no means all" of the spurious links between fragments "are metrically or semantically clumsy."[47] On this basis alone, we cannot rule out the possibility that some of Chaucer's better educated early readers might have been capable not only of appreciating but also of reproducing a creditable imitation of his verse.[48]

Finally, if Wytton did write these passages, there was no reason he should not have added them to his personal copy to enhance his own enjoyment of the text as well as that of his friends.[49] We must remember that his literary culture had no concept of authorial copyright, or authority as we understand it. On the contrary, once a medieval author had published his work, either by presenting it to a patron or by allowing a friend to copy it, he had no further control over it.[50] And, in fact, fifteenth-century scribes working in the vernacular often revised texts as they copied them, in accordance with either their own needs and sensibilities or those of their patrons.[51]

One could argue that since Chaucer left his greatest work unfinished, the earliest scribes of the *Canterbury Tales* were virtually compelled to become creative participants in the authoring process. Different scribes adopted different solutions to the problem of putting the fragments of his work together to form a complete book, creating different links and tale orders in the process. Some went so far as to add entire tales to Chaucer's collection.[52] Others went even further, from the modern point of view, when they dared to revise Chaucer's finished work. A notable example of this last type of scribal rewriting is the Harley 7333 manuscript, in which certain lines in the *Reeve's Tale* have been revised, presumably in order to avoid offending the intended readership of Leicester canons.[53] Other examples are Jean d'Angoulême's manuscript (Paris, B. N. MS fonds anglais 39), which omits both *Melibee* and the *Parson's Tale* and abridges the *Canon's Yeoman's Tale*, the *Tale of Sir Thopas*, and the *Monk's Tale*,[54] and the Helmingham manuscript, whose extensive revisions make of the *Canterbury Tales* a "new poem."[55] To my mind the most striking example of creative scribal rewriting occurs not in a *Canterbury Tales* manuscript, however, but in the Selden Arch. B. 24 version of the *Parlement of Foules*, where the scribe has rewritten the conclusion so that the formel eagle is obliged to take the royal tercel as her mate.[56]

We can infer from the examples cited above that this sort of scribal rewriting was much more likely to occur when the wishes of the intended readership could readily be taken into account, either because the scribe was taking direction from a patron or group of patrons, like Jean d'Angoulême or the Leicester canons, or because he was copying the *Canterbury Tales* for his own use, like the scribe named Wytton who copied Cambridge Dd.4.24., combining in his own person "the functions of compiler/editor/scribe/patron [and] reader."[57] Wytton's marginal comments further reveal him to have been a confirmed misogynist and misogamist.

Examples of Wytton's misogyny and misogamy are particularly frequent in the margins of the Wife's prologue. For example, opposite her boast that "no man" can "half so boldely . . . / Swere and lyen, as a womman kan" (227–28) he writes, "Verum est" (fol. 69v). Opposite her admission that women have a propensity to desire what is forbidden them (519–20, fol. 73r) and that they "konne no thyng hele" (950, fol. 78r), he likewise writes, "Verum est." Later, like the Hengwrt and Ellesmere scribes, he responds with "nota" to Jankyn's proverb that a man who "suffreth his wyf to go seken halwes / Is worthy to been hanged on the galwes" (657–58, fol. 74v). He then finds equally notable Jankyn's saying that wives are "so wikked and contrarious / They haten that hir housbondes loven ay" (780–81, fol. 75v). Similar examples also appear in the margins of the *Merchant's Tale*. Indeed, the Dd scribe seems to have particularly enjoyed the Merchant's sarcastic mode of expressing his hatred of marriage. For example, opposite the Merchant's ironic assurance, "A wyf wol laste, and in thyn hous endure / wel lengere than the list, parauenture" (1317–18), he writes "Verum," and to the Merchant's equally ironic assurance that "If [her husband] be pore she helpeth him to swynke" (1342), he responds playfully, "or to drynke" (fol. 107r).

Wytton's marginal responses also indicate a prurient interest in sexual relations between married partners, with perhaps a special interest in their sadomasochistic potential. In the margins of the *Merchant's Tale* he responds with "nota" to January's first meditation on the beauty of May, but to his meditation on the pain he must inflict upon her on their wedding night (unless God should prevent him from doing all his "myght," 1761) the Dd scribe responds with "nota bene" in the right margin and in the left margin draws a hand doodle with index finger pointing to the passage (fol. 112r). Likewise he responds with "nota" to the Wife's admission that Jankyn could always "gloose" her into bed whenever "he wolde han [her] beal chose" even though he had just beaten her "on euery bon" (509–10, fol. 72v; see figure). And there are other indications of a particular interest in the Wife's own sexuality. At the top of the same folio (72v) he draws a hand doodle with finger pointing to her proverbial remark that a "likerous mouth must han a likerous tail" (466; see figure detail), and later he responds with "nota" to the boast that her husbands told her she "had the best quoniam that myght be" (608, fol. 74r).

Wytton's marginal comments show a remarkable similarity to the *a*-group revisions in both content and implied attitude (the most notable example being that between Wytton's extreme interest in January's thoughts in anticipation of his wedding night and the sadomasochistic implications of 575–84). But this remarkable similarity can hardly be taken as proof of Wytton's authorship of the *a*-group revisions, because this type of misogyny and misogamy was commonplace in clerical culture. Wytton was not the only scribe to respond in a misogynous way to Chaucer's representation of the Wife. The Ellesmere scribe substituted "sothe" for "sithe" in l. 45, thereby transforming the Wife's orthodox defense of the Christian widow's right to remarry into a proud refusal to live celibate ("kepe chaast in al"). The Lansdowne scribe added a link to connect the Wife's *Prologue* to the preceding Squire's fragment in which he portrays the Wife as aggressive, rude, and able to swear as outrageously as the Miller. And one or more of the *b*-group scribes, who had already inherited the *a*-group variants, in-

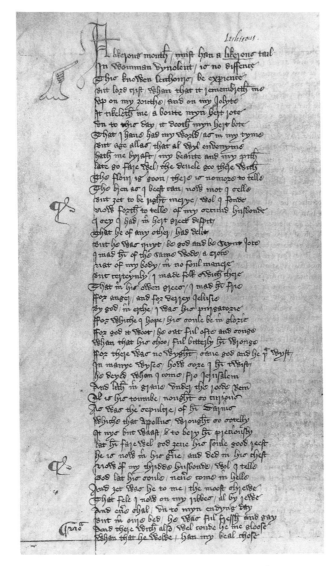

Cambridge Dd.4.24., fol. 72v. The hand points to l. 466: "A likerous mouth must han a likerous tail." By permission of the Syndics of Cambridge University Library.

serted salacious lines after the Wife's assurance to her old husbands that they "shul have queynte right ynogh at eve" (332), to reinforce the *a*-group variants' ascription to her of coarse language and casual adultery (see appendix C). [58]

Therefore, it is possible that Wytton did not compose any of the *a*-group

Detail of previous figure. By permission of the Syndics of Cambridge University Library.

variants himself but rather found them, either in his immediate copy-text or in some other manuscript of the *Tales* to which he had access; and there is some evidence to suggest that he did have access to more than one copy-text. First, his pattern of rubrication alters dramatically with the introduction of the "first" husband (452–53).[59] At this same point there is also a noticeable shift in the pattern of variants shared with other manuscripts.[60] Taken together, the two pattern shifts strongly suggest that the Dd scribe changed exemplars at this point. We cannot be certain what form his alternate exemplar took, but the fact that both shifts occur at or near the beginning of the renumbered husbands revision raises an intriguing possibility. Wytton's alternate exemplar might have been a short version of the *Wife of Bath's Prologue,* consisting of this final part, as revised by the renumbered husband variants and four of the added passages, and prefaced by the Wife's opening sentence in the first eight lines.

It would not have been difficult to create such a short version of the *Wife of Bath's Prologue.* Once the final part had been revised to represent all five husbands (and thereby keep accord with the number announced in the *General Prologue*), it would have been an easy matter to disengage it from the other two parts of the Wife's discourse and append it to her opening sentence. There is a natural break between the concluding line of this sentence, "And alle weren worthy men in here degree" (8) and the first line of her sermon on marriage ("But me was told nought longe agon is," 9). Even more important, there is a natural connection between it and the opening line of the revised third part ("My first husbonde was a reuelour," 453). Omitting everything in between—the Wife's sermon on marriage, the Pardoner's interruption, and her disquisition on how to handle rich old husbands—would cut the Wife's prologue down to half its original length; however, a clerical community of readers might have thought such a shortened text was much 'improved.' First, any clerk should have been glad to be rid of the first part, the Wife's sermon on the relative merits of virginity, celibacy, and marriage, since he could not have approved its literalist and antiascetic interpretation of scripture. Moreover, he must have been at least as unhappy as Chaucer's Friar Hubert to hear a woman preaching. Second, any clerk who happened to be an old man would have been just as glad to be rid of the second part, in which the Wife describes how she controlled her three old husbands. Certainly the Ellesmere scribe seems to have found this part sufficiently offensive to warrant a marginal outburst at l. 193: "Bihold how this goode wyf serues her iii firste housbondes whiche were goode olde men" (fol. 65r).[61] What is more, eliminating this second part would have the further advantage of removing the contradiction between the Wife's describing her three old husbands as practically impotent and then describing them all again individually as either sexually active or attractive men. However, the most important reason that a well-educated clerk would have been more satisfied with this drastically reduced and revised version of the Wife's *Prologue* is that it represents Dame Alys exactly as she should be represented—according to the antifeminist literary tradition. She is young, she is lascivious, she uses deception in courting men, and she is unfaithful to her husbands.

If it existed (and I must confess that I find the reasons for thinking that it did irresistible), such a scribal short version would surely have been popular with the clerical community of Chaucer readers. It could have circulated among them as a very slim booklet, comprising only the Wife's prologue and tale, or it could have formed part of a more substantial booklet, including the whole of Fragment D.[62] We cannot assume that such a booklet never existed simply because none has survived, for we know booklets were much more likely to have been "read to pieces" than heftier tomes like those containing the entire *Canterbury Tales*.[63]

Such a short version could not have included 44a–f, the first of the *a*-group variant passages in the *Wife of Bath's Prologue and Tale*. And yet this passage is characteristically present, together with the other *a*-group variants, in all extant *a*-group manuscripts, including Dd. If such a short version existed, therefore, someone must have decided to incorporate it into a complete text of the *Canterbury Tales* at a very early point in the transmission of the *a*-group text. It could be that Wytton himself made this decision; certainly his misogynous marginal comments suggest he would have found the short version much to his taste. It is more likely, however, that Wytton's alternative copy-text was not the short version itself, but rather a now-lost *a*-group manuscript of the *Tales* (or possibly a booklet containing the standard *a*-group text of either the *Wife of Bath's Prologue and Tale* or the D fragment), whose scribe had already incorporated the revised short version in place of the third part of the Wife's prologue.

At the same time, we cannot rule out the possibility that Wytton acquired 44a–f from a source different from that which provided the other *a*-group variants. Certainly it is different in kind from the other passages, being the only one to repeat material found in one of the other *Canterbury Tales*, and it has often been treated differently by Chaucer editors because of this. The modern tradition of treating 44a–f differently—as an authorial cancellation rather than an addition—can be traced back to W. W. Skeat, who based his landmark 1894 edition on Ellesmere. In order to explain the absence of 44a–f in that manuscript, Skeat hypothesized that Chaucer decided to cancel it after using some of the material in the *Merchant's Tale* (1427–28). However, it is equally plausible that a clever scribe, inspired by the lines in the *Merchant's Tale*, decided to add 44a–f to embellish his own copy of the *Wife of Bath's Prologue*. Such imitation of Chaucerian lines is common in the spurious links and is sometimes found elsewhere in the *Tales*.[64] Manly and Rickert have argued, on the basis of their collation of all known manuscripts, that all five *a*-group variant passages "must be considered together"; consequently, most modern editors have reintroduced 44a–f into the text proper of their editions as a late authorial addition, just like the other four.[65] If my alternative hypothesis is correct, however, Manly and Rickert's conclusion would mean that 44a–f must be considered a scribal interpolation—just like the other four—differing from them only in that it was inspired not by the antifeminist literary tradition but by a genuine Chaucerian passage in the *Merchant's Tale*.

If 44a–f has a scribal origin different from that of the other four *a*-group variant passages, could Wytton himself have added it to the *a*-group text? One of the curious features of this passage in Wytton's manuscript is that it has been visibly corrected in several places. Since "there is no comparable passage of correction" elsewhere in the Dd manuscript, Norman Blake has hypothesized that the corrections may actually be signs of Wytton's composition.[66] Against this idea, Manly and Rickert have pointed out that the passage as initially copied into Dd had all the common *a*-group errors.[67]

This suggests a contrary hypothesis, namely, that Wytton initially copied 44a–f from an *a*-group manuscript containing all the common errors and at some later time gained access to a better *a*-group text, from which he corrected the first half of the Wife's *Prologue*, including this passage. It further suggests that the scribal author of 44a–f was not Wytton himself but one of his predecessors, and not necessarily the author of the revision of part 3 of the Wife's *Prologue* either, whether or not that revision ever existed in an independent short version as I have hypothesized.[68]

As long as Chaucer editors could assume that 44a–f was an authorial cancellation, its visible correction in Dd, along with the correction of many other characteristic *a*-group errors in the first two parts of the *Wife of Bath's Prologue*, could be taken as evidence of the "authority" of Wytton's manuscript. If, however, 44a–f is not a Chaucerian cancellation, but rather a scribal invention, then the unknown manuscript that provided Wytton with the means of correcting this passage is not at all likely to have been "very near Chaucer's original,"[69] and there is no reason to accord his manuscript any authority at all.

⋅⋅⋅

As we have seen, the evidence of manuscript attestation does not strongly support the authenticity of any of the major *a*-group variants in the *Wife of Bath's Prologue*. Therefore, Chaucer editors have had to resort to other criteria to support their judgment that the variant passages are authorial revisions but that the renumbered husband variants are scribal errors. When faced with the necessity of distinguishing between authorial and scribal variants, Chaucer editors have traditionally relied upon three criteria: style, scribal practice, and meaning.[70] In thinking about the *a*-group variants in the *Wife of Bath's Prologue*, however, they have hitherto relied almost exclusively on the first two.[71] As long as they could assume that all medieval scribes were poetic dunces attempting only to make accurate copies, the criteria of style and scribal practice seemed to support their judgment. But recent research into late medieval manuscript culture shows that late medieval scribes working in the vernacular often rewrote texts, even Chaucer texts. Moreover, the degree of metrical and semantic competence demonstrated in some admittedly spurious links in the *Canterbury Tales* suggests that other links and variant passages, hitherto accepted as authorial on the grounds of style alone, may also be scribal in origin.

It is the criterion of meaning, however, that makes the present editorial judgment regarding the *a*-group variants ultimately untenable. Once the reader has succeeded in seeing behind and beyond these variants to the preexisting text and its deliberate and playful ambiguity with regard to the

Wife's chastity, it becomes clear that both sets of *a*-group variants serve a blatantly antifeminist agenda.[72] Moreover, it is an antifeminist agenda clearly marked by clerical misogyny and misogamy, for the variants succeed in obscuring the pre-existing textual ambiguity only by virtue of rewriting the Wife according to the stereotype of Estates Satire—as coarse, sexually aggressive, and adulterous. I am convinced that the author of these revisions was not Chaucer. It was probably not the scribe of Cambridge Dd.4.24, either. However, it was surely someone very like him: a highly educated and misogynous clerk, whether university don, priest or friar, making a copy of the *Canterbury Tales* for his own reading pleasure and that of his friends among the clergy.

Given what we are learning now about the lack of respect for "authority" among fifteenth-century scribes working in the vernacular, some textual critics have suggested it is no longer reasonable to attempt to recover Chaucer's original text, word for word.[73] They may be right; but as long as students and general readers must rely on printed editions of the *Canterbury Tales*, editors of these editions must decide whether or not to include the major *a*-group variants in the text proper of the *Wife of Bath's Prologue*. Until now, the inclusion of the *a*-group variant passages taken to be authorial revisions has allowed the erasure of what is most quintessentially Chaucerian in the Wife's *Prologue*: its playful and deliberate ambiguity with regard to her chastity. (Other ambiguities, just as playful, if not so evidently deliberate, are unaffected.) It is my hope that in the future Chaucer editors will omit these passages from the text proper for the same reason they have always omitted their *a*-group companions, the five scribal "errors" renumbering the Wife's husbands: because the misogynous rewriting effected by them is not the work of Geoffrey Chaucer.

Appendix A

Renumbered Husband Variants in Cambridge Dd.4.24

Once the Wife has announced that she will "speke of [her] first husbonde" (452), the sequence of renumbered husband variants is rapid, occurring approximately twenty to thirty lines apart:

> ¶ My first [Hg, El: ferthe] husbonde was a reuelour
> This is to seyn he had a paramour
> And I was yong and ful of ragerie
>
> (fol. 72r, ll. 452–55)

¶ "Now forth to telle of my secund [Hg,El: ferthe] husbonde
I sey I had in hert greet despit
That he of any other had delit
(fol.72v, ll. 480–82)

¶ "Now, of my thridde [Hg, El: fifthe] husbonde wol I telle
God lat his soule neuere come in helle
And yet was he to me the moost shrewe
(fol.72v, ll. 503–05)

¶ "My ferthe [Hg, El: fifthe] husbonde god his soule blisse
Which that I took for loue & no richesse
He somtyme was a clerk of Oxenforde
(fol.73v, ll. 525–27)

No further renumbering is necessary. One Lenten season, while the erst-while "clerk of Oxenforde" is away, the Wife courts young Jankyn. Later, after a month of mourning this "fierthe husbonde" (587), she marries Jankyn, who thus becomes her fifth husband, although never so numbered in this revision.

Appendix B

Added Passages First Appearing in Cambridge Dd.4.24

Of whiche [i.e., husbands] I haue pyked out the beste
Bothe of here nether purs and of here cheste
Diuerse scoles maken parfyt clerkes
And diuerse practyk in many sondry werkes
Maketh the werkman parfyt sekirly
Of fyue husbondes scoleryng am I
(fol. 67r, ll. 44a–f)

I bar hym on honde he hadde enchaunted me
My dame taughte me that sotiltee
And eek I seide I mette of hym al nyght
He wolde han slayn me as I lay vp right
And al my bed was ful of verray blod
But ȝet I hope that ȝe shuln do me good
For blod bytokeneth gold, as me was taught
And al was fals I dremed of it right nought
But as I folwed ay my dames loore
As wel of that as of othere thynges more
(fol. 73v, ll. 575–84)

For certes I am al Venerien
In feelyng and myn hert is marcien
Venus me ʒaf my lust my likerousnesse
And Mars ʒaf me my sturdy hardynesse
(fol. 74r, ll. 609–12)

ʒet have I Mars merk vp on my face
And also in a nother pryue place
For god so wysely be my sauacioun
I louede neuere by no discrecioun
But euere folwed myn appetit
Al were he short long blak or whit
I toke no kepe so that he liked me
How poore he was ne eke of what degree
(fol. 74r, ll. 619–26)

For which [Eve's sin] that Ihesu crist him self was slayn
That bought vs with his hert blod a gayn
Loo heere expres of wommen may ʒe fynde
That womman was the losse of al mankynde
(fol. 75r, ll. 717–20)

Appendix C

Misogynous Variants Appearing First in Other Manuscripts

First appearing in Ellesmere:

For sothe I wol nat kepe me chaast in al
(fol. 67v, l. 45)
[Hg: For sithe I wol nat kepe chaast in al]
[Dd: For syn I wol nat kepe me chast in al]

Unique to Lansdowne:

Than schortly ansewarde þe wife of Bathe
And swore a wonder grete haþe
Be goddes bones I wil tel next
I will nouht glose bot saye þe text
(fol. 87r)

First appearing in b-group manuscripts:

Be thow neuyr wroth for myn instrument
(l. 332a)

Though it be som tyme to a good felaw lent
(l. 332b)

or

But þou finde þere in anoþer mannes tent
(l. 332b)

(The last is an alternative line found only in the non-*b* MSS, Ld¹, Ry¹, and Se; however, in explicitness of language [e.g., "tente"] it closely resembles the spurious *b*-group lines added to the pear tree episode at the end of the *Merchant's Tale*.)

Notes

I am grateful to the Social Sciences and Humanities Research Council of Canada for the grant that enabled me to research and write this article.

1. Norman Blake has called the Wife's *Prologue* "the most altered piece" in the *Canterbury Tales* ("The Wife of Bath and Her Tale," *Leeds Studies in English* 13 [1982]: 45).

2. Larry D. Benson, general editor, *The Riverside Chaucer* (Boston: Houghton Mifflin, 1987; hereafter *RC*), ll. 44a–f, 575–84, 609–12, 619–26, 717–20.

3. *RC*, ll. 452, 453, 480, 503, 525.

4. Dd is one of the ten manuscripts collated with Hengwrt by the Variorum editors, not only because of its early date and status as the oldest extant representative of the *a* group but also because John Manly and Edith Rickert, the only editors to have based an edition of the *Canterbury Tales* on a collation of all known manuscripts, found that even though it was "somewhat carelessly written, some of [its] corrections give the MS authority" (John M. Manly and Edith Rickert, *The Text of the* Canterbury Tales *Studied on the Basis of All Known Manuscripts*, 8 vols. [Chicago: University of Chicago Press, 1940], 1:102).

5. The single exception is Norman Blake, who omitted the five added passages from his Hengwrt-based edition of the *Canterbury Tales* (London: Arnold, 1980), and has suggested that they may have been added by the Dd scribe himself, since his marginal notes show that he was "sufficiently interested in the Wife and in the relationship between the sexes" to have done so (Blake, *Textual Tradition of the* Canterbury Tales [London: Arnold, 1985], 135). There is a similar difference of scholarly opinion with regard to some of the major variants in the *Nun's Priest's Tale*. In his Variorum edition Derek Pearsall takes the position that both the added couplet 4060a–b and the epilogue are genuine passages later canceled by Chaucer, and that both the short and the long versions of the link (the latter adding ll. 3961–80) are likewise genuine (*The Nun's Priest's Tale*, A Variorum Edition of the Works of Geoffrey Chaucer, vol. 2 [Norman: University of Oklahoma Press, 1983], 100). On the other hand, Ralph Hanna III has cited 4060a–b as a good example of a "perverse desire" on the part of a scribe "to join

in the fun and write some poetry, too" ("Authorial Versions, Rolling Revision, Scribal Error? Or, the Truth about *Truth,*" *Studies in the Age of Chaucer* 10 [1988]: 24–25).

6. The phrase "horizon of expectation" is a key concept in H. R. Jauss's reception theory and historicist reader-response criticism. See H. R. Jauss, *Toward an Aesthetic of Reception,* trans. Timothy Bahti (Minneapolis: University of Minnesota Press, 1982).

7. I borrow the phrases "cultural literacy" and "clerical assumptions" from Mary Wack's fascinating study, *Lovesickness in the Middle Ages: The 'Viaticum' and Its Commentaries* (Philadelphia: University of Pennsylvania Press, 1990), xv.

8. At the end of her study of the *General Prologue,* Jill Mann offers a list of twenty-one "representative poems" in which estates are presented, including Chaucer's *Canterbury Tales* and Gower's *Mirour de l'Omme.* Only nine of these treat women at all (Gower's *Mirour* is not one of them), while only four, including Chaucer's *General Prologue,* treat wives in particular (*Chaucer and Medieval Estates Satire: The Literature of Social Classes and the* General Prologue *to the* Canterbury Tales [Cambridge: Cambridge University Press, 1973], 203–06).

9. Seth Lerer, *Chaucer and His Readers* (Princeton: Princeton University Press, 1993), 12.

10. The following paragraphs summarize the argument in Beverly Kennedy, "Cambridge Dd.4.24; a Misogynous Rewriting of the *Wife of Bath's Prologue?*" *Chaucer Review* 30 (1996): 343–56. In an article that came to my attention only after I had written this essay, John Eadie argues that four of the variant passages (475–84, 609–12, 619–26, and 717–20) appear to have been "designed to bring the text of WBP into line with conventional medieval attitudes to women, at least as these attitudes tended to be interpreted in clerkly circles" ("The Wife of Bath's Non-Hengwrt Lines," *Neuphilologische Mitteilungen* 96 [1995]: 175).

11. All quotations, unless otherwise specified, are taken from Cambridge Dd.4.24.

12. Eadie "Non-Hengwrt Lines," 174, points to the inappropriate "clerical piety expressed" in these lines and further argues that the Wife herself would not "simply repeat" an antifeminist commonplace such as "womman was the losse of al mankynde" without "some kind of gloss of her own choosing." In his opinion, these are the reasons why the Gg scribe omitted the passage.

13. Both revisions are still effective, however, partly because the Wife has never said that her three old husbands were actually her *first* three husbands and partly because it is only in retrospect that the reader can perceive the contradiction. Charles Owen has nevertheless suggested that the Ellesmere editor may have deliberately omitted 44a–f from his text because of this contradiction (Owen, *The Manuscripts of the Canterbury Tales* [Cambridge, England: D. S. Brewer, 1991], 12).

14. Beryl Rowland is the only critic to have observed that "at its surface value" the fictive dream is "totally out of character" for the Wife ("On the Timely Death of the Wife of Bath's Fourth Husband," *Archiv* 209/2 [1973]: 278).

15. This fourth added passage also raises the question of why a rich and otherwise apparently respectable woman would choose to boast of her sexual promiscuity. Only two critics have tried to answer this question. Beryl Rowland has argued that, like many prostitutes, the Wife suffers from both frigidity and nymphomania induced by the trauma of "precocious sexual experience." This diagnosis does not, however, explain why Dame Alys would wish to boast of her illness publicly ("Chaucer's Dame Alys: Critics in Blunderland," *Neuphilologische Mitteilungen* 73 [1972]: 391). On the other hand, Alcuin Blamires has speculated that, like the Pardoner, Alisoun suffers from exhi-

bitionism and so is driven to say what is "normally unsayable" in order to "shock" and "outrage" her audience (*The Canterbury Tales* [Atlantic Highlands, N.J.: Humanities Press International, 1987], 70–71); however, this explanation leaves one wondering why she bothered to lie about adultery earlier.

16. Mann, *Chaucer and Medieval Estates Satire*, 126, has noted that in the *General Prologue* Chaucer describes "the Wife's sexual experience . . . ambiguously . . . as 'compaignye in youth,' 'wandrynge by the weye' or 'the olde daunce.'" I have found that he continues this pattern through the use of deliberately ambiguous terms like "myrthe" (399) and "daliaunce" (565) in the Wife's prologue.

17. For a full discussion of the intertextual evidence supporting the notion that in Chaucer's time "chaumbre of venus" could refer to the heart as well as the genitals, see Beverly Kennedy, "Reambiguating the Obvious: Alisoun's 'Chambre of Venus'" (paper delivered at the New Chaucer Society, Seattle, Washington, August 1992).

18. See 217–19.

19. Most textual critics would date the first six manuscripts before 1420 and the last two before 1430. See Blake, *Textual Tradition*, 50–78, and Owen, *Manuscripts*, 9–12. However, Ralph Hanna III has asserted that Hg, Ha⁴, Cp, Dd, and El "might" all have been written before 1410 ("The Hengwrt Manuscript and the Canon of *The Canterbury Tales*," *English Manuscript Studies, 1100–1700* 1 [1989]: 73). In addition, most textual critics now agree that Hengwrt (Hg) is the earliest extant manuscript, although M. B. Parkes has observed that Corpus (Cp) may be the earliest, and the same claim has in the past been made for Harley 7334 (Ha⁴). Lansdowne (La) has to be later than Cp, if Cp was its copy-text, but Claire Thomson has recently suggested that this may not have been the case ("The Status of the Lansdowne Chaucer," Paper delivered at the 33d International Conference of Medieval Studies, Kalamazoo, Michigan, May 1998). There is no agreement as to the relative order of Ha⁴ and Cp: Blake thinks Cp is earlier than Ha⁴ (*Textual Tradition*, 11); Owen, drawing on different and more recent evidence, suggests the contrary, that Ha⁴ is earlier than Cp (*Manuscripts*, 9). They agree on the chronological position of Cambridge Dd, however: It is later than Cp and Ha⁴, but earlier than El and Gg (Blake, *Textual Tradition*, 148–49; Owen, *Manuscripts*, 11).

20. I have taken much of the information that follows from the electronic transcriptions of the *Wife of Bath's Prologue* manuscripts made by Peter Robinson, Elizabeth Solopova, and their assistants under the aegis of the Canterbury Tales Project and recently published on CD-ROM (*The Wife of Bath's Prologue on CD-ROM*, ed. Peter Robinson [Cambridge: Cambridge University Press, 1996].

21. This number includes Manly and Rickert's *c* group, descended from Corpus and Lansdowne, and the closely related and very large *d* group, descended from Petworth.

22. The eight manuscripts that have inherited both sets of variants are Manly and Rickert's *a* group (of which Dd is the oldest extant member), namely Egerton 2726 (En¹), Cardigan (Cn), Manchester English 113 (Ma) and Devonshire (Ds), and their *b* group (textually together with *a* throughout the Wife's *Prologue* [*Text of the* Canterbury Tales, 2:207]), namely Helmingham (He), New College D 314 (Ne), Caxton's first printed edition (Cx¹, standing for the now missing *b* manuscript from which he printed it) and Trinity College Cambridge R.3.15 (Tc²). Two of the four *b*-group manuscripts, Cx¹ and Tc² (which may have been copied from Cx¹), have only the first two renumbered husband variants (452 and 453), and these have been visibly corrected in Tc².

The six manuscripts that acquired one or the other set of variants by contamination fall into two groups: (1) those whose scribes picked up all five variant passages but either did not try or tried and did not succeed in correctly renumbering the husbands, viz., Christ Church (Ch), whose scribe did not try, and Cambridge Ii.3.26 (Ii), Royal 17 D.XV (Ry[1]), and Selden (Se), whose scribes all tried but had difficulty getting the renumbering right: Ry[1] gets all but 480 right; Se gets 502 and 525 right but leaves 451, 452, and 480 blank; and Ii gets them all wrong, though two of his errors, 480 and 525, happen to coincide with the Chaucerian numbering; and (2) those with all of the renumbered husband variants but none of the variant passages, viz., Egerton 2864 (En[3]) and Additional 5140 (Ad[1]), which was copied from it. The evidence of this pair of manuscripts could be interpreted to mean that the renumbered husband variants had an origin independent of the passages, and Peter Robinson has recently hypothesized that the renumbered husband variants were not present in the a-group exemplar from which Ellesmere derived its four passages, but rather entered the a-group text in a "consecutive" exemplar ("A Stemmatic Analysis of the Fifteenth-Century Witnesses to the *Wife of Bath's Prologue*," *The Canterbury Tales Project Occasional Papers* [Oxford: Oxford University Press, 1997], 2:123). Robinson's two-step hypothesis about the origin of the a-group variants does not necessarily mean that the renumbered husband revision ever enjoyed an existence separate from the variant passages, however, and as for the evidence of En[3] and Ad[1], Owen has argued persuasively that, since the Egerton scribe acquired the renumbered husband variants from the ancestor of Cn, he must have seen the five variant passages there and, for whatever reason, chose not to copy them into the margins of his own text (Owen, *Manuscripts*, 88).

    23. The four manuscripts are Sion College (Si), Additional 35286 (Ad[3]), Harley 1758 (Ha[2]), and Laud 600 (Ld[1]). The exception is Sion College, a very late (1460–90) anthology of four tales (the Clerk's, the Wife's, the Friar's, and the Summoner's) that, in addition to four of the added passages (not the same four as in Ellesmere), has acquired by contamination all five of the renumbered husband variants.

    24. Manly and Rickert, *Text of the* Canterbury Tales, 1:150, 2:196. Robinson confirms that the scribe of El had access to two exemplars and identifies that used for the second half of the Wife's *Prologue* as possibly the "ultimate exemplar of Dd and the A witnesses" ("Stemmatic Analysis," 110).

    25. See above, n. 13.

    26. M. L. Samuels has established that the same scribe who copied Hengwrt, which has none of the a-group variants, also copied Ellesmere some years later ("The Scribe of the Hengwrt and Ellesmere Manuscripts of the *Canterbury Tales*," *Studies in the Age of Chaucer* 5 [1983]: 45–65). Therefore, it is not really necessary to posit simultaneous access to an unrevised manuscript in order to explain why this scribe might have questioned variants that, so far as he knew, did not exist at the time he copied Hengwrt.

    27. It is always possible that the choices I have hypothesized here for the Ellesmere editor were actually made by one of his predecessors in the transmission process. We do not know how many early manuscripts may have been lost. Robinson avoids attributing so much choice to the Ellesmere editor by positing two "consecutive" copies of the a-group ancestor: (1) the one used by Ellesmere to copy the second half of the Wife's *Prologue*, which he identifies as the ultimate ancestor, or α, which may have contained only these four added passages; and (2) a copy of this, into which were introduced the renumbered husband variants, along with other variants not present in El ("Stemmatic Analysis," 123–26). Another way to avoid attributing such choice to the Ellesmere editor

is to accept Walter Skeat's hypothesis that 44a–f is different from the other four variant passages in being an authorial cancellation rather than an addition. Even if this were true, however, we would still be left with the question of why the Gg scribe (or one of his predecessors) omitted 717–20 as well as 44a–f. Eadie has recently argued that 717–20 was deliberately omitted by the editor of Gg because of its "total inappropriateness" ("Non-Hengwrt Lines," 174); see above, n. 12. On the other hand, Ralph Hanna III, who believes that the attribution of 717–20 to Chaucer is "probably" erroneous, observes that its omission from Ggm might be explained as a case of "eyeskip" occasioned by the repetition of "mankynde (716) . . . mankynde" (720) (["The] Editing [of] the Ellesmere Text," in *The Ellesmere Chaucer: Essays in Interpretation*, ed. Martin Stevens and Daniel Woodward [San Marino, Calif.: Huntington Library, 1995], n. 17).

28. Si included four passages (44a–f, 609–12, 619–26, and 717–20), not the same four as El; Ha² copied two into the margins (609–12 and 619–26) and allocated marginal space for a third (717–20), not the same three as in Gg; Ad³ included two (475–84 and 609–12), not the same two as were copied into the margins of Ha²; and Ld¹ included only one (619–26).

29. Manly and Rickert, *Text of the* Canterbury Tales, 2:193.

30. John H. Fisher, "Animadversions on the Text of Chaucer, 1988," *Speculum* 63 (1988): 789. It is of course possible that both hypotheses are true; certainly there is evidence to support both. Hanna has argued that the Hengwrt scribe could not have had access to Chaucer's own copy-text and that his manuscript looks very much as if it were copied from an incomplete collection of *in vita* copies of fragments of the *Canterbury Tales* ("The Hengwrt Manuscript and the Canon," 66–75). On the other hand, John M. Bowers has argued that Ha⁴ and Cp, the earliest manuscripts to include *Gamelyn* in lieu of the *Cook's Tale*, most likely derive from Chaucer's own papers, since *Gamelyn* appears only in the twenty-five *Canterbury Tales* manuscripts that use it to complete the Cook's performance, and all twenty-five clearly derive from a single source. Bowers hypothesizes that Chaucer's literary executors found *Gamelyn* "inserted at this point in the poet's final drafts . . . put there by him as a potential source for a tale, never written, to replace the abandoned account of Perkyn Revelour" (Bowers, ed., *The Canterbury Tales: Fifteenth-Century Continuations and Additions* [Kalamazoo, Mich.: Medieval Institute Press, 1992], 33).

31. Blake, *Textual Tradition*, 131–35.

32. Robinson dismisses the currently accepted hypothesis of authorial revision on the grounds that, other than the five passages, there is no evidence of authorial revision in the Wife's *Prologue* (as argued by Elizabeth Solopova in "The Problem of Authorial Variants in the *Wife of Bath's Prologue*," in *The Canterbury Tales Project Occasional Papers*, vol. 2 [Oxford: Oxford University Press, 1997], 133–42). However, Robinson's choice of an alternative hypothesis, namely, that all five passages were authorial cancellations, fails to convince on a number of counts. First, it is necessarily based on the assumption that all extant manuscripts descend from Chaucer's personal copy of the *Tales*, whereas many Chaucer editors still think it possible that parts of the *Tales* circulated during Chaucer's lifetime (the *Wife of Bath's Prologue* being one of the likelier candidates for such circulation), and Hanna has recently argued, on the basis of his own analysis of variants in the first 6,000 lines, that *all* early copies of the *Canterbury Tales* relied on "odd bunches of quires, from diverse sources and of diverse textual quality" ("Editing the Ellesmere Text," 231). Next, Robinson's hypothesis is based on the even

more questionable assumption that all five passages were part of Chaucer's original creation, whereas every previous editor or critic who has examined the passages in context has taken them to be late insertions (see the textual note to the first passage [44a–f] in *RC*). Together, these two assumptions enable Robinson to take the admittedly misogynous, repetitious, and contradictory content of the passages, along with the relatively poor quality of some of them, as reasons why Chaucer would have decided to omit them in a later revision, rather than as evidence of scribal interference (the only other possible hypothesis, once authorial revision has been rejected). Finally, having established that all extant witnesses of the passages descend from one common source, α, the ultimate exemplar of the *a* group (which he believes to have been copied directly from Chaucer's own copy), Robinson must base his hypothesis of authorial cancellation on yet another unlikely assumption, namely, that one, and only one, of the scribes who had access to Chaucer's copy (the α scribe) chose *not* to respect the author's cancellation marks (Robinson, "Stemmatic Analysis," 124–27).

33. See his critical apparatus to the forthcoming Variorum edition of the *Wife of Bath's Prologue and Tale*. I am grateful to Professor Fisher for allowing me to read parts of it prior to publication.

34. Alcuin Blamires, *Woman Defamed and Woman Defended: An Anthology of Medieval Texts* (Oxford: Oxford University Press, 1992), 99. This is an anthology of medieval antifeminist texts that also includes some of the feminist texts elicited by the tradition.

35. Feminist critics of Chaucer are sharply divided on the issue of his "feminism'"or "antifeminism," and it is clear to me, at least, that their debate has been much affected by the misogynous content of the *a*-group passages. Despite these passages, however, Hope Phyllis Weissman has argued that Chaucer critiques antifeminist stereotypes through his realistic representations of the Wife of Bath and the Prioress ("Anti-Feminism and Chaucer's Characterization of Women," in *Geoffrey Chaucer: A Collection of Original Articles*, ed. George D. Economou [New York: McGraw-Hill, 1976], 104–8; rpt. in *Critical Essays on Chaucer's* Canterbury Tales, ed. Malcolm Andrew [Toronto: University of Toronto Press, 1991], 199–24). Carolyn Dinshaw has argued that Dame Alys's appropriation of patriarchal antifeminist discourse is done "with a difference" amounting to "assertive [and, I would add, subversive] mimicking" (*Chaucer's Sexual Poetics* [Madison: University of Wisconsin Press, 1989], 120, 131). Jill Mann has argued that through the Wife of Bath's character, Chaucer gives his readers the "imagined representation of an individual engagement with" and resistance to antifeminist stereotypes (*Geoffrey Chaucer* [Atlantic Highlands, N.J.: Humanities Press International, 1991], 83). And in *Woman Defamed and Woman Defended*, Alcuin Blamires has positioned the *Wife of Bath's Prologue* at the point of "interface" between antifeminist and feminist texts, recognizing that, "even in the process of submerging the reader in a welter of misogynistic quotations," it can be read as one of Chaucer's "narratives in defence of women" (198).

36. Mann has noted the ambiguity of Chaucer's representation of the Wife's sexual experience in the *General Prologue*, see above, n. 16; and Graciela Daichmann has characterized Chaucer's representation of the Prioress as more subtly ambiguous than any previous literary representation of this stock character (*Wayward Nuns in Medieval Literature* [Syracuse: Syracuse University Press, 1986]).

37. *Le Roman de la Rose*, ed. Daniel Poirion (Paris: Garnier Flammarion, 1974), l. 13,691.

38. Eileen Power quotes the thirteenth-century scholar Jacques de Vitry as having argued that Eve "succeeded in banishing her husband from the garden of delights and in condemning Christ to the torment of the Cross" (Power, *Medieval Women*, ed. M. M. Postan [Cambridge: Cambridge University Press, 1975], 14).

39. Blamires notes that it would have been easy to excerpt this relatively brief and witty answer to "the 'woman' question" and add it "to one's manuscript notebook of quotations" (*Woman Defamed and Woman Defended*, 99).

40. For a survey of this curriculum and how it is reflected in Chaucer's text, see Robert A. Pratt, "Jankyn's 'Book of Wikked Wyves': Medieval Anti-Matrimonial Propaganda in the Universities," *Annuale Medievale* 3 (1962): 5–27.

41. Owen, *Manuscripts*, 15–22.

42. Estelle Stubbs's research is still in progress, and she is careful to qualify her preliminary findings with the caveat that "tracing groups of names through a variety of records is a treacherous undertaking." Nevertheless, she is convinced that "the constant recurrence of the same names or groups of names in records linking families, Augustinian priories, literary activity and *Canterbury Tales* manuscripts, must surely have some significance" ("Further Insights into the Provenance of Some *Canterbury Tales* Manuscripts" [paper delivered at the Thirty-Second International Congress of Medieval Studies, Kalamazoo, Michigan, 10 May 1997]). In addition to the possibility that Dd's scribe, Wytton, was a friar, Stubbs thinks it likely that the other four *a*-group manuscripts were also either owned or copied by friars. En[1] was very likely copied by two friars from Clare priory who were brothers, Thomas and Henry of Colchester. Cn and Ma have the name of a Norfolk friar, Robert Cley, copied into the margin of the *Pardoner's Tale*. Finally, although her work on Ds is not yet complete, Stubbs has found links between Clare Priory and the group of people who may have owned this manuscript at an early date. Stubbs has also found connections between friars and some of the *b*-group manuscripts and, what is even more interesting from the point of view of my hypothesis, between at least one (Ry[1]) and possibly another (Ch) of the four manuscripts that acquired all five of the *a*- and *b*-group variant passages in the *Wife of Bath's Prologue* by contamination. All in all, Stubbs has evidence linking thirteen of the nineteen manuscripts containing some or all of the *a*-group variant passages to Augustinian friars, Clare Priory, or landed families living near Clare Priory (private communication, 29 May 1997).

43. Manly and Rickert, *Text of the* Canterbury Tales, 1:104–05, have suggested that Wytton was the Richard Wytton who became master of Mickle Hall, Oxford, in 1426, connecting the Dd manuscript to Oxford through the signature "hungerford" on fol. 8, which may be that of Walter Lord Hungerford (d. 1449), in his youth a student at Mickle Hall. Estelle Stubbs observes that this Oxford Wytton could be the same man as the friar attached to Lincoln priory, whom she has suggested is the copyist of Dd. The friar was a lector at Lincoln Priory and therefore can be presumed to have spent some years away from his home priory at university (private communication, 27 May 1997). If Friar Wytton came from the area around the priory to which he was attached, as was customary, he would meet the linguistic criteria raised by Dan Mosser in objection to Manly and Rickert's identification of the Oxford don. Mosser himself has found another Wytton who fits the linguistic criteria, a Cambridgeshire man who lived until at least 1412 and worked in and around London as a priest (*The Wife of Bath's Prologue* CD-ROM).

44. Both terms are employed by Joyce Coleman in her groundbreaking book ana-

lyzing the different types of literacy that coexisted in the late Middle Ages (*Public Reading and the Reading Public in Late Medieval England and France* [Cambridge: Cambridge University Press, 1996], esp. 88–97). Wytton's "scholar[ly] interest in the text" he was copying has already been noted by Owen, *Manuscripts*, 12.

45. Manly and Rickert, *Text of the* Canterbury Tales, 2:191.

46. Blake, *Textual Tradition*, 47. Unfortunately, computer-assisted stylistic analysis cannot solve the problem, at least not yet. Stephen Reimer has attempted to distinguish the styles of Chaucer, Gower, and Lydgate using computer-assisted analysis, but has found it impossible to achieve a statistically significant result on the basis of short passages alone ("Differentiating Chaucer and Lydgate: Some Preliminary Observations," *Computer-Based Chaucer Studies*, ed. Ian Lancashire [Toronto: University of Toronto Press, 1993], 161–76).

47. Stephen Knight, "Textual Variants: Textual Variance," *Southern Review* 16 (1983): 52. The editorial assumption of fifteenth-century scribes' poetic incompetence is so taken for granted as to be almost never stated. It is sometimes implied, however. See, for example, Nicolas Jacobs's observation, "To be a scribe is not a bar to poetic talent, but scribes are not selected for it" ("Regression to the Commonplace in Some Vernacular Traditions," in *Crux and Controversy in Middle English Textual Criticism*, ed. A. J. Minnis and Charlotte Brewer [Woodbridge, England: D. S. Brewer, 1992], 63) and Ralph Hanna's description of l. 805 in *Sir Thopas* as "a piece of deliberately bad poetry" and "thus not necessarily beyond the power of a scribe to supply" ("The Hengwrt Manuscript and the Canon," 77).

48. Elizabeth Solopova demonstrates that even the very earliest scribes attempted "metrical regularisation" of Chaucer's verse; more important, she finds that one of them, the scribe responsible for the "metrical improvements" in Ha⁴, was a "skilful reviser" of Chaucer's iambic pentameter line ("Chaucer's Metre and Scribal Editing in the Early Manuscripts of the *Canterbury Tales*," in *The Canterbury Tales Project Occasional Papers*, ed. Norman Blake and Peter Robinson [Oxford: Oxford University Press, 1997], 2:157–59).

49. Joyce Coleman has shown that the dominant mode of receiving recreational literature throughout the fourteenth and fifteenth centuries was social and aural. She has also analyzed Chaucer's texts to show that he expected his works to be received aurally for the most part (*Public Reading and the Reading Public*, chapters 4 and 5). Highly educated clerics, whom she calls "scholarly-professional readers," would have been accustomed to private reading (91), but different kinds of readers might choose different modes of reception according to situation and type of literature (93). Thus, it is not at all unlikely that groups of religious clerics might have chosen to imitate the larger literate culture when receiving recreational texts like the *Canterbury Tales* by listening in groups while the most talented lector among them read aloud.

50. According to Ralph Hanna, what we call "authority" seems to have been "quite intentionally dispersed in late medieval manuscript culture," being "most of the time not the property" of the individual we would identify as the "author" ("Producing Manuscripts and Editions," in *Crux and Controversy*, 122). See also A. J. Minnis, *The Medieval Theory of Authorship: Scholastic Literary Attitudes in the Middle Ages* (London: Scolar Press, 1984).

51. See Hanna's discussion of scribal revisions designed to "meliorate" the texts of *Sir Orfeo* and the *Polychronicon*, in "Producing Manuscripts," in *Crux and Controversy*, 117–19, 122–23.

52. See John M. Bowers, *Continuations and Additions*, a useful edition of many of these scribal efforts.

53. See Barbara Kline's "Scribal Agendas and the Text of Chaucer's Tales in British Library MS Harley 7333," in this volume.

54. Jean of Angoulême's manuscript is discussed by Paul Strohm, "Jean of Angoulême: A Fifteenth-Century Reader of Chaucer," *Neuphilologische Mitteilungen* 72 (1971): 69–76.

55. Seth Lerer, *Chaucer and His Readers*, 211. Lerer believes that Helmingham was revised for use as a "household volume." Thus he focuses his discussion on those parts of the *Tales* that might usefully have been "read and heard by both children and adults" (93–94). He neither discusses the fabliaux nor mentions the fact that Helmingham adds three bawdy passages to embellish the conclusion of the *Merchant's Tale* and two bawdy lines (332a–b, quoted in appendix C)—in addition to the *a*-group variants—to the *Wife of Bath's Prologue*. More examples of creative scribal rewriting in Cn and Ne are noted by Owen, *Manuscripts*, 21–22, 58 n. 6.

56. Louise Fradenburg speculates that the ending may have been revised in this way to make the poem suitable for presentation as a wedding gift (*City, Marriage, Tournament: Arts of Rule in Late Medieval Scotland* [Madison: University of Wisconsin Press, 1991], 129).

57. Owen, *Manuscripts*, 19–20.

58. By no means all early scribes tried to rewrite Chaucer's Wife of Bath in conformity with antifeminist literary tradition. On the contrary, judging by the same sort of evidence, namely, scribal variants, links, and large-scale narrative additions, at least three scribes seem to have viewed the Wife quite positively: Cp, Royal 18 ([Ry²], whose link to the Wife's *Prologue* was copied into both Barlow [Bw] and Laud 739 [Ld²], and Northumberland (Nl). See Beverly Kennedy, "Contradictory Responses to the Wife of Bath as Evidenced by Fifteenth-Century Manuscript Variants," in *The Canterbury Tales Project Occasional Papers*, 2:23–29.

59. Whereas in the first two parts of the Wife's prologue Wytton never used paraphs to mark important segments of the narrative, not even the Pardoner's interruption, in this final part he uses them regularly. They appear at ll. 453, 480, 503, 525, 563, 587, 627, 655, 780, 829, 840, and 850.

60. Manly and Rickert, *Text of the* Canterbury Tales, 2:208–09, find that Dd switches manuscript affiliation somewhere around l. 450 of the *Wife of Bath's Prologue*.

61. He follows this initial outburst with two more marginal comments, which, since they lack the opening "Behold" (with its implied exclamation point) and the special pleading adjective "goode" to describe the husbands, appear much less emotional and more matter-of-fact: At l. 453 he writes, "Of the condicioun of the fourthe housbonde of this goode wyf and how she serued hym" (fol. 67v), and at l. 503, "Of the fifthe housbonde of this wyf and hou she bar hire ayens hym" (fol. 68r). Perhaps the Ellesmere scribe was an old man himself and less able to identify with the two younger husbands, the philandering fourth, and the wife-battering fifth.

62. Ralph Hanna's analysis of manuscript relations among the earliest extant copies of the *Canterbury Tales* offers some support for my hypothesis. In addition to the three or possibly four "full" exemplars of the *Canterbury Tales* he posits to account for the pattern of shared errors among the first seven manuscripts of the *Tales*, he adds a fifth, "loose exemplar" to account for the peculiarities of Dd in the second half of the Wife's prologue. He does not specify the length of this "loose exemplar," but does note

that it is "not evidenced elsewhere in [his] sample," which includes all of fragments 1 and 2 and the *Wife of Bath's Prologue* (Hanna, "Editing the Ellesmere Text," 229–30). This suggests to me that his posited "loose exemplar" could have been the clerical short version of the Wife's *Prologue* I have hypothesized.

63. Kate Harris, "Patrons, Buyers and Owners: The Evidence for Ownership and the Role of Book Owners in Book Production and the Book Trade," in *Book Production and Publishing in Britain, 1375–1475,* ed. Jeremy Griffiths and Derek Pearsall (Cambridge: Cambridge University Press, 1989), 165–67. It is of some interest in this regard that Ralph Hanna has identified Fragment D as one of the five "large chunks" or "booklets" acquired to make up the Hengwrt manuscript ("The Hengwrt Manuscript and the Canon," 66).

64. For example, the "modestly salacious" two-line addition to the *Nun's Priest's Tale* (4060a–b) is, in Ralph Hanna's opinion, clearly a scribal interpolation, "derived from a legitimate Chaucerian line" ("Authorial Versions," 24–25), though the editor of the Variorum edition, Derek Pearsall, disagrees with Hanna's judgment on this (see above, n. 5).

65. Manly and Rickert, *Text of the* Canterbury Tales, 2:191. F. N. Robinson followed Skeat in both the first and second of his Riverside editions; Donaldson, Pratt, Fisher, and Benson have all decided, presumably on the basis of Manly and Rickert's evidence, to reinsert 44a–f into the text proper. However, in the third Riverside edition Benson continues to insist on the difference of 44a–f by bracketing it and remarking in the textual and critical notes that it is absent from Ellesmere and may be an authorial cancellation. Although he believes 44a–f to be an authorial cancellation, Peter Robinson offers another explanation for its absence from El, see above, n. 27.

66. Blake, *Textual Tradition,* 130.

67. Manly and Rickert, *Text of the* Canterbury Tales, 2:193, 208–9.

68. This hypothetical scribal short version, if it existed, could also explain the apparent selectivity, noted above, of the Ellesmere and Cambridge Gg scribes. Ellesmere incorporates four of the *a*-group variant passages, and Gg incorporates three, but neither includes 44a–f. Both also exhibit shifts in the pattern of shared variants at the point at which the *a*-group revision of part three of the Wife's *Prologue* begins (Manly and Rickert, *Text of the* Canterbury Tales, 2:199). Therefore, it is possible that the apparent shift of exemplar in Ellesmere and Gg, like that in Dd, is connected in some way with the *a*-group version of the last part of the Wife's *Prologue.* Peter Robinson hypothesizes that El and Gg's source for the variant passages was either α, the ultimate ancestor of the *a* group, or an "intermediate" copy of α, which "contained at least the last four added passages," ("Stemmatic Analysis," 123–24); either of these might have been my hypothesized scribal short version of the Wife's *Prologue.* See above, n. 27.

69. Manly and Rickert, *Text of the* Canterbury Tales, 1:106, observe that the Dd scribe may have managed to correct many errors "by the light of his own reason." They were never able to identify the manuscript "very near the original," which they believe provided Wytton with "the original form" of ll. 44a–f (2:193), but Peter Robinson has suggested that it was the same manuscript from which Caxton later corrected his second edition, which he thinks was "extremely close to the α exemplar and may indeed have been the α exemplar" ("Stemmatic Analysis," 124).

70. Fisher, "Animadversions," 790.

71. The significant exception here is Robert Pratt, who certainly took meaning into account when tracing what he took to be a series of authorial revisions in the Wife's

Prologue ("The Development of the Wife of Bath," in *Studies in Medieval Literature in Honor of Prof. Albert Croll Baugh,* ed. MacEdward Leach [Philadelphia: University of Pennsylvania Press, 1961], 45–80). Pratt takes the five *a*-group passages to be the last in this series but apparently cannot see that they change the meaning of Chaucer's text in any significant way, for he simply quotes them without discussion. This is probably because he perceived the Wife to be sexually immoral even without the added passages; that is to say, he read Chaucer's pre-existing text so as to resolve each of the deliberate ambiguities in favor of the immoral rather than the moral possibility. He would have been culturally predisposed to resolve them in this way if, as is most likely, he shared the puritanical Victorian view that any woman who had married many times was already sexually promiscuous. For further discussion, see Beverly Kennedy, "The Variant Passages in the *Wife of Bath's Prologue* and the Textual Transmission of the *Canterbury Tales:* The 'Great Tradition' Revisited," in *Women, the Book, and the Worldly,* ed. Lesley Smith and Jane H. M. Taylor (Cambridge, England: D. S. Brewer, 1995), 97–99.

72. Even though Eadie ("Non-Hengwrt Lines," 169, 175) does not seem to perceive the ambiguity of the pre-existing text, finding rather that the Ellesmere version "does not differ all that much" from the Hengwrt version, his perception that the added lines bring Chaucer's text more into line with conventional antifeminist attitudes constitutes an important part of the argument leading to his conclusion that Chaucer himself did not add them.

73. See Tim Machan, *Textual Criticism and Middle English Texts* (Charlottesville: University of Virginia Press, 1994) and also Charles Moorman, "One Hundred Years of Editing the *Canterbury Tales," Chaucer Review* 24 (1989): 99–114.

III

AUTHORITY AND THE PRINTED WORD

The Influence of Printed Editions and Manuscripts on the Canon of William Thynne's *Canterbury Tales*

Robert Costomiris

Recent studies of William Thynne's 1532 edition, *The Workes of Geffray Chaucer* (TH[1]; STC 5068[1]), by the editors of the *Variorum Chaucer* show that Thynne's text of the *Canterbury Tales* was indebted both to previously printed editions and to manuscripts. For some of the tales Thynne appears to have consulted at least one manuscript, but for other tales he seems mainly to have followed the text of one of the earlier printed editions.[2] Such complex and shifting evidence gives the impression that Thynne had no overarching plan for his work and that he compiled his edition in a random way. This impression, based on the study of discrete portions of Thynne's text, is misleading. The study of some of the grosser characteristics of TH[1] suggests that Thynne's conception of the *Canterbury Tales* was based on Caxton's first (1477) edition (CX[1]; STC 5082),[3] which he subsequently augmented with readings from other printed editions and manuscripts. In itself, the relationship between CX[1] and TH[1] is not profound, but their connection has implications that extend to the formation of the early printed canon of the *Canterbury Tales* and to our understanding of how that canon was composed. For example, even though it is almost certain Thynne was aware of the existence of the *Tale of Gamelyn*, Thynne's use of CX[1] must be considered an important influence on the circumstances responsible for the omission of the tale from TH[1]. In turn, Thynne's allegiance to the general outline of CX[1], and the concomitant sophistication it implies about his editorial judgment, raises doubts about the evidence that links Thynne with the inclusion of the *Plowman's Tale* in the second edition of *The Workes* printed in 1542. If Thynne were as sensitive an editor as the omission of *Gamelyn* leads us to believe, it is unlikely that he would have condoned inclusion of the *Plowman's Tale* in the Chaucer canon. A more probable explanation is that Thynne himself had nothing to do with the decision to include the *Plowman's Tale* and that, contrary to established opinion, he was not involved in the 1542 publication of Chaucer's works that bears his name.

To arrive at this unorthodox conclusion it is necessary first to discuss the order of the *Canterbury Tales* and establish the relationship between CX[1] and TH[1]. The order of the *Tales* generally sparks heated debate. Regardless of the fact that few believe that Chaucer established a definitive tale order before he died, much effort has been spent defending the order of the tales found in the "best" manuscripts such as Ellesmere and Hengwrt, or in some conformation suited to the editor's expectations.[4] Certainly it is the editor's job to sort out problems of this nature, and if we assume that Chaucer would not have juxtaposed incompatible tales or made flat-footed transitions between tales, it is reasonable to hold that some orders are more likely to represent Chaucer's intentions than others. But the variety of manuscript tale orders and the incomplete and poorly constructed state of many connecting links suggest that fifteenth-century scribes were not so discriminating as modern editors believe themselves to be. Nor could they be. Evidence suggests that most early manuscripts of the *Canterbury Tales* were assembled in a piecemeal fashion, not copied in their entirety from one source, and, despite what we think of their work, many scribes must have been doing their best to assemble the tales in a reasonable way. They were probably less troubled by questions of Chaucer's intent and the possibility of spurious interpolations than they were desirous of making a complete and seamless work from a complex and often incongruous group of tales.[5]

The problem of tale order was in some ways simplified and in other ways complicated by the advent of printing. By fixing the text and the tale order in print and then reproducing it in relatively great numbers, the early printed editions lent authority to their respective tale orders. Although the tale order of an early printed edition might not have had much impact on its earliest readers (who probably had little chance or inclination to compare print with manuscript), it clearly had an effect on the way subsequent printers ordered the tales. The influence of earlier editions on later ones is evident in the relative regularity of tale order established from Caxton's second edition (CX[2]) to the printing of TH[1]. Printing did not completely resolve the issue of tale order, however, and appendix B shows that even after CX[2] the order of some sections of the printed editions of the *Canterbury Tales* remained in flux. Like their scribal predecessors, early printers and editors continued to look for a satisfactory way to order the *Canterbury Tales*, but, in addition to the possibilities offered by manuscript exemplars, they also had to consider the precedent set by earlier printed editions.[6]

The notion that Thynne was substantially influenced by Caxton's first edition of the *Canterbury Tales* was set forth by Skeat, who wrote, "It is impossible to say upon what authorities Thynne founded this edition, because we know that, as he tells us, he had access to manuscripts. Still, it is to be suspected that he made very little use of these, and followed Caxton's *first* (and worse) edition only too implicitly, apparently with the object of saving himself trouble."[7] Skeat's difficulty in ascertaining which manuscripts Thynne used is understandable given the difficulty even more thorough investigations have had in localizing Thynne's sources, but I think the motive Skeat attributes to Thynne misrepresents the process by which Thynne composed his text of the *Canterbury Tales*. If Thynne were interested only in "saving himself trouble" he might just as well have followed the tale order and text of Pynson's 1526 edition (PN[2]) of the *Canterbury Tales*, which presumably was equally accessible to him and which, in terms of layout, is more similar than CX[1] to the presentation of the tales found in TH[1]. But Thynne did not follow Pynson's order, and a more plausible explanation for his decision to mimic the tale order found in CX[1] is that he believed he was returning the *Canterbury Tales* to a more original state, in this case, the form of Caxton's *editio princeps*.

This interpretation of Thynne's rationale is consistent with the spirit in which TH[1] was produced. The 1530s in England was a time of considerable antiquarian interest, and Thynne very likely considered Caxton's first edition the essential starting point for establishing his more complete version of the *Canterbury Tales*.[8] Indeed, Thynne's great anthology, in which the *Canterbury Tales* appears as the first major work, is essentially a compilation of old works (all attributed to Chaucer), many of which had not been printed before, and some of which survive only in TH[1] or, at most, in a few manuscripts. The publication of TH[1] was presented as a chance to rescue Chaucer and the English language from oblivion and restore them to their rightful places of eminence. The preface to the anthology (addressed to Henry VIII) makes clear how the edition came together:

Wherfore gracious soueraygne lorde / takynge suche delyte and pleasure in the workes of this noble clerke (as is afore mencioned) I haue of a longe season moch vsed to rede and visyte the same: and as bokes of dyuers imprintes came vnto my handes / I easely and without grete study / might and haue deprehended in them many errours / falsyties / and deprauacions / whiche euydently appered by the contrarietees and alteracions founde by collacion of the one with the other / wherby I was moued and styred to make dilygent sertch / where I might fynde or recouer any trewe copies or exemplaries of the sayd bookes / wherunto in processe of tyme / nat without coste and payne I attayned / and nat onely vnto such as seme to be very trewe copies of those workes of Geffray Chaucer / whiche before had ben put in printe / but also to dyuers other neuer tyll nowe imprinted / but remaynyng almost vnknowen and in oblyuion.[9]

In the climate that fostered the attitude expressed in the preface it is not hard to see that Thynne might have regarded CX^1 as having greater authority than any of the intervening editions.

In the years between the printing of CX^1 in 1477 and TH^1 in 1532, the *Canterbury Tales* had been printed four times: again by Caxton in 1483 (CX^2; STC 5083), once by de Worde in 1498 (WN; STC 5085), and twice by Pynson, in 1492 (PN^1; STC 5084) and 1526 (PN^2; STC 5086). The order of the *Canterbury Tales* fragments in TH^1 and CX^1 is A, B^1, F^1, E^2, D, E^1, F^2, G, C, B^2, H, I.[10] CX^2, WN, PN^1, and PN^2 adhere to the general outline of this order but change the order of fragments F^1, E^2, D, E^1, and F^2. CX^2, PN^1, and PN^2 order this segment of tales E^2, F, D, E^1, thus placing the *MerT* after the *MLT* and continuing with the *SqT, FranT, WBT, FrT, SumT,* and *ClT* before picking up again with the *SNT*.[11] WN orders the same fragments D, E, F and thus follows an entirely different arrangement by having *WBT* follow *MLT* before continuing with *FrT, SumT, ClT, MerT, SqT, FranT*. Clearly, TH^1, which follows the *MLT* with the *SqT* and then continues with *MerT, WBT, FrT, SumT, ClT,* and *FranT*, ignored the precedent of these other printed editions, and instead followed the order of CX^1 exactly.[12]

But, since Thynne clearly had access to manuscripts, it is only reasonable to ask if a manuscript inspired Thynne to print the tales in the same order as Caxton. Six type *b* manuscripts (He, Tc^2, Ne, Ha^3, Ln, and Py)[13] order the tales very like Thynne, but due to the absence of individual tales or links connecting the tales, none of the type *b* manuscripts seems a likely source for Thynne.[14] Similarly, a host of type *d* manuscripts (Lc, Mg, Ha^2, Sl^1, En^2, Bw, Ry^2, Ld^2, Ry^1) also have the same tale order as TH^1, but again, while these manuscripts might have acted as corroborative substantiation of the superiority of CX^1, the analysis of a small section of the *MerT* makes it nearly certain that Thynne used CX^1.[15]

Near the end of the *MerT*, the Merchant describes the consummation of Damian and May's tryst in the pear tree with the following warning:

> Ladyes, I prey yow that ye be nat wrooth;
> I kan nat glose, I am a rude man—
> And sodeynly anon this Damyan
> Gan pullen up the smok, and in he throng.
> (*RC*, IV [E] 2350–53)

The opportunity to embellish the act condensed in these lines is obvious, and in TH^1 the following eight lines are appended to line 2353:

A great tent / a thrifty and a longe
She said it was the meryest fytte
That euer in her lyfe she was at yet
My lordes tent serueth me nothyng thus
It foldeth twifolde by swete Jesus
He may nat swyve worth a leke
And yet he is full gentyll and full meke
This is leuer to me than an euynsong.[16]

(fol. 39r, 2253a–53h)

On the same folio there are two more bits of spurious material. The first is a couplet that follows January's cry for help in IV (E) 2366 which reads: "For sorowe almost he gan to dye / That his wife was swyued in the pery" (2366a–66b). The second instance consists of four lines appended to "'God woot, I dide it in ful good entente' / 'Strugle?' quod he, 'Ye, algate in it wente'" (IV [E] 2375–76):

Styffe and rounde as any bell
It is no wonder though thy bely swell
The smocke on his brest lay so theche
And euer me though he poynted on the breche.

(2376a–76d)

These lines were first printed in CX[1] and were left out of all subsequent printed editions until TH[1]. Most of these lines also appear in three type *b* manuscripts (Tc[2], He, and Ne) and one type *d* manuscript (Ha[2]).[17] That CX[1] was Thynne's source for these additional lines can be deduced by a process of elimination. Ha[2] can be dismissed as Thynne's source because it reads *he prest in* in 2353a where TH[1] reads *a thrifty*, has *not* in 2353d where TH[1] has *nothyng*, adds *she said* to 2353d, which TH[1] leaves out, and has *to seche* in 2376c where TH[1] has *so theche*. Manuscript Ne follows the same readings as Ha[2] for 2353d and 2376c and can be dismissed for similar reasons. Manuscript He can be discounted because it lacks 2353g and 2353h as well as 2376c and 2376d. Only Tc[2] has the same readings for these sections of text as CX[1] and TH[1], but ultimately even Tc[2] was probably not Thynne's source because, when the *MerT* is considered in its entirety, Tc[2] lacks line 2224—a line that is found in both CX[1] and TH[1].[18] While the possibility exists that Thynne composed his text for the *MerT* from multiple sources, the most likely explanation is that he found these bawdy lines and the rest of the *MerT* in CX[1]. Having CX[1] before him, Thynne most likely took it as the source of inspiration for his own order.

Although I am stressing the connections between TH[1] and CX[1], the numerous differences between the two editions illustrate that, once the general outline for the *Tales* had been established, Thynne embellished his version by completing parts that Caxton had left unresolved. Collation shows this to be true on a small scale, but some of the most notable differences can be found in the larger chunks of text that link the tales together. The first major difference between TH[1] and CX[1] occurs between the *SqT* and the *MerT.* At this juncture in CX[1], the transition between the two tales is abrupt. The *SqT* ends with the Apollo couplet, and there follows a rubric ending the *SqT* and introducing the *MerPro.* Then the *MerPro* begins with "Wepyng and waylyng, care and oother sorwe" (IV [E] 1213). TH[1] alters this arrangement by giving to the Merchant the words that are usually attributed to the Franklin when the *FranT* follows the *SqT* (V [F] 673–708). Thus in TH[1] it is the Merchant and not the Franklin who says "'In feith Squier, thow hast thee wel yquit / And gentilly. I preise wel thy wit'" (V [F] 673–74). To make this arrangement work, all references to the Franklin have been altered to read "Merchant," resulting in a smoother transition in TH[1] from the *SqT* to the *MerT* than is found in CX[1].

Where did Thynne get the idea for this arrangement? All printed editions after CX[1] and before TH[1] have this link but place it between the *SqT* and the *FranT,* where modern readers expect to find it.[19] However, the attribution of this link to the Merchant and its placement between the *SqT* and the *MerT* can be found in fifteen type *d* manuscripts (Mg, Ha[2], Sl[1], En[2], Bw, Ry[2], Ld[2], Dl, Fi, Ii, Ht, Ra[2], Pw, Mm, and Gl), four type *b* manuscripts (Ln, Py, Ra[3], Tc[1]), and Hg and Nl as well. Many of the type *d* manuscripts as well as Nl are unlikely sources because all except Fi, Ht, and Ra[2] lack lines F[1] 679–80. The type *b* manuscripts generally come close to what is printed in TH[1], however, it is impossible to pinpoint any of the type *b* or *d* manuscripts that have the complete text, since none of them mirrors the readings in TH[1] exactly. Ht comes very close in several cases and is the only manuscript to share with TH[1] the readings *perseuerance* in 680 and *thy speking* in 681. Ht, along with the type manuscript *b* Py, are also the only manuscripts to spell *alouth* in 676 in the same way as TH[1]. But Ht, along with Fi, Ra[2], Ln, Py, Ra[3], Tc[1], and Hg, despite the fact that they share many unusual readings with TH[1], disagree with it in so many other readings that the most that one can say from this evidence is that Thynne used one or more manuscripts following the *b* or *d* tale order.[20]

The case of the Canon's Yeoman-Physician link is similar to that of the Squire-Franklin link but substantially increases the likelihood that Thynne used a type *d* manuscript. The *PhyT* follows the *CYT* in twenty-nine manuscripts, twenty-two of which have (or are thought to have had) the following fourteen-line link found in TH[1]:

Whan this yemen his tale ended had
Of this false chanon / which was so bad
Our hoste gan say / truely and certayne
This preest was begyled / sothe for to sayne
He wenyng for to be a phylospher
Tyl he right no golde lefte in his cofer
And sothly this preest had alther iape
This cursed chanon put in his hoode an ape
But al this passe I ouer as now
Sir doctour of Phisyke / yet I pray you
Tel vs a tale of some honest matere
  It shal be done / if that ye wol it here
Sayd this doctour / and his tale bygan anon
Now good men (qd he) herkeneth euerychon.
(fol. 74r)

Although this link is now thought to be spurious, it survives in whole or in part in sixteen type *d* manuscripts (Lc, Mg, Sl[1], En[2], Bw, Ry[2], Ld[2], Dl, Ry[1], Fi, Ii, Ht, Ra[2], Pw, Mm, Ph[3]), two type *a* manuscripts (Bo[1], Ph[2]), and one type *b* manuscript (Py). It can also be found in Nl, and it might have been present in Ha[2] and Ld[1]. A sixteen-line version of the link can be found in La.[21] Judging just from the numbers of manuscripts involved, type *d* manuscripts clearly predominate, and the following survey of the major variants shows that a type *d* manuscript was probably what Thynne used for this link.

The type *a* and type *b* manuscripts have many discrepancies with TH[1]. Py, the single type *b* manuscript, adds *that* to 1 and 2, adds *to* to 3 and *wil* to 9. Compared to TH[1], Py also omits *host* in 3, *yet* in 10, and *men* in 14. Bo[1] and Ph[2] make the same additions as Py in 1, 3, and 9, and, in addition, Bo[1] and Ph[3] have *that* where TH[1] has *which* in 2, and *sotheli* or *sothely* where TH[1] has *sothe* in 4. Such differences make these manuscripts unlikely sources. Not surprisingly, some type *d* manuscripts are very close to TH[1]. Most notably, Ht, Ph[3], and Ii are the same as TH[1] in 1, and Ht, Ii, and Fi are the same as TH[1] in 2. Ra[1] and Ry[1] have *sooth* in 4, which is close to *sothe* in TH[1]. Unfortunately, this neat correspondence between Ht, Ii, and TH[1] is ruffled by the fact that Ht, Ii, and Ph[3] are the only manuscripts to read *litull* in 7, where TH[1] reads *alther* and nearly all others read *a lither*. Ht, Ii, and Fi are also out of step with TH[1] in 4 and 12. Nevertheless, the inability of these type *d* manuscripts to align consistently with TH[1] cannot discount the evidence of line 9, which reads "But al this passe I ouer as now." Except for the anomalous Se, the word order of this line is exclusive to type *d* manuscripts and thus provides strong evidence in favor of their use by Thynne.[22]

The last major piece of evidence that shows the influence of type *d*
manuscripts on Thynne is the twelve-line Pardoner-Shipman link that appears in TH[1]:

> Nowe frendes sayd our hoste so dere
> Howe lyketh you by Johan the pardonere:
> He hath vnbokeled wel the male
> He hath vs tolde right a thrifty tale
> As touchyng of his mysgouernaunce
> I pray to god yeue him good chaunce
> As ye han herde / of these ryottours thre
> Nowe gentill mariner / hertely I pray the
> Tel vs a good tale / and that right anon
>   It shal be done / by god & by saynt John
> Sayd this maryner / as wel as euer I can
> And right anon his tale he thus began.
>   (fol. 79v)

This link is found in nineteen manuscripts and most closely resembles TH[1]
in fourteen manuscripts: twelve type *d* manuscripts (Lc, Mg, Ha[2], Sl[1], En[2],
Bw, Ry[2], Ld[2], Dl, Fi, Ii, Ra[2]) and two type *a* manuscripts (Bo[1], Ph[2]).[23] This
link had never appeared in print before, and, given the preponderance of *d*
manuscripts, there is a high probability that Thynne found it in a manuscript of this type. When this evidence is considered together with that
offered by the other links, I think there is ample reason to believe that
Thynne was familiar with one or more manuscripts following the type *d*
tale order. Moreover, the fact that the *MerPro* and the Pardoner-Shipman
link are separated by five tales illustrates that Thynne was acquainted with
other various distinguishing features of the type *d* manuscripts, thus supporting the view that he was familiar with more than the isolated sections
where he found the previously unpublished links.

If this analysis is correct, what are we to make of the absence in Thynne's edition of the *Tale of Gamelyn,* one of the hallmarks of type *d* manuscripts?[24] Based on Thynne's purported association with the vehemently
anticlerical *Plowman's Tale,* the occasionally anticlerical *Tale of Gamelyn*
seems like a poem that would have appealed to him, especially because
anticlerical sentiments are fairly common in the genuine *Canterbury Tales.*
Additionally, because *Gamelyn* condones the exercise of royal power by
having the king forgive Gamelyn and establish him as Chief Justice of the
Forest, it seems even more like a poem that was custom-made for an edition
of Chaucer produced by a royal household official in the period leading up
to Henry's standoff with Rome.[25] Based on the zeal with which Thynne
added other apocryphal works to the Chaucer canon and his familiarity

with type *d* manuscripts, the omission of *Gamelyn* stands out and shows how Thynne was simultaneously influenced by both manuscript and print traditions.

Although *Gamelyn* survives in twenty-four manuscripts, one of the amazing aspects of the poem's history is that it was not printed as part of the *Canterbury Tales* until Urry's edition of 1721—nearly 250 years after CX[1]. The reason for this appears to be the direct and indirect influence of CX[1] on all subsequent printed editions. It is not surprising that Caxton did not print *Gamelyn*, because CX[1] was printed from one manuscript, and CX[2] simply combined the readings of CX[1] with those of an additional manuscript that was brought to Caxton's attention.[26] Nor is it remarkable that Pynson's two editions do not have *Gamelyn*; both are primarily reprints of CX[2] that show little or no evidence of manuscript influence. De Worde clearly had access to manuscripts for his edition of the *Canterbury Tales*,[27] but the fact that the tale order of WN so closely approximates the order of the Ellesmere manuscript (in which the *WBT* follows the *MLT*) indicates that he was probably influenced by the order of a type *a* manuscript.[28] That Thynne left out *Gamelyn*, then, is perhaps not unexpected. In all of the early printed editions there was an erratic tendency to observe the precedents set by one or another of the earlier editions. Pynson and de Worde mostly observed the precedent set by CX[2] and Thynne looked first to CX[1]. None of these editions had *Gamelyn* and, given Thynne's preference for CX[1], its absence there was likely an important consideration in leaving the poem out.

However, because Thynne printed the additional links discussed above, and thereby broke with the precedent set by the earlier printed editions, it is clear he was not completely tied to the form of the earlier editions. On what other grounds might he have excluded the poem? The most obvious distinguishing quality is that *Gamelyn* is written in alliterative couplets. Although the alliteration is neither especially strong nor particularly consistent, Thynne knew that Chaucer, except for a few brief, isolated instances, never wrote alliterative verse. This quality might easily have singled *Gamelyn* out as a particularly un-Chaucerian work. The length of the poetic line in *Gamelyn* is also longer than the line used in Chaucer's poetry. But the way in which *Gamelyn* was incorporated into the body of the *Canterbury Tales* could also have been a signal to Thynne that something was amiss with this particular tale.

In the twenty-four manuscripts that include *Gamelyn*, it always follows the *CkT*. In most manuscripts *Gamelyn* is connected to the *CkT* by a two-line link, but in one manuscript there is a four-line link. In several others there is no link at all, but instead an abrupt transition from the end of the *CkT* to the beginning of *Gamelyn*. Most type *d* manuscripts have the following two-line link (or something very similar to it) appended to the last line of the *CkT*:[29] "But hereof I wol passe as now / And of yonge Gamelyn I wol telle yow." Of the type *d* manuscripts, Lc, Sl[1], Ry[2], En[2], Pw, Mm, Gl, Ht, and Ii follow these lines with a simple rubric that indicates in rudimentary fashion that *Gamelyn* is distinct from the *CkT*. Ha[2], Ra[2], and Ph[3] might have had a similar rubric but now lack it because of missing leaves. Mg, Bw, and Ld[2] have no rubric at all. Fi has the two-line link but has "The Cokes Tale" as a rubric, indicating that the Cook is starting all over again. Ii also has the link but confuses the issue even more by indicating that what we think of as the *CkT* was a mere prologue to the actual tale, which Ii conceives is *Gamelyn*. Dl and Ry[1] lack the link altogether, and these manuscripts have especially odd rubrics: Dl reads "Explicit the Cokis tale / Here begnnyht [*sic*] Gamelyn," and Ry[1] reads "Her endeth o tale of the Cooke and her / folowyth another tale of the same Cooke." If one compares this transition with the one that occurs at the end of *Thop*, the only other tale in which the teller stops and begins again in a completely different vein, the transition between *Thop* and *Mel* is so much more developed and assured that the transition between *Gamelyn* and the *CkT* looks weak. Even at its most fluid, the transition between the *CkT* proper and *Gamelyn* is so creaky that, when considered together with *Gamelyn*'s distinct prosody and its absence from the printed tradition, it could easily have caused Thynne to exclude the poem from the rest of the *Canterbury Tales*.

From the evidence examined so far, Thynne appears to have been a thorough editor whose goal to make the *Canterbury Tales* more complete involved including more linking material and fleshing out certain tales, such as the *MerT*, with additional lines. But Thynne was evidently not anxious to augment the *CkT*, despite the fact that he was almost certainly aware of the manuscript evidence supporting *Gamelyn*'s inclusion. His restraint on this matter raises doubts about his involvement with the printing of the *Plowman's Tale* in the 1542 reprint of his edition of Chaucer. If Thynne was not prepared in 1532 to incorporate a poem with manuscript support and with the comparatively tame anticlerical tenor of *Gamelyn*, why would he have admitted the *Plowman's Tale* to the canon in 1542?

The *Plowman's Tale* was first printed as an independent edition by Thomas Godfray, possibly as early as 1535 (STC 5099.5).[30] Although primarily a fifteenth-century work, parts of the poem, including the prologue that fits the poem into the framework of the *Canterbury Tales*, have been shown to be sixteenth-century additions.[31] The most common reason given to account for linking the *Plowman's Tale* with the *Canterbury Tales* is that it served the cause of Henrician propaganda.[32] The poem is vehemently anticlerical, but, more notably, it is anti-papal and pro-monarchial. In the mid-1530s, when Henry was attempting to institute the royal supremacy, it is not difficult to imagine royal approval and even encouragement for printing the *Plowman's Tale*—especially because it brought Chaucer's name into the battle on the king's side.[33] But by 1542, when the poem appeared in Thynne's second edition (TH²), the royal supremacy had been in effect for about eight years, and sweeping changes had already been instituted affecting the relationship between church and crown.[34] During this time, Henry also flexed his muscles against the pope and those loyal to the papacy by dissolving most of the monasteries and subduing the Pilgrimage of Grace. These facts call into question the expediency of including the *Plowman's Tale* in the 1540s.

The inclusion of the *Plowman's Tale* should also be considered in light of Henry's shift in the 1540s toward supporting the more conservative factions in the English church. Even after the break with Rome, Henry's attacks on the church were not always straightforward, and in 1541 he "indicated—to [Stephen] Gardiner and to the emperor [Charles V]—that ecclesiastical supremacy was negotiable, that the break with Rome was not *necessarily* final."[35] While an additional salvo against the pope was perhaps still welcome, and an anticlerical poem might have served Henry in his conflicts with insular church officials, the atmosphere of the 1540s was ambivalent, and the need to attach the poem to the rest of the *Canterbury Tales* was clearly not as urgent as it had been in the mid-1530s, when Godfray first printed it. Undoubtedly, nestling the *Plowman's Tale* among the genuine *Canterbury Tales* lent the poem greater credibility and a wider readership, and it is tempting to see such an action as part of a greater propaganda effort. Nevertheless, it is hard to argue that the political considerations of 1542 were so compelling that Thynne ignored his editorial judgment and included the poem despite its dubious authenticity.[36]

Two additional factors also decrease the likelihood that Thynne was involved in the decision to include the poem in 1542. As far as we know, Thynne was not involved with the 1535 printing of the *Plowman's Tale*, and his connection with Godfray can be documented only from the 1532 edition of Chaucer, in which both their names appear.[37] By 1542, however, the association between Godfray and Thynne had for some reason dissolved, and the inclusion of the *Plowman's Tale* in 1542 does not appear to be the result of collaboration between them.[38] In fact, the 1542 edition of Chaucer was issued by William Bonham (STC 5069) and John Reynes (STC 5070), whose two nearly identical editions suggest that the 1542 edition was an independent commercial venture.[39] Ten years had passed since the 1532 edition, and it is not hard to see that Chaucer's enduring popularity could have been the force behind another edition of his work. Therefore, the presence of the *Plowman's Tale* in the 1542 edition is just as likely to be the work of Bonham and Reynes themselves, who could have found a printed version of the poem as easily as Thynne and based its inclusion on their own commercial desire to print something new while capitalizing on Chaucer's name. Certainly the manner in which the poem was clumsily appended to the ParsT in TH[2] suggests that the decision to add the poem was hasty, with little consideration for the overall design of the Canterbury Tales.[40] It is hard to imagine that this was the work of a careful editor like Thynne.

Our knowledge of Thynne's association with the editing and printing of Chaucer's Workes is tenuous at best. The only evidence connecting Thynne with any of the three editions of Chaucer that bear his name rests on the appearance of his name in the preface to the edition and on the words of his son Francis, who writes, with suspiciously detailed hindsight, of William Thynne's involvement in printing Chaucer, his close relationship with the king, and his early efforts to print the apocryphal Pilgrim's Tale against Wolsey's will.[41] None of Francis Thynne's assertions is wholly persuasive,[42] and when it comes to the last two editions bearing Thynne's name, the issue of William Thynne's involvement in printing Chaucer's work is complicated by a biographical detail that has escaped notice.

By 1542, Thynne's status within the household of Henry VIII had improved from chief clerk of the kitchen, the position he held when the first edition appeared in 1532, to that of being one of four masters of the king's household.[43] The chief clerkship of the kitchen had gone to Thomas Weldon[44] by 1538 and to Michael Wentworth by 1540.[45] Nevertheless, the prefaces to the second and third editions (which, like the first edition, are addressed to Henry) make no acknowledgment of Thynne's changed status, but instead continue to refer to him as "chefe clerke of your kechyn." If Thynne had been actively involved in emending the first edition, is it not likely that he would have indicated his improved position by changing his title in the preface? Such a simple change would not have been difficult to achieve in the new edition, and it would have assured all readers (including Henry) that Thynne was still working on Chaucer and thereby an active supporter of the reform effort. But, as was shown above, by 1542 Henry was in a more conservative mood, and the reform effort had slowed. In such a climate, even if Thynne were involved with the 1542 edition, he might have decided to leave well enough alone and not include the Plowman's Tale. But the evidence of the preface makes it clear that there are serious doubts about Thynne's involvement with the two later editions that bear his name, and the changes effected in the 1542 edition should probably be attributed to Bonham and Reynes.

William Thynne's 1532 edition of Chaucer has long been regarded as a watershed in the printing of Chaucer's works because it brought together many spurious and genuine works by Chaucer for the first time. It has also been highly regarded for the sophistication of its editing. Yet the usual minute focus on Thynne's editing has obscured any sense of the plan that guided his work and the decisions he reached based on that plan. Thynne may have edited line by line, but the bigger picture of his work reveals more. The inclusion of important type *d* links and the omission of *Gamelyn* show how Thynne based his editorial judgments on Caxton's first edition and a variety of manuscript influences. In turn, his restraint with *Gamelyn*, combined with the political climate of the 1540s and the printing history of the later editions, strongly suggests that Thynne was not part of the decision to include the *Plowman's Tale* in 1542 and might not have had anything to do with either of the two editions brought out after 1532. This broader approach to Thynne's work, combined with the detailed collations issued by the *Variorum Chaucer*, will ultimately yield a clearer sense of what Thynne is likely to have done and not done in preparing Chaucer for print.

Appendix A

Abbreviations for the *Canterbury Tales* and Their Division into Fragments and Groups

CkT	Cook's Tale	PardT	Pardoner's Tale
ClT	Clerk's Tale	ParsT	Parson's Tale
CYT	Canon's Yeoman's Tale	PhyT	Physician's Tale
FranT	Franklin's Tale	PrT	Prioress's Tale
FrT	Friar's Tale	Ret	Retractions
KnT	Knight's Tale	RvT	Reeve's Tale
MancT	Manciple's Tale	ShipT	Shipman's Tale
Mel	Tale of Melibee	SNT	Second Nun's Tale
MerT	Merchant's Tale	SqT	Squire's Tale
MilT	Miller's Tale	SumT	Summoner's Tale
MkT	Monk's Tale	Thop	Tale of Sir Thopas
MLT	Man of Law's Tale	WBT	Wife of Bath's Tale
NPT	Nun's Priest's Tale		

Fragment I	Group A
	GP, KnT, MilT, RvT, CkT
Fragment II	Group B¹
	MLT
Fragment III	Group D
	WBT, FrT, SumT
Fragment IV	Group E
	E¹ = ClT
	E² = MerT
Fragment V	Group F
	F¹ = SqT
	F² = FranT
Fragment VI	Group C
	PhyT, PardT
Fragment VII	Group B²
	ShipT, PrT, Thop, Mel, MkT, NPT
Fragment VIII	Group G
	SNT, CYT
Fragment IX	Group H
	MancT
Fragment X	Group I
	ParsT, Ret

Appendix B

Order of the *Canterbury Tales* in the First Six Printed Editions Compared with the Ellesmere MS

CX¹	CX²	PN¹	WN	PN²	TH¹	El
KnT	KnT	KnT	KnT	KnT	KnT	KnT
MilT	MilT	MilT	MilT	MilT	MilT	MilT
RvT	RvT	RvT	RvT	RvT	RvT	RvT
CkT	CkT	CkT	CkT	CkT	CkT	CkT
MLT	MLT	MLT	MLT	MLT	MLT	MLT
SqT	MerT	MerT	WBT	MerT	SqT	WBT
MerT	SqT	SqT	FrT	SqT	MerT	FrT
WBT	FranT	FranT	SumT	FranT	WBT	SumT
FrT	WBT	WBT	ClT	WBT	FrT	ClT
SumT	FrT	FrT	MerT	FrT	SumT	MerT
ClT	SumT	SumT	SqT	SumT	ClT	SqT
FranT	ClT	ClT	FranT	ClT	FranT	FranT
SNT	SNT	SNT	SNT	SNT	SNT	PhyT
CYT	CYT	CYT	CYT	CYT	CYT	PardT
PhyT	PhyT	PhyT	PhyT	PhyT	PhyT	ShipT
PardT	PardT	PardT	PardT	PardT	PardT	PrT
ShipT	ShipT	ShipT	ShipT	ShipT	ShipT	Thop
PrT	PrT	PrT	PrT	PrT	PrT	Mel
Thop	Thop	Thop	Thop	Thop	Thop	MkT
Mel	Mel	Mel	Mel	Mel	Mel	NPT
MkT	MkT	MkT	MkT	MkT	MkT	SNT
NPT	NPT	NPT	NPT	NPT	NPT	CYT
MancT	MancT	MancT	MancT	MancT	MancT	Manc
ParsT	ParsT	ParsT	ParsT	ParsT	ParsT	ParsT

Notes

1. STC numbers are from A. W. Pollard, G. R. Redgrave, W. A. Jackson, F. S. Ferguson, and Katherine F. Pantzer, eds., *A Short-Title Catalogue of Books Printed in England, Scotland, and Ireland and of English Books Printed Abroad, 1475–1640*, 2d ed., 3 vols. (London: Bibliographical Society, 1986–1992).

2. An analysis of Thynne's text (William Thynne, *The Workes of Geffray Chaucer*, 1532) of individual *Canterbury Tales* can be found in Paul G. Ruggiers and Daniel J. Ransom, gen. eds., *A Variorum Edition of the Works of Geoffrey Chaucer* (Norman: University of Oklahoma Press, 1979–; hereafter *VC*). Donald C. Baker's work on the *Squire's Tale* suggests that Thynne used a combination of PN² or CX² and "manuscripts outside the *cd** group but related to that group. . . . These manuscripts are Dl Mc Ra¹'" (Donald C. Baker, ed., *The Squire's Tale*, *VC*, 2/12, 102). Concerning the *Prioress's Tale*, Beverly Boyd thinks Thynne used either CX², PN¹, or PN² as a copy-text, but cannot specify the manuscript responsible for the fifty-four changes that do not appear in any

other previously printed edition (Beverly Boyd, ed., *The Prioress's Tale, VC,* 2/20, 97–98). Due to the shortness of the *Manciple's Tale,* Donald C. Baker is also unwilling to speculate about the manuscript authority for the nineteen variants in TH[1], but inclines toward WN and CX[2] as the printed basis for TH[1] (Donald Baker, ed., *The Manciple's Tale, VC,* 2/10, 66–67). Derek Pearsall thinks that TH[1] generally follows WN for the text of the *Nun's Priest's Tale,* but concludes, "It seems clear that TH[1] consulted no manuscript in the process of setting up his edition of the *Nun's Priest's Tale* or that, if he did, his practice was so sporadic that the evidence will not allow its nature to be revealed" (Derek Pearsall, ed., *The Nun's Priest Tale, VC,* 2/9, 110–12). Helen Corsa's study of the *Physician's Tale* supports "Koch's conclusion that TH[1] made use of a *d* manuscript, perhaps the ancestor of *Pw,* " but was "corrected with CX[2] (or with any of PN[1]–PN[2])" (Helen Storm Corsa, *The Physician's Tale, VC,* 2/17, 77). In his discussion of the *Miller's Tale,* Thomas W. Ross insists that "Thynne is never with WN except coincidentally" and "suggests that a manuscript close to *c/d* may have been his source" (Thomas Ross, *The Miller's Tale, VC,* 2/3, 100–01). Daniel J. Ransom's commentary on the text of the *General Prologue* aligns TH[1] with WN but presents inconclusive evidence regarding manuscript affiliation (Malcolm Andrew, Daniel J. Ransom, Lynne Hunt Levy, and Charles Moorman, eds., *The General Prologue, VC,* 2/1A). James E. Blodgett writes that Thynne's text for the *Canon's Yeoman's Tale* was based on one of Pynson's editions but was augmented with readings from a manuscript in the *cd** group. See Blodgett, "William Thynne," in *Editing Chaucer: The Great Tradition,* ed. Paul G. Ruggiers (Norman, Okla.: Pilgrim Books, 1984), 46–47.

3. The sigla for the printed editions are those used by *VC.* They are: Caxton's first edition, CX[1]; Caxton's second edition, CX[2]; Pynson's first edition, PN[1]; Pynson's second edition, PN[2]; de Worde's edition, WN; Thynne's first edition, TH[1]; Thynne's second edition, TH[2]; Thynne's third edition, TH[3].

4. The most recent defense of the tale order found in Ellesmere can be found in Larry Benson, "The Order of *The Canterbury Tales,*" *Studies in the Age of Chaucer* 3 (1981): 77–120. The order of Hengwrt is defended by N. F. Blake, "The Relationships between the Hengwrt and Ellesmere Manuscripts of the *Canterbury Tales,*" *Essays and Studies* 32 (1979): 1–18. The idea that the fragmentary nature of the *Canterbury Tales* "sets us free to alter the arrangement of any or all of the MSS, to move up or down any *Groups* of tales, whenever internal evidence, probability, or presumption, requires it" was espoused by Frederick J. Furnivall in *A Temporary Preface to the Six-Text Edition of Chaucer's* Canterbury Tales, Chaucer Society, 2d ser., 3 (London: Trübner, 1868), 22.

5. For a discussion of how Hengwrt might have been assembled see Ralph Hanna III, "The Hengwrt Manuscript and the Canon of *The Canterbury Tales,*" *English Manuscript Studies, 1100–1700* 1 (1989): 64–84.

6. For a discussion of how printing did not necessarily lead to standardization of text or presentation, see Lotte Hellinga, "Manuscripts in the Hands of Printers," in *Manuscripts in the Fifty Years after the Invention of Printing,* ed. J. B. Trapp (London: Warburg Institute, 1983), 3–11.

7. W. W. Skeat, introduction, *The Works of Geoffrey Chaucer and Others* (London: Alexander Morning and Henry Frowde, n.d.), xxvi. A more recent facsimile is by Derek Brewer, *Geoffrey Chaucer: The Works, 1532* (London: Scolar Press, 1969; reprint, 1974, 1976, 1978).

8. I am grateful to Dr. Lotte Hellinga of the British Library for suggesting that Thynne's use of Caxton could have been related to the antiquarian interests of the 1530s.

For other discussions of sixteenth-century antiquarianism, see May McKisack, *Medieval History in the Tudor Age* (Oxford: Clarendon Press, 1971), 1–25, and Joseph Levine, *Humanism and History: Origins of Modern English Historiography* (Ithaca: Cornell University Press, 1987), 73–82.

9. Thynne, *Workes*, Aii^v, right col. Controversy has surrounded the authorship of the preface since the discovery of an inscription on the Clare College (Cambridge) copy of TH[1] that reads: "This preface I sir Bryan Tuke knight wrot at the request of mr clarke of the kechyn then being / tarying for the tyde at Grenewich." Whoever the author is, the preface is still valuable as a sixteenth-century view of Chaucer and the purpose of the edition.

10. See appendix A for a list of the groups and fragments of the *Canterbury Tales* and the individual tales associated with each fragment. In this paper I use the older alphabetical nomenclature for the groups of tales because, except for group B, the current system of roman numerals does not allow for the division of groups into smaller subgroups. John M. Manly and Elizabeth Rickert, *The Text of the* Canterbury Tales *Studied on the Basis of All Known Manuscripts*, 8 vols. (Chicago: University of Chicago Press, 1940), also use the alphabetical system.

11. The sigla used for the individual tales in the appendixes are those adopted by *The Riverside Chaucer*, general editor Larry D. Benson (Boston: Houghton Mifflin, 1987; hereafter *RC*), 779. All quotations from the *Canterbury Tales* are taken from *RC* unless otherwise indicated.

12. Thynne's decision to follow CX[1] should be seen in the context of the influence CX[1] had on all subsequent editions of the *Canterbury Tales*. Although the text of CX[1] was radically altered in later editions, features characteristic of CX[1], such as the sectional divisions of the *CYT*, persisted in later editions. Modern editions and fourteen manuscripts indicate that the first part of *CYT* should end at VIII (G) 971. All printed editions from CX[1] to TH[1] are at odds with this arrangement and instead indicate (using a capital or a blank line) that the division of the tale should occur at 1012. There is very little manuscript support for this scheme. Only Hk, Fi, and Ha[4] indicate that there should be a break at 1012 (Manly and Rickert, *Text of the* Canterbury Tales, 3:535). Tc[2] and He, two of CX[1]'s closest relatives, are of no use in determining if this division was more widespread because they lack the *CYT* entirely.

13. The sigla used for the manuscripts of the *Canterbury Tales* are those devised by Manly and Rickert, *Text of the* Canterbury Tales. Hanna's essay preceding *RC*'s textual notes to the *Canterbury Tales* also contains these sigla as well as a brief outline of the controversy concerning tale order, *RC*, 1118–22. The grouping of manuscripts into types *a, b, c, d*, and "anomalous" refers to the categories devised by Robert Campbell, which group the manuscripts according to tale order. See the "Order of Tales" charts on the unnumbered pages following Manly and Rickert, 2:494. These tables can also be found at the end of Benson, "Order."

14. Manuscript He lacks the *CYT* and the *ShipT*. Tc[2] places the *PardT* after the *ClT* and lacks the *PrT* and *Thop*. Ha[3] also lacks the *ShipT*. Ln and Py are closest to TH[1] in terms of tale order and cannot be discounted as Thynne's models. However, these manuscripts are textually so distinct from TH[1] that it is difficult to feel convinced that he used either of these manuscripts.

15. All of these type *d* manuscripts except En[2] precede the *FranT* with a short form of the Merchant's Endlink (IV [E] 2427–32) connected to a seven-line Franklin's Headlink. TH[1] has neither of these. Sl[1], Ry[2], and Ld[2] also end the *SumT* at 2158 and append

four lines to it that are not found in TH[1]. Bw, Ry[1], and Ld[2] also have a sixteen-line link connecting the *MerT* and the *WBT*. If Thynne used one of these manuscripts, he would have had to ignore these characteristics.

16. One need only think of the *MilT* and the coarser *RvT* to understand how the sexually explicit nature of these lines might have been considered genuine.

17. The collations of these spurious passages can be found in Manly and Rickert, *Text of the* Canterbury Tales, 6:493–96.

18. In *RC*, l. 2224 reads "Of Cancer, Jovis exaltacion." CX[1] has "And cansere of Jouis exaltacion," whereas TH[1] has "The causer of Jouis exaltation." Thynne's version makes the least sense in light of the lines that precede it, but TH[1] is clearly close enough to what is printed in CX[1] to have been derived from it. This is supported by the insertion of the word *of* in CX[1] between *cansere* and *Jouis*. Only two manuscripts (To and Ii) also support this reading; neither of these manuscripts has the spurious lines found in CX[1] and TH[1]. Of the extant sources, TH[1] is closest to CX[1].

19. Despite the fact that WN places the *SqT* between the *MerT* and the *FranT*, there may be some connection between WN and TH[1]. At the end of the *SqT*, WN has the rubric, "There can be founde no more of this for sayd tale. whyche I have ryght dilygently ser chyd in many dyuers copyes /." This is echoed in TH[1] which has the rubric, "There can be founde no more of this foresaid tale / whiche hath ben sought in dyuers places." This similarity may indicate that, to some extent, Thynne used WN. However, the numerous differences in the text of this link in TH[1] and WN support the view that Thynne based the placement and attribution of the link on what he observed in a type *b* or *d* manuscript.

20. A partial list of some distinctively different readings follows: Ht has *And* in 679 and *Now certes*, and *holi* in 682 where TH[1] has nothing; Ht also has *dame*, not *dome*, in 677. Fi omits *wel* in 674, has *this*, not *the*, in 675, and has *sir* in 676 where TH[1] has nothing. Ra[2] has *right* in 673 where TH[1] has nothing, has *allow the*, not *the alouth*, in 676, and has *a*, not *at*, in 689. Ra[3] has *alow*, not *alouth*, in 676, omits *pardee* in 696 where TH[1] omits *sir*, and has *of right*, not *aright*, in 694. Hg has *sire* in 676 where TH[1] has nothing, has nothing in 679 where TH[1] has *right*, has *speche*, not *spekyng*, in 681. Py has *lust* in 690 where TH[1] has *play* and has *me* in 706 where TH[1] has *you*. Ln has *And* where TH[1] has *So* in 676, in 684 has *it were right now fallen* where TH[1] has *it now were fallen*, and has *worthy* where TH[1] has *vertue* in 689. For a fuller list of variants see Manly and Rickert, *Text of the* Canterbury Tales, 6:568–72.

21. See Janet E. Heseltine's essay, "A Study of the Links and Some Outstanding Divergences of Arrangement in the Manuscripts of the *Canterbury Tales*," in William McCormick, ed., *The Manuscripts of Chaucer's* Canterbury Tales (Oxford: Clarendon Press, 1933), xv–xxxii, xxvii.

22. For these collations, see Manly and Rickert, *Text of the* Canterbury Tales, 7:3. See also Helen Corsa's assessment of this link in *VC*, 2/17, 43–45.

23. See Heseltine, "Links," xxvi, for an explanation of the various configurations of this link in the manuscripts and why some of them lack the link now but probably had it at one time. In Gl, Mm, Ph[3], and Pw the link follows *Gamelyn*. In Ht it follows the *ClT*.

Although Ph[2] and Bo[1] are included by Manly and Rickert in a chart of manuscripts that have the type *a* tale order, the second half of the *Tales* (i.e., the section that incorporates the Canon's Yeoman-Physician Link and the Pardoner-Shipman Link) follows the same tale order as type *d* manuscripts. For the purpose of this discussion Ph[2] and Bo[1] might usefully be grouped with the wholly type *d* manuscripts. See Charles Owen, *The Manuscripts of the* Canterbury Tales (Cambridge: D. S. Brewer, 1991), 79–81.

24. For the text of the *Tale of Gamelyn*, see W. W. Skeat, ed., *The Complete Works of Geoffrey Chaucer* (Oxford: Clarendon Press, 1897), 4:645–67, esp. 888–902.

25. Francis Thynne (William's son) writes that his father was prevented by Wolsey from printing the anticlerical *Pilgrim's Tale* and was forced to suppress an edition that antedates the 1532 edition. It is possible that *Gamelyn* was also edited out at this time. However, since no copies of an earlier Thynne edition survive, and Francis Thynne is not always the most reliable source, it is impossible to judge the veracity of his comments. By 1532, nearly two years after Wolsey's death and well into the tenure of his reform-minded successor Thomas Cromwell, the printing of a tale like *Gamelyn* would probably not have been frowned upon. See Francis Thynne, *Animaduersions vppon the Annotacions and Corrections of some imperfections of impressions of Chaucers workes (sett downe before tyme, and nowe) reprinted in the yere of oure Lorde 1598*, ed. F. J. Furnivall (London: N. Trübner, 1876), 7–10.

26. See N. F. Blake, *William Caxton and English Literary Culture* (London: Hambledon Press, 1991), 149–65.

27. Thomas J. Garbáty, "Wynkyn de Worde's 'Sir Thopas' and Other Tales," *Studies in Bibliography* 31 (1978): 57–67.

28. Although no type *a* manuscript has *Gamelyn*, as we have seen, both Bo[1] and Ph[2] have the Canon's Yeoman-Physician link and the Pardoner-Shipman link. However, if de Worde knew about these links, he was very conservative in his judgment, for, unlike Thynne, he printed neither of them. William F. Hutmacher ("Wynkyn de Worde and Chaucer's *Canterbury Tales*: A Transcription and Collation of the 1498 Edition with Caxton[2] from the *General Prologue* through *The Knight's Tale*," *Costerus: Essays in English Language and Literature*, n. s., 10 [Amsterdam: Rodopi, 1978]) believes that WN's order of the *Canterbury Tales* is a result of his attempt to correct the arrangement found in CX[2]. He bases this decision on the fact that his extensive collation of CX[2] and WN shows WN to be based on one source, CX[2] (1). Hutmacher later modifies his stand when he admits that "Wynkyn was concerned with issuing as accurate an edition as possible; and with a source other than Cx[2] at hand, possibly that which has come to be known as Ellesmere, he would naturally extend his corrections to the ordering of the tales" (21). Later still, Hutmacher concedes, "There persists the recurring notion that, though Cx[2] is undeniably the source of Wynkyn's 1498 printing, Wynkyn might possibly have concerned himself with an occasional other reading" (30). Certainly the differences between CX[2] and WN in the *MkT* and the *NPPro* suggest that WN had a source besides CX[2]. When these differences are combined with the position of group G, which is so different in El and WN, it might be more prudent to suggest that de Worde consulted more than one source.

29. Although *Gamelyn* is included in three type *c* manuscripts as well as four of the so-called anomalous manuscripts, these manuscripts are not considered here. They do not contain the Canon's Yeoman-Physician link or the Pardoner-Shipman link that are common to both type *d* manuscripts and Thynne.

30. Godfray printed Thynne's *Workes* in 1532. The STC date for the *Plowman's Tale* is 1535. Andrew N. Wawn dates the poem c. 1536 (Wawn, "Chaucer, *The Plowman's Tale* and Reformation Propaganda: The Testimonies of Thomas Godfray and *I Playn Piers*," *Bulletin of the John Rylands University Library of Manchester* 56/1 (1973): 174–92, on 175). Based on "provenance evidence," Mary Rhinelander McCarl dates

Godfray's edition at 1533, but it is unclear how she arrives at this date (McCarl, The *Plowman's Tale: The c. 1532 and 1606 Editions of a Spurious* Canterbury Tale [New York: Garland, 1997], 16).

31. Andrew N. Wawn, "The Genesis of *The Plowman's Tale,*" *Yearbook of English Studies* 2 (1972): 21–40.

32. Wawn, "Chaucer, *The Plowman's Tale* and Reformation Propaganda," 176–77. This view is accepted and expanded by Thomas J. Heffernan, who calls Thynne a "Henrician propagandist" (Heffernan, "Aspects of the Chaucerian Apocrypha: Animadversions on William Thynne's Edition of the *Plowman's Tale,*" in *Chaucer Traditions: Studies in Honour of Derek Brewer,* ed. Ruth Morse and Barry Windeatt [Cambridge: Cambridge University Press, 1990], 155–67, on 160).

33. Godfray's printing output is linked with various of Henry's causes and with the printing of Thomas Berthelet, the King's Printer from 1530 to 1547. See Wawn, "Chaucer, *The Plowman's Tale* and Reformation Propaganda," 177–84.

34. The Act in Restraint of Appeals (1533) acknowledged Henry as the supreme head of the *Anglicana Ecclesia* and limited recourse to Rome for cases involving marriage, tithes, and testaments. The Act in Restraint of Annates (1534) not only stopped the payment of annates to Rome, it also gave the king the power to elect bishops and obliged the archbishop to comply. The Dispensations Act (1534) gave to the archbishop of Canterbury the authority to issue dispensations and ended all payments to Rome. The Act for the Submission of the Clergy (1534) formalized Henry's domination by allowing him to "allow or disallow canons passed by" Convocation. The Act of Supremacy (1534) finally gave the crown many powers dealing with questions of doctrine and canon law that were formerly held by the pope. For a brief review of these statutes see A. G. Dickens, *The English Reformation,* 2d ed. (London: B. T. Batsford, 1989), 137–45.

35. Christopher Haigh, *English Reformations* (Oxford: Clarendon Press, 1993), 156–57.

36. Neither of Wawn's essays addresses Thynne's involvement with the addition of the *Plowman's Tale* to the Chaucer canon. In an earlier essay, I argued that Thynne and his audience might have believed the poem was Chaucer's due to stylistic and thematic similarities. In that essay I did not address the *Gamelyn* issue and tacitly accepted Thynne's involvement in admitting the *Plowman's Tale* to the canon. My current argument that Thynne was not involved with the *Plowman's Tale* does not refute my earlier claim that the poem might easily have been perceived by a sixteenth-century audience as Chaucer's work—especially after it was positioned before the *ParsT* in Thynne's third edition (1545–50). See Robert Costomiris, "The Yoke of Canon: Chaucerian Aspects of *The Plowman's Tale,*" *Philological Quarterly* 71 (1992): 185–98.

37. See Wawn, "Chaucer, *The Plowman's Tale* and Reformation Propaganda," 176–84.

38. Godfray's output has been dated between 1531 and 1536, but accurately dating his production is very difficult because only two of his works bear dates. See Katherine F. Pantzer, ed., *STC,* 3:69.

39. John R. Hetherington (*Chaucer, 1532–1602: Notes and Facsimile Texts,* privately printed by the author [Edgbaston, Birmingham: Vernon House, 1964], 3) writes, "There may be evidence that the book bearing Bonham's name was actually printed by Grafton (i. e., in Grafton's printing office); but if this is true, then Grafton also printed the book bearing the name of Reynes. The sheets are identical. The only observable difference is in the imprint of the title-page." This assessment is in accord with the STC

data concerning Bonham and Reynes, which states that both men were booksellers, not printers, and that virtually all the works bearing their names were produced for them by other printers. See STC, 3:25, 144.

40. This situation was improved in the last edition bearing Thynne's name. In this edition (TH³), the *Plowman's Tale* was placed before the *ParsT*, and necessary modifications were made to the beginning of the *ParsPro*. Unfortunately, it is impossible to link Thynne with this improvement, because the publication date of TH³ is assigned to the period between 1545 and 1550. Thynne died in 1546; he may have had nothing to do with this revision at all.

41. Francis Thynne, *Animaduersions*, 6–10.

42. Francis Thynne was, at most, a small child when his father died. The value of his recounting of his father's relations with Henry and Wolsey is compromised by the chronological distance between him and his material as well as by certain other inaccuracies. For example, Wolsey was out of power by 1529 and dead by November 1530. Thus, Thynne's supposed effort to print the *Pilgrim's Tale* would have had to come about when Thynne was still a fairly minor official in the king's household. Not only is there no surviving copy of this edition, it also is unlikely that the edition Francis claims existed would have been produced so close to the time of Pynson's (the King's printer at the time) 1526 edition of Chaucer. In addition, Francis Thynne mentions that the edition was composed of single columns—an unusual format for editions of Chaucer in the sixteenth century, since double columns had been the norm since de Worde's edition in 1498. (See Henry Bradshaw's comments on Francis Thynne's confusion in *Animaduersions*, 75–76.) Francis Thynne's remark about Skelton's composing *Collyn Clout* at William Thynne's house in Erith is also doubtful, because Thynne did not take up residence there until after *Collyn Clout* was printed. William Thynne's relationship with the king is the hardest thing to quantify. Certainly his numerous promotions and the gifts he received during his lifetime of work as an official of the household can be interpreted as signs of royal favor, but there is nothing exceptional about such rewards and nothing in them that indicates that Thynne was more than a competent and well regarded bureaucrat. Heffernan ("Aspects of Chaucerian Apocrypha," 165) notes the chronological distance between Francis and William but nevertheless writes, "neither he nor his father seriously doubted but that *The Plowman's Tale* belonged in the *Canterbury Tales*." Although this statement might apply to Francis, I do not think it is safe to make this claim for William Thynne.

43. J. S. Brewer, R. H. Brodie, and James Gairdner, eds., *Letters and Papers, Foreign and Domestic, of the Reign of Henry VIII*, 21 parts in 37 vols., 2d ed. (London, HMSO, 1864–1932; reprint, New York: Kraus, 1965; hereafter *LP*), 16:1488 (4).

44. *LP*, 13:1191 (ii).

45. *LP*, 16:220 (1).

Chaucer's Doppelgänger: Thomas Usk and the Reformation of Chaucer

Thomas A. Prendergast

Recently some scholars in the profession have reached a kind of consensus that Chaucer's works show little evidence of political engagement. As one critic puts it, "We find a serious, even threatening political dimension missing here."[1] At least part of this shared perception of Chaucer seems to arise from Chaucer's apparent disinterest in writing about one of the defining political moments of the fourteenth century—the uprising of 1381. One critic goes so far as to claim that Chaucer's admirers have in fact been "desperate" to extract something "appropriate" about the revolt from him.[2] This comment has itself something of desperation about it—a desperation to distance Chaucer from any overt political allegiances that might, perhaps, mar his poetical reputation. Though the governing ideal of the poet as politically disengaged has recently undergone something of a transformation, it has not so much altered the terms in which we think of Chaucer as it has reenacted an ancient debate about the viability of a political Chaucer. This debate has its origins in the early reception of Chaucer's biographies and it is to these biographies that I turn in order to explore the historical roots of our own representations of Chaucer as apolitical.

The most influential version of Chaucer's life from the early modern period was undoubtedly the biography attached to Thomas Speght's edition of Chaucer. It was the first life of Chaucer written in English and remained the standard biography until the 1840s.[3] But there were other biographies that gave alternative, even unexpected readings of the poet's career. In a manuscript dated to the late sixteenth or early seventeenth century we find a Chaucerian "Life" that begins, "He lyved some parte of Richard the second his tyme, in the lowe cuntryes of Holland and Zellande by reason of some disgrace that happenyd unto hym, as a man suspected to be spotted with the rebellion of Jack Straw and Watte Tyler."[4] Some of these curious details, as R. F. Yeager has pointed out, were undoubtedly picked up from the life appended to Thomas Speght's editions of Chaucer, but the supposition that Chaucer was involved in the 1381 uprising seems to be a bit of speculation on the part of the author of the vita.[5] Speght's life says only that "In the second yeare of Richard the second, the King tooke Geffrey Chaucer and his lands into his protection. The occasion whereof no doubt was some daunger and trouble wherein he was fallen by favoring some rash attempt of the common people."[6] The writer of the vita seems to have taken some liberties with the dating of Chaucer's troubles in order to make them accord with one of the greatest upheavals of the fourteenth century.[7]

If, then, his contemporary critics often attempted to dissociate Chaucer from overtly political acts, early modern writers seem to have approached the author from the opposite perspective: they attempted to connect him with one of the greatest upheavals of his day. This desire to place Chaucer in the tumultuous events of 1381 may bespeak a psychological need to have something to say about Chaucer—to associate him with a historical event with which the audience would have been familiar. Reinforcing this "need" might also be a kind of incredulity that a poet who lived above Aldgate (one of the gates that the rebels stormed through) and who had connections to John of Gaunt would be absent from one of the most important dates of his history. Ultimately, though, I think that the desire to locate Chaucer's participation in a concrete historical event has its roots in a much larger desire to have Chaucer politically engaged in a politically engaged time. As the life preceding Speght and other sources indicate, early editors were far from "indifferent to distractions social or political" (as one early twentieth-century critic put it); rather, they were quick to assume that Chaucer was not only politically active but also deeply implicated in the political struggles of the fourteenth century.[8]

But if early editors assumed that Chaucer was politically involved, they were not immune to the kinds of doubts that contemporary critics have about how the idea of a political Chaucer might interfere with the ideals of a poetical Chaucer. For Speght this conflict centers on Chaucer's apparent disregard for the courtiers who supported his art. After recounting the illustrious connections that Chaucer made in his lifetime (with, for instance, John of Gaunt and King Edward III's daughters Isabel and Margaret), Speght begins a disquisition on Chaucer's political troubles with a puzzling phrase, "Yet it seemeth that he was in some trouble in the daies of King Richard the second, as it may appeare in the Testament of Love: where hee doth greatly complaine of his owne rashnesse in following the multitude, and of their hatred against him for bewraying their purpose."[9] The force of the "yet" beginning this quotation cannot be overstated. Speght clearly finds it difficult to reconcile Chaucer's initial choice in following the multitude with his connections with what he later terms Chaucer's "best friends." Why, Speght seems to inquire, would Chaucer follow the commons when he had so many powerful patrons at court?

What Speght struggles with here is a conflict between inherited notions of Chaucer as a "court poet" and the "facts" about Chaucer's life, for, since 1532, the legend of Chaucer's political "trouble" had assumed the guise of truth. Chaucer's "trouble," of course, was based on Thomas Usk's *Testament of Love,* which had been read as an autobiographical account by Chaucer ever since William Thynne's 1532 edition of Chaucer's works.[10] The misunderstandings about Chaucer that followed were so great that they led Thomas R. Lounsbury to say that Usk's work "played a part more important . . . in his [Chaucer's] biography . . . than all of his writings put together."[11]

The *Testament of Love* and the Reformation Chaucer

The *Testament of Love* seems to have been written some time after an obscure scrivener named Thomas Usk became involved in the struggle for control of city government in London during the 1380s.[12] Usk had first favored the party of John Northampton and the craftguildsmen (encouraged by John of Gaunt), but when Nicholas Brembre and the merchant-oligarchs (linked to Richard II and the court) gained the upper hand and Usk was arrested, he was persuaded to betray his former confederates and so receive a pardon. His *Testament of Love* is thus a kind of Boethian apologia for his actions, in which he at once attempts to excuse himself for backing the wrong people and justify his own betrayal of Northampton. Because Usk is somewhat obscure in his *Testament* (for instance, he mentions no names and turns the aldermen of London into senators), early editors and chroniclers of Chaucer's life did not read the *Testament of Love* in the context of the Northampton/Brembre conflict. Instead, assuming that it was by Chaucer, they constructed their own notions of the kind of trouble Chaucer was in—one that pitted a sympathy for the unruly commons against Chaucer's dependence on the court.

The life attached to Speght, for instance, inflected this trouble with the notion that the "attempt" of the common people was "rash" and that Chaucer complained of "his owne rashnesse in following the multitude." To understand how and why this attempt had to be constructed as "rash" we need to turn to the "Argument" of *The Testament of Love,* which (along with "Arguments to every Tale and Booke") is also attached to Speght's editions of Chaucer's works. In it Speght claims that "Chaucer did compile this booke as a comfort to himselfe after great griefs conceived for some rash attempts of the commons, with whom he had joyned, and thereby was in feare to loose the favour of his best friends."[13] Chaucer's best friends are (as we saw above) denizens of the court and, presumably, the commons are to be opposed to members of the courtly party. In fact, if we turn to the *Testament of Love* itself we find that the protagonist made his way out of his problematic association with the "commons" only through the grace of the king, who forgave the "mikel misdede."[14]

This forgiveness might be seen to enhance the character of the poet who was worthy enough to receive it, but it comes at a cost, for, on some level, the poet must now be seen as a traitor, even if to the wrong side. Hence, it should not be surprising that the *Testament of Love* spends some time excusing those whom it terms the "converted," by citing a number of historical examples which show that "bewraying of the conspiracy" has inherent virtue.[15] Earlier, the author of the work justifies being a turncoat by saying that "every man that, by any way of right, rightfully don, may helpe any comune wele to ben saved; whiche thing to kepe above al thinges I am holde to mayntayne, and namely in distroying of a wrong; al shulde I therthrough enpeche myn owne fere, if he were gilty and to do misdeed assentaunt. And mayster ne frend may nought avayle to the soule of him that in falsnesse dyeth."[16] Speght is, unsurprisingly, somewhat apologetic for Chaucer's "rashness"; indeed he immediately takes some pains to distance Chaucer from what must have been seen as an imprudent political move: "For living in such troublesome times, wherein few knew what parts to take, no marvell if he came into some danger, nay great marvell that hee fell not into greater danger. But as he was learned, so was he wise, and kept himselfe much out of the way in Holland, Zeland, and France, where he wrote most of his bookes."[17] Speght's apologia undoubtedly speaks to the specific political struggles that characterized the later fourteenth century, but it also suggests that he and his Reformation audience would understand problems of loyalty implied in phrases like "few knew what parts to take." Indeed, Speght's acquaintance, John Stow—who helped him assemble the materials for Chaucer's biography—had had his house ransacked by the Elizabethan secret police for harboring recusant manuscripts.[18] What I suggest here is that, far from embarrassing Speght, the portrait painted of Chaucer by the *Testament of Love* may have been appealing to Speght and others who lived in a country which asked its subjects to change religions almost every decade. Indeed, by linking the fate of one's soul to the safety of the "comune wele" so clearly in the passage above, the author of the *Testament of Love* could almost be seen to reiterate the arguments that Henry VIII himself made for leaving the Church. It may, then, be no accident that sixteenth-century audiences saw Chaucer as a kind of apologist for the Reformation. Certainly his works were among the few that were explicitly exempted from the list of forbidden books in the Act for the Advancement for True Religion (1542–43). As Thomas J. Heffernan has pointed out, Thynne's 1542 edition (prefaced with a dedication to Henry VIII) had already gone a long way toward constructing a Chaucer who was an early proponent of ecclesiastical reform.[19] It is a short step to suggest that it would be pleasing for many Protestants in the sixteenth century to view Chaucer not only as a kind of proto-Protestant but as someone who, despite an initial error, eventually "converted" to the king's party.

What Chaucer's Renaissance biographers focus on, as they construct the story of Chaucer's prodigality and conversion, is Chaucer's wisdom, which inspired him to reform by removing himself from the political chaos of London. The vita from British Library Additional 5141 says that, after "the rebellion of Jack Straw and Watte Tyler . . . he travailed into Fraunce where he proffited so much in the Frenche tongue and grewe into such singularitye of knowledge in their Phrase of Speatch, and Methode of writinge, as they had hym in wonderfull admiration for his wisdome, and to this daie havinge his works in thayre owne Language they do mutch esteame them He returned out of Fraunce in the Latter ende of Ric. the 2. his reigne accompanied with a wonderfull fame of his well doinges as the unseparable companyon of his vertues."[20] By suggesting that it was Chaucer's fame (won by his "wisdom") that enabled him to return from exile, the vita seems to be following the pattern of Speght's "life," which, as we saw, suggests that Chaucer's wisdom led him to regret his earlier association with rebellious subjects and exile himself to Holland, Zeeland, and France. The uses to which the *Testament of Love* were put, then—highlighting first Chaucer's political unruliness, then his "reformation"—insist that his indisputable fame was a product of his recantation of his former, rebellious ways. The implication is that the poet would not have been well known in the fourteenth century—much less the sixteenth—if he had not followed the pattern of rebellion and reform.

Thomas Usk and the Modern Chaucer

Curiously enough, this tendency to read Chaucer in light of the *Testament of Love* did not cease after scholars had expressed serious reservations about Chaucer's authorship of this work. Instead it took a different turn. Thomas Lounsbury's reaction to the *Testament of Love* in 1892 (almost twenty-five years after Wilhelm Hertzburg first questioned its authenticity) suggests how this spurious source gave rise to what might be called a school of "character": "If, therefore, the 'Testament of Love' is to be regarded as Chaucer's, we are inevitably led to conclusions that do not tend to enhance our opinion of the character of the poet for modesty, for honesty, or even for ordinary sense."[21] Since Lounsbury is almost certain that the work is not by Chaucer, he is free to make relatively harsh judgments about the merits of its author; at the same time he uses these deficiencies to show that the work could not possibly be Chaucer's. The author of the work cannot be Chaucer, Lounsbury implies, because we all know that Chaucer is modest, honest, and sensible. This portrait ultimately translates into the solid Chaucer that, as Lee Patterson notes, defines all that is best (at least for certain nineteenth-century critics) about a socially ordered England. Indeed Lounsbury's comment that Chaucer possessed "all the qualitites that distinguish the man of affairs from the mere man of letters" recalls Lee Patterson's discussion of the conservative strain of Chaucer studies in the nineteenth century.[22] For these critics, the author of the *Testament of Love* presented a portrait of the artist that was unacceptable because it portrayed a poet who was caught up in pluralistic and individualistic ideas which threatened the social order.

By the time critics had definitively determined that Usk, not Chaucer, was the work's author, most of the writing in the *Testament* was employed to distance Chaucer from Usk as much as possible. Even a bit of praise that Usk had levied on *Troilus and Criseyde* in the *Testament of Love* provided a focus for dissociating Chaucer from his "less talented" contemporary. Hence W. W. Skeat, Usk's modern editor, asserts, "We can now readily understand that Usk's praise of Chaucer must have been more embarrassing than acceptable; and perhaps it was not altogether without design that the poet in his House of Fame, took occasion to let the world know how he devoted his leisure time to other than political subjects."[23] Skeat's fantasy about a politically disengaged Chaucer may be an attempt to avoid representing Chaucer as either liberal or conservative. As such it anticipates Pearsall's determination to find "Chaucer to be a decent sort of fellow" by avoiding "the snobbery among English biographers" or "the tendency of American biographers . . . to make a point of democratizing Chaucer."[24] The difference between Skeat and Pearsall is that Pearsall does not pretend to objectivity, but acknowledges his own bias toward a congenial image of the poet, while Skeat is still actively involved in refuting the legend of the prodigal Chaucer.

As the critical heritage moved further and further away from the memory of Chaucer as prodigal, we might expect that Usk and his work would have been forgotten. Yet, some thirty years after Skeat published his edition of the *Testament of Love*, the legend of the prodigal would be resuscitated. This time, however, the prodigal would not be welcomed home with open arms, instead Usk's prodigality became a cautionary tale used to show off Chaucer's enduring loyalty and prudence.

In his address to the Medieval Academy in 1928, Thomas Frederick Tout quoted the seemingly self-referential lines from the *House of Fame* (undoubtedly the same passage to which Skeat referred earlier) and argued that these lines demonstrated Chaucer's "prudence" because they showed that he was "indifferent to distractions, social or political":[25]

> For when thy labour doon al ys,
> And hast mad alle thy rekenynges,
> In stede of reste and newe thynges
> Thou goost hom to thy hous anoon,
> And, also domb as any stoon,
> Thou sittest at another book
> Tyl fully daswed ys thy look;
> And lyvest thus as an heremyte,
> Although thyn abstynence ys lyte.[26]

Presumably Tout would argue that sitting "domb as any stoon" until "daswed" is Chaucer's version of an argument for the contemplative life, for Tout then offers Usk as a negative exemplum of the active life. And here, for the first time, Usk's fall and subsequent death are offered as a kind of object lesson for Chaucer: "The fate of this poet turned politician may well have convinced his friend Chaucer of the wisdom of holding aloof from politics and ostentatiously proclaiming his indifference to all but the daily official task and the literary pursuits of his leisure hours."[27] Tout's assumption of Chaucer's "wisdom" or "prudence" is (as I mentioned earlier) at least as old as Chaucer's "fame." Along with this assumption is reiterated the belief that this prudence is somehow connected to Chaucer's removal of himself from the political world. What is new is the way in which Tout feels the need to define Chaucer in terms of that which he is not.[28] It is almost as if the absence of an extended autobiographical work by Chaucer (like the *Testament of Love*) leads Tout to define Chaucer in contrast to the author of the work. Tout even attempts to strengthen his argument by implying that the lesson must have been a personal one because Chaucer was a friend of Usk's—despite the fact that there is no evidence to suggest that Chaucer even knew Usk.

Tout seems to want to give his audience a progressive view of the Middle Ages, for he ends his discussion of Chaucer by asserting that the preferments and position that Geoffrey Chaucer won for his son might be seen as ample reward for Chaucer's "reticence." "People still talk of the Middle Ages as the time of the domination of an hereditary caste. [Yet] even the lay official could find opportunities for his kin, hardly surpassed by the direct avenue to power and position afforded by the church."[29] Tout's view here might be seen as characteristic of a deeply conservative, bourgeois Protestantism that constructs for its audience a man who worked his way up the hierarchical ladder by prudently keeping himself aloof from the day-to-day battles in the court. Unlike the "Renaissance Chaucer," whose reputation was at least partially based on his prodigality, Tout's Chaucer is more like the brother who stayed home and attended to his work.

Tout's suggestion that Chaucer was affected by the death of his "friend" Usk has found new life in S. Sanderlin's recent discussion of Chaucer and Ricardian politics.[30] Sanderlin suggests that Chaucer's unexplained transfer of his annuities to John Scalby in 1388 may have indicated an attempt to distance himself from the court at a time when those who challenged the power of the king—the Appellants—were in the ascendancy. Sanderlin uses the fictional connection between Chaucer and Usk to bolster his argument that Chaucer surrendered his annuity, "because of the Appellants' ruthless treatment of men who were Chaucer's known associates."[31] Sanderlin then enlarges on how Chaucer must have felt when Usk "was hanged and then beheaded with thirty strokes. . . . it was as much bad luck as his own poor judgment that got Thomas Usk killed. At the time, though, it must have been very worrying for Chaucer to see his associates purged, condemned, and executed."[32] This projected state of mind (a fictional creation by the critic) is stated as fact and ultimately provides the rationale for "what comes to be a pattern. When there was trouble, Chaucer withdrew from public life. . . . It is fairly certain that Chaucer had retired to Kent and was living the country gentlemen's life."[33] Hence, Usk—an exemplar of how not to be a poet and civil servant—defines Chaucer as the ideal civil servant, one who has the good judgment to retire to the country and perhaps (as both Skeat and Tout have suggested) spend his time on poetry rather than fickle and dangerous politics.

This ongoing tendency to define Chaucer in terms of Usk finds its fullest expression in the work of Paul Strohm, who, even more systematically than Tout and Sanderlin, compares the careers of the two writers. Yet Strohm—conscious that Chaucer may not have known Usk—resists the temptation to insist that Usk's tragic career was an object lesson. Instead he speculates that "Chaucer's career embodied for Usk a source of inspiration and precedent."[34] Ultimately, of course, this inspiration falls short of carrying Usk to his lofty goals of being a canny politician and a talented poet; hence Strohm concludes, "to poor, erratic, overardent Usk, Chaucer must have remained an elusive and constantly frustrating example, with his calmer broader-based and ultimately more successful attitude toward both the politics and poetics of faction."[35] Despite his more sympathetic treatment of Usk, Strohm, much like Tout and Sanderlin, attributes Chaucer's "success" as a poet and a "politician" to the fact that (unlike Usk) he was "wisely and systematically curtailing the extent of his factional visibility."[36] In a later article Strohm reexamines his own "implied judgments" about Usk and attributes them to the source on which he depends (the Westminster chronicler). In placing so much pressure on his own interpretive experience, however, I think that he overlooks how this bias is at least partially the result of larger institutional pressures to create Usk as a kind of *doppelgänger* for Chaucer, who, in the absence of any autobiographical work, draws off the negative qualities from the exemplary poet of the later Middle Ages.[37]

The question, of course, is What qualities does Usk possess that apparently compel critics to invoke his biography in order to dissociate Chaucer from him? For Strohm, it seems to be in part Usk's prose style, his tendency to import chunks of "self-serving and relatively unmediated discourse" into his work which reflect a "mixed literary and personal impulse."[38] His poetic and his personal sensibilities seem, in other words, to be an incomplete blend of the literary and the personal. Chaucer, "on the other hand . . . refract[s] experience into literary forms . . . he assimilates his social vision into a textual model of unresolved and unresolvable conflict."[39] Usk does not so much "refract" and therefore change experience into art as he reproduces his experience in a heavyhanded and clumsy way. This inability to "assimilate his social vision" may, in fact, suggest a kind of blindness, which led not only to his problematic text, but to an inability to see what was happening in the politically uncertain 1380s.

This aesthetico-political argument is characteristic of more recent readings of Chaucer. John Ganim's *Chaucerian Theatricality* captures the essence of this argument in a particularly forthright manner, "I said in opening this chapter that I wanted to help define Chaucer's politics, but I have ended up writing as much about his poetics. This is because my argument has been that his poetics are his politics, his politics are his poetics."[40] In other words, Chaucer's sophisticated writing somehow mirrors—or perhaps actually is in some sense—the political acumen of a poet. This current tendency to view politics and poetics as virtually interchangeable has, I would argue, both enabled the discussion of Chaucer in terms of Usk and been enabled by the idea that Chaucer was (unlike Usk) a canny player in the world of factionalism. Critics invoke Usk, in other words, to reinforce the notion that Chaucer's poetry and his career mirror one another. Though Donald Howard, for instance, begins his biography by perceptively noting that there are, in effect, two Chaucers, and that the argument for his oneness is an argument from silence, he (like other scholars, biographers, and editors), has filled this silence with speculative and circumstantial evidence that bolsters his assumption of a unified Chaucer.[41] In the absence of any biographical work like the *Testament of Love,* he boldly sets out his enabling assumption by claiming that "most of [Chaucer's] poems reflect events of his time and of his life, both public and private."[42]

In a parallel manner Tout, Sanderlin, and Strohm employ Usk's biography as a conceptual backdrop against which to portray an essentially Romantic reading of the poet's literary career as an extension of his life. Hence, by juxtaposing the account of Usk's political treachery against the account of Chaucer's removal to Kent, modern critics have inflected Chaucer's selling of his annuities (and his move from London) with a significance it might not have otherwise had: they have assumed that this action illuminates Chaucer's prudence. Such readings assume that Chaucer makes a kind of pilgrimage to Kent in order to begin his *Canterbury Tales*. Like his pilgrims, he leaves behind not only London, but its "political demimonde."[43] Implicated in such readings is not so much an accurate biographical description as the conventional literary opposition between the peaceful and apolitical country and the "avant-garde" and corrupt city.[44] Chaucer is seen to retire to a geographical place that encourages feudal hierarchies at precisely the moment when what Patterson calls the "medieval merchant adventurer" (the exemplum of the heroic bourgeoisie) temporarily asserts his power. What is interesting here is the way that contemporary readings of Chaucer's life sound so much like those earlier lives of Chaucer that showed how he "wisely" removed himself to Zeeland, Holland, and France, where "he wrote most of his books" when he got into serious trouble. It is almost as if that which we have repressed (Usk's *Testament of Love* and the Renaissance fantasies about Chaucer that it occasioned) has returned to haunt us—just at the moment when the lack of an autobiography should enable us to dispense with such fantasies.

Notes

1. John Ganim, *Chaucerian Theatricality* (Princeton: Princeton University Press, 1990), 119.
2. Derek Pearsall, *The Life of Geoffrey Chaucer* (Oxford: Blackwell, 1992), 327.
3. Derek Pearsall, "Thomas Speght," in *Editing Chaucer: The Great Tradition*, ed. Paul Ruggiers (Norman, Okla.: Pilgrim Books, 1984), 77.
4. R. F. Yeager, "British Library Additional MS. 5141: An Unnoticed Chaucer *Vita,*" *Journal of Medieval and Renaissance Studies* 14/2 (1984): 262.
5. Yeager, "Add. 5141," 265, points out that the notions that Chaucer was in trouble and that he fled to the Low Countries were probably inspired by Speght's life.
6. Thomas Speght, *The Workes of Our Antient and lerned English Poet, Geffrey Chaucer, newly printed* (London, 1598), B6v.
7. This despite the fact that on the next page of the life (C1r), Speght is careful to say that some of the *Canterbury Tales* were "translated, and penned in King Richards

daies the second, and after the insurrection of Jacke Strawe, which was in the *4. yeere* [my italics] of the same king for the Tale of the Nunnes priest, he maketh mention thereof."

8. T. F. Tout, "Literature and Learning in the English Civil Service in the Fourteenth Century," *Speculum* 4 (1929): 385.

9. Speght, *Chaucer,* B6v.

10. As Caroline Spurgeon, *Five Hundred Years of Chaucer Criticism and Allusion, 1357–1900* (New York: Russell and Russell, 1960), 1:10, suggests, William Thynne seems to have included the work in his edition because of a line from *Confessio Amantis* in which Venus purportedly tells Gower to tell Chaucer to "make his testament of love."

11. Thomas R. Lounsbury, *Studies in Chaucer* (New York: Russell and Russell, 1892), 1:181.

12. See the lucid account of these events by Paul Strohm, who argues that Usk probably wrote the *Testament of Love* somewhere between 1385 and 1387 (Strohm, "Politics and Poetics: Usk and Chaucer in the 1380s," in *Literary Practice and Social Change in Britain, 1380–1530,* ed. Lee Patterson [Berkeley: University of California Press, 1990], 85–90).

13. Speght, *Chaucer,* C6r, "Arguments to every Tale and Booke."

14. Thomas Usk, *The Testament of Love,* in *The Complete Works of Geoffrey Chaucer,* vol. 7, ed. W. W. Skeat (Oxford: Clarendon Press, 1897), 60. This application of regal support seems to be the inspiration for the assertion in Speght's life that the king took Chaucer and his lands into his protection, though why Speght chose to place this event in the second year of Richard's reign is something of a mystery. One might speculate that Speght is referring to the protection afforded Chaucer by Richard when he went abroad in 1378.

15. Ibid., 107.

16. Ibid., 27.

17. Speght, *Chaucer,* B6v.

18. Lounsbury, *Studies in Chaucer,* 154.

19. Spurgeon, *Chaucer Criticism and Allusion,* 1:84. Thomas J. Heffernan, "Aspects of the Chaucerian Apocrypha: Animadversions on William Thynne's Edition of the *Plowman's Tale,*" in *Chaucer Traditions: Studies in Honour of Derek Brewer,* ed. Ruth Morse and Barry Windeatt (Cambridge: Cambridge University Press, 1990), 155–67.

20. Yeager, "Add. 5141," 262.

21. Lounsbury, *Studies in Chaucer,* 203.

22. Ibid., 125. For Patterson's discussion of the two strains of medievalism in Chaucer studies, see Lee Patterson, *Negotiating the Past* (Madison: University of Wisconsin Press, 1987), 9–18.

23. Usk, *Testament,* xxiv. R. Allen Shoaf's edition of the *Testament* appeared too late to be considered in this essay.

24. Pearsall, *Chaucer,* 7–8.

25. Tout, "Literature and Learning," 385.

26. From *The Riverside Chaucer,* general editor Larry D. Benson (Boston: Houghton Mifflin, 1987), ll. 652–660.

27. Tout, 386.

28. Thomas Usk's own attempts to define himself might be seen as remarkably similar. As Andrew Galloway has recently noted, "Never do we know whose side

Thomas is on; but we always know whom he is against" ("Private Selves and the Intellectual Marketplace in Late Fourteenth-Century England: The Case of the Two Usks," in *Cultural Frictions: Medieval Cultural Studies in Post-Modern Contexts, Conference Proceedings* [Georgetown University, 1995]. Available at http: //www.georgetown.edu/ labyrinth/conf/cs1995/papers/).

29. Tout, "Literature and Learning," 388.

30. S. Sanderlin, "Chaucer and Ricardian Politics," *Chaucer Review* 22/3 (1988): 174. Sanderlin seems to have picked up the idea from Tout.

31. Ibid., 175.

32. Ibid.

33. Ibid., 174–75.

34. Strohm says only, "He must at least have noted the cautionary lesson of Usk's career" but quickly distances himself from this statement in a note, "as Tout, at any rate believed" ("Usk and Chaucer," 84, 106).

35. Ibid., 112.

36. Ibid., 91.

37. Paul Strohm points out that the chronicle has a decided bias toward the Appellants (Strohm, *Hochon's Arrow: The Social Imagination of Fourteenth-Century Texts* [Princeton: Princeton University Press, 1992], 160).

38. Strohm, "Usk and Chaucer," 111.

39. Ibid., 111–12. In many ways Usk serves the same purpose here that (as Carolyn Dinshaw has demonstrated) Gower has vis-à-vis Chaucer. Where critics have constructed Gower as politically self-interested, "content to follow and imitate," Chaucer is by comparison "the source of pure poeticality, language and aesthetics unpolluted by self-interest" (Dinshaw, "Rivalry, Rape and Manhood: Gower and Chaucer," in *Chaucer and Gower: Difference, Mutability, Exchange,* ed. R. F. Yeager [Victoria, B.C.: University of Victoria, 1991], 132).

40. Ganim, *Chaucerian Theatricality,* 120.

41. Donald Howard, *Chaucer: His Life, His Works, His World* (New York: E. P. Dutton, 1987), xii.

42. Ibid., xii.

43. Strohm, "Usk and Chaucer," 84. For a recent example of how these assumptions about Chaucer's removal from London make their way into critical texts not specifically concerned with Usk, see Steven Justice, *Writing and Rebellion: England in 1381* (Berkeley: University of California Press, 1994), 224.

44. Lee Patterson, *The Subject of History* (Madison: University of Wisconsin Press, 1991), 247.

Discourses of Affinity in the Reading Communities of Geoffrey Chaucer

STEPHANIE TRIGG

Sympathetic identification with the poet is one of the dominant features of traditional Chaucer studies: critical response to Chaucer often seems structured as a form of conversation with the author.[1] Current practice is far less overt and less literal about these possibilities, since the desire to speak directly with the past has been repressed from the distinctive professional decorum of the academic.[2] Yet the desire such practices betray can be displaced onto other critical modes. When we aspire to become the most attentive readers of Chaucer, for example, when we indirectly position ourselves with him, when we claim intimate knowledge of his characters, when we identify with his contemporaries as his best, most authentic readers, even when we take the titles of our books and papers from Chaucer, we assume a kind of continuity (albeit, at times, an ironic one) with Chaucerian language, and a potential conversation with the poet. Another important expression of this desire is the invocation of a community of Chaucerians: an international, diverse company of pilgrims in search of the canonical poet, but also a community that might provide a sense of institutional strength in an era of economic rationalism, when medieval studies is seen in some quarters to be struggling.

In Louise Fradenburg's diagnosis, projecting a community of readers provides a subtle form of consolation for lost authorial presence: It is another form of criticism as melancholia. She suggests that "the seeking of community in the form of undifferentiated unions or of unions predicated on identity can never be anything other than a defense against loss."[3] The history of that loss and its consolations deserves examination. The ideology of authorial presence is structured around the direct transmission of poetic authority, the intimate knowledge of, in this case, Chaucer's personality, or the even more transcendent possibility of spiritual collaboration. Invocations of authorial presence, then, are always signs of loss.

Early communities of Chaucerians displaced this sense of loss onto different forms and patterns of identification among themselves and with the poet. These patterns constitute what I call discourses of affinity in Chaucer studies, discourses that presume and promote a special relationship of understanding and empathy between the author and his editors, readers, or critics. Sometimes that relationship is predicated on something as simple as the idea of having read the same books as Chaucer. Sometimes a more complex sense of a reciprocal poetic sensibility is implied or directly claimed. Sometimes this relationship is based on a masculinity that can range from an unconscious invocation of shared gender as the basis for good reading to a more obviously homosocial sense of the difficulties of heterosexual relations.[4] Sometimes this sense of identification is based on a presumption of class or, more specifically, gentlemanly identity.

Some of these discursive patterns persist into the modern critical tradition; some are anticipated by Chaucer's fifteenth-century readers and poetic followers.[5] My principal concern in this essay is with the sixteenth-century editors of Chaucer's printed texts. These editions represent a foundational moment in the construction both of Chaucer as an "author" and of the "Chaucerian" reader. Analyzing their assumptions, language, and self-representation can reveal a great deal about the ideological work they do and provide an important complement to the study of their editorial practice and textual variants. Chaucer's first editors and printers experimented with a range of voices and expository discourses for commenting on, editing, translating, and indeed selling Chaucerian textuality. These discourses mark a distinct shift from the medieval scholastic theory of authorship and academic commentary, which was primarily taxonomic in practice. Medieval theory demarcated different authorial roles and classified the text in question from a scholarly position outside that text. In accordance with this tradition, the Latin marginalia that appear in many Chaucer manuscripts are principally concerned with identifying quotations, proverbial expressions, and biblical references, or with classifying Chaucer's role as author or compiler. Even where those commentaries reveal divergent interpretations, as in the Egerton MS 2864 and Ellesmere commentaries on the *Wife of Bath's Prologue*,[6] Chaucer's vernacular fictions are assimilated into a scholarly, Latinate tradition, affirming a cultural continuity with earlier medieval tradition.

In contrast, the fifteenth- and especially the sixteenth-century editors of Chaucer gradually apply to the "English Ovid" the modes of humanist scholarship developed around classical Latin and Greek texts, especially in Italy. This method is certainly related to the scholastic tradition, but its broader cultural agendas for the recuperation of classical and medieval texts are quite different. Chaucer's works become a productive site around which to explore the specifically English manifestations of linguistic mutability, a "source of authentic anxiety" for most medieval and Renaissance writers.[7] The sixteenth century's contempt for the prior history of the English language has been well documented. Affirming their own discontinuity from the medieval past permits Chaucer's Renaissance commentators to rescue him, as it were, from the period of ignorance that both necessitated and enabled their own labors; to develop the discourses of linguistic and historical expertise by which to mediate between the medieval past and the modern present; and to explain the poet in authoritative terms to new generations of readers. For Chaucer to be worth printing and editing, he must be redeemed as a pseudoclassical writer, worthy of commentary and elucidation. By the end of the sixteenth century, as we will see, a sophisticated editorial practice foregrounds its achievements in overcoming the otherness of Chaucer, surrounding his texts with more and more elaborate prefaces, commentaries, biographies, glossaries. It is a move with far-reaching implications for the construction of the medieval as the Other to modernism. And yet it would be misleading to lump all these editors together as if they were united by a common approach. The concept of expertise also provided a means for an editor to distinguish his work from that of his predecessors, in a self-conscious rivalry that constitutes one of the chief differences between the discourses of manuscript and printed text production. This rivalry is also often hierarchical and class-bound, organized around an increasingly great division between the intellectual and manual labors involved in book production and a growing consciousness of difference between the amateur and the professional scholar. As we will see, these editors often appeal to a readerly community of like-minded lovers of Chaucer, united by gender, sensibility, and class background. And yet because those communities are also in the process of formation, their limits and boundaries are constantly being tested and redrawn.

How could such editorial discourse in English be authorized? In whose voice could the editors speak? It is well recognized that the early printed editions borrow many elements of their formatting and presentation from the manuscript tradition. Another borrowing was the license to complete or supplement Chaucer's works with scribal or editorial additions. If the *Canterbury Tales* seemed incomplete, or if linking passages seemed to be missing, then the editor or scribe would compose or commission the missing portions of text. These extra portions would then be silently, anonymously incorporated into the final copy. They could be as short as a couplet or as long as the elaborate prologues and extra tales added to some fifteenth-century manuscripts—often with little visible indication in the manuscript.

The scribal custom of writing in a Chaucerian voice, either to complete or to supplement his texts—the distinction is difficult to maintain with rigor—was taken up by the early printers. In addition to the editorial prefaces and introductions the new medium seemed to require, many editors imitated the scribal *explicit* to commend themselves to their audience and to advertise their business. Poetic texts also gave the editor an opportunity to affirm his own authority in verse form. For example, Caxton composed a brief conclusion for the *Hous of Fame*. In his edition of 1484, his twelve-line addition is clearly indicated by "Caxton" in the right-hand margin:[8]

> They were a chekked bothe two
> And neyther of hym myght out goo
> And wyth the noyse of them [t]wo   Caxton
> I sodeynly awoke anon tho
> And remembryd what I had seen
> And how hye and ferre I had been
> In my ghoost, and had grete wonder
> Of that the God of Thonder
> Had lete me knowen, and began to wryte
> Lyke as ye have herd me endyte;
> Wherfor to studye and rede alway
> I purpose to doo day by day.
> Thus in dremyng and in game
> Endeth thys lytyl *Book of Fame.*
>
>   Explicit

Mimicking the return to books at the end of the *Parlement of Foules*, this conclusion imitates the voice of the Chaucerian narrator, the right-hand gloss the clearest indication that this voice is seen as an iterable fiction, not a sacred autobiographical signature. In his prose conclusion, Caxton affirms the distinction between Chaucer's verses and his own. "I fynde no more of this werke tofore-sayde, for as fer as I can understonde this noble man Gefferey Chaucer fynysshyd at the sayd conclyusion of the metyng of lesyng and sothsawe." In fact, Caxton's text lacks the final sixty-four lines of the poem, from l. 2094 to the end (omitting the chaotic flight of Fame's "tydynges," the pilgrims and couriers, the rush to hear the "love-tydynges," and the "man of gret auctorite"). After several lines in praise of Chaucer, Caxton adds his final benediction:

> And I humbly beseche and praye you emonge your prayers to remembre hys soule, on whyche and on alle Crysten soulis I beseche Almyghty God to have mercy. Amen.
> Emprynted by Wylliam Caxton.

Caxton imitates both a Chaucerian and a Caxtonian voice here, since some of his praise of Chaucer echoes the introduction to his second edition of the *Canterbury Tales*, written around the same time.[9]

Wynkyn de Worde's 1517 edition of *Troilus and Criseyde* is the most dramatic instance of an editorial attempt to supplement Chaucer. Even though this poem is as complete and finished as anything Chaucer wrote, in glaring contrast to the patently incomplete *Canterbury Tales*, de Worde adds several stanzas that give the visual impression of imitating Chaucer's rhyme royal, even though his lines barely scan.[10] After Chaucer's final stanza, of which I quote the last two lines here, de Worde imposes his own ideological closure on the poem.

> So make vs Jhesu for thy mercy dygne
> For loue of mayden and moder thyne benygne
>
> Finis
>
> The auctor
>
> And here an ende of Troylys heuynesse
> As touchynge Cresyde to hym ryght vnkynde
> Falsly forsworne deflouryng his worthynes
> For his treue loue she hath hym made blynde
> Of feminine gendre the woman most vnkynde
> Dyomede on here whele she hathe set on hye
> The faythe of a woman by her now maye you se
>
> Was not Arystotle for all his clergye
> Vyrgyll the cunnynge deceyued also
> By women inestymable for to here or se
> Sampson the stronge with many a .M. mo
> Brought into ruyne by woman mannes fo
> There is no woman I thynke heuen vnder
> That can be trewe and that is wondre
>
> O parfyte Troylus good god be thy guyde
> The most treuest louer that euer lady hadde
> Now arte thou forsake of Cresyde at this tyde
> Neuer to retourne who shall make the gladde
> He that for vs dyed and soules from hell ladde
> And borne of the vyrgyne to heuen thy soule brynge
> And all that ben present at theyr latre endynge
>
> A   M   E   N.
>
> Thus endeth the treatyse of Troylus the heuy
> By Geffraye Chaucer compyled and done

Ne prayenge the reders this mater not deny
Newly corrected in the cyte of London
In Flete Strete at the sygne of the sonne
Inprynted by me Wynkyn de Worde
The .M.CCCCC and xvii yere of oure lorde.[11]

The "AMEN" that appears in six manuscripts of *Troilus* is thus delayed for three stanzas, while de Worde's final verse *explicit*, "Thus endeth the treatyse . . ." encourages the illusion that he has added only one stanza, not four. The heading "Auctor" also suggests that the five books of the poem have been narrated in a different, fictional voice, which requires a further authorial conclusion to point the misogynist moral of the tale. (It suggests that "auctor" is a category still more concerned with ethical authority than writerly authenticity.) Accordingly, Criseyde is described as "vnkynde," "forsworne," "faithless," "mannes fo." In his deliberate conflation of Criseyde with the goddess Fortune ("Dyomede on here whele she hathe set on hye") and in his invocation of standard antifeminist exempla of women's victims (Aristotle, Virgil, Sampson), de Worde imitates Robert Henryson's more extensive misogynistic supplement to Chaucer's poem in the *Testament of Cresseid.*

Finally, in his loving address to Troilus, "O parfyte Troylus," de Worde emphatically positions the reader as masculine, or at least masculine-identified, in contrast to Chaucer's rhetorically similar address to his own mixed audience, "O yonge, fresshe folkes, he or she . . ." (V.1835). De Worde encourages an intimate identification with Troilus, using the difficulties of heterosexual relations to consolidate a homosocial bond between poet and reader. In this case, it is also a spiritual bond, as de Worde prays Jesus to bring Troilus' soul to heaven. The only solution, we may conclude, to the problem of faithless woman is refuge with the only acceptable female model, the Virgin. A more drastic solution was offered by Jonathon Sidnam who, around 1630, modernized the first three but not the last two books of *Troilus and Criseyde,* refusing to recount "The wanton slipps of this deceit-full Dame."[12]

Yet even though de Worde makes every claim to inhabit what we may call a Chaucerian space at the end of this poem, his final stanza also makes a careful technical distinction between Chaucer's work and his own labors. Chaucer is the learned *compiler* of the *treatyse;* de Worde is "corrector" (both textually and morally, it seems) and printer. This final verse uneasily combines the medieval scribal formula, *Explicit . . .* with the more commercial discourse of advertising, commending the book for its textual accuracy, identifying the printer's name and workshop, and dating the edition, with a visual and typographic—if not a metrical—insistence on preserving Chaucer's verse form.

Such demarcations of textual labors soon became more complex, more hierarchical, and more ideologically laden with the development of antiquarian, humanist interest in medieval English literature as a version of a classical past. Chaucer's editors increasingly present themselves as gentlemen amateurs, proud of their aristocratic patrons and concerned rather with scholarship than with profit. They do their best to distinguish their work from the commercial trades of printing and bookselling. There is no name for this new editorial author role, as we recognize it, which is analogous in part to the role of the aristocratic, amateur poet of the Tudor courts. The word "edit" and its cognates are not used in the modern sense regularly before the eighteenth century.

Chaucer is represented at this time primarily as a poet of courtly love, and his own biography and family connections with royalty and the aristocracy play an increasingly important role in sixteenth-century editions of his work. More attention is given to the discovery of "new" Chaucerian works, to the search for better manuscript sources, and to introducing the text with increasingly elaborate prefaces and letters or verses of commendation or dedication. In keeping with the conventions of humanist scholarship, the historicist agenda of these editions is clear: instead of blurring the distinction between poet and editor, instead of speaking in a Chaucerian voice (as earlier editors attempted to), the aim was to historicize Chaucer, to place him firmly in a medieval context, to mark out the historical distance between poet and editor—a distance it becomes the editor's task to bridge. The editor presents his labors as an archaeological task of recovery and restoration of Chaucer's glories. Supernumerary verses such as Caxton's and de Worde's are abandoned, since it is an important aspect of these later editions' conception of history to be perfectly clear about where the texts of Chaucer and his contemporaries begin and end. One revealing indication of this difference is the typographical convention of printing Chaucer's poems in the black-letter fonts used by the earlier editions, but using a mixture of roman and italic faces for the "modern" commentary, inserting black-letter again for quotations.[13]

This is not to say that the idea of imitating a Chaucerian voice became less popular; rather, the phenomenon took on a wider range of more specialized, more self-conscious possibilities. At one end of the spectrum is the elaborate poetic homage offered to Chaucer by Edmund Spenser in the *Shepheardes Calender* and the *Faerie Queene*. Spenser's imitations of Chaucer, and his fantasies of direct poetic descent, the "infusion sweete" of his spirit, were not without their own anxieties, but they make confident claim to and thus constitute an English poetic inheritance. An important aspect of this inheritance, however, was the notion of an aristocratic, familial (masculine) lineage of poets, which had to be exclusive to be canonical. Not all men could be true inheritors of a Chaucerian spirit, and mere printers, such as de Worde, were among the first to be excluded in a hierarchical organization of labor that privileged the intellectual over the manual and the scholarly over the commercial. A range of discourses and voices was, however, available to the sixteenth-century editor: genealogical, biographical, critical, poetic and scholarly. It was a period of experimentation with the ancillary discourses of textual studies. There are only rare signs of the later influential split between the practices and genres of editing and criticism. At this stage, the major rupture is between poetry and criticism on the one hand, and between printing and editing on the other. Printing and editing are quickly disposed in hierarchic rank: the printer is to the editor what the untrustworthy scribe (often invoked as Adam Scriveyn) is to the poet.

In 1532 *The Workes of Geffray Chaucer,* so called, were published by William Thynne, the first to collect the complete known works (with a number of others) in one volume and also the first to commission the printing to someone else. Thynne was a scholarly amateur and antiquarian, a member of the household of Henry VIII, "chefe clerke of your kechyn," as he is described in his dedicatory preface (actually written by Sir Brian Tuke). Thynne writes of the comparisons he has made between "bokes of dyuers imprints" and the "many errours, falsyties, and depravacions which evydently appered by the contrarietees and alteracions founde by collacion of the one with the other." Accordingly, he sought out other texts, lamenting the "neglygence of the people that have ben in this realme, who doutlesse were very remysse in the settyng forthe or avauncement" of Chaucer's works. Thynne's remarks seem to apply equally to Chaucer's medieval contemporaries, guilty of neglecting the poet, and to his later careless editors. He describes his own activity as the recovery and restoration of Chaucer's texts according to truer copies and exemplars, and he makes a deliberate comparison between Chaucer and classical writers in Latin and Greek.[14] Thynne presents himself as one of a company of gentlemen scholars and is careful to distinguish his work from the more mechanical activities of his printer. Thynne's colophon to the final poem names the printer without comment as Thomas Godfray. Until John Urry's text of 1721, the 1532 edition was the model for all other editions, including various reprints, the expanded edition prepared by John Stow in 1561, and the more comprehensive, more fulsome edition of Thomas Speght in 1598.

In Speght's edition, *The Workes of Our Antient and Learned English Poet, Geffrey Chaucer, Newly Printed,* we witness one of the most comprehensive affirmations of the editor's role as classical scholar. Through the classical portals framing Speght's elegant title page, we are confidently ushered into the world of humanist scholarship. An epigraph from Chaucer's *Parlement of Foules* stands opposite one from Ovid's *Metamorphoses*. In addition to some of Thynne's introductory material, Speght includes nearly thirty pages of prefatory letters, poems, summaries of all the works printed, and a *Life* of Chaucer—complete with an illustrated heraldic genealogy—framing a full-length picture of Chaucer and stressing his connections with the houses of Lancaster and Henry VII, as well as the de la Pole family. All this surmounts a drawing of the elaborate tomb of Chaucer's son, Thomas.[15]

Speght explains in his dedication, "To the Readers," that "I was requested by certaine Gentlemen my neere friends, who loued Chaucer, as he well deserveth," to repair Chaucer's memory. He had completed some of his research, "collecting" Chaucer's biography, correcting the copy from old manuscripts, summarizing each book, providing glosses and commentaries, and locating other previously unprinted works, "for those priuat friends, so was it neuer my mind that it should be published," when it turned out that a new edition of Chaucer's works was in press, three parts already printed. His friends, as well as some of "the best in the Companie of Stationers hearing of these Collections, came vnto me, and for better or worse would haue something done in this Impression." Speght thus carefully positions himself in a specific social context: one of a company of friends united by love of Chaucer, and an amateur scholar who must be coaxed into publication under the dual auspices of those "priuat friends" and the leading men of the Stationers' Company. That is, the amateur ventures into the commercial, professional world only under the assurances of his personal network, men who have already been successful in that world. This "importunitie" of his friends causes him to commit the fault of "publishing that which was neuer purposed nor perfected for open view," and he apologizes here, and at many other points, for the imperfections of the edition. This trope appears again and again in editorial and critical discourse and is a forerunner of modern academic disclaimers, perhaps even an echo of the adage *ars longa, vita brevis*. This gentlemanly reluctance to go into print becomes so conventional as soon to be the object of sixteenth-century ridicule, and is perhaps invoked ironically here.[16] At the same time, given the newness of the scholarly edition of medieval and English poetry, it is possible that Speght's modesty puts a different spin on this trope. His careful treading of the border between the private and the public serves a specific function here, in interpellating a new community of readers, an imaginary reading public who will be both sensitive to his own reluctance to print, and yet welcoming of his labors in editing Chaucer. One indication that Speght imagines his reader in this way is his inclusion of the poem "The Reader to Geffrey Chaucer," by one "H. B.," in which Chaucer speaks from beyond the grave to commend the labors of the editor. Here the reader is given a position from which to speak intimately with Chaucer, "good Geffrey," in a conversation whose theme is the rescue of Chaucer from obscurity, indeed, from exile, by his loving friend Speght.

The Reader to Geffrey Chaucer

REA.   Where hast thou dwelt, good Geffrey al this while,
        Vnknowne to us, save only by thy bookes?

CHAU. In haulks, and hernes, God wot, and in exile,
        Where none vouchsaft to yeeld me words or lookes:
            Till one which saw me there, and knew my friends,
            Did bring me forth: such grace sometimes God sends.

REA.   But who is he that hath thy books repar'd,
        And added moe, whereby thou art more graced?

CHAU. The selfe same man who hath no labor spar'd,
        To helpe what time and writers had defaced:
            And made old words, which were unknown of many,
            So plaine, that now they may be known of any.

REA.   Well fare his heart: I love him for thy sake,
        Who for thy sake hath taken all his pains.

CHAU. Would God I knew some means amends to make,
        That for his toile he might receive some gains.
            But wot ye what? I know his kindnesse such,
            That for my good he thinks no pains too much:
            And more than that; if he had knowne in time,
            He would have left no fault in prose nor rime.

In the last stanza, "Chaucer" raises the possibility of remuneration for his editor, before suggesting that Speght's aims are more noble and altruistic. Again we find the discourse of the scholarly amateur, where the relation between editor and author is one of amicable affinity. Author, editor and reader are apparently bound together by ties of love and mutual obligation and by ties of mutually flattering recognition and knowledge.

An even more specifically homosocial discourse of friendship is rehearsed in the letter "to his very louing friend, T.S." from Francis Beaumont, who speaks of Chaucer's unique ability:

to possesse his Readers with a stronger imagination of seeing that done before their eyes, which they reade, than any other that ever writ in any tongue. And here I cannot forget to remember unto you those auncient learned men of our time in Cambridge, whose diligence in reading of his workes them selves, and commending them to others of the younger sorte, did first bring you and mee in love with him: and one of them at that time was and now is (as you knowe) one of the rarest Schollers of the world. The same may bee saide of that worthy man for learning, your good friend in Oxford, who with many other of like excellent judgement haue euer had *Chaucer* in most high reputation.

"Chaucer" here serves as a mnemonic for friendship, for brotherly companionship in scholarship and patronage of "the younger sorte," and a nostalgia for university days. In conjunction with Speght's address to his readers and with H.B.'s poem, it is clear that the love it is possible to feel for Chaucer is an important aspect of the homosocial bonds that link a company of gentlemen, not only the source of Speght's own love and knowledge of Chaucer, but also the main audience for the edition, a community of male readers. And if they are not all gentle by birth (Speght was a poor scholar who depended on part-time work),[17] they are firmly wound into this genteel circle of like-minded readers. According to Pearsall, Speght's "good friend in Oxford" was Dr. Thomas Allen, fellow of Trinity College, "a renowned mathematician, philosopher, and antiquary," while Beaumont himself later became master of Charterhouse. Pearsall also reminds us that Edmund Spenser was a student at Pembroke College around this time, from 1569 to 1576.

Although he condemns some of Thynne's conclusions and errors, Speght in his address "To the Readers" gladly echoes his complaints about the printers. *They* are concerned with publicity, where *his* interests are scholarly, his labors hard, and his motives a mixture of honor and love, as "The Reader to Geffrey Chaucer" also explains. Speght writes of the pains he has taken in repairing damage caused by "injurie of time, ignorance of writers, and negligence of Printers." He asks us to accept his labors for Chaucer's sake, and after condemning all those who have neither wit nor learning, he flatteringly interpellates a wiser and more appreciative readership, to whom he humbly commends himself: "And so making no doubt of the friendly acceptance of such as have taken pains in writing themselues, and hoping wel also of all others, that meane to employ any labour in reading, I commit our Poet to your favourable affection." Speght hereby assists in the formation of a new audience, a reading (and writing) community that mirrors the editor. So much so, in fact, that Speght concludes his edition, on the final page of his "Annotations, with some corrections," with a most Chaucerian injunction to his readers to continue his own work, and a Latin epithet, to answer the lines from Ovid on the title page of the edition.

These faults and many mo committed through the great negligence of
Adam Scriuener, notwithstanding Chaucers great charge to the contrary,
might have ben amended in the text itselfe, if time had serued: Whereas
now no more, than the Prologues only, are in that sort corrected: Which
fell out so, because they were last printed. Sentences also, which are many
and excellent in this Poet, might haue ben noted in the margents with
some marke, which now must be left to the search of the Reader: of whom
we craue in Chaucers behalfe that, which Chaucer in the end of one of his
books requesteth for himselfe,
  Qui legis, emendes autorem, non reprehendas.

  FINIS

Speght's invitation was taken up with gusto by Francis Thynne, the son of
William, who in 1599 wrote Speght a letter, his *ANIMADVersions vppon
the Annotacions and Corrections of some imperfections of impressiones of
Chaucers workes (sett downe before tyme, and now) reprinted in the yere of
oure lorde 1598 sett downe by Francis Thynne*, criticizing the edition for its
errors and inaccuracies. The circumstances of this letter and its contents
have been well studied.[18] In the present context let us focus on Thynne's
assumptions about the nature of editing and the role of the critical reader.
First of all, Thynne does not publish his critique, but sends it to Speght in
manuscript form (it was first published by G. H. Kingsley in 1865 and revised by Frederick J. Furnivall ten years later for the EETS). That is, the
community of readers is still an abstract community that has not yet found
expression in a public sphere where textual and critical debate might be
exchanged. But Thynne assumes from the beginning that he, as commentator, and Speght, as editor, are engaged in the same enterprise: "The Indus-
trye and love (maister Speighte) which you haue vsed, and beare, vppon
and to our famous poete Geffrye Chaucer, deseruethe bothe comendatione
and furtherance: the one to recompense your trauayle, the other to accom-
plyshe the duetye, which we all beare (or at the leaste, yf we reuerence
lernynge or regarde the honor of oure Countrye, sholde beare) to suche a
singuler ornamente of oure tonge as the woorkes of Chaucer are."[19] Editing
and commenting on Chaucer is hard work, but it is necessary, gentlemanly
labor that brings its own rewards: *noblesse oblige*. Thynne also reminds
Speght that he had invited correction, and describes his own efforts in
terms similar to those in which he commends Speght's, terms that echo
the Horatian imperatives of pleasure and instruction while appealing to an
affinity, or amity, between editor and author, describing Speght's "Indus-
trye and love," and for Thynne's own part, the "duetye and love whiche I
beare to Chaucer."[20]

Francis Thynne himself was an enthusiastic antiquarian, but less of an amateur, perhaps, than Speght. Thynne was a self-taught expert on alchemy and heraldry whose achievements in this field were recognized only a few years before his death, when he was made Lancaster herald. Pearsall summarizes his catalogue of failures thus: "He published nothing of note, and his whole life was a history of being put upon."[21] In this context we may recall Thynne's unhappy marriage and his imprisonment for debt at the hands of his wife's relations.[22] Furnivall prints several of his letters from prison and two of his epigrams, on the best wives (dead ones), and a lament on the miseries of marriage. In his letter to Speght, Thynne invokes two other, perhaps compensatory, bonds of social obligation: the first, the emphasis on the duty owed Chaucer by the company of those who love him, and the second, that on the duty owed by a son to his father.

The Thynne family reputation is at stake here. Even though Francis Thynne was only two years old when his father died, he repeats a conversation between Henry VIII, Cardinal Wolsey, and his father, "beinge in great fauore with his prince (as manye yet lyvinge canne testyfye,)" about the inclusion of the controversial, because virulently anti-Catholic, *Plowman's Tale* as one of the additional *Canterbury Tales*.[23] The whole letter is a defense of William Thynne's own "ernest desire and love . . . to have Chaucers Woorkes rightlye to be published"[24] and a determined justification of all his editorial and textual decisions.

Here Thynne is defending his father against charges by Speght and others of wronging Chaucer with an imperfect edition: "Wherefore, to stoppe that gappe, I will answere, that Chaucers woorkes haue byn sithens printed twyce, yf not thrice, and therfore by oure carelesse (and for the most parte vnlerned) printers of Englande, not so well performed as yt ought to bee: so that, of necessytye, bothe in matter, myter, and meaninge, yt must needs gather corruptione, passinge throughe so many handes, as the water dothe, the further yt runnethe from the pure founteyne."[25] The ideological force of these polemics is blatant. Editing involves the restoration and purification of text that necessarily, over the course of time, becomes promiscuously involved with the lowly and dirty business of the printers. The textual tradition, like all patriarchal, genealogical traditions, is constantly threatened by uncertainty and faithlessness, in this instance because it depends on a commercial trade. The work of the fathers—Father Chaucer, Father Thynne—must be constantly protected and policed. Embedded in this discourse is also a strong sense of the linguistic instability of English, which rendered Chaucer progressively more illegible to his sixteenth-century readers and made the philological support offered by the editor more and more necessary and increasingly elaborate.

By the end of this century, Chaucer's works had become almost unreadable without special expertise and assistance. Speght included a glossary explaining the "old and obscure" words in the text, as well as a translation of his French phrases. This section of his edition was expanded in the revised version of 1602, to include some limited etymological information in the glossary, a number of new entries, and translations of Latin phrases. Editing had become a double act of veneration and alienation, since such apparatus inevitably has the effect of confirming the sense of historical distance between Chaucer and his modern readers. Linguistic change confirmed what was already happening: the professionalization of the editor.

A further effect of this perception of linguistic distance is gradually to make impossible the easy supplements and continuations of Chaucer's poems so popular in the manuscripts and early printed editions. Once an increased historical self-consciousness and a desire for scholarly objectivity intervene, it is no longer so easy to inhabit the Chaucerian space at the margins of his poems. The implicit claim to familiar knowledge of Chaucer takes a different form—the linguistic or historical expertise of the gentleman amateur or the learned professional, rather than the ability to generate more Chaucerian verse. This is one of the early signs of the professionalization of literary studies and is also an early indicator of their divergence from the poetic tradition of imitation, which follows a different trajectory altogether.

This does not mean that the editor is no longer attracted to the possibility of spiritual transmission of the Chaucerian voice, but that such possibilities will now be hinted at or described secondhand rather than enacted directly. The desire to speak with Chaucer or in his voice is displaced onto the various discourses and voices that proliferate around the Chaucerian text. If an editor is to "become" Chaucer, to claim any kind of allegiance with him, the becoming takes place in the framing sections of the edition: the prefaces, dedicatory poems, and so forth, clearly signed with the name of the editor or other contributor. The split between prose and poetry as vehicles, respectively, for criticism and creative or imaginative writing is not yet complete: editorial and critical discourse can still take poetic form. "The Reader to Geffrey Chaucer" is an instance of editorial self-promotion in verse that typifies these trends.

That the poetic tradition of Lydgate, Hawes, Clanvowe, Hoccleve, and most luminously, Spenser, is seen as separate from its editorial and critical strand is witnessed by Speght's approving summary of Spenser's relationship with Chaucer. Speght's remarks are spoken at a distance from the material he is discussing, in a careful tone of objective description (and careful attribution of his sources) that we would these days take for granted in academic criticism. The authoritative tone of this summary is as important to my argument as its emphasis on the friendship between the two poets:

"In his Faerie Queene in his discourse of friendship, as thinking himselfe most worthy to be Chaucers friend, for his like naturall disposition that Chaucer had, hee sheweth that none that liued with him, nor none that came after him, durst presume to revive Chaucers lost labours in that un-perfite tale of the Squire, but only himselfe: which he had not done, had he not felt (as he saith) the infusion of Chaucers owne sweet spirit, surviving within him." Speght's emphasis on the "daring" of Spenser in continuing the *Squire's Tale* can perhaps be read as a subtle critique of the older edi-torial decorum, according to which such continuations were indeed ac-ceptable. In contrast, as we saw so clearly in the Thynne-Speght-Thynne sequence, the proper name of the editor now operates in a different social and rhetorical sphere. It takes on meaning in opposition to the names of other editors, rather than complementing that of the poet in a dyadic, seem-ingly organic relationship. The necessary converse of professional rivalry is professional cooperation, in the form of the grace with which Speght seems to have accepted Thynne's suggestions and criticisms. Rightly or wrongly, and perhaps swayed by Thynne's own rhetoric of true heredity, Speght incorporated many of Thynne's proposals in the revised edition of 1602,[26] even printing Thynne's "poor poem" in praise of Chaucer.[27] This poem concludes with a characteristic, though rather incoherent, emphasis on Chaucer's poetic posterity: "Then *Chaucer* liue, for still thy verse shall liue, / T'unborne Poëts, which life and light will give." Even though the antiquarian mode has ruled out the easy continuations of Chaucer's texts so prevalent in the manuscript tradition, metaphors of spiritual poetic transmission persist.

Another curious addition to the 1602 text is an anonymous poem that seems to invoke an older, habitual continuity between poet and editor. Here Speght is commended as "the child of *Chaucers* fruitfull breine."[28] Yet the poem's insistence on "the learn'd praise-worthie peine" and "the helpefull notes" of the edition reveal a strong consciousness of the distinctive fea-tures of the editorial task. Dominant here is the idea of the editor as histori-cal scholar who can rescue the medieval poet from obscurity:

Vernishing his workes with life and grace,
Which envious age would otherwise deface;
Then be he lov'd and thanked for the same,
Since in his love he hath reviv'd his name.

Speght's two editions consistently trace over this possibility of speaking with Chaucer in a tangle of metaphors of family kinship, spiritual revival, love and duty, labor and devotion, and cultural recovery, all typical—and formative—of the discourse of affinity. Speght treads a fine line between claiming a position of privileged access to the Chaucerian word and opening up that position to his sympathetic readers. This second possibility, however, rapidly closes down as later editors become more confident of their own authority, finding comforting reflections of themselves not in their readers but in their predecessors.

The two traditions of poetic and scholarly inheritance meet again at the end of the seventeenth century in John Dryden's *Fables Ancient and Modern.* His preface provides perhaps the clearest formulation of their dominant shared metaphors, and some of the most enabling moments for literary criticism, now quite separate from the field of editorial commentary. Dryden explicitly articulates a theory of masculine parthenogenesis, the idea that poets beget and transmit their own linear traditions. "*Milton* was the Poetical Son of *Spencer,* and Mr. *Waller* of *Fairfax;* for we have our Lineal Descents and Clans, as well as other Families; *Spencer* more than once insinuates, that the Soul of *Chaucer* was transfus'd into his Body; and that he was begotten by him Two hundred years after his Decease. *Milton* has acknowledg'd to me, that *Spencer* was his Original."[29] In this passage, Dryden links the two mutually sustaining ideas that I suggest are fundamental to patriarchal literary tradition. First is the idea of lineal descent and the elite poetic family (a more benign version of Harold Bloom's agonistic Oedipal poetics). Should that continuity fail, should another medieval period of scholarly neglect intervene, for instance, then the souls of older poets might still be transfused into their spiritual descendants. This second possibility of a transcendent connection guarantees poetic continuity, the perpetuation of the male line in an elaborate metaphorical structure that denies the need for maternal involvement and effaces or elides the dangers and risks of historical change. The male poet can thus give birth not only to his own poetry, but to his own tradition, which itself can be perpetually renewed.

This mode of authorization is easily extended. Dryden invokes the same motif to license his improvements to Chaucer's poems in his translations: "I have presum'd farther in some Places, and added somewhat of my own where I thought my Author was deficient, and had not given his Thoughts their true Lustre, for want of Words in the Beginning of our Language. And to this I was the more embolden'd, because (if I may be permitted to say it of my self) I found I had a Soul congenial to his, and that I had been conversant in the same Studies. Another Poet, in another Age, may take the same Liberty with my Writings; if at least they live long enough to deserve Correction."[30] The congenial soul is one who not only shares a similar sensibility, but who also—in a pleasant fantasy—shares a similar background, even the same history. This metaphysical magic turns out to have a strong social component. It is almost as if Dryden echoes

Francis Beaumont's nostalgic Cambridge reminiscences, when he assumes that poetry derives from similar "Studies." Most important, Dryden's theory of the transfusion of souls enables him to add to Chaucer's work, to become Chaucer himself, as his translator, in order to do full justice to Chaucer's poems. Unlike Caxton's or de Worde's continuations, where the textual format blurs the distinction between text and supplement, Dryden prefaces his imitations with self-conscious justification. Acts of cultural recuperation and scholarly research are combined with the spiritual magic of the poet.[31]

Dryden's authorizing other poets to modernize his own writings both underlines and furthers the medieval tradition of asking for correction, the topos familiar to Dryden from the works of Chaucer and Boccaccio, and one which, as we have seen, plays an important role in Chaucer's own editorial history. As a rhetorical trope it partakes of the conventional modesty of the poet writing for patronage, but this modesty also plays an additional historicist role of implying the work's undoubted posterity, part of a continuous future for poetry. Dryden borrows Chaucer's petition, though not his words, to reinforce his claim to share a congenial soul. He also projects the similar "transfusion" of souls into the future, shoring up his own posterity by challenging another poet to join this select group.

Yet the line of succession is not open to everyone who would claim it. Dryden is very clear that the transmission of the inheritance he claims is open only to poets. He gives himself license to restore Chaucer's sense, which at times was "lost or mangled in the Errors of the Press,"[32] and to correct Chaucer's meter and his incomplete pentameters at the expense of Thomas Speght, "he who publish'd the last Edition of him; for he would make us believe the Fault is in our Ears, and that there were really Ten Syllables in a Verse where we find but Nine."[33] Dryden thus opens up a new, influential hierarchy that has the effect of downgrading the role of editor in comparison to all three of Dryden's roles as poet, translator, and commentator: "But this Opinion is not worth confuting; 'tis so gross and obvious an Errour." It is only the congenial poetic soul who has faultless ears for Chaucer's faulty metrics—a textbook example of strong poetic misprision.

For although Dryden claims sympathy with Chaucer, writing himself into a poetic tradition that also embraces Ovid, Homer, and Boccaccio; while he also excludes those poets and editors less worthy of his canon, he still struggles with Chaucer as a powerful father figure. The model of the *congenial* soul is a way of defusing Chaucer's influence, to appropriate him as a friend, not a rival. Another way of doing so is to infantilize Chaucer in the growth to maturity of the English language: the medieval poet is "Father of English Poetry," but Dryden excuses some of his expressions and metrical forms, since Chaucer lived "in the Dawning of our Language."[34] Or again, "We can only say, that he liv'd in the Infancy of our Poetry, and that nothing is brought to Perfection at the first. We must be Children before we grow Men."[35] If Chaucer is a poetic father figure, Dryden speedily disables him by associating him with linguistic infancy. It is an interesting reversal of the fifteenth-century poetic tradition described so suggestively by Seth Lerer, in which it is Chaucer's poetic successors who represent themselves as infantilized in comparison with their teacher and master.[36]

Dryden's preface was certainly influential on the subsequent reception of Chaucer. The twin ideas of identifying with Chaucer and of regarding his pilgrims as representative of all humanity have persisted well into the twentieth century, though Dryden's remains the clearest statement of these attitudes and an unequivocal example of the strategic, even programmatic imitation of and identification with Chaucerian voice. By the nineteenth century reprises of this motif had developed into a critical tradition independent of the poetic imitation of Chaucer. James Russell Lowell's *Conversations on Some of the Old Poets* (1845) rehearses Dryden's fantasies of spiritual proximity to the great poets in almost identical terms. Quoting Arcite's death speech from the *Knight's Tale*, Lowell, in the voice of Philip, places himself close to all three poets—Chaucer, Spenser and Shakespeare:

> The language of the heart never grows obsolete or antiquated, but falls as musically from the tongue now as when it was first uttered. Such lustiness and health of thought and expression seldom fail of leaving issue behind them. One may trace a family likeness to these in many of Spenser's lines, and I please myself sometimes with imagining pencil-marks of Shakespeare's against some of my favorite passages in Chaucer. At least, the relationship may be traced through Spenser, who calls Chaucer his master, and to whom Shakespeare pays really as high a compliment. . . . How must Chaucer have become, for a moment, sweetly conscious of his laurel, even in paradise, at hearing his name spoken reverently by Spenser and Milton and Wordsworth![37]

Lowell also engages in the familiar double strategy of giving Chaucer his affectionate devotion at the same time as distancing him: "But it is not for his humor, nor, indeed, for any one quality, that our old Chaucer is dear and sacred to me. I love to call him *old* Chaucer. The farther I can throw him back into the past, the dearer he grows; so sweet is it to mark how his plainness and sincerity outlive all changes of the outward world."[38] Ready identification with Chaucer is also seen in the ease of Leigh Hunt's marginal annotations to his copy of *The Poetical Works of Geoffrey Chaucer* in Robert Bell's edition (1854). Against the narrator's address to the reader in *Troilus and Criseyde*, V.270, "Thow, redere, maist thi self fulle wele devyne,"

Hunt comments: "There is something singularly pleasing, flattering, and personally attaching in finding one's self thus personally addressed by such a man as Chaucer, even under an individual designation so generalizing."[39]

Spiritual identification with Chaucer, fantasies of reading or writing in his presence, and the conscious affirmation of this aesthetic continuity come to a height in the rhetorical exuberance of Frederick J. Furnivall (1825–1910). Furnivall's revival of Chaucer manuscript studies, at the expense of the imperfect printed tradition, is supplemented by more personal wishes to live and work in Chaucer's presence, "to hear him talk Chronicles of kings and other pollicies, to pipe and harp and sing, and to keep honest company with me, after his cunning."[40] Furnivall's historicism took the form of tireless enthusiasm for discovering, and printing, every detail of medieval life, in order to realize as fully as possible the lives of the poets. In his edition of *Edward II's Household and Wardrobe Ordinances*, Furnivall develops his theory of biographical study as nostalgic, congenial friendship with the writers of the past: "As we delight to see, to know, our Tennyson, Ruskin, Huxley, of to-day, and get their looks, their tones, their little special ways, into our eyes and ears and hearts, to hear from an old schoolfellow or college friend, all their history, so we desire to realize to ourselves, so far as may be, the looks and life, the daily work and evening task, of the Chaucer, Shakspere, Milton, who've left us in the body, but are with us in the spirit, friends of our choicest hours, guides in our highest flights."[41] Criticism is clearly understood as a relationship of friendship or affinity, grounded in some kind of shared sensibility and background.[42]

The ideal of a literary conversation between gentlemen friends, professionals, or educated men, has proved an enabling trope for modern literary criticism. Its most familiar exponent for Chaucer criticism has been E. Talbot Donaldson, whose loving identifications with Chaucer are notorious examples, for feminist theory, of the exclusivity of this male tradition, and its assumptions that the Chaucerian reader is normatively male and heterosexual.[43] Of course, there is now an equally strong tradition of resisting such assumptions, as contemporary criticism claims its major function as critique, rather than empathetic engagement with the authorial sensibility under discussion. Feminist critical theory has been most influential here not only in providing the main exception to such ready affinity with male authors, but also in helping us diagnose these hidden agendas in the discourses of literary studies. For example, the idea of a community of readers alerts us to the fact that many of these male writers did indeed share a similar cultural and educational background, from which their female contemporaries were excluded.

Furnivall is the last editor actively to espouse an identification with his author as a basis for scholarship, although George Reinecke claims that

F. N. Robinson to some degree "modeled himself . . . on Geoffrey Chaucer," as a "gregarious, decorously jolly, and avuncular" figure;[44] and as recently as 1979, Derek Brewer was encouraging members of the New Chaucer Society to model themselves on Furnivall: "We do well to honor in him the ideals which the New Chaucer Society would wish to follow." Implicit here is the idea that in becoming Furnivall we might also become Chaucer, as if this were indeed our common aim. Brewer, for example, praises Donaldson as "that most Chaucerian figure." Describing Furnivall's internationalism, his interest in broader access to education, Brewer stresses his interest in women's concerns. Furnivall, he says, "treated everyone as equals, even women."[45]

The depth and continuity of Chaucer's reception constitute more than simply a historical curiosity, a "great tradition," as the title of a recent volume has it.[46] It can never be claimed openly that the best reader or editor of Chaucer is someone as much like him as possible, since it is a crucial aspect of Chaucer's status as a canonical writer that his appeal be universal, that none be disenfranchised as an appreciative reader for reasons of class or race, let alone gender or sexuality. However, it can be insinuated through a generalized critical method suggesting that the best response is one that effaces the most distance between author and reader, that the best reader is one who can best speak in and hear a Chaucerian voice, the one who reacts the same way as the author. The corollary argument is that if we do *not* react in the same way as Chaucer, we cannot be the true inheritors of his spirit, the congenial souls of the idealized reading community. And yet we still appeal to the idea of an international, global scholarly community of Chaucerians, perhaps seeking to hold together, under institutional pressure, the study of Chaucer, even while critical differences among us are so great. Our differences in terms of cultural capital, access to resources, and symbolic power within academic communities remain deeply dependent on our gender, our race, our nationality, our politics. The Chaucerian "community" is always divided, and never as universal or inclusive as the discourses of affinity imply.

Notes

1. My thanks to Sheila Delany, Elizabeth Fowler, and Paul James for commenting on an earlier version of this essay.

2. Stephen Greenblatt, *Shakespearean Negotiations: The Circulation of Social Energy in Renaissance England* (Berkeley: University of California Press, 1988), 1.

3. Louise Fradenburg, "'Voice Memorial': Loss and Reparation in Chaucer's Poetry," *Exemplaria* 2 (1990): 193.

4. Elaine Tuttle Hansen writes of the "homosocial couple," critic and author, in *Chaucer and the Fictions of Gender* (Berkeley: University of California Press, 1992), 46.

5. This essay is part of a book-length work in progress on such patterns, "Congenial Souls: The Reading Communities of Geoffrey Chaucer."

6. Susan Schibanoff, "The New Reader and Female Textuality in Two Early Commentaries on Chaucer," *Studies in the Age of Chaucer* 10 (1988): 71–108.

7. Thomas Greene, *The Light in Troy: Imitation and Discovery in Renaissance Poetry* (New Haven: Yale University Press, 1982), 6.

8. N. F. Blake, *Caxton's Own Prose* (London: André Deutsch, 1973), 102.

9. William Thynne also incorporated a modified version of Caxton's conclusion in his edition of Chaucer's works in 1532.

10. See also de Worde's comparable verse conclusion to his *Scala Perfectionis*, available in facsimile in James Moran, *Wynkyn de Worde: Father of Fleet Street* (London: Wynkyn de Worde Society, 1960), 17.

11. The text is a slightly modernized version of my transcription of the Huntington Library copy. See also David C. Benson and David Rollman, "Wynkyn de Worde and the Editing of Chaucer's *Troilus and Criseyde*," *Modern Philology* 78 (1981): 275–77.

12. Herbert G. Wright, ed., *A Seventeenth-Century Modernisation of the First Three Books of Chaucer's* Troilus and Criseyde, Cooper Monographs on English and American Literature 5 (Bern: Franke, 1960), 86. For an interesting commentary on Sidnam, see Clare Kinney, "Lost in Translation: The Vicissitudes of the Heroine and the Immasculation of the Reader in a Seventeenth-Century Paraphrase of *Troilus and Criseyde*," *Exemplaria* 5 (1993): 343–62.

13. Tim William Machan, "Kynaston's *Troilus*, Textual Criticism and the Renaissance Reading of Chaucer," *Exemplaria* 5 (1993): 176–77.

14. James E. Blodgett, "William Thynne (d. 1546)," in *Editing Chaucer: The Great Tradition*, ed. Paul Ruggiers (Norman, Okla.: Pilgrim Books, 1984), 36.

15. Derek Pearsall, *The Life of Geoffrey Chaucer: A Critical Biography* (Oxford: Blackwell, 1992), 295, 300.

16. Wendy Wall, *The Imprint of Gender: Authorship and Publication in the English Renaissance* (Ithaca: Cornell University Press, 1993), 1–3.

17. Pearsall, "Thomas Speght (ca. 1550-?)," in *Editing Chaucer: The Great Tradition*, ed. Ruggiers, 72–73.

18. Frederick J. Furnivall, *Mr Furnivall's Hindwords*, in *Animadversions vppon the annotacions and corrections of some imperfections of impressiones of Chaucers workes (sett downe before tyme, and now) reprinted in the yere of oure lorde 1598 sett downe by Francis Thynne*, ed. G. H. Kingsley, 1865 (revised by Furnivall), EETS 9 (London: Oxford University Press, 1875); see also Pearsall, "Thomas Speght."

19. Furnivall, ed., *Animadversions*, 4.

20. Ibid., 4–5.

21. Pearsall, "Thomas Speght," 84.

22. Furnivall, ed., *Animadversions*, xlviii–lvi.

23. Ibid., 10.

24. Ibid., 6.

25. Ibid., 5–6.

26. Pearsall, "Thomas Speght," 84–85.

27. Furnivall, ed., *Animadversions*, cvi.

28. Ibid., cvii.

29. James Kinsley, ed., *The Poems of John Dryden* (Oxford: Oxford University Press, 1958), 4:1445, ll. 32–37.

30. Ibid., 4:1457, ll. 521–29.

31. For further discussion of the relation between Dryden's preface and his Chaucer translations, see Stephanie Trigg, "Singing Clearly: Chaucer, Dryden and a Rooster's Discourse," *Exemplaria* 5 (1993): 365–86.

32. Kinsley, *Poems of John Dryden*, 4:1457, l. 530.

33. Ibid., 4:1453, ll. 338–40.

34. Ibid., 4:1451, l. 262.

35. Ibid., 4:1453, ll. 347–50.

36. Seth Lerer, *Chaucer and His Readers: Imagining the Author in Late Medieval England* (Princeton: Princeton University Press, 1995). Lerer's study concentrates on the "subjection" of Chaucer's fifteenth-century readers, and their elevation of Chaucer as aureate poet and laureate master. His focus is on Chaucer's poetic followers and imitators rather than on the commentary tradition. *Chaucer and His Readers* is an important adjunct to the present essay.

37. James Russell Lowell, *Conversations on Some of the Old Poets* (Cambridge: John Owens, 1845), 18–19.

38. Ibid., 21.

39. Comments transcribed from Leigh Hunt's copy of Bell's edition, held in the British Library.

40. Furnivall, ed., *Animadversions*, xiv.

41. Frederick J. Furnivall, ed., *King Edward II's Household and Wardrobe Ordinances* (London: Trübner, 1876), v.

42. Alois Brandl describes Furnivall's relationship to the poet: "With Chaucer he literally lived on terms of personal friendship: Chaucer's character, indeed, was perhaps most closely analogous to his own" (*Frederick J. Furnivall: A Volume of Personal Record* [London: Oxford University Press, 1911], 11). In a similar vein, J. J. Jusserand describes the "rare delight" of listening to "the voice of a man who had, it seemed, personally known Chaucer" (ibid., 92).

43. Hansen, *Chaucer and the Fictions of Gender*, 46; Carolyn Dinshaw, *Chaucer's Sexual Poetics* (Madison: University of Wisconsin Press, 1989), 30–39.

44. George Reinecke, "F. N. Robinson," in *Editing Chaucer*, ed. Ruggiers, 232.

45. Brewer reports that "Furnivall was also true to his Shelleyan prototype in pressing for what I suppose we must now call Women's Lib. When he was eighty he was a vigorous supporter of women's suffrage, conceived in ardently idealistic Victorian terms. 'Woman,' he said in 1905, 'is the beauty and glory of the world.' ... Being a sensible man, he liked women. The famous sculling club he later founded for working girls to enable them and eventually men to scull on the Thames on Sundays is the most famous if slightly comic example. At the A.B.C. tea-shop in New Oxford Street, where he did so much of his teaching, he was as charming to the waitresses as he was to lady scholars like Edith Rickert or Caroline Spurgeon" (Derek Brewer, "The Annual Chaucer Lecture: Furnivall and the Old Chaucer Society," *Chaucer Newsletter* 1 [1979]: 3).

46. Paul Ruggiers, ed., *Editing Chaucer*.

Contributors

Julia Boffey is Reader in Medieval Studies at Queen Mary and Westfield College, University of London. Her research is largely concerned with the manuscript and printed transmission of literary texts in the late medieval and early modern periods.

John M. Bowers has taught at the University of Virginia, Caltech, and Princeton University. He is currently a professor of English and chair of the department at the University of Nevada, Las Vegas. He is the author of *The Crisis of Will in "Piers Plowman"* (1986) and *The Canterbury Tales: Fifteenth-Century Continuations and Additions* (1992). His recent articles include "Controversy and Criticism: Lydgate's *Thebes* and the Prologue to *Beryn*," in *Chaucer Yearbook*, and *"Pearl* in Its Royal Setting: Ricardian Poetry Revisited," in *Studies in the Age of Chaucer*.

Robert Costomiris is an assistant professor in the Department of Literature and Philosophy at Georgia Southern University.

A. S. G. Edwards is a professor of English at the University of Victoria. He is the author of *Stephen Hawes* and the editor of *Skelton: The Critical Heritage, Middle English Prose*, and George Cavendish's *Metrical Visions*. Most recently he has coedited (with Julia Boffey) a facsimile of Bodleian Library, Oxford, MS Arch. Selden B. 24.

Mary F. Godfrey has published widely on Chaucer, medieval literature, and manuscript culture. Her current research interests include medieval drama, the use of psychoanalytic theory in literary criticism, and depictions of Jews and Judaism in medieval culture.

Carolyn Ives is finishing a doctoral program at the University of Alberta in Edmonton and is writing her dissertation, "Shifting Borders and Fluctuating Margins: The Bannatyne Manuscript and the Construction of Scottish National Identity in the Early Modern Period." Her conference papers and publications include work on concepts of authorship in the Bannatyne manuscript, the politics of scribal editing in the Bannatyne manuscript, and the role of James VI and James I in the development of Scottish and national literary identity.

BEVERLY KENNEDY has recently taken early retirement from the English department at Marianopolis College in Montreal. She has published many articles on Sir Thomas Malory's *Morte Darthur* and a book-length study, *Knighthood in the Morte Darthur* (1985; 2d ed. 1992). She has also published articles on the variant passages in and early scribal responses to the *Wife of Bath's Prologue*. She is currently at work on a book-length study of the different fifteenth-century versions of this text and their subsequent editorial reception.

BARBARA KLINE has taught at Florida International University and at Albertson College. Her articles on medieval woman mystics have appeared in *Magistra* and in a collection of essays entitled *Imagining Heaven* (forthcoming). She is currently completing research on a catalog of British Library MS Harley 7333.

EDGAR LAIRD is a professor of English at Southwest Texas State University. He is the editor (with Robert Fischer) of *Pèlerin de Prusse on the Astrolabe* (1995) and has published several studies on medieval astronomy and on medieval literature.

DAVID PARKINSON is an associate professor of English at the University of Saskatchewan. He has edited Gavin Douglas's *The Palis of Honoure* and has published in the *Journal of English and Germanic Philology* and *The Chaucer Review*.

THOMAS A. PRENDERGAST is an assistant professor of English at the College of Wooster. He has published on Chaucer and *Beowulf* and is completing a book-length manuscript entitled "Chaucer's Dead Body."

STEPHANIE TRIGG is Senior Lecturer in the Department of English with Cultural Studies at the University of Melbourne. She is the editor of *Wynnere and Wastoure* (1990) and *Medieval English Poetry* (1993), and the author of *Gwen Harwood* (1994). She is currently completing a book on the discourse of Geoffrey Chaucer criticism titled "Congenial Souls: The Reading Communities of Geoffrey Chaucer."

MÍCEÁL F. VAUGHAN is an associate professor in the departments of English and comparative literature at the University of Washington, and he recently collaborated in founding the university's new program in textual studies. Having published recent articles on the endings of both the A and B versions of *Piers Plowman*, he is now at work on the manuscripts, the printed versions, and the critical reception of Chaucer's *Retractions*.

INDEX

———◆———

Index of Manuscripts